TO WALK WITH THE DEVIL

Slovene Collaboration and Axis Occupation, 1941–1945

In the spring of 1941, when Slovenia was invaded by Germany, Italy, and Hungary, Slovenes faced at best assimilation, and at worst deportation or extermination. Still, a significant number of Slovenes would eventually collaborate with the Axis powers. Why were they so ready to work with their invaders, and why did the occupiers permit this collaboration?

Gregor Joseph Kranjc investigates these questions in *To Walk with the Devil*, the first English-language book-length account of Slovene-Axis collaboration during the Second World War. Examining archival material and postwar scholarly and popular literature, Kranjc describes the often sharp divide between Communist-era interpretations of collaboration and those of their émigré anti-Communist opponents.

Kranjc situates this divide in the vicious civil war that engulfed Slovenia during its occupation – a conflict that witnessed at its bloody climax the execution of over 10,000 Slovene collaborators and opponents of the new Communist Yugoslav regime in the wake of liberation. *To Walk with the Devil* makes clear how these grisly events continue to ripple through Slovene society today.

GREGOR JOSEPH KRANJC is an assistant professor in the Department of History at Brock University.

GREGOR JOSEPH KRANJC

To Walk with the Devil

Slovene Collaboration and Axis Occupation, 1941–1945

UNIVERSITY OF TORONTO PRESS
Toronto Buffalo London

© University of Toronto Press 2013
Toronto Buffalo London
www.utppublishing.com

ISBN 978-1-4426-4517-2 (cloth)
ISBN 978-1-4426-1330-0 (paper)

Library and Archives Canada Cataloguing in Publication

Kranjc, Gregor Joseph, 1974–
  To walk with the devil : Slovene collaboration and Axis occupation, 1941-1945 / Gregor Joseph Kranjc.

Includes bibliographical references and index.
ISBN 978-1-4426-4517-2 (bound)   ISBN 978-1-4426-1330-0 (pbk.)

1 Slovenia – History – Axis occupation, 1941–1945 – Collaborationists.   I. Title.

D802.S67k73 2013   949.73022   C2012-908152-3

This book has been published with the help of a grant from the Canadian Federation for the Humanities and Social Sciences, through the Awards to Scholarly Publications Program, using funds provided by the Social Sciences and Humanities Research Council of Canada.

University of Toronto Press acknowledges the financial assistance to its publishing program of the Canada Council for the Arts and the Ontario Arts Council.

University of Toronto Press acknowledges the financial support of the Government of Canada through the Canada Book Fund for its publishing activities.

Contents

Abbreviations vii

Alternate Spellings of Place Names ix

Map 1 Axis-Occupied Yugoslavia, 1941 x

Map 2 The Province of Ljubljana and Surrounding Regions xi

Introduction 3

1 The Battle Goes Postwar: The Historiographical Debate 13

2 Before the Deluge 30

3 Reality Subverted, 6 Apil–22 June 1941 51

4 The Emergence of Resistance, July 1941–November 1942 69

5 The Emergence of Collaboration, July 1941–July 1943 85

6 The Collapse of Italy and a New Spirit
   of German Cooperation, July 1943–December 1943 115

7 Shoulder-to-Shoulder with the German
   Armed Forces, January 1944–December 1944 141

8 The Banality of Civilian Collaboration,
   September 1943–December 1944 169

9 The Final Stand and Its Consequences,
    January 1945–May 1945   209

Conclusion: The Verdict   238

Notes   255

References   299

Index   313

Abbreviations

ARS	Arhiv republike Slovenije (Archive of the Republic of Slovenia)
AVNOJ	Antifašitičko vijeće narodnog oslobođenja Jugoslavije (Anti-Fascist Council of the National Liberation of Yugoslavia)
BBZ	code name for Vladimir Vauhnik's espionage ring
CPY	Communist Party of Yugoslavia
CPS	Communist Party of Slovenia
DOS	Državna obveščevalna služba (Četniks' National Intelligence Service)
GILL	Gioventu Italiana del Littorio di Lubiane (Italians' Fascist Youth Organization of Ljubljana)
IU	Informativni urad (Information Office of the Provincial Administration)
KA	Katoliška akcija (Catholic Action)
MVAC	Milizia volontaria anti comunista (Anti-Communist Volunteer Militia)
NDH	Neodvisna država Hrvatska (Independent State of Croatia)
NO	Narodni odbor (National Committee for Slovenes)
NOB	Narodna osvobodilna borba (National Liberation War)
NOV	Narodna osvobodilna vojska (National Liberation Army)
NR	Narodnostni referat (Nationality Report)
NS	Narodni svet (National Council)
NSV	Nationalsozialistische Volkswohlfahrt
OF	Osvobodilna fronta (Liberation Front)
ORJUNA	Organizacija jugoslavenskih nacionalista (Organization of Yugoslav Nationalists)
OSS	U.S. Office of Strategic Services

OZAK	Operationszone Adriatisches Küstenland (Operation Zone Adriatic Littoral)
OZNA	Oddelek za zaščito naroda (Department for the Protection of the People)
PO	Propagandni odsek (Propaganda Branch of the Provincial Administration)
POJ	Partizanski odredi jugoslavije (Yugoslav Partisan Detachments)
PU	Pokrajinska uprava (Provincial Administration)
PVZ	Policijski varnostni zbor (Police Security Corps, as the force was known until March 1944)
PZ	Policijski zbor (Police Corps, as the force was known from March 1944 onwards)
SL	Slovenska legija (Slovene Legion)
SLS	Slovenska ljudska stranka (Slovene People's Party)
SNOO	Slovenski narodnoosvobodilni odbor (Slovenian National Liberation Committee)
SNČ	Sodišče narodne časti (Courts of National Honour)
SNV	Slovenska narodna vojska (Slovene National Army)
SNVZ	Slovenski narodni varnostni zbor (Slovene National Security Corps)
SOE	U.K. Special Operations Executive
SZ	Slovenska zaveza (Slovene Covenant)
TIGR	pro-Yugoslav anti-Fascist resistance organization in Italy, acronym for the contested regions of Trst, Istria, Gorizia, and Reka
TOS	Tajna obveščevalna služba (Slovene Legion's Secret Intelligence Service)
UVOD	Ústřední vedení odboje domácího (Central Leadership of Home Resistance, Czech)
VOS	Varnostna obveščevalna služba (CPS Security Intelligence Service)
VS	Vaške straže (Village Guards)

Alternate Spellings of Place Names

Code: E (English), I (Italian), G (German), SLO (Slovene)
Place name most commonly used in text: Alternate spellings
Carinthia (E): Koroška (SLO), Kärnten (G)
Bela Krajina (SLO): Weißkrain (G), White Carniola (E)
Dolenjska (SLO): Unterkrain (G), Lower Carniola (E)
Gorenjska (SLO): Oberkrain (G), Upper Carniola (E)
Gorizia (I): Gorica (SLO)
Notranjska (SLO): Innerkrain (G), Inner Carniola (E)
Primorska (SLO): Littoral (E), Küstenland (G)
Province of Ljubljana (E): Ljubljanska pokrajina (SLO), Provincia di Lubiana (I)
Soča (SLO): Isonzo (I)
Štajerska (SLO): Untersteiermark (G), Lower Styria (E)
Trieste (I): Trst (SLO)
Vetrinje (SLO): Viktring (G)

Map 1. Axis-Occupied Yugoslavia, 1941

Map 2. The Province of Ljubljana and Surrounding Regions

TO WALK WITH THE DEVIL

Slovene Collaboration and Axis Occupation, 1941–1945

Introduction

After the terrorist bombings of London's transportation system in July 2005, which killed more than fifty people, British diplomat Julian Evans responded in a defiant fashion during a vigil in Toronto, Canada. He said: 'The terrorists who perpetrated mass murder know how to make bombs. Perhaps they should have spent more time studying British history. We are not a people easily intimidated. We are not a people who can be bombed into submission or into changing policies and values that we believe to be right; others have tried and failed.'[1] Evans did not elaborate on the specific historical examples he was alluding to, but he almost certainly had in mind the Battle of Britain and the Blitz, when the British, standing alone, heroically resisted Nazi Germany's repeated attempts to bomb their nation into submission.

A Slovene's memory of those very same years is not as clear-cut. Yes, there was, indeed, resistance to the Italian, Hungarian, and German occupiers, but there was also accommodation as well as outright collaboration. Slovenia, unlike Britain, did not have the considerable advantage of being an island nation defended by one of the world's most formidable navies. As a small people numbering approximately one and a half million and residing in the strategic heart of East Central Europe, the position of Slovenes was precarious well before the Second World War began. As a result of Great Power machinations during the First World War, a quarter of the Slovene population found itself living outside the frontiers of the new Yugoslav state, mostly in Italy, but also in Austria. Yugoslavia, which Slovenes joined in 1918, was a poor country riven by internal ethnic squabbles. In early April 1941, Slovenia – which the author defines as the Slovene-inhabited lands of Yugoslavia – and the rest of the country were invaded by the Axis powers.

In the perspective of the long history of the Slovenes, the invasion of their lands during the Second World War was not a novel phenomenon. Nevertheless, the popular impression that Yugoslavs were 'warrior peoples' with long traditions of armed resistance is, at least in the Slovene case, an unsubstantiated generalization. A long pedigree of irregular guerilla warfare was certainly part of Serbian history, for example, particularly during the Ottoman period; Slovenes, however, were more similar to the Czechs and their tradition of accommodating foreign powers. Slovenes enjoyed only a brief period of self-rule, in the historically hazy seventh and eighth centuries. Autonomy was replaced with the domination of Franks and Bavarians until the thirteenth century, when Slovenes came under the control of the Habsburgs who would rule over them until 1918. With the emergence and spread of a Slovene national consciousness in the nineteenth century, Slovenes safeguarded their national distinctiveness by pledging loyalty to the monarchy and, in return, hoping for recognition of their national autonomy and cultural distinctiveness. The fallacy of such a policy became tragically clear during the First World War, when young Slovenes spilled their blood on foreign battlefields, or closer to home, on the Isonzo front, for a monarchy that steadfastly refused to satisfy the national demands of the South Slavs. With the collapse of the Austro-Hungarian Empire, Slovenes were the victims of a belligerent and expansive Italy, which severed three hundred thousand of their co-nationals from the newly established Kingdom of Serbs, Croats, and Slovenes, which Slovenes joined, in part, to counter the prevailing sense of insecurity in Europe. As one of the smallest nationalities in Yugoslavia, Slovenes once again found their destiny partially controlled by others, this time by the Serb-dominated governing apparatus in Belgrade. Slovene politicians, nevertheless, managed to carve out a significant degree of self-administration and autonomy by cooperating with the plethora of governments in Belgrade, unlike the obstinate obstructionism of the Croats. Thus, on the eve of the Axis invasion and occupation, Slovenes had already developed a policy of national survival that emphasized accommodation and political engagement with stronger foreign powers. Such a strategy, while partly successful in a somewhat liberal and cosmopolitan Habsburg Empire, or in a small interwar Balkan state made up of fellow South Slav nationalities, became tragically inadequate for an Axis occupation that as its modus operandi strove, in various degrees, to eliminate the Slovenes as a national entity. Indeed, on this very issue,

Slovenia's wartime experience was unique. Slovenia was not the only territory in Europe to be trisected and occupied – an experience that was also shared by Greece. However, it was the only territory to then experience a further step: absorption and annexation into neighbouring Nazi Germany, Fascist Italy, and Hungary. In the face of such a catastrophe emerged the Communist-led Liberation Front (Osvobodilna fronta, OF) and its armed Partisan detachments, and these spearheaded what they termed the Narodna osvobodilna borba (NOB, or National Liberation War) – the violent struggle that was waged from 1941 to 1945 to liberate Yugoslavia from Axis control. The Liberation Front and the National Liberation War represented a true revolutionary development in a centuries-long tradition of diligent Slovene perseverance in response to foreign domination. On its broadest level, this book focuses on the collision of these two Slovene responses to occupation in the years 1941 to 1945.

Accommodation and collaboration with Nazi Germany or Fascist Italy were rarely spoken of in European official circles in the first two decades following the Second World War. The prevailing assumption was that Nazism and Fascism had been destroyed in 1945, and the small clique of traitors had been dealt with either through summary executions by popular (or vigilante) justice, or through official trials. Attention turned to rebuilding a Europe divided along the very different ideological lines of the Cold War. In this pervasive sense of certainty, Marcel Ophuls released his 1969 film *Le chagrin et la pitié: Chronique d'une ville française sous l'occupation* (The Sorrow and the Pity: Chronicle of a French City under the Occupation). This film represented a watershed in the post – Second World War public reappraisal of collaboration in France. The Gaullist myth of resistance, which had portrayed French collaboration as limited primarily to a band of 'Parisian traitors' was widened to include ordinary Frenchmen and Frenchwomen.[2] Since then, a number of historical works (often by foreign scholars) have emerged from formerly occupied Western European states that have reassessed the popular interpretation of resistance and collaboration as a struggle between fortitude and bravery, on the one hand, and human weakness, on the other.

This process was somewhat delayed in Eastern Europe, as well as in China, chiefly because the demonization of 'bourgeois' collaborators during the Second World War was often crucial to the Communist regimes, which based at least part of their supposed right to rule on their record of resisting fascism. Certainly, this was the case in Slovenia, where the 'regime school' of postwar Communist historians and their fellow-travellers insisted that most Slovenes overwhelmingly supported Josip Broz Tito and his Communist Party of Yugoslavia's (CPY) policy of uncompromising resistance to the Axis occupation of their country. The regime's understanding of a collaborator vacillated between definitions both narrow and wide. Collaborator, narrowly defined, targeted a relatively small clique of opportunistic politicians and Church officials who worked against the Slovene masses by using the occupiers to maintain their reactionary rule. These collaborators, the regime school insisted, were 'never [. . .] able to receive any support among the Slovene nation,'[3] conveniently absolving those whom the leading Slovene Communist Edvard Kardelj defined as 'misguided peasants.'[4] The welfare of the masses meant not only the ejection of the occupier, however, but also the fruition of the Communist revolution – an historical necessity Collaborator, widely defined, was thus taken to be any Slovene who actively worked against the Liberation Front. As Rodoljub Čolaković, the Partisan and postwar prime minister of Bosnia-Hercegovina, put it: 'Men either had to go to the communists in the fight against the greatest danger that had ever threatened the Slovene nation, or be mere lookers-on of the struggle on the issue of which depended their own fate. These men had gone with the communists regardless of the fact that they disagreed with them ideologically. Ideological disagreement at that juncture was plainly no more than an excuse for cowards and traitors.'[5] Thus, it was not surprising that when the Yugoslav Communists requested, in the immediate postwar years, that American and British governments repatriate collaborators, they lumped together not only those who had truly collaborated, but also any and all opponents of the regime, regardless of their attitude towards the occupiers. The position paper entitled *War Criminals, Traitors, and Quislings*, submitted by the American government to the United Nations General Assembly, on 12 September 1947, recommended: 'War criminals, who are chiefly enemy or ex-enemy nationals and persons who initiated and pursued aggressive war on innocent people or who committed atrocious crimes or crimes in the violation of the laws of war, are to be distinguished from quislings and traitors, who are ordinarily nationals of the requesting country. Persons accused by Yugoslavia as quislings frequently appear to be guilty of nothing more than political dissidence from the present government.' The U.S. position paper also stressed: 'The necessity for close scrutiny by the Department [of State] of the merits of each case arises from (1) the frequency with which the Yugoslavs term war criminals or traitors persons who are simply opposed to the present Yugoslav regime, and (2) the vague nature of the Yugoslav charges with respect to the time, place, character of crime, and the accused's share therein.'[6]

In comparison with the more-or-less ideologically cohesive regime school, a rival interpretation developed out of the far more diverse groupings of Slovene exiles, who left the country either during the Second World War itself or after the Communists seized final control, in May 1945. Living on four continents, this diaspora represented a fairly broad spectrum of Slovenia's pre-war and wartime political and ideological kaleidoscope. The emigrants included fascists and their sympathizers, members of the pre-war mainstream political parties, Communist dissidents, some Church officials, and members of the artistic and cultural elite, as well as ordinary civilians who for any number of reasons feared Communist rule enough to flee their homeland. Their wartime behaviour was equally diverse – a few resisted the occupiers, more collaborated, and many avoided both responses as best they could. What glued them together was their opposition to Communism, despite differences in the motivations for this rejection and its intensity.

Collectively, this anti-Communist camp (*protikomunistični tabor*), or opposition – as some collaborators referred to themselves already during the war – developed common enough interpretations of the events in their homeland during the Second World War to be characterized as an 'émigré school.' For example, they defended themselves from accusations of wartime collaboration as being merely a Communist attempt to discredit them and to downplay the extent of popular opposition to Communist rule. Those in the anti-Communist camp had, in fact, played a 'double-game,' pretending to be loyal to the occupiers so that they could resist the Communist revolution. Moreover, they claimed that they were the victims. As many in the anti-Communist camp had been among the pre-war ruling elite in Slovenia, they still saw themselves as the legitimate political representatives of Slovenes. They had been caught 'between two fires' – Tito's forces on the one side, the occupiers on the other. Miha Krek, a wartime member of the Yugoslav government-in-exile and a postwar leader of the Slovene émigré community, wrote in 1955: 'The Slovene nation and her anti-communist army during the occupation and revolution, in suffocating conditions between two, three fires, accomplished everything they could from their own strength in order to protect the freedom of their homeland, to assist in the victory of democratic forces [and] defend against communist tyranny.'[7]

After the war, regime historians, who were beholden to the 'Party line,' and émigré writers chafing at having been forced into exile by what had otherwise been a tiny, illegal Communist Party before the war, were nonetheless, able to provide relatively clear interpretations of collaboration. Motivated less by a need for historical accuracy than by their ideological predispositions to see the world in a Manichean light, both sides viewed one another as the embodiment of evil, whereas they themselves fought only for the purest of ideals. There were few, if any, troublesome exceptions in their interpretations. To regime historians, good was represented by the valiant and selfless Partisan, and evil was embodied in the occupier and his domestic lackeys. To the émigré writers, the only evil worse than the occupation was the exploitation of Slovenia's and Yugoslavia's prostrate status in order to launch a Communist revolution that embraced godlessness, fostered Soviet ambitions, and had complete disregard for human life. Beaten down by two enemies, one foreign and the other domestic, the traumatized Slovene nation was forced to seek a humiliating safety by siding *temporarily*, as the émigrés insisted, with the lesser of the two evils. In short, for the émigré, goodness was represented by the suffering Slovenes, who in the face of oppression remained true to their nation and religion, whereas Stalin's Liberation Front lackeys and the occupiers personified evil.

As Stevan Pavlowitch has pointed out, 'the horrible truth about Yugoslavia is that it is so complex that it cannot be simplified or conceptualized without also being distorted out of all recognition.'[8] This was the error of the regime and émigré schools. Their reductionism was comforting to them – it justified difficult and potentially immoral decisions taken during a perverse occupation within a moral framework of good versus evil or progressives versus reactionaries. Reductionism gave clarity to an otherwise surreal world where national loyalties, moral obligations, and the very definition of the enemy were turned upside down by an occupation whose brutality had never before been witnessed by Slovenes. When the civil war between the Liberation Front and its domestic opponents finally broke out, in 1942, this black-and-white understanding was crucial, too, to the psychological health of its participants. You could more easily kill your enemy, your ethnic brother, if he was inherently evil, foreign, and dehumanized.

If comforting, these polarized perceptions were not the truth, or they were, at best, only part of the truth. The political, ideological, social, and moral complexities of the war years undermine the black-and-white interpretations of the regime and émigré schools. In reality, the world between 1941 and 1945 was a murky grey. The Slovene Communists were never quite the monolithic front envisaged in the final stage of Hugh Seton-Watson's communization process.[9] The Liberation Front was a coalition for much of the Second World War, and although it came under increasing Communist direction and discipline, it was not a Stalinist clone despite what their opponents may have claimed in their propaganda. Similarly, if anti-Communism suggested an attractive element of intellectual cohesion and unanimity in wartime behaviour and aspirations, the reality of the occupation speaks otherwise; thus, 'anti-Communism' will be used sparingly here to avoid succumbing to the same terminological reductionism as practised by the postwar regime. Anti-Communism was not the same as collaboration, even though a good number of its adherents succumbed to it in some form. Collaboration, not opposition to Communism, during the period 1941 to 1945, is the main target of this study.

As has France and many other European states, Slovenia has had its own unique 'crisis of memory' that revealed the inadequacies of the two postwar interpretations of collaboration and resistance. The democratic revolution in Slovenia, and Slovenia's secession from Yugoslavia in 1991, accelerated the reappraisal of wartime events, the seeds of which were planted already in the 1980s, and even earlier, among postwar dissidents and critics of Tito's regime. In particular, these momentous changes allowed Slovenes, finally, to debate freely and publicly the postwar fate of approximately twelve thousand anti-Partisan Home Guard (*domobranstvo*) militiamen, who were forcibly repatriated and summarily executed by Tito's forces in May and June 1945.[10] A new generation of historians has recently emerged that has produced more critical interpretations of collaboration. Whereas the regime school was indiscriminate, the new generation of historians have made distinctions between those who accommodated and those who collaborated, and at the same time undermined the émigrés' image of themselves as selfless national martyrs.

This book contributes to this belated reappraisal of wartime events in Slovenia, and specifically the role of Slovene collaborators. While the phrase 'we must understand the past so as to understand the present' has been used ad nauseam, this work will, at least in its initial chapter, subvert this notion and, instead, propose that in order to understand the past we must understand the present. This seems apparent in any discussion of wartime collaboration in Slovenia, a topic so maligned by the ideological divisions of the postwar years that simply venturing into the period has the unfortunate historian pigeon-holed into either the Communist or anti-Communist camps – the Reds (*rdeči*) or the Whites (*beli*) – and sharing all of their presumed biases and devious purposes. Chapter 1 begins with a brief historiography of Slovene collaboration in order to understand what has been written, how it has been written, and where the history of collaboration is going in present-day Slovenia. From here, the work will revert to a chronological framework, with chapter 2 devoted to a brief survey of political and ideological developments in pre-war Yugoslavia and chapter 3 detailing the awesome speed of Yugoslavia's collapse, in April 1941, and Slovenia's trisection by its three occupiers. Chapters 4 and 5 concentrate on the rise of resistance movements and of collaboration in occupied Slovenia respectively, with a particular focus on the Province of Ljubljana, the Italian share of partitioned Slovenia – and 'heartland' of wartime Slovene resistance and collaboration. Chapter 6 examines the Italian capitulation of September 1943, a watershed event in the history of occupied Slovenia, and the subsequent German reoccupation. Chapters 7 and 8 address military and civilian collaboration with the Germans respectively. The last months of the Nazis' tottery European empire are examined in chapter 9, exploring the final showdown between the Slovene resistance and its opponents, as well as the postwar fate of collaborators. The conclusion wades into the various collaborative arrangements enumerated in the previous chapters and, as much as possible, categorizes them in terms of 'degrees' of collaboration – in search of a verdict. This is a difficult exercise, made all the more humbling because the historian *was not there*. No collection of documents could completely recreate what an individual at that time was facing when making the decision to collaborate. Moreover, all were not confronted with the same palate of choices, with the same latitude for freedom, or with the same level of understanding as to what constituted collaboration. Within the confines of this most nuanced of terms, there existed a wide array of types of collaboration, which varied as much regarding motives as in the substance of the collaborative relationships.

Since the 1970s, a handful of historians have attempted to categorize the various forms of European collaboration during the Second World War, as can be seen in the colourful chapter titles in Werner Rings' 1983 work, *Life with the Enemy: Collaboration and Resistance in Hitler's Europe, 1939–1945*, and the more recent analysis by Peter Davies, *Dangerous*

Liaisons: Collaboration and World War Two (2004).[11] Using a single term to account for diverse societal responses to occupation is an almost Sisyphean task. The historian Jan Gross has admitted as much, noting that collaboration 'puts a kind of veil over a very complex reality.'[12] Collaboration, as understood in this work, can at least be sandwiched between two conceptual boundaries. At one end lies its most extreme form – *collaborationism* – a term that the historian of Vichy France Stanley Hoffman uses to describe 'an openly desired cooperation with, and imitation of, the occupying regime.'[13] The collaborationist, thus, has a strong ideological affinity with the occupier. The opposite goal-post from collaborationism is *coercion*. Coercion relies on the brute power of the occupiers, by forcing the occupied to cooperate 'at the point of a gun.' Even though the coercion is not always represented by an actual gun, the coerced submits to the occupier's demands so as to avoid either outright physical harm or other difficult socio-economic penalties. Coercion involves so little personal choice on the part of the coerced when confronted with such massive retaliatory consequences that its usefulness in the understanding of collaboration is limited simply to its role as a definitional marker beyond which collaboration ceases to be collaboration and becomes pure slavery.

Unlike with coercion, then, collaborators had choice. They did not have to collaborate; the occupier would not directly punish them if they did not collaborate. Here we must bear in mind the dilemma that was introduced above between the historical reality that we have acquired in hindsight and the contemporary perceptions of the historical actors themselves. In short, even if *we* may know that there were no consequences in refusing to collaborate, collaborators, themselves, may have personally felt that they had no choice.

Collaboration requires the *active* engagement of the collaborator with the occupier. Those Slovenes who continued on with their lives as best they could and did not resist the occupiers – but also did not go out of their way to seek out the occupiers – may be said to have *accommodated* to enemy rule. Indeed, there is no ethical requirement for civilians to resist an occupation; thus, everyone who was not a Partisan was not by definition a collaborator. Rather, the Slovene masses often behaved very similarly to how historian Martin Conway has so lucidly described the bearing of occupied Belgians: 'Only in extremis, confronted by material desperation or the pressure of family and friends, did many individuals find themselves thrust into making – frequently almost against their will – the dramatic choices symbolized by collaboration or resistance.'[14] The concern of this work is collaboration, not accommodation, while recognizing, of course, that the divide between the two is often blurry and not at all clear.

This study aims to better reflect the world that was inhabited by occupied Slovenes during the Second World War, in order to move a step forward from the crude finger-pointing that marked postwar historiography. As a corollary, the analysis will also reveal something about the moral limitations of resistance in the context of an immoral occupation, as well as the durability of national cohesiveness. Finally, if the act of categorizing and paring away what I see as the layers of collaboration elicits the reader's objections, all the better, as it will at least motivate a much needed reappraisal of what collaboration meant during the Second World War in its narrow Slovene example and in its wider Yugoslav and European perspective. Paradoxical as it may seem, it is possible to have a more accurate understanding of wartime Slovene collaboration if its complicated, confused, and complex, yet authentic nature is revealed, rather than if a sanitized and simplistic caricature is presented that bears little resemblance to the reality of the times.

1 The Battle Goes Postwar: The Historiographical Debate

> Beneath the rule of men entirely great,
> The pen is mightier than the sword.
> Edward Bulwer-Lytton, *Richelieu; Or the Conspiracy* (1839)

Slovenia's four long years of occupation ended in early May 1945, as the Partisans, having already won the race for Trieste, entered Ljubljana to the jubilation of its inhabitants. The occupation, and most importantly, the civil war between the Liberation Front and the Slovene forces that had allied themselves with the occupiers, was seemingly over. In the euphoria of liberation, most Slovenes probably could not foresee the bloody events that were about to occur.

A week before the triumphant arrival of Tito's forces, a very different scene had greeted Ljubljana's citizens. On 3 May 1945, just five days before the end of the Second World War in Europe, the underground National Committee for Slovenia (Narodni odbor, NO), comprised of representatives of the pre-war non-Communist Slovene political parties, believed the decisive moment had come to turn against the Germans. That day, in the Sokol (Falcon) athletics hall, located in the Tabor neighbourhood of Ljubljana, the National Committee held a session of the reconstituted Slovene parliament and declared a National State of Slovenia free of German control. The Tabor Declaration further announced Slovenia's common cause with the Allied forces and reaffirmed its place in a democratic and federated Yugoslavia under King Peter II of the Karadjordjević dynasty.

With most of Yugoslavia liberated and under the control of Tito's National Liberation Army (Narodna osvobodilna vojska, NOV), the so-called Tabor Declaration was no less than a last gasp attempt on the part of Slovenia's pre-war ruling elite to forestall a Communist seizure of power. Not only did it reveal how much power the old political order had lost during the occupation, but also their passivity before the German occupiers and their fatal dependence on the Slovene anti-Partisan forces that had actively collaborated with them. To defend this fledgling Slovene national state from the approaching Partisans, the National Committee turned to a new formation that had been announced in the Tabor Declaration, the Slovene National Army (Slovenska narodna vojska, SNV). The SNV had only existed on paper, having been announced clandestinely by the National Committee on 21 February 1945. It absorbed the Home Guard based in the so-called Province of Ljubljana (Ljubljanska Pokrajina) – Italy's former share of partitioned Slovenia – and a number of smaller anti-Partisan units in the neighbouring Slovene regions of Primorska and Gorenjska. Since their establishment in late 1943, all of these units had fought, in their own words, 'shoulder-to-shoulder' with the Germans against the Liberation Front. Therefore, it was somewhat disingenuous for the Tabor Declaration to call on the 'Partisan units to suspend immediately all actions against the Slovene National Army and the peace-loving Slovene people, and, by doing this, to bring to an end the terrible bloodshed among brothers.'[1]

Pressed by the advancing Partisans, who would enter the city on 9 May, the National Committee exercised authority for only a few short days. One of the first orders to the newly formed Slovene National Army was that it was to retreat 'temporarily' to Austrian Carinthia. Approximately twelve thousand Home Guardsmen and six thousand civilians would, thus, follow the last German units and their Balkan and Eastern European auxiliaries – led by the German Colonel Oberst von Seeler – as they withdrew northwards.[2] It was not difficult to deduce the reasons behind the exodus of the Home Guards. Their collaboration with the Germans, and their refusal to respond to the Partisan amnesties in 1944 and early 1945, had clearly left them marked men. The reasons why Slovene civilians fled were more complex, as John Corsellis and Marcus Ferrar highlight in their 2005 study *Slovenia 1945: Memories of Death and Survival after World War II*:

> The Germans had been protecting a nearby paper mill for strategic reasons, so its financial director had to flee. The head of a brush factory had to go too because he once sold a batch to the Italians. He had spurned the love

of his secretary, so she denounced him. Another left because he kept his bedding firm solvent by selling mattresses to an Italian military brothel, delivering them clandestinely on a tricycle after curfew. A headmaster had to leave because he once apologized to an Italian Fascist chaplain, in order to save his pupils from expulsion for refusing to say the Lord's Prayer in Italian.[3]

For those who had actively served the Home Guard cause, such as the propagandist Franc Pernišek, the urgency to evacuate was even clearer. In his diary, on 5 May 1945, Pernišek wrote, 'The hardest moment in my life faces me: to tell my wife and children that, if we want to stay alive, we must leave home and all our possessions and go abroad to an unknown but terrible future.'[4]

Crossing into Austria through the recently completed 1,570-metre-long Ljubelj Tunnel, they surrendered and were disarmed by the British, who allowed them to camp on the fields outside of Viktring (Vetrinje), a village located on the southeastern fringe of Klagenfurt. The presence of Partisans in Carinthia, there to push Tito's claim to the territory and its Slovene-speaking minority, must have certainly unnerved the new arrivals. However, their custody in the hands of the British was promising. Surely, the non-Communist *angleži* (English) would protect them!

Beginning on 27 May 1945, the British began loading the first of the Home Guard to be forcibly repatriated onto trucks that were then driven to the railway stations at Rosenbach, Maria Elend, and Bleiburg, where they transferred to trains bound for Yugoslavia. With their charges under the impression that they were being sent to Displaced Persons camps in Italy, and secure in the conviction that their British anti-Communist 'allies' would never betray them, the deportations proceeded relatively smoothly, the last transport departing on 31 May. Upon arrival in Yugoslavia, the vast majority of these 11,700 returnees were imprisoned and beaten.[5] Their arms bound with wires, they were trucked and then marched to the edge of karst sinkholes in Kočevski Rog, Hrastnik, and Teharje, where they were summarily executed. Their bodies were unceremoniously disposed of in the inky blackness of the pits. Fortunately, a similar order to repatriate the remaining Slovene civilians in Austria on 1 June was reversed, less than twelve hours before it was to be carried out.[6] Housed in rather difficult conditions in the Austrian refugee camps of Lienz, Spittal, St Veit, and Judenburg, most of the refugees would have to wait until 1948 or 1949 before they could emigrate abroad to Argentina, Canada, the United States, Australia, and Britain.

The legal basis for the British repatriation has been a topic of fierce debate among the handful of scholars who braved official British indifference to expose the events. The Hague Conventions of 1899 and 1907 and the 1929 Geneva Convention were created to account for conventional interstate conflicts, not civil wars. Predictably, they did not specifically outlaw forced repatriations. Nevertheless, the Geneva Convention expressed its intentions towards prisoners of war in its Article 2, which states that 'prisoners of war [. . .] shall at all times be humanely treated and protected, particularly against acts of violence, from insults and from public curiosity. Measures of reprisal against them are forbidden.'[7] Since the Home Guard had been disarmed and its members effectively made prisoners of war, and since they would hardly receive a warm welcome if returned to Yugoslavia, it appears that the British should have fallen back on this key article of the Geneva Convention. Concealing the true destination of the repatriation transports was yet another infringement of the 1929 Geneva Convention, Article 26 of which states: 'In case of transfer, prisoners of war shall be officially notified of their new destination in advance.'[8] Many commentators have pointed to the Yalta Agreement concerning prisoners of war and civilians liberated by U.S. and Soviet forces that was signed on 11 February 1945, as well as similar agreements between Britain and the Soviet Union, signed on the same day, and later France and the Soviet Union, as the grounds for repatriation. Although this may be the case with regard to the repatriation of Soviet citizens, these agreements make no mention of repatriating Yugoslavs.

Nevertheless, as early as 1941 the British government was intimating that the right of asylum would not be granted, as British Prime Minister Winston Churchill declared in a 22 June 1941 broadcast, to 'that vile race of quislings who make themselves the tools and agents of the Nazi regime against their fellow countrymen and the land of their birth.'[9] Indeed, by 1944 British policy, as communicated to the British Joint Staff Mission in Washington DC on 24 June, was that 'all "allied nationals" seeking Anglo-American protection after serving in hostile military or para-military organisations of non-German origin [. . .] should be handed back to the government of the ally concerned.'[10] This policy was not without its critics and as events in Austria were about to come to a head the British Ambassador in Belgrade, Sir Ralph Stevenson, cabled the British Foreign Office in London on 27 April 1945, stating that to hand over 'anti-partisan units' that were 'completely compromised by open collaboration with the Germans' to Tito, would be 'inconsistent with traditional claim to asylum of political refugees at the end of a civil war.'[11] Churchill accepted Stevenson's suggestion, stating on the 29 April that it was 'the only possible solution.'[12]

Of course, as journalist and researcher Christopher Booker clearly revealed in his critical assessment of the repatriations from Austria, Churchill could not predict the emergency situation that would develop in May 1945 for the V Corps of the British Eighth Army that held southern Austria. V Corps was debilitated in their task of carrying out the possible forcible ejection (Operation Beehive) of Tito's army from Carinthia, whose claims to the region were in violation of the envisioned four-power (Britain, U.S., U.S.S.R., France) postwar administration of Austria, by the demands of securing and feeding hundreds of thousands of German and anti-Communist Russian, Yugoslav and other prisoners of war, including tens of thousands of civilians, with the threat of more anti-Titoist troops and refugees pouring into the overtaxed area from Yugoslavia. Military priorities prevailed, as Field Marshal Harold Alexander, the Supreme Allied Commander, Mediterranean, cabled Churchill on 16 May with his aim to 'clear the decks' in Carinthia.[13] The repatriation of the Yugoslavs and the Soviets would quickly solve at least one of V Corps' challenges. The order that set the repatriation of the Slovenes and other Yugoslavs in motion was sent by General Sir Brian Robertson, chief administrative officer of the Supreme Allied Command, Mediterranean, on 14 May 1945. It stated that 'all surrendered personnel of established Yugoslav nationality who were serving in German forces should be disarmed and handed over to local Yugoslav forces.'[14] This order was carried out – to the obvious distaste of many rank and file British soldiers tasked with its execution – between 18–31 May.

For the Slovenes, the consequences were momentous. The bloody settling of accounts in the spring of 1945 ensured that the ideological divide that had sundered the Slovene nation into two warring sides during the occupation would remain unbridgeable. For the opponents of Tito's regime, the executions of the Home Guardsmen would become their Katyn. Unlike in the case of Poland, however, the perpetrators were not a foreign army but their own ethnic kin. For the refugees and émigrés, who would come to constitute the Slovene anti-Communist camp in the diaspora, it would be ground zero in a historiographical civil war that would rage for more than four decades – one that arguably persists to the present day. Within their social, cultural, and economic organizations in the diaspora, the refugees and émigrés would preserve an alternate understanding of what the Communists denounced as 'collaboration' and of whom they accused of being 'collaborators.'

In 1945 Yugoslavia, however, their voices amounted to very little, as Tito's regime solidified its grip on power. The mass execution of the Home Guard was only one attempt, albeit a particularly bloody one, to wreak vengeance upon collaborators while simultaneously neutralizing the political threat facing the new regime by the presence of thousands of anti-Partisan militiamen and refugees residing along the borders of Austria and Italy. The interpretation of wartime collaboration and war crimes promulgated by the Communist Party of Yugoslavia was, thus, thrown into the same judicial pot as political dissidence with the new regime. The results were predictably tragic. The twinning of these two legally distinct concepts is understandable if we view the CPY as the small and illegal party it was for much of the pre-war period. The CPY's meteoric rise to power had been achieved only recently in the crucible of the Second World War, in its struggle against not only the occupiers, but also its domestic opponents – the pre-war political and religious elite. Thus, the National Liberation War became the bedrock – the 'creation myth' if you will – of the Communist Party of Yugoslavia, and the starting point in virtually all regime histories. Even historical accounts of regions where Partisan resistance was virtually non-existent are presented in the context of the NOB, for example, Ferdo Godina's 1980 work on Hungarian-occupied Prekmurje, is entitled *Prekmurje, 1941–1945: A Contribution to the History of the National Liberation War*.[15] Postwar historians went into minute detail in describing enemy offensives against Partisan units. The role of the Soviet army, which had helped liberate some regions of Yugoslavia, most notably eastern Serbia and Prekmurje, was largely ignored. Tito's 1948 break with Moscow only accelerated this autochthonous trend in wartime historiography. The significance of Anglo-American wartime support for the Partisans was equally downplayed. Like no other factor, the National Liberation War legitimized the Communists' postwar right to rule.

Not surprisingly, collaborators and the admittedly weak non-Communist resistance figured little in this straightforward narrative of heroic Liberation Front defiance of the occupiers. Rational aims were not affixed to their actions or responses to the occupation. In the colossal

900-page 1979 *Zgodovina Slovencev* (History of the Slovenes), 150 pages, or approximately 20 per cent of the work was dedicated to the four short years of the National Liberation War and the Second World War. Fewer than ten pages were dedicated to their opponents. The former priest-turned-Partisan and later historian Metod Mikuž explained this discrepancy in blunt language: 'this chapter is not very extensive, as the role of traitors in the history of the Slovene and Yugoslav people was not that important.'[16]

The regime school's view of collaboration was held by numerous historians and commentators and defined by certain shared elements. This view operated from the basic premise that the Liberation Front was the only proper manifestation of the will of the Slovene people during the Second World War. This was a continuation of the OF's insistence from its very inception that no insurgent organization could operate outside the confines of the front. As such, regime historians claimed that the OF's choice of armed resistance against the occupation enjoyed the support of the majority of Slovenes. 'Our sacred national responsibility,' wrote the Slovene Communist Boris Kidrič during the war, is rebellion.[17] The regime historian Branko Božič added to Kidrič's words, stating that 'all those who did not want to fight soon found themselves on the side of the occupier and among the traitors of the Slovene nation.'[18] Thus, the covert 'wait-and-see' approach that was initially favoured by a number of non-Communist resisters – a policy that envisioned striking only when the occupier was weakest in order to reduce unnecessary reprisals – was described as the cowardly action of 'faint-hearted people.' According to the regime school, the proponents of this more cautious approach to resistance became 'mere lookers-on of the struggle' and 'political gamblers,' driven by base self-interest in order to restore their reactionary pre-war political dominance.[19]

Collaborators and their supporters were demonized with epithets that had already been popularized during the war. They were referred to as White Guards (*bela garda*) – a term alluding to the Whites in the Russian Civil War – reactionaries, defenders of the Germans (*švabobranci*), Hungarian sympathizers (*madžaroni*), or the always vague but frightening, 'clerical fascists.' The meagre public following for collaboration was dismissed as the choice of 'misguided' or 'unschooled people.'[20]

Regime histories followed a predictable narrative. Little was written about the less-savoury aspects of the Liberation Front's wartime record. The relative passivity of the Communist Party in the months between the initial invasion of Yugoslavia, in April 1941, and the Axis attack on the Soviet Union, that June, was passed over. Slovenes, it was assumed, courageously bore enemy reprisals in their support of the Liberation Front. Victims of Communist assassinations were unquestionably 'collaborators.' Even while silence reigned over the issue of the Communists' postwar executions, regime historians such as Franček Saje and Štefanija Ravnikar-Podbevšek emphasized the bloodlust and cruelty of the 'white guard' torture chambers of Saint Urh, as well as the shadowy 'Black Hand' organization that murdered Communists and their families.[21] Moreover, regime historians refused to refer to the civil war as a *civil war*. Rather, it was seen as a tiny unresponsive reactionary clique resisting the revolutionary will of the people, with the assistance of the occupier.

The historians' craft was only one part of a larger Yugoslav Communist campaign to enshrine the 'victor's history' as *the history* of the Second World War. Communist-era Slovenia was infected with a severe case of 'monument-itis.' Elaborate monuments sprung up all over the country, commemorating known and unknown fallen Partisans and their daring exploits. As late as 1975, the thirtieth anniversary of the liberation of Ljubljana, where an enormous monument to Partisan leader Franc Rožman-Stane was unveiled, was attended by 150,000 people.[22] In the cinematic sphere, *Na svoji zemlji* (On Our Own Land) was released in 1948. The film is a heroic portrayal of a Primorska village and its support for the local Partisans who battled the Italians and the Germans under the sadistic commander Kutschera (a reference to Franz Kutschera, the SS general and Gauleiter of occupied Gorenjska) and his drunken Slovene collaborators. The première was attended by 54,800 people, and it is considered one of the most-watched Slovene films of all times.[23] The education system taught obedience and respect for the National Liberation War, as evidenced by the Young Pioneers and the mandatory portraits of Tito. Such active promotion of the victor's history in the decades after the Second World War stood in contrast to the officially forgotten execution sites in the Kočevski Forest, off-limits to mourners.

The regime school was challenged by the thousands of mostly anti-Communist Slovenes who fled and emigrated immediately after the war. Free from the censorship of Communist Yugoslavia, they ensured that the postwar executions would not be forgotten and that an alternate understanding of collaboration existed to that forwarded by the Communist Party. This emigration wave changed the face of the diaspora. Unlike previous Slovene immigrants, these new arrivals were not economic refugees but mostly political refugees, united in their hatred of the Communist system in Yugoslavia. This influx exacerbated divisions within the established diaspora communities on the issue of the National Liberation War and the Communist takeover of power. Among the most vocal of Tito's supporters in the diaspora was the American-Slovene author Louis Adamič.[24] Nevertheless, whereas reactions to Tito's Yugoslavia were important in distinguishing and defining the diaspora, it was certainly not the only compass. There was a pre-existing and, arguably, much older political division – that between Catholic and liberal émigrés. In addition, a few influential members of the so-called wartime Centre (*sredina*), among them the Slovene economist and dissident Ljubo Sirc, were as critical of the compromising stance the political right took towards the occupiers as they were of the Communist takeover.[25] This was a view held, too, by some former Slovene Četnik supporters of General Draža Mihailović's Yugoslav Army in the Homeland, who had hoped for an effective non-Communist and anti-occupier resistance force during the war.[26] As in all immigrant communities, there were also Slovenes who refrained from all political activity, kept their beliefs to themselves, and concentrated primarily on establishing a new life.

Despite this lack of political and ideological unanimity – a fragmentation that had also decisively hampered their initial opposition to the occupiers and the Liberation Front during the Second World War – most post-1945 Slovene émigrés shared a similar enough interpretation of collaboration to form their own distinctive historical school. They disseminated their views primarily through community publishers concentrated in Buenos Aires, Cleveland, and Toronto, and through the Catholic *Mohorjeva družba* based in Klagenfurt. Their publications were varied, and included the influential periodical *Zbornik koledar svobodne Slovenije*, published in Buenos Aires, newspapers, memoirs, various polemical tracts commemorating the postwar massacres, and some less than impartial histories.[27]

The most definitive of the émigrés' shared doctrines, perhaps, has been their insistence that what the Communists termed collaboration was, in fact, *self-defence*. They saw themselves as victims caught between 'two fires' – between the Communists and the occupiers. The 'two fires' theory argued that the Liberation Front's policy of immediate armed action against the occupier regardless of enemy reprisals was irresponsible and reckless, and thus, denounced their opportunistic attempt to seize power in the midst of a national catastrophe. Their own acceptance of taking up the occupiers' arms was exonerated by Liberation Front aggression, which had forced them to side with the lesser evil to defend themselves and their nation.

The émigrés further justified their compromising decision by highlighting the 'double game' they had alleged to have played on the occupiers. Indeed, as will be shown, some collaborators remained sympathetic to the Western Allies and loyal to the Yugoslav government-in-exile in London, believing that they were all united against the Red Menace. Others relayed intelligence reports on the Axis forces to the government-in-exile at the same time as their reports on Liberation Front networks were conveyed to the occupiers. The émigrés insisted that the Axis never completely trusted the loyalty of anti-Partisan forces, offering them outdated weapons, prohibiting their scattered units from unifying into larger joint actions, and periodically arresting their members. Always sharing a prominent place in the works of the émigré school was the Tabor Declaration, clear evidence, in the view of the émigrés, of their true allegiance.

Unlike Communist historiography, the émigré school recognized the conflict between the Partisans and their opponents as a civil war, yet erred in the opposite extreme by portraying it *purely* as a civil war. By doing so, the émigrés conveniently diminished collaborators' crucial dependence on their occupiers. Moreover, within the context of the Cold War, the émigrés were able to transform what had, in fact, been a 'dirty war' into a heroic fight against Communism, in solidarity with the contemporary struggles in Korea, Vietnam, and the anti-Soviet uprisings in Hungary and Czechoslovakia in 1956 and 1968 respectively. Émigré publications, thus, described the Liberation Front and the Communist Party as a 'foreign' entity that worked for the interest of international communism, not that of the Slovene nation, and stood for godlessness in a devoutly Catholic country. Partisans and Communists were morally inferior beings in émigré literature – 'lazy workers, alcoholics, squanderers, prostitutes, and known thieves, who went with the Communists, so that they could take over the belongings of honest people.'[28]

The émigrés ridiculed the Partisans' celebrated 'liberated territory' as nothing more than terrain the occupiers left unoccupied because of a lack of manpower and strategic value. The Communists were reminded of their defeatism during the April 1941 invasion and their inactivity until Operation Barbarossa destroyed the Molotov-Ribbentrop Pact.

They insisted that the popularity of the Liberation Front was a fraud: whatever small support existed for the Liberation Front arose only from their unscrupulous use of coercion against their own people and their lies of a future socialist paradise. Émigré works dismissed the torture and execution of Partisans at Sveti Urh and elsewhere as fabrications. 'Collaboration' was nothing more than a convenient Communist term to defame the good names of their honest, devotedly Catholic, and nationally conscious victims. Rather speciously, émigrés accused the Partisans of collaborating with the occupiers, pointing to the heavy weaponry acquired from the capitulated Italians that was so effectively used against anti-Partisan forces in September 1943.

Most uncomfortable for the Communist authorities, however, was the fact that the émigré school would not allow the postwar executions to be swept under the proverbial rug. An overwhelming aura of martyrdom surrounded them, enhanced by British treachery in delivering these alleged 'pro-Allied, anti-Communist warriors' into the hands of their enemies. Pointing to the British support for Greek nationalists, the émigré school highlighted the double standard practised against Slovene anti-Communists. Perhaps most significantly, the sheer scale of the postwar executions fostered a psychological defence against accusations of collaboration. The twelve thousand Home Guard victims only reaffirmed the righteousness of the émigré struggle against what they saw as an unquestionably evil regime and ideology.

A combination of ideological solidarity and government coercion ensured that regime historians projected a more unified interpretation of the war years than the more segmented émigré camp. But cracks soon appeared. Milovan Djilas became the best known dissident with his famous work *The New Class*. His 1977 memoir, *Wartime*, offered a picture of an occupied Yugoslavia gripped by ethnic and civil strife. His work examined the atrocities committed by both sides, and referred to the postwar executions as 'sheer frenzy.'[29] The best known Slovene dissident was Edvard Kocbek, the celebrated man of letters, who during the Second World War headed the Christian Socialist faction within the Liberation Front. His critical 1951 work *Strah in pogum* (Fear and Bravery) explored the moral dilemmas of Partisan resistance and earned him a ten-year ban from publishing. His memoir of the war, entitled *Tovarišija* (Comradeship), was published in 1967. It described a Slovenia wracked by civil conflict. The work challenged the regime historians' assumption of widespread popular support for the Liberation Front. Referring to the suspicious peasantry as 'a political paradox,' Kocbek wrote, 'we are liberating a people almost against their will and we are expressing our progressive concepts in the name of that people, to whom we are at present opposed.'[30] However, a series of interviews that Kocbek gave to his friends Boris Pahor and Alojz Rebula that truly frightened the Slovene Communist Party (CPS). The result *Edvard Kocbek: Pričevalec našega časa* (Edward Kocbek: Witness of Our Time) was published in Trieste in 1975. In it, Kocbek spoke candidly of the civil war and the bullying sectarianism of the Communists in the later years of the Second World War that destroyed many of the Liberation Front's self-proclaimed ideals. More importantly, he spoke openly of the 'horrific punishment of the enemy' after the war and the clumsy attempts to conceal it. Although not defending collaboration, Kocbek believed it was necessary to go public with what had happened after the war, to admit 'our guilt' and 'our crimes,' otherwise 'Slovenes will never step into the clean and clear atmosphere of the future.'[31] Thus, in the midst of the thirtieth anniversary of the liberation, Kocbek's work and an earlier far less controversial feature by the historian Dušan Biber in a Zagreb weekly, initiated a limited public discourse on the final bloody months of the war.[32] The Yugoslav regime, for its part, banned the book by Pahor and Rebula, while Kocbek was under constant police surveillance until his death in 1981.

Kocbek's re-evaluation was a prelude to the changes that were to occur in the 1980s. Tito's death, increasing economic difficulties, heightened ethnic nationalism, and a growing cultural liberalization all contributed to a re-evaluation within Slovenia of the regime view of collaboration and the war years. Eschewing the simplistic ideological caricatures of the previous four decades, collaborators and collaboration became a topic of intense interest for a new, younger generation of historians, many with no first-hand experience of the Second World War. In 1980, Dušan Željeznov revisited the trial of General Leon Rupnik.[33] Under the Italians, Rupnik served as the mayor of Ljubljana, and under the Germans, as president of the Province of Ljubljana and inspector-general of the Home Guard. Leon Rupnik was tried and executed by Tito's government in 1946. Željeznov in no way challenged the verdict that Rupnik was a collaborator and responsible for the death of many Slovenes. Nevertheless, by quoting extensively from Rupnik's eighty-three-page deposition, which he submitted to the court on 1 February 1946, Željeznov portrays a man with far more complex motivations than the figure villainized in postwar propaganda. Beginning already in the late 1970s, one of the current leading authorities on the Home

Guard, Boris Mlakar, offered a more critical and nuanced study of the anti-Partisan units in Primorska. In his 1982 work on the topic, Mlakar stated that at the end of the Second World War, the Communists shot some of them 'without due process.'[34]

A great stir was created among the diaspora by Nikolai Tolstoy's 1986 book *The Minister and the Massacres*.[35] The colourful and controversial Count Tolstoy attempted to reveal who among the British authorities in Austria was responsible both for the repatriation of anti-Communist Yugoslavs and for the handing over of anti-Soviet Cossacks and Russians to Stalin's regime. Evidently sharing the sympathies of the émigré school, Tolstoy's book quickly became their bible as up until that point few Western scholars had taken an in-depth interest in wartime events in Slovenia. Despite its popularity, Tolstoy's study had, in fact, been preceded in Slovenia by Spomenka Hribar's controversial 1984 work *Krivda in greh* (Guilt and Sin). Despite her leftist political credentials, Hribar created a stir by insisting that the Home Guard had also died for the homeland. As part of her call for national reconciliation, she demanded a monument to the Home Guard in the centre of Ljubljana dedicated to this 'tragedy of a small nation.'[36]

Two key turning points in the public re-evaluation of Slovenia's wartime experience occurred in 1990. In April that year, the non-Communist Democratic Opposition of Slovenia (DEMOS) won a majority in the first postwar multiparty elections. DEMOS then declared, in July, that Slovenia would be seeking formal independence. Already at this early stage, the outspoken periodical *Mladina* (Youth) carried stories on the Kočevski Rog executions and interviews with survivors. Long suppressed works burst into the public domain, including Ljubljana Bishop Gregorij Rožman's 1946 letter to the Pope, in which he defended himself against charges of collaboration that were levied upon him at his postwar trial in absentia. The letter appeared in the 1990 edition of *Nova revija* (New Review), an opposition journal edited by the historian Niko Grafenauer that had been causing the Communist authorities grief since it first appeared in 1982.[37] The viciously anti-Communist *Črna bukva* (Black Book) was also reissued in 1990. Initially released in Ljubljana in 1944 by Mirko Javornik, the editor of the anti-Partisan Catholic weekly *Slovenski dom* (Slovene Home), the book highlighted Liberation Front atrocities including the murder and torture of civilians, the torching of homes, and the destruction of Slovenia's cultural heritage. As a sign of how quickly times had changed, the new editors not only reaffirmed the old justifications of 'self-defence' and 'two fires,' but also dismissed accusations of collaboration as 'the most shameful cynicism of the people who for so many years themselves collaborated with Stalin, one of the greatest monsters of world history.'[38] A month before Slovenia's proclamation of independence, in June 1991, a conference at the University of Ljubljana, dedicated to the fiftieth anniversary of the outbreak of Liberation Front resistance, captured the divergent perspectives that were appearing. The conference was attended by a number of historians still loyal to the regime school, a participant from the theology faculty who defended Bishop Rožman, and Mlakar with his 'critically sympathetic' analysis of the wartime anti-Partisan opposition.[39]

On a more popular level, the 'rediscovery' of the postwar execution sites held out hope for Kocbek's desire to see Slovenes acknowledge and move beyond past crimes. Yet, it also fed a campaign by right-wing nationalists in Slovenia and abroad to invalidate the legitimate patriotism that many Partisans fought and died for, as well as any value in Slovenia's forty-year experiment with socialism. As the historian H. James Burgwyn has observed, the fact that 'the Communist regime of Marshal Tito after the war shot countless "bourgeois" enemies, liquidated thousands of rounded-up Četniks, and imposed a resolute dictatorship over the people should not obscure the idealism of many a partisan insurgent.'[40] The first mass in memory of the victims of Kočevski Rog was held next to the execution sites, on 8 July 1990. As a sign of public reconciliation, the mass was presided over by Archbishop Alojzij Šuštar, and it was also attended by the former Communist and later president of Slovenia, Milan Kučan. On a grassroots level, unofficial monuments commemorating the 'victims of communist aggression' began to go up even before Slovenia's formal independence, particularly in small rural villages in the wartime anti-Partisan strongholds of Dolenjska, Notranjska, and Bela Krajina. In these regions, which had borne the brunt of the postwar executions and yet were never able to officially commemorate their losses, this transformation of the 'monument landscape' was cathartic. Unfortunately, many of these monuments also failed to mention that their victims had once fought side-by-side with the occupiers.

Thus, the reassessment of collaboration and resistance within a changing understanding of the Second World War was not simply the result of the electoral defeat of the Communist Party of Slovenia, the unshackling of right-wing nationalists, or the independence of Slovenia. This reappraisal had begun much earlier. It arose within Titoist

Yugoslavia's more 'liberal' version of Communism, with the isolated words of 'tolerated dissidents' such as Edvard Kocbek and among historians and thinkers in the 1980s who were not satisfied with the postwar regime view.

Nevertheless, Slovenia's formal independence from Yugoslavia and its liberal-democratic character encouraged a further explosion of literature, both popular and academic, on the topic of collaborators and the anti-Partisan opposition, as well as other formerly taboo subjects from the Second World War. Alojzij Žibert's memoir, for example, chronicled the shameful physical violence and discrimination practised against the tens of thousands of 'forgotten' Slovenes who had been forcibly conscripted into the German army.[41] An increasing number of historians, among them Bojan Godeša, Mlakar, Tone Ferenc, France Dolinar, and Tamara Griesser-Pečar have written extensively on collaborators and the wider anti-Communist movement during the war.[42] Other historians have reopened the related topic of the popular courts and show trials against alleged traitors in the immediate postwar years.[43] Their efforts, if not always in accord, have nonetheless revealed some of the political, ideological, and social heterogeneity of the group that for decades had been classified by the Communists under the catch-all term of collaborators. They embedded collaboration within the context of the brutal occupation and Slovenia's regional variances. Even historians who remained largely sympathetic to the Partisans, such as Ferdo Gestrin, nevertheless, offered a less black-and-white portrayal of collaboration and resistance.[44] A 'grey' view had begun to dominate, which acknowledged that the Partisans also alienated people through their actions and behaviour.

Among this newly available literature, there was a marked increase in apologist and polemical works that misrepresented the Second World War collaborator as a type of proto-independence fighter and precursor to the recent struggle against Communism. The organization New Slovene Covenant (Nova Slovenska zaveza), made up in part of Home Guard veterans, and its quarterly journal *Zaveza* (Covenant), which has been published since December 1991, is just one example of a revisionist campaign describing the Liberation Front and its Communist successor as genocidal.[45] The release of Stanko Kociper's biography in 1996 was dogged with controversy. As Leon Rupnik's personal secretary and son-in-law, and as one of the chief propagandists of the Home Guard, Kociper defended Rupnik's record and steadfastly refused to admit that he or his force had collaborated. Falling back on predictable arguments, Kociper stated that Liberation Front atrocities forced the Home Guard and other Slovene anti-Partisan units to seek the assistance of the occupiers in order to defend themselves and their nation.[46] For its part, the Catholic press continues to defend the wartime record of the Church and urges the rehabilitation of Bishop Rožman.[47]

A number of historians and writers including Draga Ahačič and Gregor Tomc have warned against this rehabilitation of the émigré–Home Guard view of the Second World War, and its equation of collaborators as the wartime defenders of democracy.[48] The historian Oto Luthar has denounced what he sees as a dangerous revisionism among historians such as Mlakar and Griesser-Pečar, in which collaboration with the occupiers 'is understood as functional opposition to the [Communist] revolution and hence as morally and politically justified.'[49]

Despite the attention that rehabilitated émigré – Home Guard perspectives have recently received, unfettered Partisan legends also persist, particularly among the still influential but shrinking National Liberation War veteran groups.[50] This often-bitter clash of seemingly polar opposite views of collaboration and wartime events is not all that different from the equally acrimonious national reappraisal that occurred in France in the 1970s and 1980s following the release of *The Sorrow and the Pity* and the sensational trials of René Bousquet, Maurice Papon, and Paul Touvier. The scholarly literature stands testament to similar re-evaluations in many formerly occupied European states and, more recently, in Asia.[51] This process is related, as it is in the Slovene case, to the passing of regimes that had based a significant part of their legitimacy on their wartime record of resistance, as well as the passing of a generation that was personally moulded by the Second World War. Slovenia's reckoning with its wartime past was delayed by its regime and the recalcitrance of its émigrés, a significant but hardly unique experience in East Central Europe. The hope is that this debate about Slovene collaboration will lead to a more inclusive view of the various experiences of the Second World War, not one of moral equivalency, but rather one that reveals war crimes perpetrated by either side for what they were.

There is method to the apparent madness of a book on collaboration vaulting over the actual events of the Second World War, and starting with an examination of historical interpretations whose underlying events have yet to be introduced. Such a methodology emphasizes that the discussion and debate surrounding Slovene collaboration over the past six decades has hardly ever been a purely academic exercise – assuming such an idealistic enterprise exists. Instead, emotions and ideological allegiances, fed by traumatic events, continue to impact the historical record of these years. By highlighting these potential distortions, a discussion of historiography should assist in inoculating the historian from the seductive ideological arguments that revisionists and some émigrés have used to explain away collaboration in Slovenia. Anti-Communism was not synonymous with collaboration. Although there were many collaborators who were deeply opposed to Communism, there were collaborators for whom anti-Communism was only one of a number of motivating factors. Moreover, there were also opponents of the Liberation Front who refrained from collaborating, and some who chose exile or were imprisoned by the occupiers. In a similar vein, an assessment of the historiography offers a glimpse of the sheer stubbornness of the National Liberation War's guardians, who insist that the wartime actions of the Liberation Front and their ideological rigidity could not have driven some Slovenes into the arms of the anti-Partisan units. The safety of time and nostalgia's inevitable inaccuracies have also distorted eyewitness memories of those years. Retrospective heroism did not always mean that actual heroic events had occurred. Decisions and options that may have appeared so straightforward in the 1970s, 1980s, or 1990s were not that clear-cut in 1942, 1943, or 1944. Moreover, both the regime and émigré schools often failed to base their arguments on rigorous assessments of the historical material. They resorted to selective choices of documentation to buttress preconceived ideological narratives, and émigrés were additionally burdened by being denied physical access to many of the surviving documents that were archived in Communist Yugoslavia. With these cautionary observations in mind, it is necessary to return to the difficult period between 1941 and 1945 to examine anew, and in closer detail, the relations between Slovenes and their occupiers, and the story of their collaborators.

2 Before the Deluge

> My heart seized for a moment when I saw those lands where I will perhaps spill my blood and lay down my life. However, when I gazed upon our beautiful littoral, when I watched the sea, the tension released and my resolve hardened even more, that I am prepared to sacrifice myself so that our enemies do not seize our beautiful lands.[1]
>
> Franc Rueh, Moj dnevnik, 1915–1918

This diary entry was written by a young Slovene soldier from Dolenjska while he was stationed on the Isonzo front. The enemy was Italy, but the year was 1915. In a war that took over thirty thousand young Slovene lives and exacted a casualty rate of 2.75 per every hundred inhabitants – one of the highest percentages of the Great War – the First World War was assumed to be the war to end all wars.[2] The Adriatic landscape that moved a young Franc Rueh to such patriotic poetry would, however, not be liberated. Along with a considerable portion of Slovene-inhabited territory, it would be awarded to Italy in postwar peace treaties. Yet, this injustice was only one of innumerous affronts that the Great War bequeathed to interwar Europe, as it swayed and lurched in its economic, social, national, and psychological malaise towards the century's second great slaughter that started in 1939. Few Slovenes could predict in 1918, 1928, or even 1938 what destiny would deliver on 6 April 1941. Nevertheless, the behaviour of Slovenes under Axis occupation was conditioned by their experiences in 1918, 1928, and 1938 – indeed, by the entire tumultuous period of the Great War and the interwar era. This chapter examines the ideological and political faultlines that existed before the deluge of April 1941. The Axis invasion and occupation was certainly a turning point in twentieth-century Slovene history, and popular responses to it, including resistance, collaboration, and accommodation can be better understood by placing them within the historical continuum that pre-dated it.

The December 1918 birth of the Kingdom of Serbs, Croats, and Slovenes ended Slovenia's seven-century-long political relationship with the House of Habsburg. However, virtually until the end of the Great War, most established Slovene politicians and their parties pledged loyalty to the Austro-Hungarian Empire. Indeed, in the late nineteenth and early twentieth centuries, Slovenes had enjoyed the fruits of a policy of organic work that had strengthened the social and economic positions of Slovenes and, ultimately, their national consciousness and cohesiveness. Many of these successes, including rising education levels, agricultural modernization, and increasing industrialization, were at least partly dependent on a unified empire. The Slovene Catholic political movement, and particularly the Slovene People's Party (Slovenska ljudska stranka, SLS), which in 1908 became the ruling party in the mostly Slovene-speaking province of Carniola, had originally emerged as one of the most active proponents of national self-strengthening and economic modernization. Yet, as the historian Ivo Banac noted, in the lead-up to the First World War the Catholic parties of central Europe, Slovene included, 'were increasingly losing their reformist edge and becoming a pillar of Habsburg order.'[3] In addition to the traditional challenge of liberalism, the Slovene People's Party and the Catholic movement were confronted by the more radically reformist Marxists and socialists. Yugoslavism, which had matured from its Illyrian roots of the 1830s and 1840s, also gained increasing adherents in Slovenia, particularly among the young and intellectuals who were frustrated with what they saw as the Dual Monarchy's aggressive intentions in the Balkans and its reticence in recognizing South Slav autonomy. Support for Yugoslavism before the First World War must not, however, be overstated, as the historian Carole Rogel has argued, 'the [Slovene] parties continued to expect their respective Yugoslav programs to be realized within Austria. They also expected the empire to continue to expand southward, and that someday soon even Serbia (independent since 1878) would be a part of it. In their minds, secession from Austria was not a working option.'[4]

With the outbreak of the First World War, the Slovene political establishment reaffirmed its loyalty to the Habsburgs. SLS leader Ivan

Šuštersič, a particularly unrepentant Serbophobe, stated on 5 July 1914 that 'the heavy hand of the Slovene soldier, Slovene boy will crush the skull of that Serb, within which lives gluttonous megalomania.'[5] Even the younger Father Anton Korošec, the future proponent of Yugoslavia and SLS leader, 'promised loyalty to the death in 1914.'[6] Italy's irredentist designs and its 1915 attack on Austro-Hungarian territory populated by ethnic Slovenes appeared to have convinced Slovene politicians that they needed the protection of the Dual Empire more not less. Austria's penchant for responding with force to signs of internal dissension and disloyalty, however, led to the closing of Slovene cultural institutions, the arrest of intellectuals and politicians, and the execution of 469 Slovenes for treason in the first fourteen months of the war alone.[7] In addition to martial law, the desperate material deprivation in the empire, particularly in the last two years of the Great War, further undermined civilian support for the war and the monarchy.

Leading Slovene politicians began to openly flirt with a reconfiguration of the empire that would benefit the South Slavs only after the reopening of the Imperial Parliament in 1917. On 30 May 1917, the Yugoslav Club, consisting of the empire's Slovene, Croat, and Serb politicians, including Šuštersič and Korošec, signed the May Declaration (Majniška deklaracija). It called for 'all territory of the Monarchy, where Slovenes, Croats, and Serbs live, to unite under the sceptre of the Habsburg-Lorraine dynasty into an independent national body, which will be free from foreign rule and based on a democratic foundation.'[8] The May Declaration stated clearly that a solution to the South Slav question was to be found within the confines of the Habsburg Empire, but its unanimous call for reforms precisely when the empire was involved in a life-and-death struggle for its very existence was indicative of the impatient mood of its traditionally loyal Slovenes. More ominously, on 20 July 1917, the émigré Yugoslav Committee and the Serbian government signed the Corfu Declaration, calling for a constitutional, democratic, and parliamentary Kingdom of Serbs, Croats, and Slovenes under the Serbian Karadjordjević dynasty.

Tensions grew in the autumn of 1917 and early 1918, as the declaration movement (deklaracijsko gibanje) provided a surge of popular support for the May Declaration. Tens of thousands of Slovene civilians, especially women and youth, gathered signatures for the document, adding to it their hope for a speedy end to the war. The opposition of the emperor and the Viennese government to this movement, and the growing conviction in the final months of the war 'that the Habsburg

Empire was going down in defeat [. . .] pushed even more Slovenes, Croats and Serbs into an "external" variant of Yugoslavism' – one that had been promoted in the initial years of the war by only a handful of vocal South Slav émigrés.[9] Within the influential Slovene People's Party, division grew between those such as Šušteršič who were committed to finding a solution to Slovene national demands within the empire, and younger members led by Father Korošec who were pushing for a Yugoslav solution.

The Dual Monarchy's defeat and ultimate disintegration in November 1918, combined with the predatory designs of a resurgent Italy, vindicated the strategy of Korošec and the other Slovene supporters of South Slav unity. The task of nation building in the new Kingdom of Serbs, Croats, and Slovenes, however, was a sobering epilogue to the idealism of 1918. In addition to the daunting harmonization of the new state's banking, transportation, legal, and military systems that had for centuries been oriented centrifugally, the country was bitterly divided over its political character. Most 'Slovenes accepted the new state,' but they were 'at the same time eager to preserve their distinct language and culture.'[10] Thus, along with the Croats, they advocated for a federated configuration to the Serbian 'unitarist' or 'integralist' vision for Yugoslavia, which ultimately, prevailed in the Vidovdan Constitution of 28 June 1921 – so named because it was approved by the Constitutional Assembly on the Serbian feast day of St Vitus, a holiday that also marks the epic 1389 Battle of Kosovo between the medieval Serbian and Ottoman empires, as well as the 1914 assassination of the Archduke Franz Ferdinand that sparked the First World War. Unlike the Croats, however, who increasingly toyed with a separatist solution to their frustrated demands for federation in the interwar era, none of the 'major Slovene political parties nor Slovene intellectuals were anti-Yugoslav.'[11] The critical project, therefore, for the Slovene political establishment, in an interwar environment hostile to Europe's smaller peoples, was striking a balance between greater Slovene cultural and national autonomy and the preservation of Yugoslavia's territorial integrity and the relative security that it provided.

This critical project was severely hampered at the very outset by the postwar territorial settlements that defined the boundaries of the new Yugoslav state. The November 1920 Treaty of Rapallo cashed in on the secret incentives embodied in the 1915 Treaty of London, and rewarded Italy's decision to enter the war on the side of the Allies with extensive territorial concessions in areas also claimed by Yugoslavia.

Italy received virtually the entire former Austrian littoral crown land (Österreichisches Küstenland) or, as the Italians referred to it, Venezia Giulia – a name that insinuated a much more organic connection between this peripheral region of *Italia irridenta* and the rest of Italy. In Slovene, the littoral was known as Primorska – the designation that this study will also use – and included the northern Istrian peninsula, the city of Trieste and its Slovene-inhabited hinterland, and the old province of Gorizia (Gorica) extending up the Soča River to the town of Kobarid and beyond. In addition to Primorska, the Italians were also awarded the western portion of the predominately Slovene-inhabited former Austrian duchy of Carniola (the present-day Slovene region of Notranjska), and its main towns of Idrija and Postojna.[12] Croatian-inhabited lands that were ceded to Italy included the southern half of the Istrian peninsula, the islands of Cres and Lošinj, the Dalmatian town of Zadar, and some minor Dalmatian islands. All told, some half a million Slavs found themselves under Italian rule in this ethnically mixed region, of which approximately three hundred thousand were Slovenes.[13]

With Mussolini's rise to power, the region's Slavs felt the heavy brunt of Fascist rule, including enforced Italianization. Slovene and Croat cultural and political life was muffled in the campaign to assimilate the Slavs, which included among other measures, the encouragement of Slovene emigration, particularly of its educated classes, to central regions of Italy.[14] To escape persecution, a number of Croats and Slovenes emigrated to Yugoslavia or abroad. Much more violent resistance to Fascist rule was led initially by ORJUNA (Organizacija jugoslavenskih nacionalista, or Organization of Yugoslav Nationalists), which was formed in Split in 1921, followed, in the late 1920s, by the pro-Yugoslav anti-Fascist resistance organization in Italy called TIGR (an acronym for the contested regions of Trst, Istria, Gorizia, and Rijeka). Made up of Slovenes and Croats, TIGR called for the national liberation of Italy's South Slav minority, and it is considered to be one of the first anti-Fascist resistance organizations in Europe. TIGR established contacts with both Yugoslav and British intelligence; however, frequent arrests and executions bedevilled its capacity throughout the 1920s and 1930s. In the 1930s, TIGR increasingly fell under the influence of the political left, and during the Second World War, many members joined the Liberation Front in Primorska.

A significant number of Slovenes found themselves under Austrian rule during the interwar era. For almost a year following the capitulation of Austria-Hungary, in November 1918, a series of armed border skirmishes between the new Yugoslav state and Austria attempted to delineate the frontier. The Kingdom of Serbs, Croats, and Slovenes claimed mostly Slovene-inhabited southern Carinthia. In September 1919, the Treaty of Saint-Germain agreed that sovereignty in southern Carinthia should be decided by plebiscite, and the region was divided into two zones, a southern Zone A with a Slovene majority and a northern Zone B with a German-speaking majority. The vote was initially held only in Zone A, on 10 October 1920, and the decision was 60 per cent to 40 per cent in favour of remaining within Austria.[15] This result made it unnecessary to hold a plebiscite in Zone B. A significant number of Slovenophones voted in favour of Austria, concerned perhaps with the comparatively undeveloped economic and political state of affairs in the new South Slav state. Besides highlighting that linguistic and ethnic identities were not the only markers in deciding political allegiances in interwar Europe, the loss in the plebiscite would ultimately leave over fifty thousand Slovenes in the republic of Austria.[16]

Slovenes organized themselves into a Political and Economic Association of Carinthian Slovenes and were granted two seats in the Carinthian provincial assembly (Landtag). Interwar Austria, however, largely ignored safeguards for the protection of minorities written into the Treaty of Saint-Germain. Many of Carinthia's Germanophones joined the Carinthian Homeland Service (Kärntner Heimatdienst), a right-wing German nationalist organization that was opposed to cultural and political concessions to the Slovenes. Under the increasingly bellicose German chauvinism of interwar Austria, the Slovene minority suffered from cultural assimilation and random, although yet still relatively isolated acts of violence. Assimilative pressures reached their peak after the Anschluss of March 1938, when the Slovenes of Austrian Carinthia found themselves citizens of the German Reich. Carinthia's Germanophones were particularly enthusiastic about Hitler, reputedly producing the greatest number of Nazi Party members in all of the Third Reich – accounting for some 10 per cent of the province's population.[17] Among these native sons who would play a significant role in the German occupation of Slovenia were the Nazi war criminals Odilo Globocnik and the future high commissioner (Gauleiter) Friedrich Rainer. Indeed, even today, Carinthia remains the stronghold of the late Jörg Haider's far-right Austrian Freedom Party, which, among its other questionable policies, opposes official bilingualism in southern Carinthia.

With approximately one-quarter of the ethnic Slovene population residing outside of the borders of the Kingdom of Serbs, Croats, and Slovenes, and facing repressive and assimilative pressures, it is not surprising that SLS leader Korošec realized that 'even the worst Yugoslavia was for Slovenes a far better solution than no Yugoslavia at all.'[18] The SLS's opinion mattered, as it was the 'natural governing party' in Slovenia, having won every election with an absolute majority, except in 1920 when it won a relative majority. Its program stood for 'Slovene national and linguistic uniqueness and a Catholic social and cultural orientation' and, thus, was opposed to both liberalism and more especially, Marxism.[19] Engaging Slovenia's devout Catholics, the SLS's electoral base was quite broad and included peasants, a considerable portion of workers, and the petty bourgeoisie, as well as some intellectuals.

Monopolizing the religious vote was not the only factor behind the SLS's electoral successes. The party had a very capable leader in Father Korošec – the only non-Serb prime minister of Yugoslavia in the interwar era – and his chameleon-like ability to negotiate advantages for Slovenia with various Belgrade regimes. Indicative of this was the SLS's flexibility on a number of key issues. Initially, like the Croats, the SLS favoured a federated Yugoslavia and Slovene political autonomy, but eventually it accepted centralism. Generally supportive of the democratic development of Yugoslavia, the SLS was also 'the only political party which officially supported King Alexander's dictatorship introduced in 1929'[20] – which among other measures, changed the country's name to Yugoslavia, suppressed political parties, and centralized the administration of the country into nine provinces (or *banovine*) named after geographical landmarks. Having fallen out with the king in 1931, who introduced a 'bogus parliament' reliant on his authority, the SLS issued its famous 'Ljubljana Points,' in 1932, which reverted to the party's initial platform of greater autonomy for Slovenes in a democratic Yugoslavia.[21] The political weather vane made another turn in the wake of King Alexander's assassination in 1934, as the SLS dropped its official support for the Ljubljana Points and joined the coalition government of Milan Stojadinović's Yugoslav Radical Union (1935–39). Even though the Radical Union's pro-Axis foreign policy was generally frowned on by Yugoslav public opinion, the SLS still managed to win 78.7 per cent of Slovene votes in the last election of the interwar era, in December 1938, albeit one that was far from free.[22] Thus, it is precisely these opportunistic tendencies, much maligned by the SLS's political opponents, that 'secure[d] a degree of administrative "overprivilege"' for Slovenes in interwar Yugoslavia.[23] Far more ominous was the fact that the SLS carried 'their abilities as parliamentary bargainers from the Habsburg era' through the interwar period and into the perilous world of the occupation, with all its fateful implications for collaboration.

Standing in opposition to the Slovene People's Party were the Slovene Liberals, who unabashedly supported a unitary Yugoslavia. Indeed, some Slovene Liberals went as far as calling for linguistic and cultural synthesis with the Croats and Serbs – a position shared by the famed writer Oton Župančič – which left them open to attacks of being 'un-Slovene.'[24] The Liberals can be considered to have been the second largest political party in Slovenia, although they never managed to surpass the almost 30 per cent share they received in the 1920 elections.[25] Standing to their left, the Social Democrats shared with the Liberals the idea of Yugoslav integralism as the surest path to protecting the workers, who they claimed to be representing. Thus, with the exception of a faction of the Social Democrats led by Zvonimir Bernot, who called for greater federation,[26] the SLS was the one major interwar political party that at least in its pronouncements, if not always in practice, appeared to stand up for Slovene autonomy and distinctiveness within Yugoslavia.

Yet, as secure as these established parties appeared in the electoral results of the interwar era, it was the fringes of the interwar Slovene political spectrum that would play an inordinately influential role during the occupation. On the far left was the Communist Party of Yugoslavia. Founded in 1919, and committed to the political centralism and unitarism of the Kingdom of Serbs, Croats, and Slovenes, the CPY managed to poll the third largest number of votes in Yugoslavia in the 1920 elections for the Constituent Assembly. The Kingdom's government, concerned about rising social instability and buoyed by the suppression of the Hungarian Soviet Republic, banned the CPY in 1921, after young extremists known as 'Red Justice,' acting on their own initiative, assassinated the Interior Minister Milorad Drašković. The CPY remained outlawed until the 1941 Axis invasion. Hardly surprising, popular support for the CPY eroded as the organization's membership declined from a high point of 120,000 members in 1919 to below three thousand in the late 1920s.[27]

Communist attitudes towards the structure and viability of Yugoslavia fluctuated widely during their underground existence, largely reflecting the dictates of the Comintern in Moscow. The Resolution on

Yugoslavia, adopted at the Fifth Congress of the Comintern in 1924, had Serbia in its sights when it ordered the CPY to break the country into the independent republics of Croatia, Slovenia, Macedonia, and later, Montenegro.[28] The CPY would maintain its position on the dissolution of Yugoslavia through the late 1920s and the period of King Alexander's royal dictatorship, which on this issue alone, would place them in the company of the fascist Ustaši and the Bulgarian revisionism of the Internal Macedonian Revolutionary Organization. In line with the Comintern's 1934–39 strategy of Popular Front alliances with other like-minded anti-fascist European parties, the CPY was forced to reverse its position on Yugoslavia's break-up. In its place, the CPY offered each constituent Yugoslav people the right to self-determination within a federated state, as a unified Yugoslavia and army appeared far more effective in assisting in the defence of the Soviet Union from the rising menace of Nazi Germany than did a collection of small independent Balkan states. Despite the cooperation inherent in the Popular Front policy, Tito 'wielded his broom' during the late 1930s, purging party members in an effort to form the CPY 'in the Soviet mold of a monolithic party.'[29]

The Communist Party of Slovenia (CPS) was founded in 1937 as a branch of the CPY. Its leading members included Edvard Kardelj, Franc Leskovšek, and Boris Kidrič. In his seminal 1939 work, *Razvoj slovenskega narodnega vprašanja* (The Development of the Slovene National Question), Kardelj seemed to presage the future resistance activity of the CPS. He affirmed the importance of 'small' nations like Slovenia and the oppression that they suffered, a concept that had often been dismissed as regressive by Marxists. Indeed, only with the liberation of these small states from oppression – a task that Kardelj assigned to 'the vital, liberating role of the Communist Party' – could the utopian aim of a 'common humanity' be achieved among the plethora of nationalities.[30]

Standing at the opposite end of the Slovene interwar political spectrum were a motley array of far-right movements and parties that espoused admiration for European fascism and its leaders, and mouthed their typical xenophobic hatreds of Jews, Freemasons, and Communists. One of the earliest far-right Yugoslav organizations was ORJUNA, which advocated for integral Yugoslavism and a nationalist dictatorship to replace the ineffectual parliamentary system. Its Slovene chapter was known for its violent confrontations not only with Communists, which in the mining town of Trbovlje in 1924 left several dead, but also its disruption of SLS rallies.[31] After ORJUNA's dissolution in the wake of King Alexander's seizure of power, the torch was taken up by Boj (Battle), which emerged from an association of Yugoslav First World War veterans. Highly supportive of King Alexander, Boj received royal backing for its declared commitment to 'defend Yugoslav unity from revolutionary, social, and narrowly nationalistic movements.'[32] Although Boj and its pro-royalist right-wing partners, Yugoslav Action, claimed not to be fascist, their programs contained the ideological hallmarks of fascism: the adoption of fascist symbols and salutes, fervent anti-Communism, corporatism, and antiparliamentarism.[33] Internal divisions between Boj's left and right wings led to its dissolution in 1935.[34]

The Yugoslav far right was resuscitated with the establishment, in January 1935, of the pro-fascist Zbor (Rally) movement. Zbor was composed of a number of smaller associations including Boj's right-wing remnant and Yugoslav Action – which had earlier absorbed the far-right Slovene organization Borci (Fighters). Dimitrije Ljotić was chosen as leader of Zbor because of his previous short service as minister of justice during King Alexander's dictatorship and his continued contacts with the court.[35] Early in his life, Ljotić had came under the influence of Charles Maurras, the antisemitic counter-revolutionary founder of Action Française whose writings would inspire French and other European fascists, as well as the ideologues in the Vichy government.[36] Zbor's program called for a corporatist reorganization of Yugoslavia that would instil an integral Yugoslav national identity. Both Jews and Communists were incompatible with this goal. Ljotić echoed Nazism with his call for 'the racial and biological defense of the national life-force and the family,'[37] and his antisemitism became 'undisguised and unrestrained.'[38] Germany's envoy to Yugoslavia Viktor von Heeren enthusiastically supported Zbor, offering it German financial aid as early as 1935 and infiltrating its ranks with German agents.

Zbor remained on the electoral fringes in the 1935 and 1938 contests, mustering a measly 1 per cent of the vote; however, its influence was wider than the election results would suggest. For example, Ljotić's connections with Milan Nedić, the minister of the army and war in the late 1930s and the future leader of the collaborationist administration in occupied Serbia, allowed Zbor's organ *Bilten* (Bulletin) to be illegally printed and distributed among the Yugoslav Royal Army. Through such channels and the legal status of his party, Yugoslavs, including Slovenes, could read Ljotić's rather erroneous 1939 prediction that Hitler was 'an instrument of God's providence' and Slavdom's saviour.[39]

These two fringes of the political left and right accounted for only a small minority of the allegiances of interwar Slovenes. In the meantime, increasing pressure was being exerted on Yugoslavia in the 1930s to make common cause with the fascist states, and Slovenia was in a particularly vulnerable position. After the March 1938 Anschluss of Austria, Slovenia was bordered on the west by Fascist Italy, on the north by Nazi Germany, and on the east by a pro-Axis irredentist Hungarian state. In the wake of King Alexander's assassination, in Marseille, in October 1934, successive Yugoslav governments would lean further to the right in an attempt to appease these neighbouring revisionist and fascist states and disengage their support for separatists within Yugoslavia. In the process, regional diplomatic and defensive safeguards against revisionism, embodied in the Little Entente and the Balkan Pact, were effectively dismantled. The rightist Stojadinović government, which included the Slovene People's Party, led this change. In January 1937, Stojadinović's government concluded a rapprochement with Bulgaria, and in March, with Italy. Even more disconcerting was Stojadinović's expressed admiration for Mussolini and Hitler and his aping of fascist trappings, such as being greeted with calls of '*Vodja, Vodja!*' (Duce, Duce!) by his green-shirted supporters.[40] Despite Ljotić's taunts that Stojadonović was 'merely an imitator of Mussolini and the "hero and martyr" Adolf Hitler,' some disenchanted founding members of Zbor migrated quite comfortably to Stojadinović's governing coalition.[41] The Great Depression and the subsequent German economic penetration of Yugoslavia, the hesitation of Western democracies, and the fear of the Soviet Union and Communism, also contributed to this shift in Yugoslav diplomacy.

The right-wing drift of Stojadinović's government exacerbated ideological polarization in Slovenia. As members of Stojadinović's governing coalition, the Slovene People's Party was implicated in this slide and, among its other traits, was 'not bashful in displaying [. . .] anti-semitism,' although it 'stopped short of the nightmarish biological variety found in German Nazism.'[42] SLS membership in the Stojadinović government only accelerated an internal process within the SLS that was characterized in the 1930s by 'ideological-political splits and disintegration.'[43] This trend was hastened with the creation of the Communist-led Popular Fronts in 1935. It seemed not only to the Communists, but also to some SLS members and affiliates, that the ability to organize the Slovene population for a potential future war with its fascist neighbours had shifted from the SLS and the established Slovene parties to the political left.⁴⁴ Pre-eminent among them were the Christian Socialists led by their famous leader Edvard Kocbek, who splintered away from the SLS and cooperated with the Yugoslav and Slovene Popular Fronts in the second half of the 1930s. In the eyes of its youthful membership, the SLS establishment had moved into a neo-conservative and corporatist direction in which they 'obviously approved or apologized for authoritarian and totalitarian dictatorships that were being established in Europe.'⁴⁵ The SLS had become blinded by its fear of liberalism and its fear of Communism, which the calving of the party only seemed to confirm. These fears were pushing the SLS to ignore its democratic responsibilities and to cooperate with governments involved in 'the suppression of general voting rights, parliamentary democracy, [and] individual autonomy.'⁴⁶

The SLS's anti-Communism was more than an opportunistic ploy to trump a political opponent. After all, the CPY and CPS were both outlawed organizations, and their popular support, even if growing in the late 1930s with the formation of the Popular Fronts and their opposition to European fascism, could hardly be viewed as imminently threatening. Moreover, the 1939 Molotov-Ribbentrop Non-aggression Pact scuttled the Popular Fronts and sowed confusion and dismay among Communists throughout Europe, despite the forward march of the Soviet frontier after the partition of Poland. The CPY's assurances that it remained committed to Yugoslavia's independence were deflated by the Comintern's newly minted anti-war stance. The historian Dimitrije Djordjević calculated that the CPY reached a low point of only a thousand members in 1939 before rebounding to twelve thousand members on the eve of the Axis invasion of Yugoslavia – a rally attributed, in part, to Tito's organizational skill and popular anxiety over war.⁴⁷ Instead, the SLS's anti-Communism was an integral component of the party's world-view. In their propaganda, Slovene Catholic and national traditions were facing a colossal struggle against atheistic, internationalist revolutionaries. The seduction of fascism's strident anti-Communism was apparent in the May 1933 edition of the SLS-friendly Catholic daily *Slovenec* (The Slovene): 'Fascism undoubtedly has many agreeable traits even for the Catholic. Let us remember its endeavour for moral elevation, its suppression of the class war, and its establishment of a corporatist nation. Whatever is positive in fascism is taken from Christianity, and in this course fascism must absolutely be a part of the anti-Bolshevik front.'⁴⁸ In Korošec's mind, the anti-Bolshevik struggle transcended the political field and had to encompass the entire

Slovene people. In 1936, he remarked publicly that the police and prisons alone could not suffocate Communism. Rather, he declared that the 'idea must challenge the idea,' and 'Church and school [. . .] political parties, cultural and social associations, as well as economic organizations and their entire membership' must take part in this ideological battle.[49]

Korošec's call to arms was heeded by right-wing student organizations that were affiliated with the Slovene People's Party. The two main organizations were the Academic Club Straža (Sentinel) and the Mladci Kristusa Kralja (Christ the King Youth), both founded in the early 1930s. The ideological leader of Straža was the enigmatic Monsignor Lambert Ehrlich, a professor of theology at the University of Ljubljana. Born in Žabnice, in what had become Italian territory after the First World War, Monsignor Ehrlich had spent his younger formative years in Carinthia. It was for his expertise on Slovene minorities that he was included in the Yugoslav delegation at the Versailles peace talks, where he advocated for the inclusion of Slovene ethnic territory into Yugoslavia. Modelled along the lines of the Spanish Falange, Erlich's Straža Club was very active at the University of Ljubljana, where it achieved notoriety for its admiration of fascist principles.[50] In 1937, *Straža v viharju* (Sentinel in the Tempest), the group's official organ, wrote that 'fascism has been advantageous to those countries, where Catholic forces in public life have been demoralized and disorganized by liberalism. Without this tempest these nations, these countries would find it difficult to save themselves from Communism.'[51] Unique to previous far-right movements in Slovenia, which because of their promotion of Yugoslav integral nationalism were most often chapters of broader pan-Yugoslav movements, the Straža group advocated for Slovene nationalism and independence.[52]

The Mladci Kristusa Kralja, often known simply as Mladci or Tomčevi mladci after its founder Ernest Tomec, was a key organizer of the Slovene Catholic political and youth movements, and similarly attracted to aspects of fascism. In its publication *Mi mladi borci* (We Young Fighters), one finds excerpts from *Mein Kampf*, as well as praise for Nazi puppets like Monsignor Joseph Tiso, who 'saved Slovakia from the terrorist fist of Freemasonic ministers.'[53] Antisemitism also defined the Straža and the Mladci, and they equated the Jews with Western capitalist excesses and Bolshevik revolution alike.

Both active at the University of Ljubljana as well as in high schools, the Straža and the Mladci struggled in the 1930s for the leadership of the student wing of Catholic Action (Katoliška akcija, KA), a contest that the less extreme *Mladci* would win, in 1937. Catholic Action was the collective name for a European-wide apolitical laymen's movement of the Catholic Church that was to act 'as an "apostolate of the laity" under the direct guidance of the ecclesiastical authorities,' in order that 'Christian values be rooted deeply in modern society.'[54] The Catholic Action umbrella incorporated Catholic organizations and unions of students, workers, farmers, and teachers. Although not a political party, the Slovene KA in the 1930s certainly behaved like one. It became increasingly hierarchically organized and often crossed the blurry divide into politics by inveighing against the secularizing and anti-Catholic politics of Marxism, socialism, and liberalism. The KA worked in close accord with the Catholic establishment, particularly Gregorij Rožman, who was made bishop of Ljubljana, in 1930, and the ruling Slovene People's Party, whose two interwar leaders – Korošec and his successor Franc Kulovec – were both priests.

The Church in Slovenia had waded deeply into the ideological and political waters of the interwar era. It, predictably, saw Communism and its Popular Front incarnation as the greatest threat to organized religion. Bishop Rožman's hagiographic biographer Jakob Kolarčič described him already in the 1920s as being against the 'spirit of worldly, materialistic ideas.'[55] As bishop, Rožman was alarmed by the Spanish Civil War and battled 'organized atheism' in his sermons, in his written words, in conferences of priests, and in youth organizations.[56] A 1936 conference of Church deans, for example, was dedicated to 'The Communist Danger and Defence against It,' and one of its keynote speakers was Dean Matija Škerbec from Kranj, a committed anti-Communist, whose postwar writings were classics in the repertoire of émigré school literature. In justifying his ideological opposition to Bolshevism, Rožman, and indeed, most interwar Catholic-oriented politicians and activists, referenced the frequent papal encyclicals and statements that punctuated the era.

The fear of atheist Communism was not unique to Catholic officials in Slovenia. As the historian Niall Ferguson has caustically observed, 'a list of all the treasonous clerics who flirted or did more than flirt with fascism would be a book in its own right.'[57] The Catholic Church in Europe was disturbed by what it perceived to be Marxism's and socialism's increasing popularity among the disgruntled European working classes and within intellectual circles, particularly during the economic devastation of the 1930s. This fear was compounded, as it struggled to stem the Church's diminishing role and significance in a modernizing world. The historian John Cornwell has suggested that as early as the 1880s and 1890s, Pope Leo XIII (1878–1903) was apprehensive about the emerging ideology of socialism, referring to it as a 'pest [. . .] which so deeply perverts the sense of our population, derives all of its power from the darkness it causes in the intellect by hiding the light of eternal truths and corrupting the rule of life laid down by Christian morality.'[58] His successor Pius X (1903–1914) was so fearful of the modern that he was 'driven into a position of profound opposition to even the more moderate aspects of social and political modernity at the beginning of a new century, including the benefits of democracy.'[59] Pius XI (1922–1939), like most Western statesmen, was particularly concerned with the growing popularity of Communism during the Great Depression. His 1931 papal social encyclical *Quadragesimo anno* – which marked forty years since Leo's encyclical *Rerum Novarum* (1891) identified the menace of rampant capitalism, socialism, and liberalism – reaffirmed the twin dangers of liberalism and Communism to human dignity. His 1932 encyclical *Caritate Christi*, 'On the Present Distress of the Human Race' painted an apocalyptic image of Communism feeding off global economic turmoil:

> Profiting by so much economic distress and so much moral disorder the enemies of all social order, be they called Communists or by any other name, boldly set about breaking through every restraint. This is the most dreadful evil of our times, for they destroy every bond of law, human or divine; they engage openly and in secret in a relentless struggle against religion and against God Himself; they carry out the diabolical program of wresting from the hearts of all, even of children, all religious sentiment; for well they know that, when once belief in God has been taken from the heart of mankind, they will be entirely free to work out their will. Thus we see today, what was never before seen in history, the satanical banners of war against God and against religion brazenly unfurled to the winds in the midst of all peoples and in all parts of the earth.[60]

Of all of Pius XI's anti-Communist diatribes, perhaps his most quoted statement emerged from his 1937 encyclical *Divini Redemptoris*, which Bishop Rožman made reference to in his own 1940 *Zakonik Ljubljanske škofije* (Statutes of the Ljubljana Bishopric): 'Communism is something essentially evil, therefore in no case should one cooperate with it if one is concerned with Christian civilization.'[61] Like Rožman, Pius XI's belief that Bolshevism was 'the great peril of the modern world' would be reaffirmed by the outbreak of the Spanish Civil War and the victory of the Popular Front in France. Pius XII (1939–1958), a former secretary of Pius XI, would share much of his predecessor's intense fear of Communism, as Cornwell wrote, 'Pacelli [PiusXII] and Ratti [Pius XI] were well known to each other, and of one mind in their hatred and fear of Bolshevism.'[62]

The Vatican set a dangerous example of cooperation with the European dictators. The Holy See claimed that their agreements with Mussolini and Hitler in 1929 and 1933 respectively were meant to protect the autonomy of the Church and the freedom of worship, as well as to validate Rome's control over the Church hierarchy in the two respective states. The 1929 Lateran Agreement, for example, ensured the presence of religious education in elementary schools, the hanging of crucifixes, and legal parity for Catholic private schools. In return, the Church was to discourage the interference of priests in the social and political affairs of the state. In the ensuing March elections in Italy, Church officials largely supported Mussolini.[63] Similarly, in the 1933 Concordat, Hitler promised religious autonomy to Germany's Catholics and the upholding of Vatican law. Other circles in the Vatican saw Hitler's virulent anti-Communism as a welcomed bulwark against the spread of Bolshevism. In return for these concessions, Hitler managed to skilfully neutralize the political opposition of the Deutsche Zentrumspartei, the Catholic German Centre Party, by insisting that the Church remove itself from the political and social arena.[64] Compared with Pius XI, whose disillusion with Hitler's repeated violations of the Concordat led him to issue his 1937 encyclical *Mit Brennender Sorge* that portrayed Nazism as an evil ideology comparable to Communism, the legacy of his successor Pius XII is still shrouded in emotional controversy. Much of this is because of Pius XII's unwillingness – or his own perceived inability – to unequivocally and publicly denounce Nazism and its collaborators, and in particular, the murder of Europe's Jews.

Taken in its totality, the Vatican's obsessive anti-Communism and its engagement of Europe's fascist dictators to safeguard the Church's jurisdiction proved a dangerous precedent to follow for Slovene Catholic officials and the dominant Slovene People's Party. Their decisive alignment against the political left and their accommodation with the right reverberated in a society where religious study was a standard subject in state schools, where Church attendance – particularly in the countryside – was culturally expected, and where the Catholic hierarchy from the local parish priest up to the bishop enjoyed an inordinate degree of not only spiritual but secular and political influence.

It would be far too simplistic, however, to conclude that this alignment of the Slovene political and religious establishment went unchallenged by the interwar masses. Slovenia was changing in the two decades before the Second World War, and with modernization came fissures in its perceived Catholic homogeneity. A growing number of non-Communist intellectuals, such as Župančič, argued that 'the narrow received definition of Slovenehood, centred on Catholicism, melancholy, and certain political or artistic movements, was egocentric and useless.'[65] Education levels were increasing, and Slovene illiteracy, which in 1921 stood at only 8.8 per cent, was virtually eradicated by the outbreak of war.[66] The stereotypically placid agriculture way of life was also diversifying. Compared with most other regions of rural Yugoslavia, better access to modern farming techniques and markets allowed for a self-sustaining if not always prosperous agriculture system based on family-owned farms. Slovene industrialization continued to expand; in 1918, it was already four times greater in output than Serbia's and twenty-two times greater than Montenegro's and Macedonia's.[67] Urban manufacturing and the establishment of Slovenia's first university in Ljubljana, in 1919, attracted an increasing number of the rural poor and the ambitious youth. Cities achieved the not entirely undeserved reputation in the eyes of many conservatives as bastions of immoral secularism and breeding grounds for communism and other foreign ideas; generational schisms ruptured along political and ideological lines. Rudolf Hribernik-Svarun, a former Partisan and colonel-general in the Yugoslav People's Army, remembered his father's angry reaction when he found out that his son had been skipping mass to converse with a local Communist in Horjul: 'Don't you ever try to influence me with things, which you pick up God knows where. The last time I tell you! Either you will go to church, or you will no longer eat at this table.'[68] The violence and destruction of Axis conquests, their bullying stance towards Yugoslavia, and their shameful treatment of Slovene-speaking minorities in Italy and Austria left many Slovenes wary of the Yugoslav policy of rapprochement.

The interwar era was formative for the future responses that Slovenes would take towards the occupiers. The Slovene People's Party displayed its penchant for negotiation and compromise in working with Belgrade administrations of various political stripes – the governments produced during Yugoslavia's decade-long experiment with parliamentary democracy, King Alexander's personal rule, and the right-wing Stojadinović government. As the price for entering into coalition with the latter, Father Korošec and his party were willing to abandon the 1932 Slovene Declaration that they had devised in the darker days of royal dictatorship and its call for significant Slovene national autonomy in a federated Yugoslavia. Certainly, the SLS could point to concrete benefits in their political engagement, not least of which was a say in the direction of the national government. However, its critics also correctly observed that the SLS's chameleon-like political opportunism was placing the party in uncomfortably close proximity to states and ideologies that held dangerously little regard for Slovenes and their national distinctiveness. It also allowed the Communists and the Popular Fronts to exploit public misgivings about this too close company with European fascism. Although the Molotov-Ribbentrop Pact placed the Popular Fronts on temporary hiatus, future Liberation Front members would characterize their initial recruitment as having less to do with sympathy for Communism than disaffection with established politicians' inability to confront the threat of fascism.[69] At the opposite end of the spectrum, fascist apologetics that appeared in some publications of the Slovene political right before the Second World War would reappear in the propaganda organs of Slovene collaborators during the occupation.

In short, the civil war that erupted between the Liberation Front and its opponents during the occupation years, and the slide of the latter towards open collaboration, did not emerge out of nothing. The battle lines were already loosely drawn in the ideological polarization of interwar Slovene politics and society. This sundering was also apparent in much of Yugoslavia, as it was in interwar Europe as a whole, in the rightward slant of Yugoslav politics, the accelerated persecution of the CPY, and in the campus clashes between right- and left-wing students. Just as numerous Zbor members and their associates, including Minister of the Army and War Milan Nedić, would find homes within the wartime collaborating apparatus in Serbia, many of Ehrlich's and Tomec's followers would join the ranks of collaborating anti-Partisan militias in Slovenia.

The rapid German conquests of 1939 and 1940 only reaffirmed in the minds of established Slovene politicians that negotiation and, if required, concessions, could steer the ship of state safely out of dangerous international waters. As Korošec recounted to his friend, the editor of *Slovenec*, Ivan Ahčin: 'We must have patience. A great deal of patience. War is inevitable. If we are lucky enough to avoid it, Yugoslavia will have much importance in a number of years. However, we must be prepared, to give Germans more of our harvest, that German transports will ply the Danube and Sava, and on dry land maybe even German divisions. It is not inconceivable that there will sit in Belgrade some sort of German commission. But if we remain outside of the war, we will save the country and everything else.'[70] In fact, Germany, unlike Italy, appeared willing to maintain the status quo in the Balkans in 1940 in order to pursue its more pressing military objectives, not least of which were invasions of Britain and the Soviet Union.

Perhaps seeking insight as to how a Slavic state could survive in Hitler's new European order, Father Korošec visited President Tiso in Bratislava, on 27 April 1940. The two men appeared to be cut from the same stone. They had known each other from the Habsburg era, both were priests, and both headed identically named 'People's Parties' that fused Catholicism with nationalist politics. The substance of the meeting remains unknown. Nevertheless, it seems that Korošec was interested in the structure of the Slovak state, which, at the very least, appeared to be a viable model should Germany attack and disassemble Yugoslavia.[71]

No matter how well-intentioned Korošec's policy of rapprochement (*zbližanje*) with Nazi Germany may have been, it quickly ran into the same moral and ethical dilemmas that other European regimes faced in their negotiations with Hitler. In October 1940, Korošec – the new education minister in the Cvetković-Maček government – inaugurated the first of two anti-Jewish laws. The first law placed restrictions on all Jewish businesses dealing with wholesale foods – a significant industry among Croatian Jews – and the second imposed a numerus clausus on Jews in higher education to be no greater than their proportional share of the general Yugoslav population. Both of these laws struck at the civil equality and legal protection of Yugoslav Jews, rights that had been repeatedly reaffirmed by various interwar Yugoslav governments at a time when their co-religionists were systematically stripped of their legal protections in other East Central European states. When Korošec was faced with the resistance of fellow government ministers, he threatened to resign if the decrees were not passed, claiming they would seriously undermine his rapprochement with Germany.[72] Axis pressure was apparent in the timing of these decrees; nevertheless, the ingrained antisemitism of the Slovene People's Party should also not be discounted as a factor. The laws did pass, but they were only partially implemented before the Axis invasion.

After Father Anton Korošec's death, in December 1940, SLS representatives under the leadership of the priest Franc Kulovec faced Hitler's demands that Yugoslavia join the Tripartite Pact. In early March 1941, the Slovenes of Yugoslavia were surrounded on three sides by fascist powers or signatories of the pact. At the Crown Council meeting of 6 March, Father Kulovec, concerned that Slovenia would be the first to fall in an Axis invasion of Yugoslavia, was the first to suggest signing the treaty, stressing that there was no choice in the matter. To emphasize his point, he added '*Qui habet tempus habet vitam*' (He who has time, has life).[73] As a meaningless concession, the Slovenes and the Croats insisted that by signing the pact, 'they were prepared to renounce it once Yugoslavia's forces were built up to the point that they could defend itself.'[74] Following the final Crown Council meeting of 20 March, when the fateful decision was taken to join the Tripartite Pact, the weary Yugoslav regent Prince Paul told the American minister in Belgrade Arthur Bliss Lane that if 'war came, he was certain that the Croats and Slovenes would not fight. He had been urged to sign the pact by the Croats and Slovenes, the other two regents, and the opposition Yugoslav Nationalist Party.'[75]

The consequences of Yugoslavia's formal acceptance of the Tripartite Pact, on 25 March 1941, are well known. On 27 March, Serbian officers, supported by British intelligence, overthrew the regency in a military coup and declared the seventeen-year-old King Peter II to be of age. This event has been portrayed in popular history as an uncompromising rejection of the Tripartite Pact; however, the first priority of the new government of General Dušan Simović was to appease an obviously irate Hitler. Hardly soothed, Hitler ordered an immediate invasion against the upstart Balkan state. Shortly after the coup, the SLS leadership sought out Vladko Maček to see what position his Croatian Peasant Party would take in the ever more likely event of an Axis attack. According to Godeša's research on the period between the coup and the invasion, the Slovene People's Party preferred a Croat–Slovene state solution if Yugoslavia was dissolved, preferable, in fact, to a Slovak-like independent Slovene state under German auspices.[76]

Despite this frantic preparation for an anticipated post-invasion Slovenia, the Slovene People's Party took a dramatically uncompromising position on how it should behave towards its occupiers in the event of war. On 30 March 1941, at the governor's (ban's) palace in Ljubljana, the SLS diplomat Reverend Alojzij Kuhar announced: 'in the case of an enemy occupation, no member of the party, neither high nor low, will ever collaborate with the enemy, neither directly, nor indirectly, neither inure someone to collaboration, even though the pressure may be very strong and life hanging in the balance.'[77] The true test of this pledge would come in seven short days.

3 Reality Subverted, 6 April–22 June 1941

> For those of us whose wartime experiences included nothing remotely resembling the horrors of a Nazi occupation it is perhaps unbecoming to attempt to judge those who felt that the price of armed resistance was too high.[1]
>
> <div align="right">Fred Singleton, <i>Yugoslavia</i></div>

Fred Singleton's comment re-emphasizes the need to contextualize decisions taken in the past *within* the past. Without a deep appreciation of Axis brutality in Slovenia, it is rather 'unbecoming' for twenty-first-century observers to cast moral verdicts on the behaviour of occupied Slovenes, instinctively associating patriotic valour with resistance and selfish cowardice with collaboration and accommodation. The decision to resist or collaborate in occupied Europe was hardly ever a simple choice between what was right and what was wrong. Each option was fraught with danger, not only for the individual, but for his or her family, friends, locality, and nation. The Axis invasion of Yugoslavia suddenly and brutally subverted reality and basic human security. This chapter revisits that world.

On 6 April 1941, the Yugoslav sky began to rain German bombs. The Axis invasion's grim herald was a devastating air raid attack on an undefended Belgrade that killed more than five thousand people including the SLS leader Father Franc Kulovec. The terrifying speed of the Axis onslaught left Yugoslavia's citizens dazed and confused, as its army melted away. The German army crossed Yugoslavia's frontier from several directions – from Austria, Hungary, Romania, and Bulgaria – assisted by the Italian air force. As Kulovec had correctly predicted, Slovenia would be the first to fall. Prekmurje's flat Pannonian plain made it all but defenceless, and it was occupied by the Germans on the first day of fighting. (The Germans would cede Prekmurje to the Hungarians ten days later.) On 8 April, all regions north of the Drava River were taken, including Slovenia's second-largest city Maribor and the city of Ptuj. On 10 April, Italian forces crossed the frontier in the west and marched essentially unimpeded to Ljubljana. By the afternoon of 11 April, the same day that Hungarians entered the fray, an Italian flag fluttered from the castle overlooking Slovenia's capital.

Other regions of Yugoslavia held out only marginally longer. Regent Paul's worst nightmares of national disunity were confirmed when, on 10 April, the German occupation authorities announced the creation of the Independent State of Croatia (Neodvisna država Hrvatska, NDH). Governed by the Ustaša and its leader Ante Pavelić, it would manage to repel even the German military authorities with its zeal in massacring Serbs and Jews. King Peter and his government went into exile, reaching London via a circuitous route that took them through Greece, Egypt, and Palestine. This 'treasonous' decision to 'abandon' Yugoslavia would be later exploited in Liberation Front propaganda. In their absence, the humiliating capitulation to the Germans, on 17 April 1941, would fall to two representatives of the Yugoslav General Staff. As a final insult, two days later, the Bulgarians joined the ranks of the Axis powers occupying Yugoslavia.

With the military subjugation of Yugoslavia, the Axis forces dismembered the carcass. Germany annexed (although not officially) the Slovenian provinces of Štajerska, Gorenjska, and the Mežiška valley[2] (the tiny Slovene portion of Carinthia). Together these lands represented approximately 65 per cent of the territory, 75 per cent of the population (798,700), and almost three-quarters of Slovenia's pre-war industry.[3] Italy received the rest of the region of Dolenjska (with the exception of the German-occupied Ljubljana-Zagreb railway that ran along the Sava River valley), Bela Krajina, and Notranjska. Italy was awarded the capital of Ljubljana; however, the German frontier ran through the northern suburbs of the city, annexing parts of the Šiška and Bežigrad neighbourhoods. From these territorial acquisitions, the Italians created their Provincia di Lubiana (Province of Ljubljana) and annexed it to the Kingdom of Italy, on 3 May 1941, although special permits would be required to cross from it into Italy proper. About 25 per cent of Slovenia's pre-war industry, as well as much of its cultural, political, and administrative elite were located within this province's boundaries.[4] Ljubljana's 1941 population of about a hundred thousand people – now swollen with some seventeen thousand refugees fleeing German-occupied Slovenia – comprised almost a third of the province's population of 336,279 people.[5] Prekmurje and its regional capital of Murska Sobota, which Hungary annexed on 16 December 1941, was the smallest portion of occupied Slovenia. With 102,867 mostly rural inhabitants, it was also the poorest region, containing only 2 per cent of Slovene industry.[6] With these annexations, Slovenia was wiped off the map of Europe.

The grounds on which the three occupiers annexed Slovene lands were predictably questionable. Statistics on the pre–Second World War Volksdeutsche population in Slovenia are problematic, partly because of how nationality was recorded and because of the ethnic biases of the census takers themselves. For example, the 1931 Yugoslav census revealed 28,998 Germans in Drava Province (a *banovina* that comprised virtually all of Yugoslav Slovenia), and the statistical office of the German Kulturbund in Yugoslavia noted a population of 28,075 in January 1941, whereas German organizations outside of the country claimed a population of 110,000 Germans in Slovenia.[7] Germans formed a disproportionate share of the urban population in some Slovene cities, but particularly in the Štajerska towns of Maribor and Celje, where they were also economically influential; however, their physical presence alone could not be used to claim Slovenia for Germandom, surrounded as they were by some 1.5 million Slovenes. Instead, the Nazi occupiers drew on the so-called *Windisch/vindišari* theory that was popularized by Helmut Carstanjen in his work *Sprache und Volkstum in der Untersteiermark* (Language and Nationality in Lower Styria), published in Stuttgart in 1935. According to this theory, 'in addition to the Germans and a small number of nationally conscious Slovenes,' Štajerska was populated by the 'Wenden or Windisch people who spoke a dialect similar to the Slovenian language but were German-oriented.'[8] This claim, along with Slovenia's long historical relationship with the Habsburg Empire, allowed Lower Styria to be considered a 'German border march' (*deutsche Grenzmark*). Hitler's belief that these were German lands was evident in his 14 April 1941 decree that Gorenjska and Štajerska were to be annexed to the respective Austrian provinces of Carinthia and Styria and thoroughly Germanized. The Nazi *Tagespost*, published in Graz, reported Hitler's words during his visit to Maribor, on 26 April 1941: 'Machen Sie mir dieses Land deutsche, so deutsche, wie die übrige Steiermark' (Make this land German for me, as German as the rest of Styria).[9] Although formal annexation to the Third Reich never occurred, this did not stop ambitious Germanization.

The Hungarians also subscribed to the *vindišari* theory, claiming that the Slovene-speaking inhabitants of Prekmurje were Wends of Celtic extraction and, thus, ethnically distinct from Slovenes.[10] This theory suited the Hungarian occupiers and bolstered their claim over a region that they had ruled over until 1918, but which was only populated by some fifteen thousand ethnic Hungarians.

Italy's claim to the Province of Ljubljana was weakest of all, as it could not be justified by any recent historic possession of the region or by any pseudo-racial theory. There were only 458 Italians living amid 340,000 Slovenes. Rather, Mussolini relied on his notion of *spazio vitale* (living space), the nebulous Italian counterpart to Nazi Germany's *Lebensraum*.[11]

The initial reaction of the Slovene population to the invasion was generally one of shock and numbed acquiescence, while the political leadership such as remained struggled to understand Slovenia's fate. On 10 April 1941, the governor (*ban*) of Drava Province, Marko Natlačen, urged the population of Ljubljana to remain orderly and calm as further resistance was futile: 'Let us guarantee at this moment that order and peace, which is traditional to us [. . .] Now, that our army has left, the greatest sin to the nation would be if civilians used weapons against foreign military forces or against domestic national minorities [. . .] May order and peace temper us. Let us show that at these fateful hours and days, we know how to be disciplined. Do not flee, endure, and persevere!'[12] It appeared that this call was heeded in Ljubljana, as well as elsewhere in Slovene lands. In each of the urban capitals of trisected Slovenia – Ljubljana, Maribor, and Murska Sobota – the occupying troops were greeted not with hostility, but with passivity and occasionally with warmth. The former Partisan Rudolf Hribernik-Svarun observed in his memoir that the initial fear of the Italian troops marching towards Ljubljana dissipated, as some Slovene villagers of Horjul began 'returning greetings to them.'[13] In his diary entry of 25 April 1941, Italian Foreign Minister Galeazzo Ciano described the almost numbed atmosphere that hung over Ljubljana: 'The people have a distraught air but are not hostile.'[14] An Italian officer, Francesco Semi, corroborated Ciano's impression with his own: 'One month has gone by, since our units marched into Ljubljana. The city, which was already at the beginning peaceful, is today even more peaceful.'[15]

The initial reaction in Maribor was also generally positive, considering that the more than five thousand ethnic Germans, who constituted some 15 per cent of the city's population, could be counted on to offer a particularly warm welcome to the German army.[16] Already in April 1941, the promising propaganda slogans of the Germans seemed to be vindicated, with a decrease in unemployment and increases in wages. In particular, the suburban poor and the unemployed of Maribor, disillusioned with life in Yugoslavia, were 'at first very satisfied with the new conditions.'[17]

A more shocking situation prevailed in Murska Sobota. A report sent in August 1942 from SLS representatives in Slovenia to Miha Krek, vice-premier of the Yugoslav government-in-exile, claimed that if a plebiscite had been held during the initial ten-day German occupation of Prekmurje, a majority would have asked for union with the Reich. 'All was Hitlerite,' the report noted, with swastika flags festooned everywhere.[18] The source of this enthusiasm lay partly in the unique economic conditions of Prekmurje. An impoverished agrarian region, interwar Prekmurje relied greatly on the income its seasonal labourers earned working in Germany. Some of these individuals, exposed to Nazi propaganda during their German sojourns, credited that country's economic turn-around to Hitler's policies and his elimination of Jewish 'influence' – a tragic lesson for a region that was the heart of Slovenia's tiny Jewish community.[19] With the transfer to Hungarian control, some middle-class and some older inhabitants, reeling from Yugoslavia's sudden collapse, may have been influenced by nostalgia for the 'good old days' of Hungarian rule and the hope of an economic recovery and, thus, passively adjusted to the new 'old order.'

The speed and trauma of the invasion, cravings for economic windfalls, hope for a quick return to order and calm, and an instinctive and powerful desire to survive the calamity all appear to have provoked these less-than-hostile reactions to the invasion and initial occupation in very different regions of Slovenia. 'Reluctant accommodation to overwhelming force' was not unique to Slovenes, as the historian Rab Bennet submitted, but 'was a Europe-wide response.'[20] The historian Vojtech Mastny found that 'the initial German invasion was met with a surprising amount of tolerance, even goodwill and friendliness by the Czech people.'[21] The Czechs, like the Slovenes, at first obeyed the new order and refrained from resistance. Fresh memories of the great catastrophe that disfigured an entire generation just two decades earlier also played a role, as the historian Werner Rings argued: 'Intense as the sudden shock may have been, however, it was swiftly surmounted. Although emotional turmoil lingered beneath the surface for a long time, it was submerged by the strong desire for peace that had become as natural since the "futile war" of 1914–1918 as the passage of the seasons. Hadn't everyone learned, yet again and from personal experience, that anything was preferable to war?'[22]

The remaining Slovene political establishment grappled with the disorganized situation as best it could. With many leading SLS politicians including Franc Snoj, Alojz Kuhar, and the party's presumptive heir, Miha Krek, in exile, political leadership at home fell de facto to Natlačen and the mayor of Ljubljana, Juro Adlešič. On the opening day of the invasion, Natlačen formed a coalition of legal pre-war parties called the National Council (Narodni svet, NS), whose aim was to maintain the territorial unity of Slovenia. As an illegal party, the Communists were not asked to join. In line with the SLS's musings in the days leading up to the invasion, Natlačen still hoped for some type of Croat – Slovene state solution should Yugoslavia's territorial integrity appear untenable to the occupiers. However, Maček's rejection of the German offer to head a Croatian puppet state and the establishment of the Independent State of Croatia, on 10 April, forced Natlačen and the National Council to their second line of defence: a unified Slovenia under the control of one occupier. Holding to this position, on 11 April, the National Council proclaimed over Radio Ljubljana that it was the only sovereign authority representing the Slovene nation. Partition was to be avoided at all costs, as it would further fragment Slovene ethno-territorial unity and paralyze her economy. With this goal in mind, Natlačen entered negotiations with German authorities in Celje from 12 to 14 April.[23] As Natlačen later reported, the Celje delegation 'came to offer truce, that Slovene territory remain a unified whole, and that the National Council would watch over it as the supreme authority for peace and order.'[24]

Nothing came of the Celje entreaties. Indeed, on 17 April, the new Italian high commissioner of the Province of Ljubljana, Emilio Grazioli, dissolved the National Council. The strategy of the remnant Slovene politicians, thus, shifted from maintaining territorial unity to lessening the demands of each of the occupiers. As the occupational policies of the three invaders became better known, it was clear that only the Italians held out any hope for those who wanted to see the survival of a Slovene national identity.

On the heels of Hitler's stated aim to make Štajerska and, by implication, Gorenjska and Slovene Carinthia German again, the two territorial units fell under the administrative apparatus of the Austrian provinces of Styria and Carinthia respectively and their Gauleiters Siegfried Uberreither and Franz Kutschera. In December 1941, Friedrich Rainer would replace Kutschera as Gauleiter of Gorenjska and the Mežiška valley. Both Gauleiters had unlimited powers in their respective territories and acted as 'Hitler's plenipotentiaries' in charge of strengthening 'Germanity (*Deutschtum*).'[25] They would exercise their powers with destructive vigour. As in Germany, some of the first victims were the mentally and physically challenged; almost six hundred would be taken from Štajerska and euthanized near Linz.[26]

Indulging in the fascist fetish for mass organizations, the Germans called on all Slovenes in Štajerska and Gorenjska to join the Heimatbund and Volksbund respectively. These bodies were to assist in Germanization and in the mobilization of labour and military recruits. On 14 April 1941, Gauleiter Uberreither proclaimed: 'The hour of decision for every individual has arrived. All Štajerci [inhabitants of Štajerska], who acknowledge Adolf Hitler and his Reich, will be able in the following days to offer their tender for acceptance into the Steirischer Heimatbund. Steirischer Heimatbund will be one great organization that will cover all good-thinking Štajerci.'[27] Over 90 per cent of the population of Štajerska and Gorenjska joined the Heimatbund and Volksbund, organizations that were 'voluntary' in name only.[28] Refusing to join brought unfriendly attention, just as a German pamphlet urging Slovene membership in the the charity branch of the Nazi party (Nationalsozialistische Volkswohlfahrt, NSV) intimated, 'Your membership in NSV is a sign of your trustworthiness.'[29]

The Nazis, wary of the understandable opportunism of the new members, carried out racial and political assessments of virtually the entire Slovene population in the spring and summer of 1941. Whereas the German minority was given full Reich citizenship, the majority of Slovenes – *vindišari* – were given 'revocable' citizenship, with the option of full citizenship in ten years. Approximately one-quarter of applicants were rejected, as they were found to be 'racially inappropriate' (Class IV) or 'prominently anti-German' (Mark E).[30] Their fate was anticipated in a document composed by Reinhard Heydrich, head of the Main State Security Office, who as early as 21 April 1941, recommended expelling a quarter of a million Slovenes.[31] Thus, the Slovenes were included in Nazi plans for a racially reorganized Europe that saw its most grotesque vision in Generalplan Ost and the industrialized genocide of the Holocaust.

The plans for deportation were hammered out in a series of meetings between German, Croatian, and Italian officials in May and June 1941, with Serbia and the Independent State of Croatia chosen as the human dumping grounds.[32] There were to be three waves of expulsions, beginning with the national intelligentsia, followed by Slovene 'settlers' who had moved into the two regions after 1914, and finally, the Slovenes inhabiting a frontier belt approximately twenty kilometres wide between Štajerska and Italian-occupied Slovenia and the NDH. This buffer zone would then be repopulated by an immigration of Volksdeutsche (ethnic Germans), including twelve thousand Gottscheer (Kočevari) from the Kočevje area of the Province of Ljubljana. The deportations began as early as 7 June and were brutal in their execution. Families were given little time to pack a maximum of thirty kilograms of personal possessions and some currency before being deposited on the charity of local officials in Serbia and the NDH.[33] The deportations would operate in fits and starts until their official end on 12 August 1942. They would also extend to Austrian Carinthia, where some 178 ethnic Slovene families were deported in April 1942.[34]

Soon, however, problems arose. In July 1941, local Nazi officials in Gorenjska protested the expulsions because they removed valuable labour resources, urging that further deportations be delayed until the end of the war.[35] In addition, the indiscriminate manner by which deportees were chosen panicked the larger population and led to an upsurge in resistance. The ensuing organizational chaos, particularly the diversion of transportation, ensured that Heydrich's lofty goal of deporting one-third of German-occupied Slovenia's population was never carried out. This did not mean that the Slovenes had been saved: in the spring of 1942, Himmler declared that Slovenia should be added to Generalplan Ost, with the remainder of the unrepentant Slavs to be deported after Germany's victory in Europe.[36] Some fifty-five to eighty thousand Slovenes were deported to Croatia and Serbia, and after expulsions were prohibited to these two regions, in the fall of 1941, to Germany.[37] Although this number was only one-quarter of the initial target, the fact that many of the deportees were members of Slovenia's cultural elite weakened Slovene resistance to future Germanizing policies. Schools were left without Slovene teachers, parishes without priests. According to Bishop Rožman, in the period between 8 July and 25 August 1941, out of a total of 275 priests in 142 parishes in German-occupied Slovenia, 152 had been arrested, one had died, and sixty-six had been deported. This left only fourteen active and ten retired priests – and some two hundred thousand souls with no priestly assistance.[38] In this respect, the deportations were to some extent successful, as resistance in Štajerska and Gorenjska never reached the proportions that it did in the Province of Ljubljana.

The remaining Slovenes were to be Germanized. All connections with Yugoslavia and Slovene national culture and identity were to be severed. Yugoslav administrative departments were replaced with German political commissars. The regional administrative headquarters of Štajerska and Gorenjska were located in the Slovene towns of Maribor and Bled respectively; however, their main headquarters were in Graz and Klagenfurt, the provincial capitals of Austrian Carinthia and Styria. The central command of Germany's occupational forces in Slovenia, which included police, gendarmes (military units that carried out police duties) and the regular armed forces, was located in Salzburg. For political persecutions and deportations, the Main State Security Office (Reichssicherheitshauptamt) in Berlin, which included the feared state secret police (Gestapo), criminal police, and security service (Sicherheitsdienst), set up regional branches in Maribor and Bled. As early as mid-April 1941, 643 gendarmes along with 2,390 Sturmabteilung (SA) – the dreaded 'brownshirts' – arrived to provide 'order.'[39]

Slovene youth were deemed critical to Germanization, and as a result, Slovene teachers were deported and replaced with over a thousand, mostly Austrian instructors who taught only in German. The Slovene language itself was attacked, and personal names, street signs, place names, and names of commercial businesses were changed to their German equivalent. Libraries were closed and Slovene books were burned, cultural organizations were prohibited and national monuments were destroyed or removed.

The initial Hungarian occupation was somewhat less exacting than that by the Germans. There were far fewer deportations, but nationally conscious Slovene intellectuals and administrators such as Josef Klekl, a priest and the regional SLS leader, were interned in Hungary, as were many so-called Slovene colonists who had settled in Prekmurje after the First World War.[40] Although this occupation was not as brutal as the forced Germanization taking place across the Mura River, the Hungarians, nevertheless, aimed to make Prekmurje – renamed Muravidék – Hungarian. This was evident in the decision to partition and attach Prekmurje to the Hungarian counties (*megye*) of Vas and Zala and their respective regional capitals of Szombathely and Zalaegerszeg. However, Magyarization was to be achieved ideally 'with nurturing and propaganda' and without the use of force.⁴¹ The Hungarians tolerated the daily use of 'Wendish,' but like the Germans they banned Slovene schools and brought in Hungarian teachers. The Hungarian Educational Organization for Prekmurje (Vendvideki Magyar Közmüvelödesi Egyesület) was tasked with Magyarizing the Slovenes by offering Hungarian language lessons. The Hungarians particularly targeted the Slovene Protestant minority, as well as some older Slovenes and the middle class of tavernkeepers, merchants, and larger craftsmen – 'people, who before and during the First World War visited Hungarian schools, served in the Hungarian army, and were already under their denationalizing influence.'⁴² These attempts at co-opting elements of the Slovene population were assisted in the initial two years of the occupation by a favourable upturn in the economic fortunes of this poor region. Living conditions improved, and peasants were able to sell their products more easily and at a higher price in comparison with interwar Yugoslavia.⁴³

A different situation prevailed in the Province of Ljubljana, which was under the civilian administration of Grazioli and the military supervision of General Mario Robotti, the commander of the XI Corps of the Italian Second Army. In comparison with German- and Hungarian-occupied Slovenia, Italian rule was initially relatively tolerant. True, the fundamental laws of the Italian state were extended to the newly annexed province, as were the tentacles of the Fascist party. But Slovene remained the language of instruction in the province's schools, with Italian as an 'optional' instruction in higher schools, although Fascist influence infused the teaching of history and geography.⁴⁴ In addition, all official decrees were to be given in both languages. Despite Italy's annexation of the province, Slovenes did not have to serve in the Italian military. Significantly, the Italians also left the Church structure intact, ensuring that a number of Catholic cultural and social organizations continued to function. Nevertheless, Italian culture assumed a prominent place in the province, as evident in the distribution of Italian newspapers, films, and concerts. Indeed, the boycott of these already in the fall of 1941 would be one of the first signs of resistance among the Slovenes.⁴⁵

The period from 5 April to 22 June 1941 was not marked by any Slovene political collaboration with the German or Hungarian occupiers – as neither of them were willing to consider such a policy at this time. Nevertheless, the Province of Ljubljana was already revealing itself as the future centre of Slovene collaboration. In issuing his 10 April appeal to the inhabitants of Ljubljana, Natlačen appeared to reaffirm Kuhar's March 1941 warning against collaboration: 'The second greatest sin would be denunciation, which is incompatible with human decency. Denunciation is such a heavy sin, that the nation will never be able to forgive it. That is why among us there will be no denunciation!'[46] Yet, the more lenient policies of the Italians were not missed by Slovene politicians, and the modicum of autonomy in the Province of Ljubljana appeared ever more attractive in light of the brutal oppression in Štajerska and Gorenjska. On 25 April 1941, Ciano remarked on a visit he had from a visibly upset Natlačen: 'I see the ex-governor of Slovenia. I have known him since the times of Stoyadinovich. He is unhappy over the fate of that part of Slovenia, which has remained under the Germans. Grazioli tells me that the treatment of the population is actually worse than cruel. Armed robberies and killings occur every day. Churches and convents are looted and closed.'[47] Indeed, Ciano's diary affirmed that the province's autonomous legislation was designed to win over the Slovenes:

> April 26, 1941. With the Duce we prepare the decree for the annexation of Ljubljana. It will be an Italian province with broad administrative autonomy, both cultural and fiscal. Our humane treatment of the Croats [sic], as compared with the Germans' inhumane treatment, should attract their sympathy to us [. . .]
> April 29, 1941. With Buffarini I prepare a political map for the creation of the Province of Ljubljana. It is inspired by very liberal concepts. It will have the effect of attracting sympathies for us in Germanized Slovenia, in which the worst abuses are being reported.[48]

In the eyes of Slovene politicians, the Province of Ljubljana appeared to be a refuge for their ravaged national culture, and the Italians appeared least hostile towards working with them, despite the Italian leadership's lack of unanimity on the question of collaboration. Unlike the mass dismissal of many Slovene government and civil officials in Hungarian- and especially German-occupied Slovenia, Italian officials were awarded the highest administrative positions but retained Slovenes in low to mid-level positions, offices where bureaucrats were in short supply. The historian David Rodogno has estimated that the High Commissariat had some twenty-three hundred Slovene civil servants on its payroll.[49] This included mayoral positions. For example, Juro Adlešič remained in his pre-war position of mayor of Ljubljana until

June 1942, when he resigned and was replaced with General Rupnik. Indeed, Natlačen approved this situation at the outset of the occupation, when he ordered all mayors to remain at their posts until the invaders requested actions of them that were deemed 'dishonourable or against our nation.'[50]

Thus, in return for the relatively light demands of the Italians, Slovene officials were willing to cooperate in the administration of the province. Chastened by the German rejection of the Celje negotiations and their violent occupation, Natlačen and other political leaders agreed to take part in the advisory committees (*sosveti*). The *sosvet* was a committee of fourteen members, which the Italians chose 'from the productive groups of the Slovene population' to advise the high commissioner in the administration of the province.[51] The Italians appointed Natlačen, the Liberal Ivan Pucelj, the rector of the University of Ljubljana Matija Slavič, and eleven members from the business community, many of whom were members of the Slovene People's Party, to take part in the inaugural *sosvet* called on 26 May 1941. By participating, the Slovene officials were, according to their postwar supporters, accepting 'the elementary protection of national life'[52] offered by Italy in an attempt 'to save, what is savable.'[53] In retrospect, the initial Italian leniency was merely a more gradual route of Italianizing and incorporating the Province of Ljubljana into the Fascist system. Yet, in the initial post-invasion chaos, the Italians appeared to be throwing a life-line to the Slovenes. Rupnik recalled Grazzioli's assurances, in 1941, that as long as the Slovenes were 'sober and intelligent, that the possibilities for the Slovene nation are far from hopeless [. . .] that he would intervene with the Duce to expand Ljubljana's autonomy towards the west, possibly to our ethnic borders, and that they will, he hopes, come to some agreement with the Germans.'[54] Kocbek recounted the words of Luigi Salvini, director of the Italian Cultural Institute in Zagreb, who told him that 'Italy has saved the head of the Slovenians, we returned Ljubljana to you, be conscious of this and hold it before your eyes, that we will in time tie the Province of Ljubljana with Gorizia and Trieste. Understand this as well, that only with the assistance of Italy will you come in possession of Carinthia.'[55] Few Slovenes would have shared Salvini's utopian predictions. Nevertheless, the promise that Italy might intercede on behalf of Slovenes in other occupied regions was plausible, especially as Italy appeared disgruntled with its apportioned share of Slovenia. In addition, Rome permitted Bishop Rožman to intercede to the Vatican on behalf of oppressed Slovenes in Gorenjska and

Štajerska. Such hopes may have motivated Slovene officials to take part in the advisory committee, although the Italians saw it as 'a paper creation without any real consulting role.'[56] However, it did serve a propaganda purpose coincident with Ciano's designs, and Grazioli, eager to display Italian largesse, took the committee on a tour of Rome in June. After meeting with Mussolini, on 8 June, Natlačen offered on behalf of the advisory committee thanks for the 'special opportunity, that we can personally repeat our sincere expression of our respectful devotion and the complete loyalty of the entire population.'[57] Natlačen also extended an invitation for the Duce to visit the province, which the nation would be 'happy and proud' to host. Despite these felicitations, Natlačen recognized the advisory committee as toothless, and citing Italian reprisals and arrests of completely innocent Slovenes for Partisan attacks, resigned in September 1941.[58] Mussolini did not name another advisory committee until June 1943; the membership of that committee included, among others, Leon Rupnik. It was never called into session.[59]

As was the case before the Second World War, the Slovene political establishment and Slovene Church officials cooperated closely. From the outset of the invasion, Catholic prelates, relying on a traditional deference to religious authority in wartime, had interceded with the Axis forces to spare civilians and to allow the Church to operate unhindered. Their expectations were shattered. When Maribor Bishop Ivan Tomažič pleaded on behalf of arrested priests to Uberreither, the Gauleiter threatened to arrest him, warning, 'You will have to decide between Hitler and the Pope.'[60] Relations between the Slovene Church and the Italian occupiers were much warmer. As early as 23 April, Rožman made a 'courtesy call' – as he described it in his response to his postwar trial in absentia – to the Italian High Commissariat in Ljubljana. Bishop Rožman claimed that he did not, as was charged by postwar Yugoslav courts, offer his and the priesthood's wholehearted support to the Italians.[61] Far more incriminating was his congratulatory note to Mussolini on the incorporation of the Province of Ljubljana into the Kingdom of Italy, which circulated prominently within the local newspapers: 'Excellency! A decree has been published today, via which the Slovenian territory occupied by the Italian army has been incorporated into Italy. When I consider this, I thank your Excellency [. . .] I express absolute loyalty and ask God to bless you and our aspirations for the welfare of our people.'[62] Rožman claimed that Grazioli and his censors altered his original memorandum to the Italian leadership,[63] which while acknowledging the religious and national freedoms in the province, requested that they be extended to other Slovene regions under Italian control.⁶⁴

To regime historians, Bishop Rožman's memorandum, as well as others that he would compose to the occupiers in the coming years, was testament to the Church's pathetic servility towards all higher authority. According to Father Metod Mikuž, collaboration was the logical conclusion of the Ljubljana bishopric's policy of 'what will be, will be' and 'that all rule is ordained from God.'⁶⁵ Rožman and his supporters interpreted his and the Church's early willingness to engage the occupiers in a different light. As a native of Austrian Carinthia, Rožman was well aware of the discrimination that Slovenes faced there and in Primoska before the Second World War, and he fully understood German brutality in Gorenjska and Štajerska. Like Slovene politicians, Rožman and his officials saw the Province of Ljubljana as a refuge in the storm: it was critical that Slovenes have a voice in preserving these privileges, and to achieve this, required communication and accommodation with the Italians. To cut off all relations and pretend that the occupation had not occurred was irresponsible to Rožman's mind. Basic spiritual services still needed to be delivered in these trying times: mass needed to be performed, sacraments needed to be given, and the training and education of priests had to continue. In even greater demand were the charitable institutions affiliated with the Church. All such activity required the permission and the good will of the Italians. They seldom permitted them without something in return. For example, Bishop Rožman claimed that when he approached the Italians, on 17 April, to allow priests to break the curfew so that they could tend to the sick, he was pressured to first recognize the Italian occupation authorities, otherwise they would 'interpret his silence as an aggressive act.'⁶⁶ Furthermore, his frequent calls for Slovenes to remain calm and obey Italian laws were, according to Rožman, required by the Italians as the price for permitting refugees from the German-occupied zone to settle in the Province of Ljubljana.⁶⁷ Similarly, Rožman's intercessions on behalf of arrested and deported priests in Gorenjska and Štajerska had to be made through the Vatican, as there was no direct communication with the German occupiers. Yet, this, too, rested upon the good will of the Italian High Commissariat.⁶⁸ Dolinar summarized the situation like this: 'The bishop as the highest representative of the Church could not act as if the occupation regime was not in his bishopric. Economic, personal, and social matters of the bishopric could not have been solved without them. That is why he was bound "to recognize the regime and collaborate with it for the temporary and permanent advantage of the people" in all those matters that impinged on the relationship between the Church and temporal authority regardless of its ideological orientation.'[69]

Outside of the Province of Ljubljana, active collaboration in the period between Yugoslavia's collapse and the start of Operation Barbarossa was confined primarily to the German and Hungarian minorities. Well before the invasion, Nazi intelligence had used the Swabian-German Cultural Association (Schwäbisch-Deutscher Kulturbund) as a source of information on Yugoslavia's civil service and government institutions.[70] As elsewhere in occupied Europe, ethnic Germans embraced the new Nazi order, some spied for the Gestapo, and others joined the ranks of the new administration.[71] However, few ethnic Germans were given senior positions in the bureaucracy of occupied Gorenjska and Štajerska. According to Tone Ferenc, there was only one ethnic German among the staff of twenty commissioners who assisted each of the two Gauleiters, and only two among the twenty political commissars. All the rest were Austrian Germans.[72] Ethnic German – owned industrial and manufacturing works, such as the Ehrlich family's textile factory, converted to military production, and their workers were required to join the Kulturbund.[73] No more than a hundred Volksdeutsche (0.3% of their population) fought within the Partisan ranks.[74]

Many ethnic Hungarians in Prekmurje, particularly their influential urban leaders in the town of Lendava, were also strong exponents of the Magyarization of the region. The pre-war and wartime mayor of Murska Sobota, Ferdinand Hartner, distinguished himself as a committed Hungarian sympathizer (*madžaron*) by advocating for Prekmurje's inclusion into Hungary in the initial days after the invasion.[75] Josip Biro, an ethnic Hungarian from Lendava, was part of a similar deputation and, after the war, was sentenced to one year forced labour for his efforts.[76] Others would be found complicit in deporting Slovene colonists, as well as spying on and denouncing Slovenes for the Hungarian military.

Resistance, like collaboration, was slow to develop in the chaotic conditions following the Axis invasion. In the spring of 1941, armed resistance appeared little short of suicidal in the face of the occupiers' overwhelming military superiority. Nevertheless, it was the established political parties that took some of the first tentative steps in organizing an underground resistance in Slovenia, a pattern followed elsewhere in occupied East Central Europe, including in the Protectorate of Bohemia and Moravia and in Poland. These initial efforts were centred in the Province of Ljubljana, where much of the remaining pre-war elite resided and where the relatively lax Italian occupation proved least disruptive. Unfortunately, pre-war political partisanship bedevilled the early resistance, and the result was a number of separate organizations, each affiliated with a political party or movement. The earliest and strongest formation was the Slovene Legion (Slovenska legija, SL), the underground wing of the Slovene People's Party, which formed in May 1941. Within a few months of its founding, the Slovene Legion, led by Rudolf Smersu, had risen to a network of approximately five thousand members. The Slovene Legion also recruited a number of right-wing Catholic student groups, such as Straža.[77] SL cells spread over much of the Province of Ljubljana, and had committees in Gorenjska, Štajerska, Prekmurje, and Primorska. Each member was obligated to swear the following oath:

> I [name of member] swear before omnipotent God, that I will be from today onwards a loyal member of the Slovene Legion, whose objectives I am familiar with, that I will fight and work with my strength within its framework and according to its program for the freedom and independence of the Slovene nation, that I will accurately carry out its instructions, requests, and orders, that I will never betray its secrecy, its existence, its work, or its members. I realize that God's punishment and the nation's revenge await me if I break this oath. So help me, God!derived[78]

In August 1941, liberal-oriented members belonging to the Sokol gymnastic club, and who had not sided with the Liberation Front, formed their own underground military wing, the Sokol Legion.[79] The Sokol Legion was much smaller than the Slovene Legion, numbering fewer than a thousand members. It, too, had its own oath, which, owing to its liberal orientation was far more explicit in its support of Yugoslav integralism and Mihailović: 'I [name of the member] swear before all that is dearest to me, that I will cooperate in the liberationist action of the Sokol Military Committee, that I will bravely and courageously fight for the liberation of all areas of Slovenia and for the rise of a great Yugoslavia, that I will keep silent all that I know of the organization, and that I will never betray anything to anyone, and that I will without question, accurately and loyally, accomplish all the orders of my Sokol military superiors. In this may God help me. *Zdravo!*'[80] Similar to the Sokol Legion in political orientation were even smaller resistance groups including the National Legion (Narodna legija, NL), which formed out of the earlier resistance group Blood Brothers (Pobratim), led by Anton Krošl, a professor at the Ljubljana Academy of Commerce; not surprisingly, it tended to attract liberal-minded intellectuals. Another similar informal grouping was the Officers Group (*Častniška skupina*), consisting of former Royal Yugoslav Army officers. These last liberal and pro-Mihailović resistance cells were later known colloquially as the Blue Guard (*plava garda*) to differentiate them from the White Guard – the Slovene Legion – that remained under the leadership of Slovene political parties, and specifically the Slovene People's Party.

All of these legions, like their political leaders, eschewed immediate armed resistance in favour of covert preparation for a future rebellion, when the Axis forces had weakened, or in coordination with an envisaged liberation by the Western Allies. Their initial activities included caching weapons from the recently defeated Yugoslav forces, some of which were hidden in churches.[81] Emphasis was placed on intelligence gathering, and the intelligence so gathered was passed on to the Yugoslav government-in-exile in London by radio or letters via the Vatican and Istanbul.[82]

In comparison with their later resistance activities, the Communist parties of Yugoslavia and Slovenia remained relatively passive during this two-and-a-half month hiatus before Germany's attack on the Soviet Union. The Molotov-Ribbentrop Non-aggression Pact was still in force, despite the obvious Axis preparations for war against the Soviets. The Comintern instructed all of its European progeny to maintain an anti-war stance and the increasingly precarious posture that the war was caused by imperialist machinations. Nevertheless, already at this early stage, the CPY and the CPS revealed their penchant for initiative independent of the Comintern. Confronted with invasion, on 10 April 1941, the CPY's Central Committee took the 'aggressive' step of forming a Military Commission headed by Tito.[83] On 26 April, the Communist Party of Slovenia formed the Anti-Imperialist Front – the forerunner of the Liberation Front. Although its name reflected the reality of the Nazi-Soviet Non-aggression Pact, the CPS also distributed anti-occupier propaganda in the run-up to Operation Barbarossa.[84] Indeed, the speed with which the Partisans launched sabotage acts after Axis armies invaded the Soviet Union, on 22 June, suggests that considerable military planning had already been well under way.

Nevertheless, the truly transformative event for the CPY and the CPS was not the Axis invasion of Yugoslavia. Burgwyn's argument that 'without an Axis invasion, prewar Yugoslavia, although hardly an enlightened democracy, would have been free of both Communists and Četniks'[85] is only partially sustainable. The emergence of the Osvobodilna fronta and all the fateful political consequences associated with it were also critically predicated on Hitler's attempt to suffocate the world's only attempt to date at building socialism – the Soviet Union.

4 The Emergence of Resistance, July 1941–November 1942

Partisanism is not the same as communism. It is necessary to differentiate between communists and other partisans, as there were among them many honest Slovene boys, who went into the liberation war with the best intentions.

Archbishop Franc Rode, Kočevski Rog, 22 July 1997

The Axis invasion of the Soviet Union on 22 June 1941 marked an important watershed in the Slovene wartime experience, as it did across much of occupied Europe. Until then, both the nascent non-Communist underground organizations and the Anti-Imperialist Front eschewed active resistance against the occupiers. Operation Barbarossa, however, destroyed this unanimity, as the Anti-Imperialist Front – now the Liberation Front – together with Communist resisters across Europe, rushed to defend the Communist motherland and embarked on a campaign of immediate armed resistance against the occupiers. Although the non-Communist underground and the Liberation Front shared more objectives than either side cared to admit – including their opposition to the occupation, their hope for a postwar enlarged and unified Slovenia (*Zedinjena Slovenija*) encompassing Slovene minorities in Austria and Italy, and a reunified Yugoslavia – the Liberation Front's active resistance raised the bar of patriotic responsibility to a height that their rivals would not and could not reach. Moreover, despite the Comintern's initial reservations, the Communist Party of Yugoslavia increasingly took the position that their liberation struggle could be the catalyst for a successful Communist revolution in Yugoslavia. This deduction was not lost on the pre-war political establishment who, for the first time, toyed with the ugly spectre of a tiny and illegal Communist Party seizing power with its vigorous call-to-arms. Indeed, after June 1941, it would be the Osvobodilna fronta and its Communist leadership, the only organization with 'boots on the ground,' that would increasingly speak for the national liberation of Slovenia and Yugoslavia.

The wait-and-see approach of the Slovene non-Communist resistance, which saved a general armed revolt for the end of the war when the enemy would be weak, was standard practice for most occupied European countries and their governments-in-exile, including the Polish government and its Home Army (Armia Krajowa) and much of the French resistance. The Yugoslav government-in-exile made its position very clear in a 22 July 1941 broadcast over the airwaves of the British Broadcasting Corporation (BBC), urging 'the Yugoslav people to avoid battles and to await the signal from London.'[1] Operation Barbarossa, unfortunately, changed the equation, and as with the Popular Fronts in the late 1930s, the vanguard of the anti-fascist movement once again became the preserve of the political left. The passive and accommodating policy of the mainstream political representatives in Slovenia enabled the small, rag-tag Partisan forces to fill the vacuum of active resistance. As Sirc observed, 'the old politicians had prevaricated, enabling the Communists to accuse them of collaboration.'[2] The former Slovene Četnik Ivan Korošec remarked that, in Slovenia, 'democracy organized and waited [...] remained on the defensive. And this is already by its very nature defeated.' 'All great decisions entail risk,' he continued, 'In a burning house, you should not think that by jumping through the window you might break a leg.'[3] Yet, passivity was not collaboration, despite the claims of the Liberation Front and the Communist Party of Slovenia. What were the circumstances that led to collaboration? In order to discern these factors, we expand first on the emergence of active resistance in Slovenia.

The Communist Party of Yugoslavia wasted little time in initiating armed resistance following the launch of Operation Barbarossa. On 27 June, the CPY's Politburo became the General Headquarters of the People's Liberation Partisan Detachments. Chaired by Tito, its staff included two Slovenes – Kardelj and Leskovšek – both of whom were organizing resistance in Slovenia.[4] The call for 'coordinated sabotage' and a Partisan war against the occupiers was issued by CPY headquarters as early as 4 July. Some 220 acts of sabotage were recorded in Serbia during the same month, and shortly thereafter, the Partisans seized their first substantial territory by taking the Serbian town of Užice and its munitions factory, declaring the liberation of the 'Užice Republic.'[5] Reflecting this growing confidence and Tito's propensity for a clear centralized chain of command, the General Headquarters was transformed into Supreme Headquarters to oversee the resistance work in the various regions of Yugoslavia.[6]

In Slovenia, the first signs of the formation of Liberation Front committees appeared as early as August 1941, although the final form of the OF was not established until the fourth assembly of the Higher Plenum of the Osvobodilna fronta, on 1 November 1941.[7] The highest authority of Partisan resistance was the Supreme Plenum, otherwise known as the Slovenian National Liberation Committee (Slovenski narodnoosvobodilni odbor, SNOO), which was struck on 16 September. The Liberation Front, like its Anti-Imperial Front predecessor, was a genuine front and was made up of a rather diverse group of parties, movements, and individuals. Ferenc counted as many as eighteen distinct groups in total, although the most important were the left wing of the Christian Socialists led by Kocbek, some Sokol Legion members, and a number of left-leaning intellectuals, as well as some ex-Yugoslav Army officers. A handful of priests also joined, notably Bishop Rožman's former archivist Father Metod Mikuž, who was appointed religious adviser to the Partisan command.[8] Their cooperation, despite the disparity of their programs and outlook, was best expressed by Kocbek in July 1942: 'We Christians do not fear cooperating with Communists because we believe in their humanity.'[9] The membership of SNOO's executive reflected this diversity. In addition to the CPS members Kidrič and Kardelj, the front was also represented on the Catholic side by the Christian Socialists Tone Fajfar and Kocbek, by the writer and essayist Josip Vidmar, and by the Sokol members Franjo Lubej and Jože Rus. In this regard, the Slovene branch of the Partisan movement was far more 'open' than were its Yugoslav counterparts, where political sectarianism – for example, in Montenegro – was more pronounced. Nevertheless, the historian John Lampe's view that only in Slovenia could resistance forces confront the occupying forces 'with something like a united front' is perhaps overstating the coalition character of the Osvobodilna fronta.[10] Most of the non-Communist legions and their political leadership did not join the OF and, in fact, would be fighting one another within the year.

In the summer of 1941, the occupiers appeared all but indestructible. German armies were inflicting colossal routs on the Russian front, Britain stood alone, and the United States had not yet entered the war. The OF's Partisan army, thus, began from a very humble core of committed fighters, who were able to ignore the fact that the odds of success for an indigenous liberation movement were remote or who honestly believed that the Red Army would soon appear. Kocbek described some of these initial eager recruits as 'Sunday trippers,' with little understanding of the hardships they had signed up for.[11] As Ivan Korošec pointed out, it was much easier for a man to remain at home. The forest was dangerous. Hounded, hungry and cold, lacking medicine and proper hygiene, Partisan life certainly dissuaded the sober-minded.[12] Consequently, only two thousand joined their ranks in 1941.[13] These numbers obviously contradicted Kardelj's boast that the Slovene nation had risen 'with one will' in April 1941 to defend its freedom and that 'from the first day in our country, the occupier was welcomed with war.'[14] Edvard Kocbek's interviewers succinctly summarized this dissonance between postwar Communist Party mythology and the reality of post-invasion public sentiment: 'The average Slovene person, who was unaffected by the collapse of the first Yugoslavia, even worse, who in Štajerska and in Dolenjska awaited Hitler with excitement, and in Ljubljana Province looked upon the Italian occupier initially with warm kindness, could not become overnight the carrier of an awakened national consciousness. National consciousness sent a minority into the forest – perhaps even smaller than [the group] which loyalty to the Party sent into the forest.'[15]

As the repression against the Slovenes increased, however, first under the Germans and Hungarians and belatedly under the Italians, the Liberation Front ranks expanded to forty-five hundred in 1942 and fifty-five hundred before the Italian capitulation in September 1943.[16] The movement relied particularly on the young and, significantly, women – attracted to the OF's message of female emancipation that appeared in its journal *Naša žena* (Our Woman), which began publication in 1942.[17] Some undoubtedly joined out of dissatisfaction with the failings and passivity of the pre-war political establishment. Nevertheless, it appears that many of these recruits did not join the Liberation Front in order to support the program of the Communist Party of Slovenia.[18] Their homes burned, family members shot and imprisoned, or facing service in the German army, for some, the only choice was to join the OF insurgents. In primarily rural Dolenjska, former Partisan

Emil Weiss-Belač stated that many recruits did not understand what orthodox Communism stood for, since one could count the number of factories in the region on one hand. Rather, this was 'a war for an independent, free Slovenia.'[19] The CPS seemed to have recognized this, as the 'Communists could not hope to attract the peasants – without whom they could not achieve victory – by advocating traditional communist objectives.' Instead, 'their chief appeal was to nationalist, democratic and federalist sentiments,' an emphasis on Pan-Slavism and on a unified Slovenia.[20] Indeed, this ideological disparity between the Partisan command and the rank and file persisted into the later stages of the war, by which time the Liberation Front had become an unabashedly Communist organization. A February 1945 report by an agent of the American wartime intelligence agency, the Office of Strategic Services (OSS), chronicled a detachment operating in the border region between Gorenjska and Austrian Carinthia. The rank- and file of the unit was described as being composed of 70 per cent upland Slovenes, 'pious, though not necessarily churchly,' devoted to the land, and largely unmoved by political and ideological issues; another 30 per cent was made up of Carinthian Slovenes, who saw the Partisans 'as harbingers of ethnic unification.' According to the report, their program was simple: to drive the Germans out and to give Slovenia freedom and a wide degree of autonomy in a postwar Yugoslavia. A large number of the rank and file apparently fell asleep during the weekly political lectures hosted by the political commissars, as they were considered 'dull affairs': 'In general, source felt that the political commissars were outwardly endeavouring to focus the attention and interests of the unit's soldiers towards the East, while the men themselves appeared reluctant to turn their thoughts towards matters more distant than the boundaries of Slovenia, or for that matter, the limits of their own farm.'[21] Indeed, despite the concerted efforts to promote allegiance to the Soviet Union, the British Special Operations Executive (SOE) agent Lieutenant Colonel Peter Moore concurred, in a February 1945 report, that many rank and file were 'very grateful towards America and Britain to the embarrassment of the Partisan authorities.'[22]

In addition to these patriotic motivations, Kocbek admitted that a criminal element also joined the Partisans, exploiting the riches that wars offer to the unscrupulous.[23] Forced mobilization was widely practised, contradicting the 'revolutionary solidarity' that was so often spoken of in postwar regime histories.[24] In short, Slovenes would join the Liberation Front in the initial years of the occupation for a whole array of reasons, many of which had little to do with supporting the establishment of a Communist Slovenia.

Recruitment for a Partisan army was useless if the body could not be sustained with arms, supplies, and intelligence. This role fell to a larger mass auxiliary contingent made up mostly of civilian sympathizers known as the National Defence (*narodna zaščita*). Membership in the National Defence cut across gender lines and professional lines, and was particularly well represented in Ljubljana – earning the city the moniker of 'Red Ljubljana' among its opponents. The National Defence recruited on behalf of the Liberation Front, distributed propaganda, collected intelligence, and helped organize the production and transportation of arms to the Partisans, who operated primarily in the countryside.[25] Besides allowing ordinary unarmed Slovenes to play a productive – and in some cases life-altering – role in the liberation of their own people, their service helped to broaden and widen the organizational reach of the Liberation Front across Slovene society.

One of the earliest OF attacks on the occupiers occurred in Gorenjska, on 22 July 1941, near the small village of Rašica, located on the outskirts of Ljubljana. The Liberation Front would develop far more slowly in German-occupied Slovenia, despite evidence of popular sympathy for the resisters. An SLS internal report from August 1942, for example, stated that although there definitely were a large number of OF sympathizers in the Štajerska town of Ljutomer, no Partisan movement had yet emerged.[26] The historian Marjan Žnidarič's examination of OF resistance in Maribor found that approximately 10 per cent of the population was sympathetic towards the OF and offered material support, and only 3.2 per cent (or 1,750 individuals) supported the OF in an active sense.[27] The mines and industries of the Zasavje region of Štajerska, centred on the town of Trbovlje, were a hotbed of socialist and Communist agitation. Kocbek bemoaned the fact that, up until mid-1943, only 'a scant percentage of proletarians' actively joined the Osvobodilna fronta.[28]

This initial passivity in German-occupied Slovenia was understandable. The ethnic cleansing and deportations of Slovenes in Gorenjska and Štajerska was concentrated in the first year and a half of the occupation, and although stoking anger, it also disrupted the organization of the nascent underground. In September 1941, Field Marshal Wilhelm Keitel, head of the High Command of the German Armed Forces, promised that fifty to a hundred hostages would be executed for every German soldier killed by Partisans (and, indeed, this was taken to its maximum ratio by the German commander in Serbia, General Franz Böhme, of a hundred hostages for every German killed and fifty hostages for every German wounded). The collective punishment also impacted Slovenia.[29] Between 30 July and the end of December 1941, 306 Slovene hostages were executed; 391 were executed between 3 January and 21 May 1942; and 976 were executed between 3 June and 4 November 1942.[30] Adding to this misery was the deportation to Germany of some eight thousand family members of the executed, and the incineration of numerous villages.[31] Indeed, even the head of the XVIII SS Military District, SS-Obergruppenführer Erwin Rösener described the peak of the reprisals in 1942 as *blutdürstig* (bloodthirsty).[32] In total, the German occupiers imprisoned forty thousand Slovenes for political reasons, sent fifteen thousand to concentration camps, and shot almost three thousand 'hostages' as part of the Nazi's well-honed policy of collective punishment.[33] The historian Tim Kirk speculated that because Gorenjska and Štajerska were considered part of the Reich, they were compared with resistance in the Reich. On this level, Partisan actions 'indicate[d] a qualitatively different type of confrontation between regime and resistance' and highlighted 'the weakness of the mainstream organized resistance both in Germany itself and in occupied Austria.'[34] It also helps explain the Germans' draconian responses to what were otherwise still fairly isolated OF attacks and sabotage in these two Slovenian regions.

In addition to these repressive measures, the Germans also shut the valve on potential Partisan volunteers by incorporating most civilians into a number of Nazi mass organizations. The Heimatbund in Štajerska and the Volksbund in Gorenjska enlisted tens of thousands of Slovenes (and some ethnic Volksdeutsche) into the Wehrmannschaft – 84,700 and 28,052 men between the ages of eighteen and forty-five respectively.[35] The Wehrmannschaft was organized along the lines of the Nazi SA and aimed to not only offer basic militarily training to the enlisted men, but also to Germanize them. Dressed in the SA's signature brown uniforms, they were used primarily for guard duty and for fighting the Partisans, but they appear not to have been a permanently armed formation. Most of the men would continue with their civilian positions until a summons arrived, which obliged them to report to the nearest unit.[36] The most trustworthy were recruited into various Alarmkompanien, which were permanently armed but smaller units. The Wehrmannschaft was organized along municipal lines, and virtually every town had its own garrison. The Wehrmannschaft in Gorenjska, unlike in Štajerska, was dissolved by the Germans shortly after its creation in the winter of 1941–1942, ostensibly because it exhibited considerable sympathies towards the relatively stronger OF presence in Gorenjska.[37]

Far worse than Wehrmannschaft service was enlistment in the Wehrmacht, which became mandatory in March 1942 in Štajerska and in September in Gorenjska. Unlike the Wehrmannschaft, the German army required service away from home. The latest research suggests that close to ninety thousand Slovenes were called up for conscription into the Wehrmacht.[38] As Rösener stated in his trial, German-occupied areas were considered annexed territory, and the enlistment orders of 1942 were an opportunity for Slovenes to display their German patriotism.[39] The penalty for desertion was death, and if the individual deserter was not located, his family members would be threatened.[40] In addition to these German military and paramilitary formations, some thirty-three thousand Slovenes joined the Hitlerjugend (Hitler Youth), and tens of thousands of others were drafted into the Reich Labour Service (Reichsarbeitsdienst).[41]

Membership in all of these various military and civilian organizations could hardly be considered collaboration, for the same reasons that membership in the Heimatbund and Volksbund could not be considered collaboration: refusal invited suspicion, imprisonment, deportation, or execution – effectively making it forced mobilization. This, however, was not always the position of Yugoslavia's postwar Communist regime. A number of former conscripts were beaten, imprisoned, and mistreated at war's end. As Žibert claimed, his crime was 'that I did not love my homeland enough because I did not fight with the Partisans.'[42] In the mind of the new regime, forcible mobilization still left open the possibility of desertion.

In addition to reprisals and intimidation of potential recruits, geography played a role in the weak Partisan resistance in German-occupied Slovenia. The Julian Alps in Gorenjska helped conceal a much more active resistance than in Štajerska. A number of attempts in 1942 to infiltrate resisters into Štajerska from the main OF base of operations in the Province of Ljubljana were largely unsuccessful.[43] The experience of the OF's Pohorski Battalion is instructive. Formed in September 1942, on the relatively confined forested massif of Pohorje, the unit of less than a hundred men was able to carry out only a few futile acts of arson and resistance before being surrounded and wiped out by a superior

German force, the following January. A solid footing for resistance in Štajerska came only in 1944, after a Partisan contingent from the Province of Ljubljana managed to fight its way into Štajerska via a circuitous route through the Independent State of Croatia.[44]

Conditions in Prekmurje were even less ideal for resistance. The Liberation Front in German-occupied Slovenia could at least count on a population that hated the occupier, even if fear often tempered active assistance. In Prekmurje, however, the Partisans faced a largely passive and apolitical population. As the Yugoslav diplomat Rudi Čačinovič concluded in his study of wartime Prekmurje, 'the conditions in Prekmurje were not revolutionary.'[45] As late as August 1943, the impression among the non-Communist underground in Ljubljana was that 'in general, Communism in Prekmurje is very weak.'[46] An initial modicum of economic stability and the 'preventative' arrest and exile of any troublesome national intellectuals left Prekmurje Slovenes without an effective anti-Hungarian leadership. The remaining Slovene intelligentsia were unwilling to resist in Prekmurje, and many decided to complete their studies in Hungary, a decision that invited the derision of the local OF leader Štefan Kovač, who instructed: 'Now is no longer the time to study, but the time to fight!.'[47] Prekmurje's geography, like that of the Netherlands, was also an obstacle. Isolated by two national borders from the OF nerve-centre in the Province of Ljubljana, the largely flat, agrarian, and open geography made resistance difficult.

The zeal of the young OF leadership in Prekmurje appeared to have blinded it from these severe logistical deficiencies, as seen in Kovač's impatient upbraiding of a cautious and reluctant friend, in October 1941: 'You wait until everything will be over and that you will then enjoy freedom. Now is the time to begin! Now is the time to show the occupier, who and what we are! In a few weeks, the Red Army will already be in Prekmurje.'[48] Thus, Prekmurje witnessed only two brief and abortive rebellions in October 1941, when Kovač was killed, and October 1944, after the Germans and the Arrow Cross had taken power. Apart from these two episodes, Prekmurje refrained from resistance, and most ethnic Slovenes remained loyal to the conservative political Catholicism propounded by Father Josef Klekl, their imprisoned leader.[49] Indeed, Prekmurje, unlike the rest of Slovenia, would be liberated by the Red Army, not by the Partisans.

The Slovene population of Primorska region, unlike Prekmurje, was far more committed to resisting its oppressors. Along with Austrian

Carinthia, Primorska remained outside the frontiers of the Kingdom of Serbs, Croats, and Slovenes in 1918, and it also faced a great deal of discrimination by the ruling nation, in Primorska's case, Fascist Italy. Twenty years of national repression had left Slovenes bitter and resentful towards Italy, contributing, as Mlakar noted in his pioneering study of collaboration in Primorska, 'to the situation, that all social differences, party divisions, and the like stepped into the background, in the first place came the struggle against Fascism and the expression of national consciousness.'[50] The fledgling Liberation Front was able to feed off of this animosity and recruit men who would prefer to enter the forest rather than serve the Italian army in Europe or Africa – their duty as Italian citizens. As the historian Bogdan Novak noted, 'at this time the Communists did not propagate ideas for a new social order and did not come into the open as Communists.'[51] Support for the OF should also be understood as an extension of Primorska's interwar resistance to Italianization and Fascist rule that was spearheaded by TIGR. Although TIGR was never invited to join the Liberation Front – a sectarian suspicion that would see its former membership placed under Communist surveillance for years after the Second World War – many TIGR members joined anyway, sobered by a series of Italian arrests and executions in 1941 that had decimated its organization. Nevertheless, despite the sympathy of the Slovene population and some favourable mountainous and forested geography, Italian security organs had had decades to spread their tentacles, which limited the OF's effectiveness in the period before the Italian capitulation. In the summer of 1942, there were only a hundred Slovene Partisans in Primorska.[52]

Thus, in the late summer and autumn of 1941, Liberation Front activity was largely suppressed in most occupied regions of Slovenia. It survived primarily in the Province of Ljubljana, where many of the enumerated factors that bedevilled resistance activity elsewhere were less acute. The concentration of the national elite (many as refugees from German-occupied Slovenia), a forested and hilly karst topography, and a relatively lax initial occupation allowed the resistance to establish footholds in the province. As already noted, as early as May 1941, the Slovene legions, as well as a number of other non-Communist underground organizations, were established in Ljubljana. They avoided outright armed resistance in the understandable belief that such acts were suicidal in the dark days of 1941, preferring to organize their forces for a future strike against a weakened occupier; nonetheless, they were programmatically opposed to the occupation and sympathetic to the Western Allies.

Intelligence gathering was one of the key roles of these early resisters, and with their assistance, Ljubljana became a hub of the so-called BBZ (*Berliner Börsen-Zeitung*) espionage ring which was operated by the pre-war Yugoslav military attaché to Germany, Vladimir Vauhnik. (The letters 'BB' were the Cyrillic initials for Vladimir Vauhnik, while the 'Z' stood for Zagreb.) From 1941 to its dissolution in 1944, the BBZ sent information that was collected in Ljubljana by courier routes operating in three regions of Europe to the Yugoslav government-in-exile and the Western Allies via Milan and Switzerland. One channel connected Ljubljana with the Balkans, via Belgrade, Split, Zagreb, and Trieste; another collected information in Italy via the axis Rome-Ancona-Bologna; and a third was channelled through Munich-Vienna-Berlin. There are several reasons why the Province of Ljubljana and its capital became – in Vauhnik's somewhat exaggerated and self-serving characterization – one of the 'largest knots in the espionage web of the Western Allies in all of Central Europe.'[53] Ljubljana was a major railway hub for traffic between Central Europe, Italy, and the Balkans, and a careful observer of rail traffic could, therefore, glean a great deal of intelligence that would be useful in predicting future Axis movements on the battlefields. It was the capital of a semi-autonomous and politically largely unimportant province that did not attract aggressive counterespionage efforts. According to Vauhnik, despite their lack of any real power, the presence of native administrators and officials assisted espionage activity. For example, a passport from the Province of Ljubljana allowed the bearer to travel almost anywhere in Central Europe, and Slovene functionaries, as well as an active black market, facilitated the acquisition of these passes and passports.[54] Alcohol and cigarettes, staples of the local black market, were valuable wartime currencies that allowed the intelligence networks to purchase information. Finally, the Slovene, Serb, and Croat refugees, as well as other displaced central Europeans, including Jews who used the province as a way station on the road to relative freedom in Italy, were important intelligence sources in their own right. Many, in fact, were knowledgeable and influential members of their respective pre-war political and administrative elites.[55]

The peculiar characteristics of the Province of Ljubljana facilitated the emergence of non-Communist underground organizations and intelligence networks. They also offered tantalizing prospects for the

OF's armed resistance, which initiated sabotage and guerilla attacks on Italian units in the fall and winter of 1941. Not surprisingly, the initial Italian leniency changed, largely as a result of the Slovenes' 'lack of gratitude,' and became increasingly draconian. As Burgwyn has summarized, 'violent repression and reprisals were not stimulated, as in the case of the Germans, by cold-hearted triumph over a terror-stricken enemy whose helplessness invited contempt, but an inability [of the Italians] to control insurgency.'[56] Beginning as early as September, Grazioli instituted an Extraordinary Tribunal, which imprisoned any Slovene found with subversive literature or materials, and sentenced to death those involved in violent attacks against Italian officials.[57] These regulations were strengthened with the convening of a military tribunal on 7 November. German and Italian counter-insurgency operations in the autumn of 1941, combined with a harsh winter, scuttled half of the thirty-one OF companies that had formed in Slovenia until then and prevented them from securing any significant territory.[58]

Italian repression only grew in the following year. In January 1942, Ciano recorded the increasingly violent solutions that were being suggested in order to quell the restive Slovenes: '[Aldo] Vidussoni [leader of the University Militia and secretary-general of the Fascist Party] comes to see me. After having spoken about a few casual things, he makes some political allusions and announces savage plans against the Slovenes. He wants to kill them all. I take the liberty of observing that there are a million of them. "That does not matter," he answers firmly, "we must imitate the Askari [native soldiers from Italy's African colonies] and exterminate them!" I hope that he will calm down.'[59] Indeed, the Italian authorities decided not to leave anything to chance and relied ever more on a military solution to insurgency. On 19 January, Mussolini granted General Robotti permission to suppress the growing resistance in the Province of Ljubljana, a responsibility that had belonged to Grazioli's civilian administration.[60] Critical of Grazioli's 'lenient' approach to suppressing insurgency, in February 1942, construction began on the infamous Ljubljanska *žica* (wire), the line of guard posts and barbed wire that would encircle Ljubljana and effectively turn the city into a massive prison camp. The barrier aimed to physically separate the leadership of the resistance as well as its National Defence activists, who initially resided mostly in Ljubljana, from their armed units and their base of operations in the surrounding countryside.[61] A 5 p.m. curfew was imposed, and civilians were barred from congregating in groups of more than three individuals.[62]

Despite these measures, in early 1942, Yugoslav Partisan Supreme Headquarters ordered the Liberation Front to increase the number of armed units in the province, as well as their attacks and sabotage. The Slovene Partisans duly responded with increased activity in April, May, and June. This surge coincided with the Italians' Plan Primavera, which saw the withdrawal of Italian troops from smaller outposts in villages, where they were susceptible to OF attacks, to larger garrisons. This strategic withdrawal left large swaths of the province void of a permanent military presence, which was quickly filled by the Liberation Front. In the spring of 1942, Grazioli observed that the Partisans and the OF's administrative organs controlled approximately two-thirds of the province's territory.[63] On 18 May, Ciano also remarked on the deteriorating security situation in the province: 'In Slovenia things are not going so well. The High Commissioner asks us to send twenty-four thousand men. It appears that the streets of Ljubljana are now unsafe for our troops; every doorway and every window hides potential danger.'[64]

Increasingly equating Slovene civilians with insurgents, Robotti's solution was to carry out mass 'preventative' arrests of civilians to keep them from joining the insurgency. This began in March 1942, with the incarceration in Italian concentration camps of approximately two hundred former Yugoslav Army officers and six hundred non-commissioned officers.[65] Robotti also introduced Nazi-style collective punishment, on 21 April, with the practice of holding known Communists or sympathizers as hostages to be shot if required in reprisals for attacks by the insurgents. The Liberation Front responded with its own decree, on 1 May, that for every hostage shot, the OF would execute the representatives of the Italian occupation – soldiers, gendarmes, policemen, government officials, and ominously, Slovenes deemed to be collaborating with the occupiers.[66] Paying little heed to such threats, the Italians would carry out larger arrests in Ljubljana in June and July, in which virtually every male of military age was interrogated, and approximately three thousand were arrested.[67] This last action forced the OF leadership to move out of the city to join its units in the field.

With Ljubljana sufficiently pacified, the Italian military turned its attention to the countryside. To truly crush the insurgency, OF-liberated territory had to be brought back under Italian control. By the early summer of 1942, the Liberation Front was sending units out from their main logistical base on the 1,000-metre-high forested karst massif of Kočevski

Rog in Dolenjska to other parts of occupied Slovenia including Primorska, the Julian Alps, and Štajerska. The Italian military's response was its 1942 summer offensive, which raged from 16 July to 4 November, certainly the most vicious Italian operation perpetrated in the main against Slovene civilians. Mussolini made the motive behind the campaign very clear during a meeting with his military brass in Gorizia, on 31 July:

> All our original optimism and good treatment of the Slovenes have been dashed by the German attack on the Soviet Union, which has induced them to declare their solidarity with the Russians. I wonder if our policy was wise. One can say only that it was ingenuous [...] I think that it would be better to pass from a friendly manner to strong-arm methods [...] At issue is our prestige. I do not fear the word. I am convinced that we must meet the 'terror' of the partisans with iron and fire. The depiction of Italians as sentimentalists incapable of being tough when necessary must cease [...] This population will never love us.[68]

It is not far from the truth to state that the counter-insurgency plans of Deputy Chief of the Italian Army Staff General Mario Roatta and Chief General Robotti 'amounted to a declaration of war against the people of Yugoslavia – especially Slovenes.'[69] It was an overwhelming show of military might, involving additional Italian units from Montenegro and other regions outside the Province of Lubljana, and amounting to some seventy thousand troops, or one Italian soldier for every five civilians in the province.[70] The province was effectively encircled by Italian and, for the occasion, German troops who agreed to launch an operation along the province's eastern frontier with Štajerska. The plan aimed to brutally excise the insurgency by disrupting the support mechanisms that allowed the twenty-five hundred to three thousand Partisans to be fed, armed, and hidden. As in Ljubljana, in the eyes of Italian military planners, this support network was the Slovene civilian population. Air raids and indiscriminate artillery shelling preceded Italian assaults. Several villages and individual homes suspected of harbouring Partisans were burned, their property and farm animals impounded. All civilians and particularly those of fighting age, defined as between sixteen and sixty years of age, with even the slightest suspicion of cooperating with the Partisans were arrested and sent to concentration camps.[71] Anyone caught with a weapon or ammunition was shot on the spot. A report from the Ribniška valley at the height of the Italian offensive noted: 'If they do not have specific information about who in the village is a Partisan, they collect all the men and send them to Italy.'[72] These would be the first of some twenty to twenty-five thousand[73] Slovenes that the Italians would imprison in the concentration camps of Rab, Gonars, Renicci, and elsewhere, which represented 7 to 8 per cent of the Slovene population of the Province of Ljubljana.[74] Thousands died in the squalid prison camps from hunger and disease – fifteen hundred on the island of Rab alone.[75] According to the Italians, daily caloric intake for 'repressed internees' on Rab was limited to 877 calories, 1,030 calories for the 'protected' who did not work, and 1,541 calories for the 'protected' who worked.[76] The brutality and systematic character of the Italian campaign can only be defined as a crime against humanity.

The cruelty of the Italian summer offensive would not be repeated in the remaining months of the Italian occupation, as Italian military reversals in North Africa and on the eastern front diverted attention and sapped the morale and strength of their troops. Nevertheless, the relatively tolerant early months of the Italian occupation would not be reinstituted. The emergency situation that prevailed in Slovenia during the summer offensive was evident in the absence of any Slovene delegates to the first meeting of the Anti-Fascist Council of the National Liberation of Yugoslavia (Antifašitičko vijeće narodnog oslobođenja Jugoslavije, AVNOJ) held in the Bosnian town of Bihać, in late November 1942. While the delegates discussed ways in which People's Liberation Committees could effectively administer the daily needs of liberated Yugoslav territory, Kardelj and his comrades were on the run. Yet, despite the deaths of some two thousand Partisans and civilians, the summer offensive failed in its strategic goal of silencing the insurgency.[77] The Liberation Front's leadership managed to mostly extricate itself from the encircled Kočevski Rog in August 1942, finding temporary refuge in the hills above Polhov Gradec, west of Ljubljana. By April 1943, the Partisan leadership had returned to Kočevski Rog, where they constructed Baza 20 (Base 20), a collection of some twenty-six barracks that housed, among other things, the Slovenian National Liberation Committee, the Central Committee of the Communist Party of Slovenia, schools, and a propaganda office with printing presses – a sure sign of the failure of Italian counter-insurgency. In postwar Partisan memoirs, the baptism by fire that was the summer offensive only reaffirmed the determination of its core members to continue the fight. The significance of the summer offensive was not, however, simply the moral and strategic bankruptcy of Italian repressive measures. It was precisely during the summer offensive that the Partisans first faced organized Slovene anti-Partisan forces, heralding the start of a vicious civil war whose repercussions Slovenes still reside with today.

5 The Emergence of Collaboration, July 1941–July 1943

The Slovene nation hates the occupiers; however, it hates its own Judases a thousand times more, who have stepped into the ranks of the occupiers.[1]
Edvard Kardelj, October 1942

In the popular memory of anti-Communist Slovene émigrés, 17 July 1942 stands as a watershed. They claim that on that date, in the village of Šentjošt nad Horjulom, located in the postcard-perfect green hills west of Ljubljana, local men spontaneously resisted the Partisans who had come to rob and murder.[2] This motley group of resisters would come to be recognized as the first *vaške straže* (Village Guards, VS), even though two additional units in Sveti Vid and Loški Potok had been formed a month earlier.[3] The July 1942 Šentjošt rising appears far more dramatic and memorable for it occurred at the start of the Italian summer offensive, a catastrophe that VS members claimed was the direct responsibility of the reckless and ineffectual Liberation Front resistance. In August, the Šentjošt Village Guards and the almost two dozen additional VS units that had formed in the interim, were given General Robotti's official permission to join the Italian-sponsored Anti-Communist Volunteer Militia (Milizia volontaria anti comunista, MVAC), the umbrella organization founded in June 1942 under which all anti-Partisan units in the Province of Ljubljana and in other Italian-occupied regions of Yugoslavia were grouped.[4] To understand what led Slovenes to turn on one another with the assistance of their shared occupiers and why this occurred in the Province of Ljubljana, it is necessary to reconsider the aftermath of Operation Barbarossa, when resistance strategies within the Slovene underground fatally diverged.

Just as the relatively tolerant Italian occupation of the Province of Ljubljana allowed the Partisans to establish a foothold, the same tolerance made cooperation with the Italians in the province appear as a potentially profitable exercise. Apart from a handful of Communists with a messianic conviction that the tanks of the liberating Red Army would soon be rolling across the verdant Slovene countryside, the vast majority of Slovenes prepared for a long occupation. The political elite of Slovenia, which was relatively well informed on the progress of the larger European war, was pessimistic about the prospects of liberation in the short term. The rapid German advance across the Balkans and the unprecedented scale of the victories on the Russian front in 1941 and 1942 only confirmed these convictions. Indeed, when faced with the collapse of Yugoslavia, was it not the responsibility of the political representatives still remaining in Slovenia to negotiate for the protection of Slovene citizens? Leon Rupnik stated in 1941: 'Looking at our Western allies I finally came to the position, that they were not even on the European continent, that up to now we had been used too much as cannon fodder and that the world capitalist allies had as much, or even less care for the Slovene nation, than they did for the Hottentots.'[5] Rupnik was by no means alone in this estimation. With an Allied victory remote in 1941, many leading Slovenes saw the necessity of 'walking with the devil.' In biding their time, and, as they saw it, preserving Slovene lives and culture, the non-Communist political and religious elite believed they had to engage the occupiers.

At the very least, a policy that sought 'to save what is savable'[6] had a chance to succeed in the Province of Ljubljana, unlike in the other regions of Slovenia where *there was little to be saved*. In retrospect, it is clear that Italian policies ultimately aimed to assimilate the Slovenes and incorporate the province into Fascist Italy. As Rodogno noted, 'there was to be no further misunderstanding as to the real extent of Slovene autonomy: it was a mere propaganda device and it was to remain a dead letter.'[7] Yet, in 1941, the Italians were the only occupying force willing to countenance the recognition – even if it was merely a ploy – of a Slovene identity. The province's autonomy, however precarious and restricted, could be seen as a symbol of hope, for only in the Province of Ljubljana was a Slovene still viewed as a Slovene and not as a German, a *vindišar*, or an *Untermensch,* who needed to be deported and eradicated. In addition to the refugees from German-occupied Slovenia, who were allowed to remain in the province, various Slovene athletic clubs and other non-political cultural and religious organizations continued to operate, albeit within the framework of the Italian Fascist Party and with the understanding that they would contribute to the rapprochement (*zbližanje*) of Italian and Slovene culture. These signs of Slovene national existence, presided over by a bureaucratic and administrative apparatus that was still somewhat 'Slovene,' was a source of optimism and a carrot for further cooperation.

The Province of Ljubljana offered the most opportunities for collaboration where greater pragmatism prevailed on the part of the Italians, unlike in German- and Hungarian-occupied Slovenia, as well as in Primorska, where collaboration was officially rejected. Collaboration, as Gross wisely concluded, 'must be an occupier-driven phenomenon,' for if the occupier is unwilling to countenance collaboration with the occupied – even if the latter is willing to do so – collaboration cannot occur.[8] Consequently, a number of former politicians, religious leaders, businessmen, and bureaucrats who were able to largely avoid persecution only in the Province of Ljubljana, engaged and cooperated with the new Italian administration. In return for behaving in an orderly manner, the Italians promised an administration that Ciano described as 'very liberal.' Thus, 'order' became the first collaborative offering to the Italians. What many could not foresee in 1941 was that Natlačen's appeal for 'order and peace' would require ever closer cooperation with the Italians if it was to be maintained in a security environment that would deteriorate sharply after the emergence of Liberation Front resistance.

Most of the top echelons of the pre-war bureaucratic and administrative elite were removed and replaced with Italian officials. Similarly, the Italians attempted, with mixed success, to disband or incorporate Slovene unions and civil society associations into their Fascist equivalents. On 8 August 1941, for example, the Italians created the Provincial Workers Union, a mass organization that was to represent all trade unions in the Province of Ljubljana. However, the lower and middle bureaucracy in the province remained overwhelmingly Slovene, a concession to administrative stability and functionality. These ordinary civil servants who continued to rise in the morning and trod off to work were, in one sense, the 'foot-soldiers' of the Italian occupation. They ensured that bureaucratic and administrative changes were implemented at the level of the average Slovene on the street, and they had both the experience and the linguistic abilities to do so.[9] They made certain that sporting clubs adhered to the conduct and membership of the Italian National Fascist Party and the Italian National Olympic Committee.[10]

They supervised theatres that now played Italian movies[11] and ensured that newspapers were printed and distributed. In addition, many Slovene educators and school officials in the province dutifully implemented many of the Italian-sponsored curriculum changes, even in the face of initial opposition from their own pupils. For example, only 10 percent of elementary-school students in the city of Ljubljana joined the Italians' Fascist Youth Organization of Ljubljana (Gioventu Italiana del Littorio di Lubiane, GILL).[12] Similarly, only 98 out of 2,474 Slovene students joined the Organization of the University of Ljubljana (Organizzazione Universitaria di Lubiana), the fascist organization of university students.[13] Yet, far from condoning such resistance, a number of Slovene school officials urged their students to adhere to the new rules, which, at the very least, guaranteed that the Slovene language was used in instruction. The Ljubljana high school Principal Marko Bajuk, for example, upbraided the later president of the Society for Slovene Studies in the United States Metod Milač and his fellow students for reciting 'Our Father' in Slovene against the wishes of their Italian professor, who demanded that the prayer be said in Italian. Milač stated that Bajuk 'did not spare us, telling us how we endangered the entire status of school curricula, which we still enjoyed, unlike other occupied regions of Slovenia, where even speaking Slovene in public is prohibited.'[14] Similarly, for Ivan Dolenec, the principal of the Novo Mesto Gymnasium, the initially lax Italian occupation meant that his 'school operated almost unaffected' in comparison with the German repression 'that we thought impossible for the twentieth century.' It convinced him of the need to preserve and defend Slovene education in the Province of Ljubljana.[15]

Dolenec's and Bajuk's single-minded commitment to protect Slovene education during the occupation could be interpreted as more heroic than servile. Other bureaucratic duties carried out by Slovenes, however, were more questionable. Kocbek, who was arrested by the Italians in 1942 while attempting to leave Ljubljana to join the Partisan insurgency, was shocked to see former Yugoslav policemen serving as office clerks and telephone operators in the police station.[16] This was not unique only to Ljubljana, as former Yugoslav policemen in Gorenjska were also summoned to join the German police, yet were only given the lowest functions.[17] In 1942, there were some 233 former Yugoslav public security agents still at work in the Province of Ljubljana, 190 gendarmes, and 187 members of the financial police.[18] Rather than concentrate on their stated role of helping the needy, the Italians' network of some forty-nine welfare centres in the province only threw fuel on the smouldering civil war by recruiting spies and informers among the local population and arranging their transfer to Italy proper in the event that they were discovered.[19]

Throughout the fall and winter of 1941, Bishop Rožman maintained his contact and communication with the Italians. He continued to intercede on behalf of deported and imprisoned Slovenes, and occasionally also on behalf of Liberation Front members.[20] Rožman was even reported to have successfully intervened in 1941 to keep baptized Croatian Jews in the province.[21] From exile, in 1956, Rožman described the process: 'there came tearful wives and mothers, worried fathers and frightened children asking: help, intercede, negotiate with the enemy rulers, so that they release "ours." After this there came interventions after interventions, pleas and beseeching to the rulers, which we refused and disliked, but for our suffering countrymen, we risked even these humiliatingly and nauseatingly unattractive steps, sometimes successful, sometimes not. Our spirits overflowing with bitterness.'[22] The Italians were wary of the nationalist proclivities of Slovene priests.[23] Their willingness to countenance Rožman's and his priests' intercessions was, thus, predicated on their active promotion of civil order in the province, a requirement that Rožman and his clergy largely obeyed.

Rožman's tactic of engaging the Italian occupiers while avoiding open criticism of them was not a unique response for a Catholic official in occupied Europe. His diplomatic and cautious behaviour was similar to Pope Pius XII's muted protests against Nazi and Fascist atrocities during the Second World War, particularly in response to the Holocaust. In Croatia, the Catholic Church led by Archbishop of Zagreb Alojzije Stepinac maintained a publicly supportive relationship with Pavelić's regime during its initial period of rule when it was committing some of the worst atrocities against Jews and Serbs. Stepinac would eventually come out publicly against Ustaša massacres. Nevertheless, for Cornwell, the Church leadership failed 'to dissociate themselves from the regime, to denounce it, to excommunicate Pavelić and his cronies.'[24] Pius XII's defenders claimed that he 'believed that quiet diplomacy and private action would save more lives than public protest.' Meanwhile, his subordinates, including those in Slovenia, had as their example the Vatican's willingness to maintain relations with dictators like Mussolini, Hitler, and Pavelić, and its failure to openly denounce their crimes.[25] Not surprisingly, Rožman and his clergy's stance towards the Italians was very similar, relying on backroom interventions while publicly calling on Slovenes to obey the new order and avoid the 'blindness and shortsightedness' of what was increasingly seen by them as a *Communist* insurgency.[26]

Indeed, the outbreak of Partisan resistance had complicated the modus vivendi that non-Communist Slovene leaders had sought to achieve with the Italians during their interactions in the spring and summer of 1941. This initiated a process that would end in a vicious triangular struggle between the occupiers, their anti-Communist collaborators, and the Liberation Front. The non-Communist Slovene leaders, along with the Italians, scrambled to understand who they were and to stake out positions towards their policy of immediate armed action. Clearly, the non-Communist political representatives and their affiliated underground legions preferred, at most, a policy of passive resistance. They did not sanction their members to form actual armed units but rather remained party-affiliated armies-in-waiting. Their aim was to prepare the necessary intelligence, provisioning, and recruitment networks that could allow Slovenes and their distinctive culture to survive until the envisioned liberation by the Allies. For a small and politically trisected nation, it was a more prudent policy in the eyes of its proponents than the Liberation Front's antagonistic and suicidal fight against overwhelming odds.

This was also the policy that General Draža Mihailović followed, who in January 1942 was named the minister of the army, navy, and air force by the Yugoslav government-in-exile and the head of the Yugoslav Army in the Homeland, and thus, the nominal leader of the various non-Communist underground legions in Slovenia who remained loyal to the London government. Mihailović was able to form a small armed group of resisters, in the summer of 1941, with a base in the Ravna Gora plateau southwest of Belgrade near the frontier with Montenegro. As a servant of the government-in-exile, Mihailović largely followed their orders of 22 July and abstained from guerilla activities. He did allow himself, however, in the late summer and fall of 1941, to be pushed into sabotage activities 'now and then against his better judgement in order not to leave the resistance entirely to the Communist-led guerillas' – in fact, some of his commanders occasionally cooperated with the Partisans against his orders.[27] The German massacre of over two thousand Serb civilians in Kragujevac, in October 1941, in reprisal for a joint Četnik–Partisan ambush that killed less than a dozen Germans, confirmed for Mihailović what a series of failed meetings between the two resistance movements had already anticipated – Tito was ideologically incompatible with his movement and his policy of an immediate armed uprising was reckless and irresponsible.[28] Mihailović, thus, became almost completely inactive against German forces, and by early 1942, the Partisans accused his Četniks of collaborating with the Italians in Montenegro. Formal ceasefires with the far more suspicious Germans would first occur only in November 1943.[29]

For their part, Slovene Communists and regime historians never sufficiently contested the merits of this passive policy and usually resorted to slander. To the regime historian Branko Božič''s claim that the choice was 'either we unite and liberate ourselves, or we give in and die,'[30] Dolenec countered:

> To me it was clear: in these conditions a small nation could bleed to death, and no one can ask a small nation to sacrifice everything in an unequal war, at the same time that the great allies, England and America, wait peacefully to throw the Germans to the ground with the least loss of their own blood. I did not doubt the final outcome of the war; I was, however, against that a few thousand Slovenes would throw away their lives without any advantage and to kindle among themselves a bloody hatred. Without advantage? Yes! Because of our armed uprising the war will not be over a minute sooner, and our borders will not be improved by a centimetre.[31]

The difficulties that the Liberation Front faced in recruiting and provisioning their Partisan fighters in 1941 and 1942 suggest that the policy of passivity and accommodation was practised not only by the pre-war establishment but also by some of the Slovene masses, particularly the rural population. Coercion and sheer brutality could account for this behaviour in German-occupied areas. Understanding its apparent prevalence in the Province of Ljubljana, where Italian violence was minimal before the Italian summer offensive of 1942, is somewhat more complex. Kocbek commented on civilian aloofness in the village of Hinje in May 1942: 'Their disposition bothered me, which spoke stubbornly that nothing bad has happened to the world.'[32] Italian administrators of the Province of Ljubljana also noted that certain OF propaganda slogans such as the freedom of thought and religious choice 'elicited a muted response from a population that preferred the existing social order and the authority of the parish priests.'[33] Djilas derided this behaviour as the product of the peasants' 'clerical' upbringing,[34] but Kocbek conceptualized it as the 'traditional peasant suspicion of outsiders' and their regional orientation as opposed to their national allegiance.[35] Although correct in part, Kocbek failed to recognize the peasants' acute insecurity – reliant as they were on their lands for their survival and lacking the mobility of urban populations and professions. Provisioning both the occupiers and the resisters, most often against their will, the peasants unfortunately, bore the reprisals of either side for their apparent collusion with the 'enemy.' In this context, the peasant was motivated to protect his immediate surroundings – his family, his home, his produce, his livestock, and his village – with whatever means possible.

Passivity and accommodation was in no way unique to the Province of Ljubljana or the Slovene masses. The historian Mark Mazower, in his work on the Greek occupation, described how resistance appeared as just another encumbrance to the peasantry. Most often 'they wanted nothing more than to be left alone; and it took a visit from German troops, burning and looting, to make them change their minds and look more tolerantly upon EAM's [the Communist-led Greek Liberation Front] vision of social cooperation.'[36] Some Greek peasants threw their lot in with EAM as a result of German reprisals, but others would identify the rebels as the source of their misfortunes. The response of the president of the German Protectorate of Bohemia and Moravia, Emil Hácha, to the Czech government-in-exile, which had branded him a traitor for his November 1941 radio broadcast that urged Czechs to remain calm, avoid armed resistance, and submit to the Germans, bore a striking resemblance to Dolenec's earlier definition of passivity: 'Mr Beneš [the pre-Munich President of Czechoslovakia] [. . .] does not see, as I do, the tears of mothers and wives who address their desperate pleas to me because their sons and husbands fell into disaster having been seduced by deceptive radio broadcasts. He is in a position to permit himself illusions, to build castles in the air, and to paint alluring pictures of the future [. . .] For us, there is no way but to face reality with resolution and to soberly act in accordance with bare facts.'[37] This 'shielding' of the masses was also the rationale behind the Vichy regime, as evinced by Admiral Françoise Darlan's words in 1941: 'Let us know how to reduce the effects of defeat and think of the France of tomorrow. Do you think that the armies of occupation will consent to reduce their requisitions if they have the feeling that our hostility persists? Do you think that they will permit our farmers to return to their farms if they feel France is still the hereditary enemy? Do you think our prisoners will be liberated if it appears that they will only increase Germany's enemy?'[38] In Denmark, the future Danish resistance fighter

Aage Bertelson noted that, initially, 'we were all in favour [...] my wife included, of the so-called collaboration policy'; yet, another prominent Danish resister, Erling Foss, wrote in January 1942, 'Anyone who tried to commit sabotage today would probably be condemned by a majority of Danes.'[39] The German-occupied Channel Islands were, as the title of the historian Madeleine Bunting's work makes clear, a 'model occupation.' Thus, in the initial months of the occupation, accommodation and passivity was a European-wide strategy of *awaiting* rather than *instigating* liberation through immediate armed action.

What complicated this widespread European passive approach to occupation in Slovenia, and in much of Yugoslavia, was the early development of what would eventually become a very strong armed resistance force and one that was, unlike in most areas of East-Central Europe, Communist in orientation. To take the example of the Protectorate of Bohemia and Moravia, 'cooperation with the regime ensured survival, it made sense to toe the line,' and as 'many Czechs saw it, resistance, as called for by London, meant choosing a worthless death over embarrassing complacency.'[40] In the aftermath of the assassination of the head of the Main State Security Office, Reinhard Heydrich, in May 1942, and the bloody German retribution visited upon the villages of Lidice and Ležaky, it is not surprising that the Czech ÚVOD (Ústřední vedení odboje domácího, Central Leadership of Home Resistance) complained to its government-in-exile that they 'could have little impact on the outcome of the war,' that 'the front remained far away,' and that their leaders in the safety of London did not understand the police state that was the Protectorate.[41] Without a strong and aggressive Communist movement constantly shifting the markers on what was *considered enough resistance*, the assessment of the ÚVOD was sound.

For the Liberation Front, which was carrying most of the load of resistance and sabotage in Slovenia – and paying the price in blood – such passivity quickly became understood as treason. The Province of Ljubljana, in particular, offered a crucial ingredient to those Slovenes accommodating the Italians that was far less common in German-occupied Slovenia and in the Protectorate of Bohemia and Moravia at this time – choice. Slovenes were not forced to cooperate with the Italians. Indeed, Natlačen resigned from the advisory committee (*sosvet*), and he was not imprisoned as a consequence. There was another avenue for occupied Slovenes – Partisan resistance – but one who's ideological and political colourings made many Slovenes nervous. Thus, in the eyes of the Liberation Front, Slovenes cooperating with the

Italians disavowed the Partisans and chose and sought out the occupiers: and were collaborators for it. In August 1941, the Central Committee of the Communist Party of Slovenia formed the Security Intelligence Service (Varnostna obveščevalna služba, VOS). Engaged in intelligence gathering and espionage, VOS was the disciplinary organ of the CPS, assassinating representatives of the occupation and, increasingly, their Slovene collaborators. What had essentially been a war of words between the Liberation Front and the non-Communist politicians and legions escalated, on 4 December 1941,when VOS operatives assassinated France Fanouš-Emer, ostensibly for having recruited former Yugoslav officers and Catholic Action followers into anti-OF organizations.[42] In February 1942, VOS agents executed the wealthy Slovene industrialist, banker, and president of the Union of Industrialists Avgust Praprotnik for allegedly denouncing Partisans to the Italians.[43] A financier of the Slovene People's Party, Praprotnik's larger crime was adding his signature to the congratulatory memorandum signed by Natlačen and other leading Slovenes in the aftermath of the 3 May annexation of the Province of Ljubljana and having served as an adviser to the High Commissioner. In May, Kardelj reported to Tito that, on average, sixty people were 'liquidated' each month.[44]

VOS assassinations removed whatever remaining good will there was between the Liberation Front and non-Communist representatives. Their assassination of Natlačen, on 15 October 1942, which cost the lives of an additional twenty-four hostages subsequently executed by the Italians in reprisal for his murder, only reaffirmed what the latter had suspected all along – that the OF was committed to fomenting a Communist revolution within Yugoslavia. To better coordinate their activities against the OF, non-Communist parties 'which, though prohibited, continued to operate surreptitiously on a limited scale' met at the end of April 1942 and formed the Slovene Covenant (Slovenska zaveza, SZ).[45] The Slovene Covenant became the central interparty organ of the non-Communist camp, consisting of a three-member executive committee and a seven-member plenum. As the largest pre-war party, the Slovene People's Party dominated the SZ, which was represented by Miloš Stare, a former SLS deputy and Miha Krek's trusted adviser. The SZ, although united in its opposition to the Liberation Front, was a motley group, diverse in their political and social ideologies, riven by generational schisms, and with differing attitudes towards accommodation with the occupiers. In addition to the SLS, the SZ was made up of a number of liberal and socialist parties that had run afoul of the Liberation Front and the Communist Party of Yugoslavia. These included the Yugoslav National Party, the People's Radical Party, the Independent Democratic Party, Črtomir Nagode's Stara Pravda (Old Justice), and Christian Socialists like Andrej Gošar and Jakob Šolar who, uncomfortable with the SLS's stance towards the Italians, formed their own 'centrist' Catholic movement called Združeni slovenci (United Slovenes).[46] Organizationally, the SZ officially adhered to the orders of the London government, which also provided a monthly stipend. On military matters, the Slovene Covenant, which oversaw both the Slovene and Sokol legions, was subordinate to General Mihailović. Major Karel Novak, Mihailović's representative in Slovenia, played a key role in the SZ's inception and operation, but future developments would increasingly diminish his influence and that of his Slovene Četniks.[47]

Despite its heterogeneity, the Slovene Covenant remained dedicated to the Allies, a postwar federated and democratically resuscitated Yugoslavia under King Peter, and the program of a unified Slovenia. On 7 May 1942, the SZ announced its program under the title 'The Duty of the Slovene in the Liberation War':

> The enemy in the country must be made to feel that he is the aggressor, who we do not recognize or welcome [...] Preparations for national liberation must only be organized according to what will be best and according to the conditions prevailing in Slovenia. That is why a numerically small nation must protect Slovene lives, homes, and belongings as much as possible, without selling out our nationality, or submitting to the enemy [...] Whoever directly or indirectly denounces native people or their affairs to the occupier, is a traitor [...] Whoever today from party or ideological reasons kills someone or threatens someone's life, is the enemy of the nation [...] Whoever organizes their liberationist work according to the orders of some non-national or foreign organization or force, [or] yokes our nation to foreign work, is a traitor.[48]

This document underscored the passive resistance that had become an article of faith for the Slovene Covenant and the non-Communist legions, as it had for Mihailović after Kragujevac (and the Czech UVOD). It advocated preparations for a future resistance, but also openly criticized the Liberation Front's sectarianism, albeit without specifically naming the organization. As for its opinion of the occupiers, the SZ made its position even clearer in a 30 May 1942 declaration: 'Germans and Italians are our enemy, and that is every German and every Italian, be they a Fascist or a Nazi, right-wing or centre, Communist or bourgeois democrat.'[49]

Italian reprisals in the spring of 1942 were largely indiscriminate, and Slovenes opposed to the Liberation Front as well as the apolitical were caught up in their mass arrests. This was seen in the 'preventative' arrests that the Italians carried out against former Yugoslav Army officers and non-commissioned officers in March and April 1942. In June and July, the Italians indiscriminately arrested young men of military age in Ljubljana in an attempt to sever the OF leadership from the rank and file in the countryside. Some of those deemed 'friendly' to Italy such as the Italians' Fascist Youth Organization of Ljubljana (GILL) were rounded up and sent to prison camps; in other cases, Slovene informants singled out the wrong people or satisfied vendettas against their personal enemies.[50] Combined with the Italians' brutal summer offensive of 1942, Slovenes, and not only those among them who were committed anti-Communists, were increasingly suspicious of the costs of Partisan resistance. According to Burgwyn, some twelve hundred Italian troops were killed battling the Liberation Front in Slovenia, a casualty rate that was 'modest when compared to the devastating toll exacted on other fronts.'[51] Although such statistics were unavailable to Slovenes critical of OF tactics, the repercussions were clear in the disproportionate violence unleashed by the once relatively lenient Italians. For its part, the OF dismissed protests against the costs of armed action as a desperate attempt to 'throw sand in the eyes of the people.'[52]

Faced with a growing realization that it was not only the Italians but also the Partisans and their revolutionary program that were to blame for the escalating violence in 1942, anti-Communist leaders had to consider the daunting question of how best to respond. As early as February 1942, according to Godeša, anti-Communist politicians were discussing how best to fight the growing Partisan insurgency without the Italians intervening – a proposal that pleased Grazioli, but which he would not act on for a number of months.[53] It fell on Monsignor Lambert Ehrlich, in April 1942, to once again suggest that Slovenes should assist in pacifying the insurgency. Ehrlich was not a natural ally of the occupiers. He issued some of the first documented reports of Nazi atrocities against Slovenes and petitioned the Italian authorities to permit pastoral services to Slovenes imprisoned in Italian concentration camps.[54] He was, however, an opponent of the Liberation Front uprising. On 1 April, Ehrlich sent a critical letter to the Italian high commissioner. He wrote that although the situation under the Italian occupation had initially been tolerable, 'today the conditions have completely changed and it appears that the Slovenes under German occupation in some ways have it better than under the Italians.'[55] He urged the Italians to release all innocent Slovenes, to cease the burning of villages and reconstruct those that had been destroyed, and to give Slovenes greater control over anti-Communist propaganda. Such demands were valid, even brave. Yet, Ehrlich took the fatal step into active collaboration with his suggestion that Slovenes be permitted to form a security force to fight the Partisans.[56] In a less explicit memorandum to the Vatican, on 14 April, that was also approved by Rožman, Ehrlich argued for increased cooperation between Italian officials and the 'legal representatives of the Slovene people':

> There are no ties between the Italian authorities and the Slovene representatives, and there is not one single Slovene personality who would be able to influence the measures and procedures of the Italian rulers. As a result, the Italian administrative and police personnel cannot carry out their functions successfully, because they do not recognize the inhabitants, the terrain, the mindset or the language of the nation. All searches, important negotiations, questions, [and] interventions have to be carried out with some [unqualified] interpreter, because there are no Slovene personnel in competent positions. That is why our destiny, including the destiny of everyday life is in the hands of foreigners who do not want to understand us. That is why for a more successful administration and security service, it is necessary that there be at least a minimum of cooperation between the Italian authorities and the legal representatives of the Slovene people who enjoy their confidence.[57]

These suggestions, influenced at least in part by the fear that Partisan resistance could only provoke a more violent Italian response in the future, earned Ehrlich and two of his students their liquidation by VOS, on 26 May 1942.

Between the execution of Ehrlich and the emergence of the Village Guards, in mid-July, elements within the Slovene Covenant, particularly Major Novak, again urged for the creation of an effective armed alternative to the Liberation Front that would also be opposed to the Italians. The meagre result was the so-called Štajerski Battalion, a Slovene Četnik unit, which departed Ljubljana for its operational terrain in Dolenjska in the middle of May 1942. As recounted by Ivan Korošec, one of its original members, the unit was woefully undermanned and underarmed, consisting of eleven soldiers and six officers.[58] The chief explanation for this was the SLS leadership's refusal to support the battalion – a product of personality conflicts with Novak as well as its steadfast commitment to a policy of passivity. (The Greater Serb pretensions of the wider Yugoslav Četnik movement were also not helpful.) As Korošec quipped, the 'democratic' parties 'were all shut in their own party programs, calculated to come ahead after the war and not knowing the way to overcome the period of occupation.'[59] Before embarking from Ljubljana, Novak nevertheless, optimistically declared the 'battalion' proof of the nation's right 'to exist outside of the OF,' but urged the contingent 'not to attack the occupier uselessly, in order to avoid national victims.' As for the Partisans, Novak wanted the unit to avoid battles with them, but to respond if attacked.[60] For six weeks, the battalion masqueraded as a Partisan unit from Štajerska, hence its name, and cooperated with the Partisans in two attacks against the Italians in Ratež and Zajc na Gorjancih. However, this was a dangerous game. On 27 May, the Liberation Front declared it would execute anyone attempting to organize Slovene armed units outside of the OF organization.[61] By early July, the unit's real identity was uncovered. Hounded by the Partisans and unable to mobilize sufficient recruits in an OF-controlled countryside, the Štajerski Battalion sought refuge among the Italians. The Italians accepted their collaboration and, in August 1942, 'legalized' this erstwhile Četnik force – which by then had grown to 640 men – with the rather foreboding name of the Legija smrti (Legion of Death).[62] The unit peaked at some fifteen hundred members. Known best for its aggressive pursuit of Partisans in the southeast of the province, the Legion of Death also organized a short-lived police force in Ljubljana called the Guardia Civica (*mestna straža*), disbanded in January 1943.[63]

The subordination of the Štajerski Battalion to the Italians, as well as the emergence and incorporation of the Village Guards into the Anti-Communist Volunteer Militia, marks the beginning of Slovene armed collaboration with the Italians and a critical rupture in the Slovene political arena. In manpower, the MVAC quickly came to rival the Partisans. It reached its peak in July 1943, with 6,134 men scattered among 107 garrisons, 953 of which belonged to two Legion of Death battalions.[64] The MVAC were auxiliary units, used to complement the main Italian military forces in the province. Although their units were usually under the command of Slovene officers, real authority resided in the nearest Italian garrison. As Ehrlich had argued, their main strategic value to the Italians was their knowledge of the local language and their familiarity with the geographical terrain. They also provided Italian intelligence with information on OF activity.[65]

The formation of the Village Guards and the Legion of Death and their inclusion into the Anti-Communist Volunteer Militia put the non-Communist political representatives in an awkward position. There was undoubtedly an organic element to the creation of the Village Guards. Ciril Žebot, an economist and a wartime leader of Straža, described the Village Guards as 'spontaneous and regional self-defence units' opposed to Partisan attacks and requisitioning.[66] Yet, there was also orchestrated assistance from non-Communist political bodies both in recruitment and organization. As an SLS situation paper issued to Miha Krek in June 1942 stated, 'the Italians are prepared to give guns to the people to defend against Partisans. The latter is, however, a very dangerous game, but it has the possibility of great success, if it will be correctly carried out.'[67] There is no conclusive evidence confirming a formal agreement between the Slovene Covenant and the Italian military. Nevertheless, the SZ and its strongest representative, the Slovene People's Party, had an undeniable influence on the Anti-Communist Volunteer Militia. Some of the MVAC's Slovene 'command' and its rank and file were Slovene and Sokol Legion members, as well as former Yugoslav military officers.[68]

Understandably, the creation of the Anti-Communist Volunteer Militia caused a rift between non-Communist Slovene politicians at home and in London. Some, like Gošar and Nagode, were appalled by the drift to military collaboration with the Italians. Other politicians still residing in Slovenia, however, in particular the Slovene People's Party, believed that London did not fully appreciate the quandary non-Communists found themselves in. For them the MVAC was envisioned as a stop-gap solution to the threat posed by two enemies, the occupiers and the Liberation Front. Stare summarized this idea in a 3 January 1943 report to London: '*vaške straže* [Village Guards] are in no way collaboration with the occupiers, but appeared as a result of the following: Slovenia has two enemies, Communism and the Italians. Currently, it is not possible to fight the Italian occupier with a gun, but there is a desire to fight against the Communists, to prevent their terror and the occupier's reprisals.'[69] He also pointed to a rift between the Italian military and civilian wings, which he believed they could exploit. As an unconvincing consolation, Stare added that the MVAC only required military cooperation with the Italians not political ties, which had ended when Pucelj and Natlačen resigned from the advisory committee (*sosvet*).

The Italians were also not completely convinced of the MVAC's loyalty. An SLS report from the fall of 1942 stated that 'the occupier is very afraid that there is some kind of relationship or some ties between this organization and Slovene political people.'[70] General Robotti, in particular, had 'serious doubts about the loyalty of Catholics and national-liberals' in the Province of Ljubljana, and he 'was reluctant to accept Slovene military assistance.'[71] Indeed, the summer offensive had not endeared the Slovenes to the Italians, and the various legions had a command structure that was, as one of their orders noted, 'affiliated with the Yugoslav soldiers that stand under the leadership of General Draža Mihailović. From the leadership of the Yugoslav Army we receive orders and without question fulfil them.'[72] The Slovene Legion's internal correspondence throughout much of 1942 identified the Italians as their enemies. A directive from 19 July ordered SL members to help all Slovenes who remained homeless as a result of Italian actions and 'to collect accurate information on all traitors who cosied up to the occupier to the harm of the nation, and on Communists.'[73] On 1 August, after the creation of the Village Guards, a Slovene Legion order directed its ranks to assist in the upcoming harvest and to hide foodstuffs, as 'we will not fatten the occupying armies. Produce was to be sold to Slovenes and only under duress to the occupiers.'[74] Subsequent SL directives, however, lost some of their anti-occupier edge and were replaced increasingly with anti-OF rhetoric. The release of Yugoslav officers, in late 1942 and early 1943, from squalid Italian prison camps on condition that they join the MVAC, which Bishop Rožman had urged, added another potentially disloyal element to their ranks.[75] Partly in response to these persistent suspicions, the Italian command insisted that the Village Guards remain fragmented into smaller units. VS units were not allowed to merge into larger offensive bodies, nor were they permitted a unified Slovene command or general staff.[76] The VS were literally to 'watch their villages,' as Stare reported: 'as a result of a lack of trust, the Italians do not allow for the free movement of the MVAC units, but are stuck in their own areas which the Partisans can take advantage of.'[77] The VS were also given substandard arms, and their uniforms were a rag-tag mixture of civilian and Italian military attire.

Italian suspicions were somewhat warranted. The Anti-Communist Volunteer Militia was infiltrated by the intelligence networks of the Slovene non-Communist parties, including Vauhnik's BBZ.[78] They were, thus, able to keep detailed records of Italian atrocities, particularly during the 1942 summer offensive.[79] The non-Communist political parties also attempted to counter the fragmentation of the MVAC with the creation of the secret five-member War Council (Vojni svet) made up of high-ranking pre-war officers including Novak, Vauhnik, Captain Anton Klinar, Lieutenant-Colonel Ernest Peterlin, and Colonel Ivan Prezelj (alias Andrej) – the last two having been only recently released from Italian camps. It sought to unify the scattered VS commands under one consolidated leadership. Part of this vision was the creation of a 'paper' Slovene national army, consisting of nineteen illegal battalions that would strike out against the Italians at the opportune moment.[80]

There was certainly significant behind-the-scenes intrigue to Slovene military collaboration with the Italians. Émigré historians and commentators tended, however, to overemphasize the VS's apparent hatred of the Italians and, thereby, underplayed the depth of their actual cooperation with the Italians. All scheming aside, the Village Guards, the Legion of Death, and their Slovene political representatives never openly opposed the Italians during their occupation of the Province of Ljubljana. Instead, the Italians provided them with arms, however substandard, and the vitally important night passes that allowed MVAC members to break curfew. There were numerous joint Italian – MVAC operations in the Province of Ljubljana – which émigré writers often seemingly forgot to mention – from the summer of 1942 to the capitulation of the Italians, in September 1943. For example, an operation in March 1943 to oust Partisans from the village of Toško Čelo on the outskirts of Ljubljana involved ninety Italians and twenty members of the Village Guards.[81] During these operations, the Italians relied on the MVAC to identify OF members and sympathizers, and it was standard procedure for MVAC to hand custody of captured Partisans or OF sympathizers to the Italian security forces.[82] Mutual respect and even cordial relations between the MVAC and regular Italian soldiers was not nearly as rare as émigrés maintained. Two VS died in joint VS–Italian operations, in September 1942, and their funeral in Trebnje was attended by a number of Italian troops along with their military band.[83] Most compromising, perhaps, was the cooperation of MVAC units in the mass arrests of Christmas 1942 in Ljubljana.[84] Stare reported that Italian troops, 150 members of the Legion of Death, and the Guardia Civica (*mestna straža*) blockaded the city on the night of 21–22 December 1942, allegedly to forestall an intended OF assassination campaign.[85] Approximately 550 suspected Communists and their sympathizers were arrested. On 2 January 1943, the Carabinieri commander Amedeo Tommasini commented on the MVAC's poor behaviour during the searches, reporting that they had committed 'abuses of every kind,' while at the same time, the Fascist Giovanni Domenis wondered why the MVAC allowed suspects to languish so long in prisons awaiting interrogation.[86]

The wartime supporters of the Anti-Communist Volunteer Militia insisted that they were simply trying to restore 'peace and order' in the province which the Liberation Front had apparently undermined. One should not underestimate, however, the windfall for the occupier of this seemingly benign goal. A calm environment and the assistance of native collaborators to achieve that end required fewer occupying troops, allowing them to be redeployed to critically important fronts in the larger European theatre. It would also facilitate the movement of goods and provisions across Slovene territory, which linked Germany and Italy and their possessions in the Balkans.

Similarly, the romanticized view of the Village Guards as soldier-farmers – simple, industrious, and pious Slovenes who were protecting their families and farms from the Red Terror – that still persists among Slovene opponents of the Liberation Front – needs to be qualified. An analysis of the age and professions of the 1,386 men who joined the Legion of Death reveals that almost half (45.6%) of them were twenty-one years old or younger, and over 80 per cent were under the age of thirty. Thus, like with the Liberation Front, mostly young Slovenes fought within the ranks of the anti-Partisan units. In addition, slightly over 50 per cent were farmers, but about one-fifth were classified as workers, contradicting Liberation Front claims that they themselves monopolized the allegiance of the working class. Only 2 per cent classified themselves as students – symptomatic of the wider support for the OF among politicized Slovene students.[87]

Moreover, émigré writers propounded the view that only the purest of ideals motivated Slovenes to join the MVAC – patriotism and the defence of the Catholic values of Slovenes. They did not view their actions as tantamount to collaboration, but rather as self-defence. The MVAC was certainly made up, in part, of the victims of Partisan activity. This included men whose family members or friends had been arrested or killed either by the Partisans or as Italian reprisals for OF resistance.[88] Rudolf Hirschegger, a former VS and Home Guardsman from Polje, wrote that the Liberation Front 'pushed us to the edge of the most bitter decision: take arms from the occupiers – the enemy, to protect our very lives and homes.'[89] However, in addressing motivations, the historian is unfortunately confronted by the same reality that was described by the Czech émigré and political scientist Jan Triska, in the introduction to his father's First World War diary: 'There are no opinion polls or statistical surveys documenting the feelings of soldiers in the trenches, only anecdotal evidence such as my father's diary.'[90] Nevertheless, there is sufficient evidence to tentatively conclude that motives beyond heartfelt ideological opposition may have moved Slovenes to join the MVAC. Individuals who were already members of the various non-Communist legions, especially the Slovene Legion, were often 'obliged' to join the MVAC, despite its voluntary nature.[91] In comparison with the Partisans' outlawed existence, the Village Guards appeared a less burdensome and dangerous option for surviving the war. The Village Guards served relatively close to home and were typically given a thirty- to forty-day discharge for fieldwork.[92] Petitioning for the release of imprisoned family members and friends or those deported to Italian concentration camps was a potential benefit of service in the MVAC. For example, the vicar of Kostanjevica, Franc Šeškar, asked the local VS unit, on 14 October 1942, to intercede on behalf of six of 'our people' who had been mistakenly accused of aiding the OF, pleading 'do all in your power to get them back.'[93] The overall success of these petitions is difficult to assess with the available documents.

Devotion to the Catholic Church may have influenced the decision to join the MVAC. The militia bore a heavy religious stamp, portraying itself as the protector of Catholic Slovene culture against a foreign atheistic creed. Bishop Rožman and parish priests routinely denounced the Liberation Front, which Rožman described from exile in Klagenfurt, in 1946, as the 'greatest danger to Christianity and for the Christian life of my nation [...] that had ever before existed in [its] 1,300-year history.'[94] Rožman would often quote Pope Pius XII and earlier papal encyclicals to justify his stance. Local parishes, such as Šmihel, organized prayer hours in support of the MVAC, 'for the humiliation of the enemy, and the victory of the Church.'[95] Bishop Rožman took a more incriminating step when he allowed military chaplains under the leadership of Father Ignacij Lenček to serve in MVAC units, although he also allowed Father Anton Ilc to act as a spiritual vicar in areas liberated by the Liberation Front.[96] On 2 August 1942, Rožman instructed his chaplains: 'I permit that you go as military chaplains on your own request. Your work is to shepherd souls and nothing else. I especially emphasize that it is often necessary – as much as possible – to sermonize, [and] to give opportunities for the sacraments. Weapons are to be carried only for self-defence, never for any other actions.'[97] Military chaplains held services but also disseminated anti-Communist propaganda. In September 1942, chaplain 'Vesela' requested from Novo Mesto standard religious paraphernalia such as rosaries and chalices for the host, but also the texts *Rdeče mreže* (Red Webs) and *Ukrajina joka* (Ukraine Cries).[98] In postwar trials, priests were accused of fighting on the side of the anti-Partisan forces, although Rožman insisted that the Church led an ideological war rather than a military war against communism.[99] In the heat of battle, however, the division between ideological and actual organizational assistance may not have been as clear-cut. For example, Anton Šinkar, a military chaplain who was captured during the critical Grčarice battle between the Liberation Front and the Četniks, in September 1943, following Italy's capitulation, testified at the ensuing Kočevje trials to having been present at the execution of a number of Partisans. In his defence, he claimed not to have watched the actual executions.[100] According to the Liberation Front and its wartime propaganda, Chaplain Karel Wolbang of Šmihel was the epitome of a 'clerico-fascist.' He was accused of having taken part in the execution of OF couriers and, rather fantastically, of having directed the September 1943 German aerial bombardment of Novo Mesto from the city's bell tower.[101] However, Wolbang's sermons certainly transcended simple pastoral duty in urging his men to arms: 'The military is now our calling. As Catholics we have to be good soldiers.'[102] The resonance of such advice on the local, rural, and devout population as well as on impressionable Catholic youth groups cannot be underestimated. Indeed, the Anti-Communist Volunteer Militia was further radicalized by the recruitment of members of Straža and the youth-wing of Catholic Action, perhaps most clearly seen by the emergence of a martyrdom creed. This was best exemplified in a well-known exchange between Jaroslav Kikelj, a young Catholic Action member, and its leader Dr Tomec, which was said to have allegedly occurred one hour before VOS assassinated Kikelj and his mentor, Monsignor Lambert Ehrlich:

TOMEC: 'Be careful, that they do not kill you!'
KIKELJ: 'Then I will go to heaven!'
TOMEC (SURPRISED): 'Directly to heaven?'
KIKELJ: 'Yes, Mr Professor, directly to heaven.'[103]

As the civil war intensified, and shocked in particular by the assassination of Ehrlich, Bishop Rožman's position towards the Liberation

Front hardened.[104] His memorandum to General Robotti, on 12 September 1942, in which he gave advice on how to fight the Partisans certainly went beyond his religious domain of responsibility:

> From the sound part of the Slovene people, who have declared themselves ready to seriously work together with the Italian authorities for the purpose of re-establishing order and destroying subversive and rebellious elements, the following is proposed to the military authorities:
> 1. We should be allowed to establish protective armed units under Slovene command in rural areas. The names of the members and commanders of these units will be supplied to the military authorities. The command will be responsible for the members of the protective units and their behaviour. The commanders of these units will be selected from men worthy of trust, to fully guarantee that the arms will be used exclusively against rebellious elements that endanger the land either with arms or revolutionary propaganda [...]
> 2. We are convinced that without the establishment of the proposed system of protective units, no self-supporting and lasting order can be maintained. The soldiers have already dispersed the camps and groups of the rebels, but many of them are still in the woods and in villages, where they are camouflaged as peace-loving citizens. Such persons are not known to the Italian armed forces. Because of their unfamiliarity with the language and the difficulty of finding those who help those who hide in the woods, it will be very difficult to find the culprits. But for the local young men such difficulties are non-existent or can easily be overcome [...]
> 5. In addition to the protective units stationed in rural areas, it would be necessary to establish a few central units under the command of former Yugoslav officers. The task of these units would be to keep wooded areas under surveillance and prevent the formation of armed Partisan groups.
> 6. To achieve the given objective, it would be necessary to bring back some young, dependable former Yugoslav officers from prisoner-of-war camps, but in an unobtrusive fashion, as if letting the officers home on furlough. Their names would be proposed by us.
> 7. In regard to Ljubljana, the following is proposed as urgent: [...] We should be allowed, so to speak, to establish a Corps of Secret Police of 500 men, to be armed with revolvers. We can give assurances that within six weeks, dangerous elements would be found, arrested, and turned over to the authorities. Those persons who have false identification cards and who freely circulate in the streets would be identified and arrested with the help of the citizens. In this way Ljubljana would become a peaceful

and orderly city in which there would be no more Communists. At the same time everything would be done to remold public opinion with the help of strong and continuing anti-Communist propaganda.

These sincere proposals show the good will of the majority of the population and create the possibility of achieving the given objective in a manner that must also please the authorities. His excellence, General Roatta, has said that the people must now choose between order and Bolshevism. We have chosen order, and propose the only way that in our humble opinion will be effective and certain to achieve complete order in active collaboration with the authorities.[105]

Bishop Rožman's *Pro memoria*, sent to High Commissioner Grazioli on 26 September, condemned a number of abuses that the Italians had perpetrated in Slovenia, urged them to restore personal as well as national and cultural liberty, but again, intimated that such reforms would give rise to 'forces, which would help with the general pacification of the province.'[106] Not surprisingly, Rožman's conciliatory policies towards the Italians earned him the praise of General Roatta, who 'expressed pleasure over the archbishop's [sic] lively role in leading "civilization and religion" in the crusade against Bolshevism.'[107] It is true that these compromising communications were written while the Italian summer offensive was in full swing, a desperate time when thousands of innocent Slovenes were arrested and abused. Nevertheless, the question remains: did this justify Rožman's suggestions that Slovenes take part in hunting down fellow Slovene resisters? Indeed, reading Rožman's memorandum, there is a sense that he did not consider Partisans to be fellow Slovenes but rather Communists, first, and misguided Slovenes a distant second. His memorandum describes them as 'subversive and rebellious elements,' 'rebels,' 'camouflaged as peace-loving citizens,' 'culprits,' 'dangerous elements,' and 'Communists.' The dehumanized and foreign Liberation Front was contrasted with what Rožman termed 'the sound part of the Slovene people,' that is, the anti-Communist Slovenes who were a 'majority of the population.' By suggesting a surgical excising of the Communist cancer from the otherwise healthy and obedient body politic, Rožman believed that order would return to Slovenia. The Slovene Partisan, not the disproportionate Italian military response, bore responsibility for the violence.

In the fall of 1942, with the Province of Ljubljana serving as the battlefield between two opposing ideological and political projects, winning over the civilian population became a pressing concern for the Liberation

Front and its opponents. The interwar era had already established allegiances and biases in certain segments of the population. Only a few priests supported the OF, despite the inclusion of Mikuž in the Plenum of the Liberation Front. The pre-war business and property-owning class were also generally opposed to the political left – their pro-worker agitation in the interwar era had won them few converts. The wartime archives of the Slovene People's Party contain lists of the party's trusted people in various parts of the province, and they included many small and large business owners – millers, sawmill owners, wood merchants, industrialists, and property owners.[108] For many of them, political instability was anathema, and a cautious, passive but cooperative approach towards the occupiers was viewed as a necessity if they were to survive the war economically. For the neutered pre-war political and administrative elite, the precarious dual objectives of suppressing the Liberation Front while avoiding compromising public fraternization with the Italians offered the tantalizing prospect of the resumption of power once the war ended. This was the SLS's position in the homeland, as evident in Stare's communications and in the behaviour of the Slovene legions. With one fell swoop, the non-Communist political camp hoped that the MVAC and the occupiers would knock their Communist competitors from the postwar political race.

The inability to quash the Liberation Front and the deepening civil war made Stare's 'dangerous game' all the more perilous. Not only the OF, but also the Italians increasingly saw wavering as a sign of disloyalty. Yet, collaboration with the hated Italians was also unacceptable to many Slovenes, regardless of their attitude towards Communism. As the liberal Ljubo Sirc recalled: 'I was so angry about this new turn of events, not understanding how anybody could venture to collaborate with the Italians that I spoke out furiously against it when some of us met again at Dr Nagode's. To my amazement, this earned me a sharp rebuke from Judge Benedik, a sober and calm man, who accused me of meddling in matters I did not fully understand.'[109] Sirc's reminiscences continued, capturing the divisiveness that collaboration invoked: 'A nationalist leader, a respected university professor, told me in June 1943 that it could hardly be wrong to collaborate with the Italians at a time when they could be considered potential allies. My opinion was that the Italians should change sides first. Until they did, our own people, who were keen to fight the enemy, would not understand our dealings with them. The professor laughed and said that the Western Allies would no doubt occupy Slovenia and they would most certainly not support the Communist Liberation Front.'[110] Shrinking away from political and bureaucratic offices that were now tainted with open armed collaboration with the Italians left the podium free for new opportunistic political creatures. For example, Adlešič's resignation as the longtime mayor of Ljubljana, in June 1942, ushered in Leon Rupnik's bizarre rise to power. The occupation turned the political arena into quicksand, swallowing some of the pre-war establishment, while offering opportunities to those enterprising individuals willing to take the outstretched hand of the occupier.

The allegiance of the civilian masses in the Province of Ljubljana, particularly the rural populace, in the evolving civil war was more difficult to anticipate. The Church undeniably exerted a strong influence over the countryside and relayed its opposition to Communism from the pulpit. Yet, Slovenes of seemingly equal piousness in other regions of Slovenia, such as Primorska, largely supported the Liberation Front and denounced collaboration.[111] On the other hand, Slovene peasants were, like rural populations everywhere, highly protective of their land. The bogy of Communist collectivization resonated strongly in the countryside. Already in the 1930s, the Slovene peasantry was conscious of the horrific conditions in Ukraine, which the Slovene People's Party exploited, in part, to garner rural support.[112] Yet, the countryside of much of the Province of Ljubljana, particularly the rocky karst soils of Suha Krajina and Notranjska, was among the poorest in Slovenia. Certainly, the promises of prosperity and social justice made by both the Liberation Front and by the Communist Party of Slovenia would have appealed to them. As Rebula and Pahor concluded, however, 'Suha Krajina, the poorest region, according to sociological absurdity was also the most anti-Partisan, neither was the terrain completely safe in Bela Krajina.'[113]

More than pre-existing socio-economic or ideological factors, the position of the rural masses in the Province of Ljubljana towards the civil war was more often influenced by the immediate dictates of survival. After all, it was the rural areas of the province, not the city of Ljubljana that was always firmly under Italian control, that bore the brunt of OF resistance and Italian counter-insurgency. Plan Primavera, in the spring of 1942, allowed the Liberation Front to move into rural isolated areas that had been abandoned by Italian forces – these were the same regions that were targeted a few months later in the summer offensive. The occupiers, the Liberation Front, and the Anti-Communist Volunteer Militia all used these areas as a source of provisioning, manpower, and if necessary, retribution. The violence employed by all factions in this ever-shifting jigsaw puzzle of 'occupation' and 'liberation' ensured that rural allegiance was often reduced to whoever was holding the gun at any given moment. Not surprisingly, support often varied between villages and even individual families, depending on their experiences with a particular faction. Gestrin's survey of the villages surrounding the heavily forested Krim massif south of Ljubljana, for example, found 10 per cent of the village of Iška Vas serving in the Partisan ranks, while nearby Ig and Tomišelj villages had only 3 per cent and 1 per cent of their population serving respectively.[114] Overall, however, it appears that in the Province of Ljubljana, support for anti-Partisan forces was strongest in the amorphous front-line areas of rural Dolenjska and Notranjska. There were numerous reasons for this, but the reprisals of the occupiers and requisitioning were chief among them. Living off of the land, Partisan requisitioning in these areas was deeply resented, where large families and poor soils meant that hunger was present in the best of times. The veteran Partisan Hribernik-Svarun described requisitioning from resistant populations: 'It always weighed heavy on our hearts, whenever with a retaliatory or a deterrent intent, we took steps to dispossess a traitor of his possessions, and even more so, if it happened to people who did not commit treason, but were not prepared to sacrifice anything for the common struggle.'[115] In his old age, Hribernik-Svarun remained convinced that such measures were justified: 'More than four decades later, the young certainly have a hard time placing themselves in the situation, in which we were forced to encroach upon the possessions of the traitors, so that the Liberation Front would continue and win.'[116]

The Suha Krajina area of Dolenjska stands as a classic example of how local self-preservation dictated allegiances. Its peasant population had initially offered food and shelter to the nascent Partisan force that had sought refuge on the nearby Kočevski Rog massif in late 1941. As Weiss-Belač remembered, Suha Krajina was, in many ways, cut off from the world 'and up until the Italian offensive was all for the Partisans.'[117] Indeed, Italian violence in 1942 would tear Suha Krajina out of its isolation, its civilian population punished for harbouring 'bandits.' Yet, reprisals would not dissuade the Partisans, as Kardelj famously declared: 'In war, we must not be frightened of the destruction of whole villages. Terror will bring about armed action.'[118] Such reasoning, and the increasingly aggressive requisitioning required to secure provisions from suspicious locals, eroded the initial tolerance of the Liberation Front in a manner not unlike that of Dalmatia, as described by Lieutenant John Hamilton of the OSS Hacienda Mission in 1944:

> The majority of the farmers resent the high-handed manner in which the Partisans operate. Also, and this is the crux of the entire situation, it is the farmer or rather the civilian peasant and his family, who are doing the work and paying the penalty too. Partisan elements are billeted with the farmers everywhere. They feed the Partisans; they supply the Partisans with livestock, horses and wagons for transport. In return, they are left behind whenever there is an enemy drive through the country [. . .] This leaves the farmer holding the bag. The Germans, or local fascists, plunder his farm, rape his women, burn a few homes and move on. Then the Partisans return and the cycle is ready to commence anew.[119]

The conduct of MVAC forces also alienated local populations. The poor behaviour of members of the Legion of Death, which included womanizing, drunkenness, and requisitioning, led some villagers to conclude that the Legion of Death was no better than the Partisans.[120] Italian officers, and even General Roatta, were disappointed with the poor discipline of some of the Anti-Communist Volunteer Militia, who 'resembled goon squads,' were 'insubordinate and rowdy,' and pillaged.[121] MVAC officers recognized the vacillation in civilian support and denounced looting among their ranks in their bid to win local support.[122]

The shifting patchwork of local support for the Liberation Front and their collaborating opponents underscores that localized and regional conditions during the occupation were significant in moulding civilian responses and attitudes. National concerns surely existed; however, in catastrophic crises such as military occupation, ordinary Slovenes could and did operate on the basis of what was better for their own families, or indeed, themselves, than for their nation. With the ship of state sinking, it was often every man for himself. Treason was not a genetic aberration more common to an inhabitant of the Province of Ljubljana than Primorska or, to expand the comparison further, more common to a Norwegian than a Pole. Rather, regional experiences helped condition localized responses towards the Liberation Front, the occupiers and, of course, collaborators. More specifically, four principal factors can be identified as impacting upon the degree of regional acceptance of collaboration in the period up until the Italian capitulation: a region's historical relationship with the occupying nation; the harshness of the occupying force; the prominence of Partisan armed resistance and civil strife in the region; and finally, the latitude for legal collaboration in the region.

In Primorska and Koroška respectively, post – April 1941 Italian and German rule was hardly different from the chauvinistic oppression that they had experienced during the interwar era. Instead, the emergency conditions of war led to an escalation in oppression. The Italian offensive against Partisan-liberated territory in Primorska, in November 1942, which saw boys as young as thirteen to fifteen years of age mobilized into the Italian military, witnessed an uptick in OF recruitment as a consequence.[123] Similarly, only a few members of the Slovene minority in Austrian Carinthia actively collaborated with a Nazi regime that had deported Slovenes and suppressed their national identity. Indeed, even some priests supported anti-German actions.[124] Slovenia proper, cognizant of the national discrimination experienced by Primorska and Koroška in the interwar era, avoided a similar fate until April 1941. However, as noted in chapter 3, initial reactions to the invasion were hardly all negative. Subsequent civilian attitudes towards the occupation and, by extension, collaboration were moulded by the occupiers' policies in the ensuing months. As already highlighted, the initial occupation was most lenient in the Province of Ljubljana. Here the relative peace and a semblance of autonomy were seen by a number of influential Slovenes as worth protecting, and gave rise, as Ciano hoped, to greater receptiveness towards the Italian occupiers. Leon Rupnik concluded as much when he became mayor: 'For all of this, Italy has only asked for our loyalty and our peaceful disposition and our cooperation.'[125] When the initial Italian leniency was eroded by the more militaristic and draconian policies embodied in the 1942 summer offensive, Slovenes in the province could be persuaded that the OF insurgency, in part, provoked this change of policy. In comparison, German oppression and, to a lesser extent, Hungarian oppression, pre-dated the emergence of the Liberation Front and was a policy in its own right. In short, there was little or less to protect in Gorenjska, Štajerska, Koroška, Primorska, and Prekmurje than in the Province of Ljubljana.

Furthermore, Partisan armed resistance and the ensuing conflict between OF forces and the Italian military and their Slovene auxiliaries was centred in the Province of Ljubljana. At least until the Italian capitulation, the civilians in the province were most likely of all occupied Slovenes to suffer from Italian reprisals for harbouring 'bandits' or at the hands of the Partisans themselves. In comparison, largely because of the 'no-nonsense' approach of the Germans and geographical obstacles, the Partisan movement was weak in Štajerska and to a lesser extant in Gorenjska, and virtually non-existent in Prekmurje. The Liberation Front had made some inroads into Primorska, but a stronger OF presence would only be established after the Italians pulled out of the war.

Until the Italian capitulation, the Germans and the Hungarians did not permit the formation of the same grassroots and relatively autonomous collaborating units as the Italians allowed with the Village Guards and the Legion of Death. The Wehrmannschaft was hardly a voluntary unit; at best, it allowed the servicemen to remain near their homes and avoided the uncertainty of conscription into the Wehrmacht. Moreover, self-identifying Slovene units were ideologically anathema to German and Hungarian nationalists, who refused to recognize the very existence of a Slovene nationality. Unlike the newly annexed Province of Ljubljana, in Primorska the Italians also prohibited the formation of Slovene collaborating units, as it would 'recognize that this region's twenty year experiment was a failure,' in short, that its inhabitants were not Italians.[126] As a result, German- and Hungarian-occupied Slovenia, as well as Primorska, were initially spared the worst of the emerging civil war, and thus, also had a more charitable impression of the Liberation Front. An assessment of public sentiments in Gorenjska, in 1942, found the townspeople of Kamnik strongly opposed to the war against the Liberation Front in the Province of Ljubljana, as well as to all cooperation with the occupiers.[127] The population of Radovljica was equally supportive of the Liberation Front.[128] Most Slovenes of Primorska heralded the OF as national liberators, but there did exist a nucleus of opposition. It was best described as a true 'centre,' composed of individuals who although opposed to OF tactics were also resolutely against any collaboration. Indeed, many had been arrested by the Italians during the interwar era as leaders of the Slovene community. Most of Primorska's non-Communist intellectual and bourgeois leadership, such as the underground Slovene National Council in Trieste led by Jože Ferfolja, were oriented towards the Western Allies and the London government-in-exile and, by extension, were also sympathetic towards the Četniks whom they saw along with the Liberation Front as harbingers of national unification.[129] The OF, unfortunately, did not countenance criticism very well, and a number of VOS assassinations of suspected OF opponents, in the spring of 1943, contributed to a growing schism between Partisan supporters and opponents that the Germans would attempt to exploit after they occupied the region in September 1943.

Thus, the comparative strength of collaboration in the Province of Ljubljana is, in part, to be explained by its relatively unique experience under Italian occupation. Unlike Primorska, its inhabitants did not suffer directly from interwar Italian oppression. After April 1941, the province was the only relatively autonomous region where the Slovene nationality was still recognized. The Province of Ljubljana was the nerve-centre of the Liberation Front – which some inhabitants identified as the cause for the deterioration of this initial autonomy – and the region where civilians were most likely to experience first-hand the deleterious effects of the developing civil war. Finally, and critically, the Province of Ljubljana offered the most opportunities for Slovenes to openly act on their anti-OF sentiments by joining collaborating units or administrative offices that sought to suppress it.

Slovenes outside of the Province of Ljubljana were not allowed to form collaborating anti-Partisan armed units that were identifiably Slovene; however, this does not mean that collaboration was completely absent in these regions in the period up until September 1943. Collaboration did take place in other occupied parts of Slovenia, but on an ad hoc, individual level rather than as an accepted policy of the occupiers. Slovenes who owned shops, or manufacturing and industrial firms, found themselves in a particularly difficult position. The fear of having their business confiscated by the occupier – and the Germans, in particular, expropriated a number of industries, banks, and enterprises belonging to the Yugoslav state and private individuals – inclined many to cooperate, even though it often assisted the occupier's war effort. But fear was not the only motivator. Opportunism played a role, especially as economic conditions initially improved under occupation. As part of the Reich, 'the German occupying authorities tried to raise the standard of living and improve the technology of industrial and agricultural production. Unemployment was ended.'[130] Compulsory and illegal labour brigades were utilized by all three occupiers – evident in the building of military fortifications and the felling of trees along rail lines to dissuade Partisan activity. A good deal of employment, however, was not forced. For example, Karel Glazer of Maribor joined the Kulturbund and also offered the services of his construction company to the Germans. He repaired their barracks, prisons, and factories.[131] Textile factories in Kranj switched to making airplane parts, while the Germans increased the production of steel plates and wire at a rolling mill in Javornik that employed four thousand workers.[132]

In addition to strictly economic relations, unscrupulous and frightened Slovenes (the distinction rarely being absolute) entered into a number of more compromising alliances with the German and Hungarian occupiers. Some joined the administrative and security branches as interpreters. Srečko Pukl, employed by the secret police in Maribor from June to December 1941, insisted that he only served an administrative function. Yet, was his position merely administrative when it involved writing out card indexes of Slovene deportees?[133] Others enlisted as prison guards, such as Jože Jarman of Ptuj, who would later be convicted of beating Slovene prisoners.[134] Slovenes joined the German and Hungarian gendarmerie, albeit usually at their lowest levels. Some, like Ivan Družin, who enlisted in the German gendarmerie in Radgona in June 1941, were even given six-month training courses at the gendarme school in Vienna.[135] A few local Slovene politicians were able to remain at their posts after the invasion. For example, Slovenes could serve as village mayors in German-occupied Slovenia – the upper limit of administrative autonomy for occupied Poles, as well – if no Germans were available.[136] Such was the case with the mayor of Sveta Barbara v Halozah, who was, thus, seen as complicit in the deportation of Slovenes.[137] Other Slovenes went a critical step further and denounced their co-nationals, becoming informants for the Gestapo or for the Hungarian secret police.

Once again, it was largely individuals or scattered groups that took part in these mostly localized acts of collaboration, as any officially sanctioned and widespread collaboration would obviously conflict with Germany's and Hungary's aggressive pursuit of ethnocide. Thus, in the period between the April 1941 invasion and the capitulation of Italy, it is not surprising that there was no Slovene version of a Marshal Pétain in German- or Hungarian-occupied Slovenia. There was also no version of the Anti-Communist Volunteer Militia in these latter regions. Thus, the real story of Slovene collaboration in the period between April 1941 and the capitulation of Italy is the story of why only a small territory gave rise to forces that gripped the guns of the occupiers and turned them on their brothers and sisters.

6 The Collapse of Italy and a New Spirit of German Cooperation, July 1943–December 1943

The German nation will value your worth according to your success.[1]
                                                                                               Odilo Globocnik, 26 November 1943

By all accounts, 1943 was a pivotal year in the Second World War. On 1 February 1943, German General Friedrich Paulus surrendered to Soviet forces at Stalingrad. The last great German offensive on the eastern front, the great tank battles at Kursk in July, failed. As the historian Robert Parker concluded: 'Until the summer of 1943 Hitler could still reasonably hope to win [. . .] After the summer of 1943 he could only hope to delay defeat until the allies fell apart.'[2] Fortune was also not smiling upon the Italians. In July 1943, the Allies invaded Sicily. In reaction, Marshal Badoglio and his conspirators overthrew Mussolini in a coup d'état. Italy's final surrender would come some two months later, on 8 September, after Allied troops landed on the Italian mainland.

Realizing that the Germans could be defeated, resistance movements across Europe – and not only Communist organizations – in Denmark, France, Italy, Poland, and elsewhere saw an increase in membership and activity. Yugoslavia and Slovenia were no different. Taking advantage of the Italian collapse and the subsequent stretching of German occupational forces, the OF's liberated territory grew in size. From approximately fifty-five hundred members before the Italian surrender, Slovene Partisan ranks swelled to twenty thousand after the capitulation and to some thirty to thirty-five thousand individuals by mid-1944.[3] Indeed, Partisan recruitment spiked across Yugoslavia, reaching some hundred thousand members by the fall of 1943.[4] During the same period, Tito's army received the recognition he had sought from the

Grand Alliance as the only force in Yugoslavia actively fighting the occupiers. Considerable material support would follow. Even the seemingly moribund Četnik forces attempted to shake themselves free, at least in Slovenia, from collaboration and to distance themselves from the Italians.

Yet, 1943 was not only a benchmark for the anti-fascist struggle. In Slovenia, there was a parallel expansion in armed collaboration with the Germans. The number of Slovenes in anti-Partisan units would almost triple within a year, from six thousand in mid-1943 to almost seventeen thousand in mid-1944. After the Italian capitulation, these units would also expand geographically, moving beyond the Province of Ljubljana into neighbouring Gorenjska and Primorska. To account for this rise in resistance and collaboration, it is necessary to return to the Province of Ljubljana in the summer of 1943 and the weakening grip of the Italian occupation.

July 1943 marked an anniversary most Slovenes preferred not to remember – one year of fratricidal conflict between the Liberation Front and its Slovene opponents. Ideological polarization only widened in tandem with its mounting victims. By accepting the Dolomite Declaration on 1 March 1943, the OF's Supreme Plenum effectively neutered the front's coalition character. The declaration recognized the Communist Party of Slovenia as its leading force, making official what had already become accepted practice. Only the CPS could retain its distinctive organization within the front, and all OF activity outside its confines was to cease. The OF's opponents, as well as some of its disenchanted members, interpreted the Dolomite Declaration in a manner similar to what the historian Hugh Seton-Watson famously described as the 'monolithic regime' phase in the communization of postwar Eastern Europe, characterized by one Communist-managed front, with one hierarchy and one discipline.[5] To its supporters, the declaration was a necessary strategic decision in a time of war, which maintained discipline within the front and avoided the sectarian divisions that bedevilled its opponents. In short, the Liberation Front and the Communist Party of Slovenia effectively became one and the same.

Indeed, the Dolomite Declaration did highlight the lack of unanimity within the non-Communist camp. Each constituent party in the Slovene Covenant maintained its own organization and political agenda. In addition to divisions between political parties, there was significant tension between Novak – the Covenant's military leader and under whom all party-affiliated paramilitaries were officially subordinated – and the Covenant's political leaders. The political influence of the Slovene People's Party over the Village Guards inevitably clashed with Novak's assumed military predominance.[6] Novak had greater control over the Legion of Death, which the bulk of his Četnik and Blue Guard (*plava garda*) followers had joined, but his overall influence in the Slovene Covenant was never as strong as he had hoped for it to be. Discussions held in April 1943 to clarify command and control between the SZ and Novak were unsuccessful, largely because Novak's proposals would have converted the SZ into a mere organ of the Yugoslav Army in the Homeland.[7] As the only major Slovene party not affiliated to a pan-Yugoslav party, the Slovene People's Party and its platform of political autonomy was especially incompatible with Novak's attempt to subordinate the remnants of Slovene political life under the military arm of the exiled Yugoslav government.[8]

The London government, which was wary of the Anti-Communist Volunteer Militia as well as the growing independence of the Liberation Front, urged a rapprochement with the Partisans.[9] In comparison with the Slovene Covenant, and in particular the SLS, Novak was far less intransigent on seeking common ground with the Liberation Front. In the spring of 1943, he was unsuccessful in coordinating operations with the Partisans of Gorenjska. According to the OF, Novak was as headstrong in negotiations with it as he was with the SZ, insisting that it be subordinate to him and cease operations against the occupiers until conditions were suitable for success.[10] With Četnik units collaborating with the occupiers in a number of large-scale anti-Partisan offensives in Bosnia and Montenegro in the first half of 1943, that these overtures failed is hardly surprising.

In the spring of 1943, General Mihailović urged Novak to do what the Štajerski Battalion had been unable to accomplish a year earlier – raise a credible non-Communist force in preparation for a strike against the Italian occupier. There were reasons to resuscitate dormant resistance plans. Allied interest in the Balkans was growing, as the American OSS joined the British SOE in fomenting Yugoslav resistance. As the historian Walter Roberts concluded, 'after the victories in North Africa and in view of the contemplated landings in Italy, operations in the Balkans ranked second only after the Italian islands and Corsica and Crete.'[11] Indeed, the Americans and the British had discussed the question of a possible Balkan invasion route in the run-up to the August 1943 Quebec Conference, and Novak wanted his non-Communist force to be ready to link up with this anticipated movement. We now know that such talk was mostly smoke and mirrors to camouflage the Allied assault on France. At the time, however, it convinced not only Hitler, but also Mihailović and Tito.[12]

Novak was confronted with a number of logistical obstacles. First, he needed men. Although he could count on a few hundred of his officer-heavy Četnik followers, Novak needed to poach men from the Village Guards. Četnik intelligence had kept abreast of the MVAC, ascertaining their numbers, distribution, morale, and political orientations.[13] In June, Novak envisioned collecting a force of about two thousand men from MVAC units in Notranjska and Dolenjska to operate in the Mirna valley. He and his followers cajoled the reluctant Village Guards to join the 'Leadership of the Yugoslav Army in Slovenia,' reminding them that 'MVAC is not the Yugoslav Army' and that 'ties with the occupiers were only a pretense to obtain weapons.'[14] Others, like the Četnik 'Jarko,' attempted to frighten the Village Guards into action: 'This is the last chance. Italians are on the ground. The Partisans aim to kill all Catholic families in case of an Italian capitulation, especially those who are members of the Catholic Action. Therefore, all boys must head to the forest to stop this.'[15] Yet, a number of VS commanders, Slovene Legion activists, and some priests disagreed and worked against Novak's plans, which they considered to be premature and dangerous. VS commander Lieutenant Ivan Boh replied that 'almost half were young married men who joined the *vaške straže* to defend their village and their homes, and it is not believable that they would now all of a sudden leave their region and their families to the mercy of the Communists.'[16] The logistical task was also daunting, how to feed and provision two thousand men without reverting to the 'Partisan methods' of stealing? Finally, there was also the question of how the Italians would react if a large number of men took to the forest. The Anti-Communist Volunteer Militia was ostensibly formed as a response to two enemies – the Liberation Front and the occupier – and that situation had not yet changed. On 18 June, the Slovene Legion announced that it would continue to expand SL units but would not obey Novak's orders. Rather ironically, their declaration ended with the words, 'The Slovene Legion is and will remain an integral part of the Yugoslav Army!'[17]

The Italians were aware of the tensions between Novak and the SLS-dominated MVAC. On 15 June, the intelligence branch of the Italian Second Army noted: 'Like all Četnik detachments dependant on Mihailović, they [Novak's Četniks] do not have a program that would be directly hateful to us,' although it cautioned against allowing MVAC members to join.[18] These predictions were borne out when, in July, Novak and a tiny force of fifteen men took part in negotiations with General Gastone Gambarra, Robotti's successor, in Vrhnika. Novak agreed to avoid skirmishes with Italian troops if they allowed his men to carry arms, to purchase food and arms from them, provided travel permits, and gave them permission to recruit among the Anti-Communist Volunteer Militia.[19] Although the Italians preferred that the Village Guards did not join the Četniks, they permitted individuals to go of their own free will. 'Many will not go anyway,' General Lubran confidently, and as it turned out, correctly predicted.[20]

It did not take long for the Anti-Communist Volunteer Militia to ascertain Novak's 'special' agreement with his purported enemies, reporting that the Italians did not fire nor did they allow the Village Guards to fire upon Četniks who had settled in Iška vas.[21] Consequently, for some MVAC members, there was little incentive to join an organization that in their relations with the Italians appeared virtually identical to their own. As one MVAC member curtly observed, 'Some are asking, why the pressure on the boys to leave MVAC for the illegal, which is legalized, that is, into the same situation in which the boys have been in for the past year?'[22] Nevertheless, splits developed between former army officers, where much of Novak's support resided, and the rank and file. In early July, Major Janko Debeljak, who had authority over the Legion of Death battalions, began preparations for the underground. Most of his men, however, refused to go. As one replied, the boys did not 'bring their heads into the Legion, so that the officers could bowl with them.'[23] As a result, Novak was only able to increase his Četnik force to some 350 men.[24]

Novak and his Četniks were more successful in their prediction of Italy's imminent collapse. On 25 July, Marshal Pietro Badoglio replaced Mussolini. Unfortunately, for Novak, this news did not award his forces with more men, and the envisioned 'exodus' to the Četniks remained a trickle limited primarily to Milan Kranjc's 2nd MVAC Battalion and a number of officers from the Legion of Death.[25] Despite a latent hostility towards the Italians, the majority of MVAC members stayed put until the Italian capitulation overwhelmed them. Discussions among the Slovene Covenant's plenum, on 5 August, revealed divisions over what to do in the event of an Italian collapse and a German takeover. Novak, his Četniks, and the 'official SLS' were inclined to 'enter the forest' – that is, to resist. The Liberals were split between resistance and remaining where they were within the Anti-Communist Volunteer Militia. The Slovene Legions offered a compromise solution. One part of the MVAC was to remain at their posts and fight the Partisans. Another part of the MVAC would enter the underground. A third group, a compromise between the two previous strategies, would enter the forest 'but not too far.'[26] VS member Alojz Brulc summarized the rank and file's suspicions in abandoning the fight against the Liberation Front: 'I think that our relations with the Blues [Četniks] as our relations with the Germans and Italians are governed by this: The Village Guards are our self-defence against Communism and therefore our only defence against total destruction. This and nothing more and nothing less. Communism means to us a more certain death than the German or the Italian occupation. Therefore we must fight against them.'[27]

This lack of unanimity contributed to the bizarre scenes that unfolded when, on 8 September, the Italians finally capitulated. The Italian mayor in Vrhnika, for example, called all his men together, including the MVAC, thanked the Slovenes for their effort, offered a comradely toast 'Long live Slovenia – Long live Italy,' and then promptly departed.[28] In a few cases, as in Novo Mesto, MVAC units actually retreated with the Italians.[29] For the majority of the units in the Anti-Communist Volunteer Militia, now officially renamed the Slovene National Army (SNV) and commanded by Lieutenant-Colonel Peterlin, the Italian capitulation caught them without a decisive plan on how to proceed. This paralysis was revealed in the different solutions proposed at a meeting of leading non-Communist officials in Ljubljana the next day, 9 September. The SLS industrialist Ivan Avsenek was behind an immediate exodus into the underground, while Peterlin urged all SNV units to remain where they were. Holding a rather common but mistaken belief, Vladimir Vauhnik of the BBZ suggested that the SNV link up with the inevitable Anglo-American assault on Trieste. In the end, the advice of Colonel Anton Kokalj, a former Yugoslav Army officer, was adopted. Older members of the SNV were to remain at their posts and form a gendarmerie, but younger SNV members were to enter the forest and form larger detachments in cooperation with the Četniks. They were to avoid attacking the Partisans and 'energetically defend the nation.'[30] The order only lasted one day, however, as the Germans entered Ljubljana that evening, severing communications between many of the SNV's leaders in the city and the rank and file in the field. Confusion reigned. Many of the units remained ignorant of the orders. Others assumed that there would be some type of joint actions between the SNV, the Četniks, and the Partisans against the Germans.[31]

In retrospect, the MVAC's dependence on the Italians had lulled them into a fatal passiveness. Fearing 'eventual reprisals' for a stance that could be construed as hostile to the occupiers, former commander Josip Dežman explained that the Anti-Communist Volunteer Militia was unable to react resolutely and in unison to the Italian collapse.[32] Admitting what many postwar émigrés refused to concede, collaboration with the Italians 'discredit[ed] [. . .] our positive elements' in the eyes of the Allies who, for strategic reasons, were forced to throw their support behind the Partisans.[33]

In contrast, the Partisans had strict orders to disarm the Italians and to capture or destroy any remnant Četnik or MVAC units. Indeed, the disarmament of Italian forces – an opportunity the Slovene National Army and the Četniks were less able to exploit – proved profitable for the Partisans. All but two of the sixteen Italian divisions in Yugoslavia adhered to the Allied request that they surrender to the Yugoslav Partisans.[34] In fact, several thousand Italian soldiers would join the Yugoslav Partisans as part of the Garibaldi division.[35] More critical to events in Slovenia was the seizure of heavy artillery, which would be critical in OF sieges of their more stationary opponents.[36] The first of these showdowns occurred in the village of Grčarice. Located some twelve kilometres west of Kočevje, the settlement was relatively isolated and mostly empty after its Volksdeutsche inhabitants were relocated to Štajerska in 1941. In coordination with a larger Croatian Četnik detachment from Lika, some 130 Slovene Četniks hoped to carve out a base where they could await an Anglo-American invasion.[37] Unbeknownst to them, the Lika unit had already been attacked and dispersed by the Partisans, and the Allied invasion of the Balkans would never materialize. Cut off from their leadership – Novak remained in German-occupied Ljubljana – the Partisans' howitzer attack on Grčarice, which took place on 9 and 10 September, made short work of Četnik resistance. Ten defenders died, eighteen were wounded, and the rest surrendered.[38]

Of the former Anti-Communist Volunteer Militia, over seven hundred ended up garrisoned inside the medieval castle of Turjak, located some twenty kilometres southeast of Ljubljana.[39] Severed from communications with commander Peterlin, who remained in Ljubljana, most believed they were to await further orders to link up with an anticipated Anglo-American invasion along the Adriatic.[40] Although the walls of the castle provided better security than the houses of Grčarice, the Partisans' heavy weaponry still forced its surrender, on 19 September, after five days of fighting. Many of the captives were pressed into Partisan service. Scores of them, and in particular their leadership, were executed–immediately or, along with the Grčarice prisoners, after having faced revolutionary justice at the Kočevje trials that took place from 9 to 11 October.[41] A more fortunate group of several hundred MVAC members, led by the more experienced Četnik commander Dežman, refused to be encircled in Turjak and made a strategic retreat via the nearby village of Zapotok. Joined by two small Četnik detachments, the Zapotok group was able to fight its way north towards Ljubljana, where they surrendered to the Germans. Most of the remaining former Legion of Death, which was concentrated in the eastern part of the province, was also able to repulse Partisan attacks and retreat towards Ljubljana.[42] Grčarice and Turjak smashed the ranks of the former Anti-Communist Volunteer Militia and the Četniks; their remnants, however, would become the nucleus of an enhanced German-sponsored anti-Partisan fighting force.

On the heels of these victories against their domestic opponents, and strengthened with new recruits and arms, the OF liberated a considerable swath of former Italian territory in the Province of Ljubljana and Primorska. This was part of Tito's broader push to capitalize on the Italian surrender, which resulted, among other gains, in the liberation of most of Dalmatia. The Germans' key concerns were reoccupying Ljubljana and securing the main transportation routes to the coast. Unless it threatened these strategic interests or German garrisons, liberated territory remained largely in the hands of the OF, although it would still weather some last remaining German offensives. The Partisans were able to seize temporary control of larger less important towns such as Novo Mesto and Kočevje until the Germans reoccupied them, in October. The OF used this breathing space to further cement its authority as a government-in-waiting. In October 1943, Kočevje hosted the Convention of Delegates of the Slovene People, which affirmed the Liberation Front as the only legal national authority on Slovene national territory and condemned the traitorous work of the anti-Partisan units, Rupnik, and, significantly, the exiled Yugoslav government in London.[43] It also elected the delegation that would attend the second meeting of the Anti-Fascist Council of the National Liberation of Yugoslavia (AVNOJ), held in the Bosnian town of Jajce between 21 and 29 November. At this historic second session of AVNOJ, the Slovene delegates agreed to join a new federated Yugoslavia, and a nine-member National Committee for the Liberation of Yugoslavia was confirmed as the provisional government, with Tito as marshal of Yugoslavia and prime minister. The meeting denounced the Yugoslav government-in-exile and outlawed King Peter's return until a referendum confirmed the status of the monarchy. The Christian Socialists Edvard Kocbek and Tone Fajfar, along with Father Metod Mikuž attended the second session of AVNOJ. Kocbek placed his own unique conciliatory stamp on the proceedings, when he spoke of 'Communists and Catholics working together.'[44] With the Partisans in control of approximately half of Yugoslavia, and the lives of some five million people, AVNOJ was the 'coming out party' of Tito's movement.[45] The sheer impressiveness of their accomplishments – and the confidence with which they displayed them in Jajce – was crucial in winning final Allied support for Tito over Mihailović. In February 1944, the first Soviet mission would finally arrive at Partisan headquarters.

As in the rest of Partisan-held Yugoslav territory, the Liberation Front also used its temporary control of regional urban areas to root out its domestic political opponents. In addition to the trials of captured MVAC and Četnik leaders in Kočevje, in October, retribution and retaliation were carried out in a far less judicious manner. In Novo Mesto, political opponents were arrested. A few, such as Canon Kek, who was defended by principal Dolenec for his interventions on behalf of imprisoned professors and students during the Italian occupation, were executed.[46] This settling of accounts sobered some civilians' heightened expectations of the Partisans. According to a MVAC assessment from February 1943, as much as 90 to 100 per cent of Novo Mesto's population had originally supported the Liberation Front, with merchants offering food, women donating knitted sweaters and socks, and the propertied classes providing money.[47] OF behaviour during its brief liberation, in addition to the Germans' violent reoccupation, in October 1943, which included a devastating aerial bombardment, eroded some of their initial enthusiasm. The result of these two turbulent months was summarized in a Home Guard report which states, 'The people are as soft as wax and one could do what one wanted to among them, as long as they maintained order and peace.'[48]

The OF's twin agenda of liberation and retribution also played out in Primorska. The Slovene population, exhausted from a quarter of a century of Italian discrimination, as well as a handful of anti-Fascist Italian Partisans, greeted the Osvobodilna fronta as liberators. The Partisans seized virtually all of Primorska, with the exception of coastal cities such as Trieste. On 16 September, the OF declared Primorska to be part of a free Slovenia and a federated Yugoslavia – an objective that was formally accepted by AVNOJ, in November.[49] Liberation Front propaganda spoke of socialist brotherhood between Italians and Slovenes. Their irredentist demands, and their arrest and execution of hundreds of Italian Fascists and their sympathizers, however, cooled relations between Slovene and Italian Partisans and their respective Communist parties.

The Germans could not tolerate this situation for long. The rail lines and viaducts of Primorska and the Province of Ljubljana carried troops and war materiel heading to German lines in southern Italy and the Balkans. The Vienna-Ljubljana-Trieste corridor, for example, was the main transport route for fuel and gas from Romania and Galicia, and coal from Silesia.[50] As early as 10 September, Hitler created the Operation Zone Adriatic Littoral (Operationszone Adriatisches Küstenland, OZAK) out of the provinces of Udine, Gorizia, Trieste, Pula, Rijeka, and Ljubljana, with the city of Trieste as its administrative capital. OZAK's ethnically diverse population of two million was 43 per cent Italian, 32 per cent Slovene, 20 per cent Croatian, and 3.5 per cent German.[51] Hitler appointed Friedrich Rainer, the former Gauleiter of Gorenjska and the Mežiška valley, as 'supreme commissar' for the OZAK, with Dr Wolsegger as vice-supreme commissar and Regierungspräsident or president of the civil service. SS Obergruppenführer Odilo Globocnik was chosen to head the SS and police in the OZAK. This was a homecoming of sorts for the man that the historian Michael Allen has described as 'the vilest individual in the vilest organization ever known' for his leading role in Operation Reinhard, which saw the murder of over one million mostly Polish Jews in the death camps of Majdanek, Treblinka, Sobibor, and Belzec, in 1942 and 1943.[52] Born in Trieste in 1904 of Kaisertreu parents of Slovene ancestry, Globocnik was capable of making speeches in Italian and Slovene.[53] He wasted little time in his new posting, as he and his 'veteran' accomplices rounded up the remaining Jews of Trieste and the OZAK. In October 1943, Globocnik had the old rice mill on the outskirts of Trieste, the Risiera di San Sabba, converted into a detention centre complete with a crematorium. Thousands of Jews, Partisans, and other political dissidents would be interrogated, tortured, and murdered at San Sabba.

As Ferenc rightly observed, the 'Germans pursued a policy of occupation [in the OZAK] that was less ambitious than that in northern Slovenia.'[54] The Germans took immediate steps to fortify and defend the coastline from an anticipated Allied invasion and silenced political dissent; however, they did not attempt to forcibly Germanize the civilian population as they had in Štajerska and Gorenjska, nor did they conscript them into the German army (although, in practice, voluntarism meant a choice between military or labour service). Despite Berlin's discomfort with local collaboration, Rainer attempted to engage the local population, realizing that the Germanization campaign that bore tepid results in Gorenjska would never be accepted in an area where Germans constituted only a tiny minority.[55] Indeed, the unrest that such actions could provoke would unnecessarily destabilize this strategically important region at a time when Germany's frontiers were contracting and occupation troops were at a premium. Rainer turned, instead, to the tried and tested strategy of 'divide and rule.' Slovene hostility towards the Italians, he believed, could convert them 'into possible collaborators or, at least, passive participants of the Third Reich.'[56] Thus, Rainer and the Germans became unlikely 'advocates of ethnic diversity in the Adriatic.'[57] They removed several irritants of Italian Fascist rule, opened some Slovene schools, and appointed Slovene administrative officials. Rainer boasted 'that no other occupied territory had such good officials and such a good administration,' pointing to subsidies for theatres, musical groups, and radio.[58] However, these concessions were not uniformly implemented across the Operation Zone Adriatic Littoral. Very little changed in the Province of Trieste, where Italian Fascists still wielded considerable authority. In contrast, in the Province of Gorizia, where Catholic-oriented Slovene intellectuals were concentrated, a Slovene was appointed to the vice-mayoral position, and a Slovene secondary school, some forty primary schools, and a Slovene newspaper were established.[59] Nevertheless, these privileges were conceived in the waning days of German power. To see what was in store for the Slovenes had the Germans not been defeated, the Slovenes of the OZAK needed only to look to Gorenjska and Štajerska. Indeed, it is assumed that the Operation Zone Adriatic Littoral would have become part of the Third Reich had the Germans triumphed.[60]

As part of his *divide et impera* policy, Rainer retained the relative autonomy of the Province of Ljubljana and, in some ways, heightened it. Some connections with Italy were severed, although the province continued to use the lira and import Italian food.[61] Part of the OZAK, the Province of Ljubljana, nevertheless, remained largely administratively distinct from Trieste. For example, police and 'anti-bandit' operations in the Province of Ljubljana were under the control of SS-Obergruppenführer Rösener's Security Police and Security Service for Carinthia, based in the Gorenjska tourist town of Bled, rather than under Globocnik. Similarly, the OZAK's propaganda department, headed by SS-Hauptsturmführer Franz Hradetzky, did not have branch offices in the Province of Ljubljana. This would help give Slovene collaborators in the province an inordinately important role in propaganda. Perhaps most critically, although the OZAK's six provinces were administered by prefects appointed by Rainer, only the Province of Ljubljana was 'governed' by a Slovene; all the rest were governed by Italians. Rainer's apparent magnanimity must be qualified, as he also assigned German (in fact, mostly Austrian) advisers to supervise the prefects and their officials.[62]

With the creation of the Provincial Administration (Pokrajinska uprava, PU) of the Province of Ljubljana, in September 1943, Leon Rupnik was chosen to be its prefect, a title that was shortly elevated to president. Rupnik took up his responsibilities on 22 September, under the supervision of Hermann Doujak, Rainer's trusted political adviser in the province, and economic adviser Friedrich Jacklin.[63] Born in the village of Lokve, east of Gorizia, in 1880, Rupnik spent his formative years as a soldier in the Austro-Hungarian Army, enlisting at the age of fifteen and eventually becoming an officer during a loyal service that spanned twenty-three years. In 1919, Rupnik joined the Yugoslav Army as a staff major, climbing the ranks to become a lieutenant-general and the chief of staff of the First Army Group at the time of the Axis invasion. In the 1930s, he led construction of the so-called Rupnik Line, a string of fortifications designed to protect Slovenia from an Axis assault that would share the same fate as France's Maginot Line. Rupnik left the army shortly after the April 1941 invasion and, as a civilian, moved to German-occupied Celje and then to Ljubljana. The degree to which Rupnik identified with Nazi ideology remains a contentious issue. Milko Vizjak, a lieutenant-colonel in the Home Guard, testified that Rupnik was sympathetic towards the Nazi Party and preferred that Slovenia become a German protectorate much like Slovakia.[64] Others, like Rupnik's friend and the mayor of Vrhnika, Ignacij Hren, claimed that Rupnik never approved of Nazism.[65] In his deposition at his postwar trial, Rupnik admitted to having had initial sympathies with the Germans, which he attributed to his Austro-Hungarian upbringing and the influence of the Nazi press and Nazi literature. Yet, he concluded, 'regardless of my sympathies to the German nation I always proudly and openly pronounced myself as a Slovene before the Germans,' claiming that his experience of German barbarity in Celje following the invasion cured him of his illusions and committed him to the autonomy of the Province of Ljubljana.[66] The CPS's Security Intelligence Service (VOS) remained unimpressed with Rupnik's professed patriotism and attempted to assassinate him already in September 1941.

In June 1942, Rupnik became mayor of Ljubljana and cooperated with the Italians in their attempt to suffocate the Liberation Front. In retaliation, the Yugoslav government-in-exile stripped him of his general's rank. Rupnik's defence was that he could do more in discussions with the Italians than he could in opposition. As evidence, he pointed to his intercessions among the Italians to free imprisoned Slovenes, while his personal secretary and son-in-law Stanko Kociper claimed that Rupnik assisted some Jews in reaching the relative safety of Italy.[67]

Directly responsible to the OZAK's supreme commissary, the Provincial Administration ran the day-to-day administrative affairs of the province, although its authority was restricted only to the towns and countryside garrisoned and patrolled by German or anti-Partisan units. Giving Slovenes a role in running their occupation was part of Rainer's aim to 'organize and calm nationality conditions, organize the self-defence of the population against Bolshevism, and mobilize the economic might of the administrative region for Germany's final victory.'[68] Rainer did not see the Province of Ljubljana as a miniature Slovene puppet state, but rather as a loyal, albeit characteristically Slovene, province of the German Reich akin to 'the old [Austrian] duchy of Carniola,' a model that Rupnik also embraced.[69]

The Provincial Administration certainly had a Slovene character. Its operational language, propaganda, and cultural programs were mostly in Slovene, and the majority of its staff were Slovenes. Departments of the PU had responsibilities for economic affairs, education, communication, propaganda, transportation, customs, culture, health, and to a certain extent, justice. The PU was affiliated with several home-grown anti-Communist organizations, such as the Committee for Dolenjski Refugees, headed by former SLS member of the Yugoslav parliament Deacon Karel Škulj, which provided shelter and sustenance for those displaced by the Liberation Front. The semi-official Workers Anti-Communist Action, established on 3 December 1943, and led by Franc Žužek, aimed to create a united anti-Communist bloc among Slovene unions.[70]

In addition to establishing collaborative civilian institutions in the Operation Zone Adriatic Littoral, the Germans followed the example of their former Italian allies and sponsored their own Slovene anti-Partisan forces. Their losses in the Soviet campaigns and the capitulation of Italy made the German less choosy as to who their allies were in the last years of the Second World War. In addition to regular German units, Yugoslavia would be occupied by a motley array of Cossacks,

Volksdeutsche – many speaking almost incomprehensible German dialects – and volunteers from Yugoslavia's 'White' Russian émigré community. Germans had been collaborating with Slavic Croats since 1941 (whose own 'racial experts,' incredulously, claimed were of Gothic origin), and more recently, with Bosnian Muslims. In Serbia, Germans cooperated with the Quisling Milan Nedić, his collaborating Serbian State Guards, and the Serbian Volunteer Corps, which was created in 1941 out of Dimitrije Ljotić's Zbor movement. In November, after the Italian capitulation, the Germans departed from their rigid stance towards the Četniks, signing the first of several non-aggression pacts with their leaders.[71] Indeed, as the historian John Connelly pointed out, 'Nazi policies towards all Slavic groups were flexible and opportunistic' – German collaboration with Slavic Slovenes was, thus, hardly unprecedented by the fall of 1943.[72] Moreover, because the OZAK was considered occupied rather than annexed territory like Štajerska, the existence of Slovene units would not be immediately construed as a failure of German denationalization measures against Slovenes.

Hounded by the more numerous and better armed Partisans, the demoralized remnants of the Slovene anti-Communist forces had a strong incentive to seek assistance from the Germans. The survivors of the September clashes became the nucleus of the Slovene Home Guard Legion (Slovenska domobranska legija) – the name was shortened to the Slovene Home Guard on 30 September – and it would operate exclusively in the Province of Ljubljana. The idea for the force was first broached in secret negotiations between representatives of the Slovene People's Party and Rösener in Ljubljana, on 16 September 1943.[73] Rainer also played an important role in the negotiations and urged Rupnik to help organize the Home Guard.[74] However, Rupnik's announcement unveiling the Home Guard, which called upon all eighteen- to thirty-five-year-old Slovenes who were 'honest thinking and concerned with the welfare of the Slovene nation' to enlist, was considered far too 'nationalist' by the German censors.[75] As a result, the German propaganda office unilaterally released an altered proclamation one day later, on 23 September, signed by the still undefined 'Leadership of the Slovene Home Guard.' The Anglo-American plutocracy, it announced, was attempting to deliver Slovenia into the hands of Bolshevism:

> In order to prohibit this, the great German military forces have come to protect us on the orders of the Führer. The German soldier and officer fight courageously and gallantly. Courage, honour, and trust are for them

sacred concepts. Dishonour and cowardice are alien to them. With its strong fighting force, Germany is the only fortress against bolshevism and capitalism [. . .] Under the leadership of our Slovene leaders, who will command us in our maternal language, we will destroy the Bolshevik murderers and arsonists in our nation [. . .] The German army and police will support us with loyal comradeship.[76]

With this call for recruits issued, confusion persisted in regards to the leadership of the Home Guard. Rupnik claimed that Rösener discussed the issue with him and future Slovene commanders of the Home Guard including Peterlin, Kokalj, Vizjak, and Lieutenant-Colonel Franc Krener.[77] Yet, shortly after taking on the position of commander-in-chief of the Home Guard, in October 1943, Rupnik was stripped of the title. The reasoning behind this is unclear, as Rupnik did not show any signs of anti-German behaviour. His first order to the Home Guard, on 30 September, for example, was submissive to German authority, commanding that 'whoever [. . .] is not directly tied to cooperation with the German army or the police is an armed bandit, and must be attacked and destroyed without delay,' urging his men to hand over captured Partisans to the closest German army or police garrison.[78] Only in September 1944, during a ceremony in Ljubljana marking the one-year anniversary of the Home Guard and German – Slovene cooperation was Rupnik readmitted to a leadership position with the title of inspector-general of the Home Guard.[79] Despite its prestigious ring, the position of inspector-general was largely ceremonial. Its responsibilities included official reviews, the maintenance of a cooperative relationship between the Home Guard and the Germans, and supervisory control over discipline, as well as the amorphous duty to participate 'in all principal affairs of the Slovene Home Guard.'[80] The inspector-general, as the name suggested, was also expected to carry out announced as well as unannounced inspections of the Home Guard, from which he was to submit proposals to the Germans on how to improve its organization and development. However, the first two points of the inspector-general's official duties left little doubt as to where ultimate power lay:

1. The Inspector-General is immediately subordinate to the Higher SS and Police Leader in Military District XVIII.
2. According to the instructions of the Higher SS and Police Leader, he executes inspector rights over all units of the Slovene Home Guard and the Police Committee in Ljubljana.[81]

Rupnik admitted as much at his trial, stating, 'The instruments of assault, that is the *vaška straža*, the Home Guard, and the police were never under my executive control, but in the occupiers' hands and – partaking in his own finger-pointing – 'in the hands of reactionary politicians.'[82] Vizjak also confirmed that the inspector-general was only a 'formal position.'[83] Although he may have lacked unbridled control over the Home Guard, Rupnik nevertheless used his considerable influence to spew pro-German, anti-Bolshevik, and antisemitic propaganda. He also actively recruited for the Home Guard and urged Slovenes to cooperate with the Germans. For example, on the eve of a joint German – Home Guard campaign, in September 1943, to clear OF-held territory, he announced: 'Honest Slovenes! Celebrate, the hour of your liberation from the bloody Bolshevik paradise nears! Cooperate with the German army and the Home Guard detachments! [. . .] The Germans are not your enemies, only communist bandits are your enemy [. . .] They will be your strong protectors, who will also provide you with all the necessities of life.'[84]

To better coordinate the various units (police, army, and Home Guard) that were fighting the Partisans in the Province of Ljubljana, on 30 September 1943, Rösener established the Command Staff for the Suppression of Guerillas Ljubljana (Führungsstab für Bandenbekämpfung Laibach), which parallelled Globocnik's Führungsstab für Bandenbekämpfung OZAK. Under Rösener's guidance, the internal structure of the Home Guard was grouped around two departments, an organizational headquarters (*organizacijskega štaba*) and a propaganda branch.[85] In October, Rösener chose Lieutenant-Colonel Franc Krener to head the organizational headquarters, with Lieutenant-Colonel Milko Vizjak as his assistant, and Lieutenant-Colonel Ernest Peterlin as the chief of staff.[86] Unlike Rupnik, the younger Krener did not owe his military training to the Austro-Hungarian Army, but rather to the Yugoslav Army. This service would land him, along with other high-ranking former Yugoslav officers, in an Italian concentration camp. After his release, Krener remained active within the Četnik ranks until he was persuaded to take on the role of organizational leader. Liberal in his political leanings, there was little love between Krener and the SLS establishment, who generally saw him (in the words of one of his lieutenants) as 'one big holy ego, a disaster for the Slovenes.'[87] Despite his pro-Četnik orientation and his contact with Slovene political figures, Krener gave the Germans little cause for concern with his otherwise dutiful and loyal, and rather plodding, service to the Home Guard.

On all accounts, the Home Guard was a far more effective anti-Partisan force than the Anti-Communist Volunteer Militia. Initially organized into companies and battalions, the Germans would reorganize its ranks several times, as it reached a height of some 13,500 members in the summer of 1944, with Mlakar noting that the total number of officially enlisted may have been as high as seventeen thousand.[88] Like their MVAC predecessors, the Home Guard was composed of mostly younger men, with slightly over 50 per cent in April 1944 under the age of twenty-four and over two-thirds under the age of thirty.[89] The Home Guard was also better equipped, dressed, and trained, with mobile battalions that would come together for larger offensive actions. It developed special niche forces such as one that operated armoured trains.[90] As with the Village Guards and the Legion of Death, Slovene officers from the Slovene Legion and the former Yugoslav Army commanded individual Home Guard units in the Slovene language.

Fighting the Liberation Front was the principle purpose of the Home Guard. Joint German – Home Guard offensives, in October and November 1943, forced the Partisans out of most major towns in the province. Home Guard intelligence was critical in unravelling OF networks and was separated into two branches, internal and external. Internal intelligence was directed at the Home Guard's own ranks to root out Communist infiltrators – and a significant number of Home Guardsmen facing disciplinary charges were, in fact, accused of OF sympathies or being 'politically untrustworthy' – but also to ensure proper discipline and behaviour. External intelligence was directed against the Liberation Front, identifying them and their sympathizers and establishing their numbers and morale, as well as the location of their headquarters and hospitals.[91]

The claim of émigrés and other revisionists that the Home Guard was only fighting a civil war with the permission of the occupiers would have some credence had the Home Guard devoted its attention only to the Liberation Front. Unfortunately, the Home Guard assisted the German war effort in areas that were only partially or even not at all related to the OF insurgency. Although the Home Guard defended the principal rail lines, roads, bridges, electricity-generating stations, fuel depots, and other infrastructure from OF sabotage, these assets were also of critical importance to the overall German war effort and served fronts further afield in Italy and the Balkans.[92] The Home Guard policed the perimeter of Ljubljana under orders to weed out OF 'saboteurs' and 'spies,' but it also established a special detachment to survey post offices and postal services, censoring letters and packages, as well as telegrams and telephone conversations.[93] Home Guard propaganda urged Slovenes to volunteer for labour units that were used both in Slovenia and in Germany, and it searched for escaped members of Organisation Todt (the Reich's construction and engineering group founded by Minister for Armaments and Munitions Fritz Todt) and other forced labourers constructing defences in the OZAK and northern Italy.[94] Perhaps most damning was the Home Guard's involvement in the arrest and deportation of Ljubljana's few remaining Jews in the autumn of 1944 to Auschwitz and Mauthausen. Such was the fate of the Pollak family, owners of a wholesale business trading in grains and milling products, who had their home raided by the Home Guard, on 13 September 1944.[95] Without all this assistance, many more German troops and officials would have been needed to service the occupation – precious resources that were freed for other duties and other fronts.

Embodied in their slogan 'Mother-Homeland-God' (*Mati-domovina-Bog*), Home Guard ideology – as much as one can be synthesized – was a blend of nationalism, conservatism, Catholicism, anti-Communism, and disturbingly, antisemitism not unlike the Hlinka Guard in Slovakia. A number of their members and leaders saw the Home Guard as a Slovene national army, or the foundation for a future one; for the Germans, it was never more than an auxiliary police unit. The Germans armed and paid the Home Guard, which remained operationally subordinate to the German military and police authorities. German superiority and command were also enshrined in rank and jurisdiction. For example, Home Guardsmen were required to greet German officers of equal or higher rank.[96] At checkpoints encircling Ljubljana, the Home Guard could only search Slovenes, and German troops were responsible for Germans.[97] Such practices could hamper the Home Guard from carrying out its duties, as in the case of its railway security unit that complained of German troops and officers smuggling 'whole suitcases full' of tobacco and cigarettes, but 'against this we cannot do anything.'[98] Ill-discipline among the Home Guard, such as looting, was judged according to the German National Penal Code, and recognition of service or bravery was honoured with German medals; there were no specific Home Guard decorations.[99] Promotion was the duty of German officers, notably Rösener.[100]

In addition to the Home Guard, which was military or paramilitary in character, the Germans also created a Slovene-staffed police force for everyday criminal matters in the province. Subordinated to the

German Security Police and Security Service for Carinthia, the Police Security Corps (*policijski varnostni zbor*) was established in October 1943 and was absorbed as much as possible within the German policing apparatus. Members of the Police Corps (*policijski zbor*, PZ, as it was later shortened to), were mandated to take German language courses and, whenever possible, to provide German translations of reports, intelligence, and texts. The Police Corps, like the Home Guard, had no jurisdiction over German nationals, military or civilian. German nationals violating curfew, for example, which the Police Corps were tasked with enforcing, were not allowed to be taken into Police Corps custody.[101]

The Germans appointed Lovro Hacin, the pre-war director of the Ljubljana police, chief of the Police Corps, although he and his organization were supervised by a German adviser, the chief of the Gestapo in Ljubljana Paul Duscha. Hacin amalgamated religious devotion, anti-Communism, and fascist sympathies into his ideological outlook. Indeed, his religious fervour at times bordered on the extreme, and a strong theocratic undercurrent permeated his notions of policing. His officers, for example, were ordered to report all cases of foul language, especially those against the Church, and to reprimand violators with 'preventative measures' – a law that the Ustaša also enforced to the delight of Archbishop Stepinac.[102] Dismissive of the Italians, referring to their police as 'useless,' Hacin admired the Germans.[103] A VOS analysis described Hacin as a 'Germanophile convinced that the Germans will win. Proceeds unobjectively.'[104] Hacin provoked the hostile audience at his postwar trial with his defiance and lack of remorse in serving the Gestapo, stating, 'Maybe, I was loyal and I am not ashamed of this.'[105] Yet, despite his eccentricities, Hacin grounded his behaviour in the concept of passivity, claiming that it was in line with former Yugoslav Prime Minister Milan Stojadinović's view that 'the only smart politics [is] that a small country cannot put itself up against large forces.'[106] Despite the fact that his defence pleaded clemency on the grounds of his 'religiously fanatic upbringing,' Hacin would receive the harshest punishment – death by hanging.

Former Yugoslav police had also served within the ranks of the Italian police. Still, the Police Corps was given greater autonomy in order to suppress communism in 'close and coordinated cooperation with the German armed forces, and with the Slovene Home Guard.'[107] Rupnik remarked at his trial that police personnel in the Province of Ljubljana were almost identical to that of pre-war Yugoslavia, and older and retired policemen and intelligence officers were considered particularly trustworthy by the occupiers.[108] The Police Corps branched out quickly to most major towns and was essential in screening citizens and ensuring that personal documents were in order.[109] Although most inhabitants would welcome the suppression of certain 'disorders' – such as pursuing thieves or subduing rowdy tavern patrons – the duties of the Police Corps went further, culminating in either direct or indirect assistance to the occupier. Like the Home Guard, the police guarded infrastructure considered strategically important to the Germans including water works, post offices, telegraph stations, telephone lines, roads, canals, bridges, foreign consulates, and prisons and their inmates. The Police Corps played a critical role in reducing sabotage on the province's rail lines with the creation of a Railway Police unit in January 1944.[110] Given the power to shoot at any suspicious individuals who violated the 'exclusion zone' on either side of the Kočevje-Ljubljana rail line, it did not take long before railway workers began to complain about trigger-happy police![111] The police suppressed demonstrations, the painting of political slogans, and the possession of all manner of 'unsatisfactory literature,' that is, leftist material.[112] Rumour mongering was grounds for arrest, as was insulting the Germans, the Home Guard, or the Police Corps.[113] Franciška Malnar, for example, was arrested for 'indecent behaviour in insulting the Home Guard army in a public place' when in a drunken state she yelled, 'Damned Home Guard' at an officer.[114] The Police Corps pursued escaped labourers from Organisation Todt,[115] as well as military recruits who were ignoring their call-up orders.[116] It directly assisted the occupiers in air defence by suppressing looting, compiling damage reports, and notifying the Germans of what regions had been hit by aerial bombardment.[117] As the war progressed, the Police Corps was also occasionally called on to engage the Partisans in armed combat.[118]

One of the Police Corps's most helpful contributions to the occupation, and the role that would make it a de facto political police force, was the dismantling of OF support networks. This was primarily the duty of the Police Corps's secret police branch, which according to OF intelligence, was made up of approximately a hundred individuals led by Maks Loh, with centres in Ljubljana, Kočevje, and Novo Mesto.[119] One of the key tasks of the secret police branch was to produce indexes of 'suspicious individuals,' short-hand for OF sympathizers, and to conduct surveillance on them.[120] To gather information, the Police Corps organized a network of local informants.[121] The PZ also spied on its own rank and file and on offices of the Provincial Administration, including city hall, the water works, exchequer's office, mayor's office, post office, translation office, the Justice Department, the prosecutor's office, the High Court, and others.[122] Health care workers, teachers, university professors, industrial workers, and bank employees were also scrutinized – in what was becoming a Slovene-administered police state. Perhaps most chilling was the order for the police to identify hostages against whom 'repressive actions' would be taken in the event that public security was endangered 'by certain elements,' namely, the Liberation Front.[123]

Judging from daily and weekly reports, from November 1943 to April 1945, the number of political prisoners incarcerated in Ljubljana's Belgian barracks prison complex dwarfed those of criminal prisoners (see Table 6.1). These figures appear to substantiate Hacin's estimate at his trial that some six thousand Slovenes had been imprisoned in his jails, although a certain Hauptscharführer Simon was in charge of the prisons and courts.[124] Approximately one-third of the political prisoners and slightly over half of the criminal prisoners were women. Prostitution was the most common criminal charge against women, which was convenient shorthand for collaboration with the Partisans. The Police Corps constructed transport lists of hundreds of political prisoners bound for German labour and concentration camps and assisted in the actual deportations.[125]

The Slovene civil war that had been restricted primarily to the Province of Ljubljana would spread after the Italian capitulation – albeit in a less ambitious form – to neighbouring Primorska and Gorenjska, spurred on by the creation of two additional German-sponsored local anti-Partisan units: the Slovene National Security Corps (Slovenski narodni varnostni zbor, SNVZ) and the Gorenjska Self-Defence (Gorenjska samozaščita). Instituted in November 1943, with its headquarters in Trieste, the Slovene National Security Corps was directly subordinated to Globocnik. The inspector-general and later commander of the SNVZ was the Yugoslav Army Colonel Anton Kokalj, who was dispatched from Ljubljana by the Slovene People's Party.[126] Established in Primorska, a region that not only had no collaborating precursor like the Anti-Communist Volunteer Militia but that was generally pro-Yugoslav and anti-Fascist in outlook after two decades of Italian national oppression, it is not surprising that the Slovene National Security Corps was dogged with chronic recruitment problems. At its height, in the summer of 1944, the SNVZ numbered only about two thousand men, with most of its officers coming from the Province of Ljubljana.[127] The SNVZ's combat potential was, accordingly, comparatively small and, judging from the Postojna unit, its ranks were generally made up

Table 6.1 Political prisoners and criminal prisoners in Ljubljana's Belgian barracks prison complex, 6 November 1943 to 14 April 1945

6 November 1943–14 April 1945	Political Prisoners	Criminal Prisoners
6 Nov. 1943	120	53
2 Dec. 1943	403	58
1 Jan. 1944	707	53
1 Feb. 1944	651	19
4 March 1944	744	28
1 April 1944	585	31
6 May 1944	399	16
3 June 1944	535	17
1 July 1944	614	18
6 Aug. 1944	651	9
3 Sept. 1944	641	5
7 Oct. 1944	450	11
4 Nov. 1944	366	11
3 Dec. 1944	446	3
7 Jan. 1945	486	82
10 Feb. 1945	646	12
3 March 1945	540	10
4 April 1945	285	3

Source: Daily and weekly reports of the condition of political and criminal prisoners at the Belgijska vojašnica, 6 Nov. 1943 to 14 April 1945, doc. 45344–6, 45429–33, 45499–507, fasc. 85; doc. 45986–46005, 46525–42, fasc. 86; doc. 46990–47006, 47129–32, 47230–43, 47345–61, 47492–508, fasc. 87; doc. 47608–23, 47721, 47802, 47900, 47996, 48084, 48132, 48224, fasc. 88, AS 1876, ARS.

of older men.[128] Despite their small number, Mlakar estimated that the SNVZ killed some dozens of Primorska's OF activists, especially in the Pivka, Idrija, and Vipavska valleys.[129] The SNVZ, and particularly its strike battalion, were most effective when supplementing German patrols and offensives. Like the Home Guard and the Police Corps, the Slovene National Security Corps guarded strategically significant infrastructure in Primorska and was also obliged to hand over any captured Partisans to the nearest German command.[130]

The Slovene National Security Corps' most important contributions to the German war effort was in propaganda and intelligence work. The SNVZ issued numerous anti-Communist periodicals, leaflets, and posters in an attempt to undermine Primorska's sympathies for the Liberation Front. It provided Germans with interrogation reports of captured Partisans and their supporters, locations of OF hideouts, and tips on suspicious activities.[131] Like the Home Guard, the Slovene National Security Corps constructed lists of OF organizers at the village level, with accompanying descriptive notes such as 'dangerous,' 'propagandist,' or 'husband is a Communist.'[132]

The Germans held the Slovene National Security Corps on a far tighter leash than it did the more numerous Home Guard. Globocnik ensured that the SNVZ and Kokalj were 'directly subordinate to me and receives all directions from me,' and that they were 'subordinate to the Higher SS and Police Leader, in all questions of pay, financing, uniforms, arms, and equipment.'[133] The SNVZ was required to execute all orders issued by regional German forces. To assist interoperability, a three-week training course was envisioned for the rank and file and six weeks for officers. Like the Home Guard, the Slovene National Security Corps was issued only German medals for bravery according to the German *Vorwundetenabzeichen* (Badge of the Wounded). The SNVZ used German raised arm salutes to greet German officers, and the Germans were responsible for punishing errant behaviour in the SNVZ, including desertion.[134]

Perhaps most remarkable was the German decision to create a Slovene anti-Partisan force in Gorenjska. Unlike the Operation Zone Adriatic Littoral, Gorenjska was considered part of the Third Reich, and its Slovene inhabitants were slated for Germanization. The Partisans had a stronger presence in mountainous Gorenjska than in Štajerska, and this accounts, in part, for the German willingness to countenance such a unit. The first garrisons of the Gorenjska Self-Defence (*samozaščita*) were set up in December 1943. At its height in 1945, the Gorenjska Self-Defence had approximately twenty-five hundred members, distributed in over forty units.[135] Its ranks were also made up of older men (some six hundred were thirty-four years of age or older) as most young men had already been mobilized into the Wehrmacht or into German labour brigades.[136] The Gorenjska Self-Defence operated more like the Anti-Communist Volunteer Militia, guarding local towns and their environs from Partisan incursions and breaking up OF civilian support networks. It protected transportation lines, gathered intelligence, and disseminated anti-OF propaganda.¹³⁷ The later development of strike battalions centred in Škofja Loka and Kranj, and led by Franc Erpič, allowed the Gorenjska Self-Defence to engage in more wide-ranging offensive actions against the Liberation Front. With the Germans, they largely prevented the Partisans from penetrating the lowlands where population centres and transportation lines were concentrated.

Like the Slovene National Security Corps and the Home Guard, the Gorenjska Self-Defence was conceived, in part, with the participation of anti-Communist politicians, in particular, the SLS deputy and Slovene Legion organizer Albin Šmajd, the pre-war president of the Chamber of Agriculture Jože Lovrič, Anton Megušar, and the former editor of the newspaper *Slovenec* Tine Debeljak. In February 1944, these men would form in Ljubljana a Regional Committee for Gorenjska in order to maintain contact between the Gorenjska Self-Defence and anti-Communist forces in the Province of Ljubljana.¹³⁸ Real power, however, was concentrated in the hands of the Gorenjska Self-Defence's German commander – the Austrian Gestapo sergeant SS-Oberscharführer Erich Dichtl, who, in turn, was subordinated to SS-Obersturmführer Alois Persterer of the Carinthian Security Police and Security Service in Bled. Nevertheless, the 'political line' of the Gorenjska Self-Defence was supervised by the head of the Gestapo in Kranj, SS-Obersturmführer Rudolf Messner. Cognizant of Gorenjska's sensitive political status, it is not surprising, then, that only the Gorenjska Self-Defence would be under the direct command of a German, as opposed to the Operation Zone Adriatic Littoral, where there was at least a veneer of 'Slovene' control over the Home Guard and the Slovene National Security Corps.

Slovene involvement increased with the arrival, in May 1944, of Slavko Krek, nephew of Miha Krek, who presented himself as Leon Rupnik's secretary.¹³⁹ By autumn, a Slovene representation of sorts known as the Centre was established in the city of Kranj. Led by Krek, it would act as an interface between the Gorenjska Self-Defence and the German command and assist in the recruitment and organization of units, administering the discharge and transfer of personnel and the supply of weapons and ammunition. Centre's propaganda, led by Alojz Perne, attempted to portray the Gorenjska Self-Defence as a Slovene force. For example, it issued a 1944 Christmas address stating that the Gorenjska Self-Defence stood for 'the desire to return to all that is beautiful and indigenous in our nation,' defending all that was 'Slovene and Christian.'¹⁴⁰

Despite the Centre's efforts, of all the German-sponsored Slovene anti-Partisan forces, the Gorenjska Self-Defence had the least amount of room for independent actions and development. The submissiveness of the force was apparent in a memorandum issued by Dichtl on 6 November 1944: 'The volunteers of the Gorenjsko *domobranstvo*[141] [Home Guard and Self-Defence were at times used interchangeably] demonstrated that they are prepared to fight with us against communism for their homeland and for a free Europe. Our shared responsibility is to save Europe from communism, to establish order and peace in Gorenjska, and to destroy banditry.'[142] He continued, noting that the Gorenjska Self-Defence has 'voluntarily expressed the wish to be led by the Security Police, [and] therefore is subordinated disciplinarily, militarily, and in every other respect, in arming and in provisioning.' Units of the Gorenjska Self-Defence were responsible to the nearest German security police posts, located in most major towns in Gorenjska, such as Kranj, Škofja Loka, Kamnik, and Radovljica. 'Independent actions,' it was emphasized, 'must be avoided if possible.'[143] If they had to be carried out without prior permission, a report of important successes, discoveries, or loss of property had to be filed as soon as possible with the nearest police post. Arrests, confiscation, and searches of homes were to be carried out only with the knowledge and under the authority of the Gestapo. Dichtl alone had responsibility over reorganizing units of the Gorenjska Self-Defence, including establishing strike battalions. The Germans also chose commanders and established their system of rank. Individual unit leaders were in charge of maintaining weaponry, sufficient ammunition, and uniforms, as well as general order and cleanliness within the companies.[144]

Thus, as 1943 gave way to the last full year of occupation, one Slovene anti-Partisan force, the Anti-Communist Volunteer Militia, had collapsed only to be replaced by four new formations – the Home Guard, the Police Corps, the Slovene National Security Corps, and the Gorenjska Self-Defence. Armed collaboration spread from the Province of Ljubljana to Primorska and Gorenjska, and civil war would follow in its wake. The Slovene Četniks, the only anti-Communist faction that had at least attempted to belatedly distance themselves from the Italians, were crippled by the defeat at Grčarice, the resignation of Novak and his departure to Italy, and news that Četnik units in other parts of Yugoslavia had signed ceasefires and were collaborating with the Germans.

Yet, despite the fact that these Slovene anti-Partisan units appeared to be standing shoulder-to-shoulder with the Nazis in their shared fight against the Liberation Front, the Germans – like the Italians before them – remained wary of their creations and their ties to Slovene politicians, who if certainly opposed to the Liberation Front were also no great friends of the Third Reich. At their height, these anti-Partisan forces had a combined strength of over eighteen thousand men, a size that unnerved some German commanders. The Germans, Vizjak recalled, had established a numerus clausus, insisting that thirteen thousand Home Guard members were sufficient to maintain peace and order; anything larger could threaten them and would most certainly be harder to control.[145] Vizjak claimed that the Germans often escorted Home Guard officers and kept a close eye on any political machinations.[146] The Germans and, in particular, Rösener insisted that anti-Partisan units in the Provinces of Ljubljana, Primorska, and Gorenjska remain separate from one another and from any residual Četnik activists. They were not permitted to spread into neighbouring Štajerska.[147] Yet, despite these operational restrictions that would see the Slovene National Security Corps prohibited from sleeping in Home Guard barracks in Ljubljana and even denied entrance into the province, they would become increasingly difficult to enforce.[148] Weak SNVZ recruitment forced their commanders to poach from the Home Guard, while Slavko Krek shared intelligence reports with the Slovene Legion and the Slovene People's Party in the Province of Ljubljana.[149] In fact, to conceal their cooperation, the Gorenjska Self-Defence was secretly referred to as 'posts outside the region' in Home Guard correspondence.[150]

Still, these tensions remained largely concealed under the slogans of cooperation trumpeted in German and collaborating propaganda. For the Western Allies and, increasingly, for members of the Yugoslav government-in-exile, collaboration with the Nazis – for whatever reason – sullied and blackened all who participated in it. The Germans understood this, and in 1944, with their military fortunes failing, they would attempt to increase the dependency of their Slovene collaborators by demanding from them ever more compromising assistance and, as we shall see, oaths of allegiance to the Third Reich. A Slovene's decision to collaborate, to resist, or to do nothing was grounded in these inherent tensions: Do we rely materially on the Germans even though we risk alienating the Allies? Does the fear of a successful Communist revolution outweigh the alarm over Nazi hegemony? Does service to my country supplant my personal safety and that of my family? Yet, as the Second World War slowly ground to its conclusion, the last option – to do nothing – became increasingly difficult, as each side in this violent quagmire sounded the familiar refrain *'kdor ni znami je proti nam,'* which means 'whoever is not with us is against us.'

7 Shoulder-to-Shoulder with the German Armed Forces, January 1944–December 1944

> Events in Slovenia were politically completely internal within the framework of a civil war. Since this was the time of an occupation and because only the Communists used it for their own aims, it makes no legal sense to ask where one received the guns, rather it raises the question [of] who carries the historical responsibility for all of the nation's bloody victims.[1]
>
> Stanko Kociper, POW Camp Wolfsberg, Austria, 1947

Stanko Kociper's tired response to the accusation of his British interrogator that the Home Guard had voluntarily accepted arms from the Nazis would have been harmless enough had he been an irrelevant rank-and-file member of the force. However, as head of Home Guard propaganda in 1943 and part of 1944, and as the son-in-law and personal secretary of Leon Rupnik, when Rupnik was president of the Province of Ljubljana, Kociper's justification for collaboration mattered and would be projected in countless propaganda pronouncements. Describing events in Slovenia from 1941 to 1945 as simply a civil war made it only too easy for collaborators to minimize the assistance of the occupiers. Indeed, from emigration they would continue to proclaim themselves to be martyrs, having fought to save Slovenia from the totalitarian grip of Communism. Yet, as this chapter will reveal, in war there is rarely a morally pristine side, and even less in collaboration. Collaborators certainly fought their internal Partisan enemies; they also assisted the occupiers in numerous ways. This analysis of the final full year of occupation in Slovenia also examines who responded to the call for military collaboration and suggests some plausible reasons why they did so. Finally, this examination will not take place in a chronological void, nor will it sever Slovenia – as Kociper conveniently did – from the wider course of the Second World War. We will follow the shrinking frontiers of the German Reich and assess whether there was any credence to the collaborators' oft-cited claims of a double game – feigning subservience while biding their time for the final strike against the occupiers.

The year 1944 ushered in a stalemate in German counter-insurgency efforts in Yugoslavia, which had peaked in the autumn of 1943. The German's seventh and last offensive against Tito's headquarters petered out in June 1944. In Slovenia, the persistent German fear of an Allied amphibious assault on the upper Adriatic and the importance of the Vienna-Ljubljana-Trieste railway for the Italian front pushed the Germans into aggressive anti-Partisan operations in Primorska already in the last week of September 1943. The German month-long campaign in the Province of Ljubljana, which began in mid-October, aimed at clearing the Partisan VII Corps from towns with rail links of secondary importance including Novo Mesto and Kočevje. The Partisans were forced to retreat. They did, however, damage the rail infrastructure with some lines linking the province to Croatia severed for the duration of the war. Moreover, the Partisan retreat was not permanent everywhere, and in the following months they would regain control of some of their lost territory. In the ensuing stand-off, the Germans and their Slovene anti-Partisan auxiliaries guarded the main transportation routes of the Operation Zone Adriatic Littoral (OZAK) and garrisoned their principal connecting towns and cities, while the Liberation Front and its People's Liberation Committees administered the villages and small towns that dotted the surrounding countryside and its forested and mountainous hinterlands. This deadlock was broken only periodically and, in most cases temporarily, by joint German – Home Guard offensives. Liberated territory in the OZAK made up in size what it may have lacked in strategic value. In Primorska, the Partisans held much of the forested karst interior as well as the mountains of the upper Soča valley, while in the Province of Ljubljana most of Bela Krajina and large parts of Notranjska and Dolenjska were under OF control. In total, perhaps half of Primorska and the larger share of the Province of Ljubljana were in OF hands by mid-1944.

The expansion of OF recruitment and the establishment of a secure base of operations in the OZAK, combined with the Allied decision to switch material support from Mihailović to Tito in the course of

1943, also gave a much needed boost to Partisan forces in Gorenjska and Štajerska. Of the two, Gorenjska provided more of the necessary inaccessible terrain with units established in the Julian and Kamniške mountain ranges, as well as in the mountains of Koroška. Štajerska was hobbled by less suitable country and a German administration intolerant of even the weakest OF activity. Most of the men of military age had been conscripted either into the Wehrmacht or the Wehrmannschaft. The latter was used to supplement anti-Partisan operations, although its unreliability and heavy losses in battles with the Partisans in the upper Sava valley led to its merger with the Nazi Volkssturm militia, in the fall of 1944, and its eventual dissolution, in April 1945.[2] Despite being augmented in 1944 by the arrival of Partisan units from the Province of Ljubljana, including veteran commanders, commissars, and organizers, the Liberation Front in Štajerska remained fragmented into small units separated by German-patrolled territory. In June 1944, during his tenure assisting Partisan sabotage, OSS Major Franklin Lindsay estimated that the Partisans in the Fourth Zone (Štajerska) numbered only two thousand men.[3] With Lindsay's help and Allied air drops, the Partisans were able to carry out a few significant attacks on rail lines, all the more important as the Štajerska town of Zidani Most was the hub for lines radiating to Central Europe, Italy, and the Balkans.

Separated from OF headquarters in Kočevski Rog by almost insurmountable distance and cursed with its flat and open terrain, the Partisan presence in Prekmurje was virtually non-existent. With the exception of an abortive OF uprising, in October 1944, Prekmurje remained free of insurgency until its liberation by the Red Army, in April 1945.

The year 1944 witnessed a shift in the priorities of the Liberation Front and the wider Yugoslav Partisan movement. Despite their tenacity and ability to rebound from periodic German offensives, by 1944, the Partisans appeared to have diverted considerably more resources towards defeating their internal enemies than in beating the occupiers. Supplemented with a relatively steady supply of Western arms and provisions, and conscious that it was only a matter of time before Germany collapsed, the Communist vanguard was increasingly preoccupied with amassing strength for the final showdown with the anti-Communist opposition. Indeed, with Belgrade liberated by the Partisans and Red Army already in October 1944, Croatia and Slovenia were certain to follow soon. This development was not lost on OSS and SOE agents in Yugoslavia. Their reports, which a year earlier had publicized the heroism of Tito's army and which were instrumental in its winning of Allied support, now exuded an air of cynicism. Major Linn Farish, the OSS's senior liaison officer with the Partisans, who in October 1943 lauded the military prowess of Tito and recommended immediate assistance, had completely changed his tune by June 1944, concluding that the Communists were primarily concerned with destroying their domestic opponents: 'It is not nice to see arms dropped by one of our airmen to be turned against men who have rescued and protected their brothers in arms [referring to Mihailović's Cetniks].'[4] Reuben Markham of the American Office of War Information was scathing in his appraisal of the Yugoslav situation in August 1944, reporting that 'we are literally spending the money of the American taxpayer to spread communism in Yugoslavia; we are supporting a guerilla army that does little fighting against the Germans and has made no appreciable progress for six months.'[5] Lindsay agreed, reporting on 15 January 1945 that the Partisans in Slovenia had obstructed his intelligence gathering and had not offered a sufficient contribution to the disruption of German communication lines between Italy, the Balkans, and the Reich, 'particularly considering the supplies, and man-power available to the Partisans and the weakness of the German opposition. This was especially true after September when the Partisans almost completely failed to hold the initiative.'[6] Describing his tenure with the Partisans of Gorenjska and Carinthia, Lieutenant Colonel Peter Wilkinson concluded, in April 1944, that 'Partisans for their part never stick their necks out. For the most part the German sticks to the roads and the Partisan to the mountain tracks: possibly by tacit agreement.' The only exception to this rule was 'when the German police and S.S. units go looking for them in the forests.'[7]

It was to curtail this endemic – if not always active – Partisan insurgency that the Germans sought collaboration with Slovene military and civilian representatives. In 1944, they would give the Germans little cause to doubt their decision, as they grappled with an opponent that was gaining in strength and committed to their destruction. In the Province of Ljubljana, joint German–Home Guard operations proved effective, at least in the short term, in hindering OF activity. On 16 March 1944, an offensive in the Novo Mesto – Kostanjevica region managed to destroy the fourth battalion of the OF's Cankar Brigade, killing 107 Partisans and only twelve of the Home Guard.[8] To replicate such successes, the Home Guard was reorganized several times during its existence. In May 1944, it was grouped into more effective strike battalions with east, west, north, and central units located in Novo Mesto, Rakek, Ljubljana, and Grosuplje respectively. Trained by German instructors, the Home Guard's growing professionalism won them additional victories in 1944. In August, the Home Guard dispersed the Partisans from Žužemberk, and in the autumn it helped clear much of the OF-controlled Loška valley. Less successful was the attempted German – Home Guard penetration of Bela Krajina in November, which saw a Home Guard unit moving from Novo Mesto defeated near Semič.

Aside from military engagements, Home Guard intelligence worked closely with the Provincial Administration's intelligence branch, the Police Corps, and the German political police. By March 1944, thirty-one Home Guard intelligence offices were located in regional centres throughout the Province of Ljubljana, including Vrhnika, Grosuplje, Velike Lašče, Šentvid, Novo Mesto, Kočevje, and Ribnica.[9] Relying on agents and a network of informants, these intelligence offices issued detailed lists in Slovene and in German of thousands of Partisans and their supporters along with their positions within the Liberation Front.[10] Some of these lists were organized along village or even family lines, with comments such as 'the entire family, Communist.'[11] Suspected Partisans captured during Home Guard operations would at times be interrogated by Home Guard intelligence officers before being turned over to the German security service, with suggestions added to their reports on how to proceed, including imprisonment in Germany – often in Dachau – or mobilization into labour battalions.[12] One such report on Viktor Turnšek, a suspected OF member, ended with the ominous advice: 'Therefore, deal with Turnšek as you would if you met Kidrič, Kardelj, Roba [sic], or Kocbek, and others.'[13] Torture appears to have been employed during interrogations. A Home Guard report from 1 July 1944 described rumours circulating in public of 'beatings and cruel behaviour in prison during interrogations.' The likely source, according to the report, was the release of prisoners or their transfer into the general prison population with visible evidence of torture on their bodies. The report concluded that more could be achieved with other methods, such as withholding food or cigarettes, or threatening the family of the accused, adding 'if in some rare cases you find it useful to strike, then let this be carried out when he is alone.'[14]

Compiling anti-Partisan intelligence fell within the general confines of the Home Guard's mandate; pursuing downed Allied airmen and surrendering them to the Germans did not. These allegations, which can be substantiated in Home Guard archives, were very damaging to the international reputation of the Home Guard. A report from 22 July 1944 stated that the Home Guard was pursuing survivors of an American Liberator crash near Borovnica. Eventually, five Americans were captured and turned over to the German authorities.[15] A captured American airman was reported to have been surrendered to the Germans in Šentvid, in March 1945.[16] Vizjak, a lieutenant-colonel in the Home Guard, confirmed this practice at his trial, stating that the Home Guard handed over all captured Allied airmen to the Gestapo.[17] On 26 May 1944, the OSS Alum Mission stated that from captured 'White Guard archives' it had obtained the following order from Franc Krener: 'Up to now parachutists have been dropping into Croatia, Bosnia, and Serbia, and recently are dropping into the Province of Ljubljana. In point of fact, many are coming equipped with radios, sabotage tools, arms, and ammunition. You are hereby ordered to arrest such men and tie them up when caught to prevent their escape. Then obtain their containers and address them all to the Honourable Police Chief at Command Headquarters' of the Anti-Bandit Fighting Unit.[18] This was confirmed by Lieutenant-Colonel Krener's subordinates, one of whom noted in his memoir that Krener contacted his base warning, 'For one pilot we will not risk the Home Guard.'[19]

In addition to this highly compromising show of Home Guard subservience, a certain degree of comradery pervaded its relationship with the Germans. Germans, for example, attended Home Guard commemorations such as the anniversary of the establishment of the Village Guards.[20] German and Slovene commanders also exchanged Christmas and New Year's greetings, in which they paid their respects to the fallen and promised even greater cooperation in the coming year.[21]

The Police Corps, too, appeared to be on good terms with the Germans, in line with Lovro Hacin's motto of 'Slovene nationalism, German friendship, and the war against Communism.'[22] Vid Bevc, the commander of a Ljubljana detachment, in May 1944, boasted that relations with the Germans 'are in every case friendly.'[23] Membership requirements for the police force reflected Nazi racism, for in addition to being between the ages of nineteen and forty, healthy, tall, a citizen of the Province of Ljubljana, anti-Communist, and possessing an 'unsullied past' and 'spiritual ability,' a policeman needed proof of Aryan descent.[24] The Police Corps may have won some additional credibility in German eyes with their sometimes rather brutal treatment of OF members and their sympathizers. In dealing with 'unruly' prisoners, regulations permitted the Police Corps to place them in solitary confinement, withhold their food for a day, or place them in chains.[25] Of course, the Police Corps, like the Home Guard's intelligence officers, also went further. Rupnik claimed to have warned Hacin not to use torture in police interrogations. Hacin's response was that such methods were used by police throughout the world.[26]

In Primorska and Gorenjska, the Slovene National Security Corps (SNVZ) and the Gorenjska Self-Defence (*samozaščita*) carried out German orders in 1944, largely without incident. In November 1944, the SNVZ strike battalion was reminded of its operational subordination to the Germans in an upcoming action: the 'systematic burning of settlements' were 'only to be carried out with the permission of the leadership of the Higher-SS.'[27] Indeed, an almost ridiculous degree of deference to the Germans was evident in an incident that occurred in the Primorska town of Idrija, on 19 August 1944. Partisans in German uniform entered a fuel depot and stole a large amount of gasoline. The SNVZ guard did not find it necessary to question the 'Germans,' nor to record the licence plate of their vehicle. The SNVZ commander noted that for future reference, a German uniform alone did not permit such activities![28] Both units cooperated in larger German-led anti-Partisan offensives. Two of the most ambitious were Operation Frühlingsanfang and Operation Winterende, which, in anticipation of the Allied penetration of the Operation Zone Adriatic Littoral, struck heavy blows against Partisan units in Gorenjska and northern Primorska, in March and April 1945.

Perhaps the most damaging display of submissiveness on the part of Slovene military collaborators was the oath of allegiance to the German armed forces that the Home Guard and the Police Corps swore on 20 April 1944, and again on 30 January 1945. Adding to the shame was the fact that 20 April was Hitler's birthday and 30 January that year marked the twelfth anniversary of the Nazi seizure of power. On the day of the first oath, hundreds of Home Guardsmen and Slovene police officers stood neatly uniformed in precise rows in the Ljubljana sports stadium; swastika flags fluttered on the perimeter. Ljubljana Bishop Gregorij Rožman, claiming his presence was required by his pastoral duties, administered mass prior to the oath-taking ceremony. Insisting that he refused to be present at the actual swearing-in – and would not have attended at all had the oath been to Hitler – by the time he had cleared away his religious paraphernalia, the ceremony had already begun.[29] On a raised podium draped with a swastika, SS-Obergruppenführer Erwin Rösener, along with Krener, greeted the assembled men with the ubiquitous *'Heil!'* to which the Slovenes responded *'Zdravo!'* (Hello!). The assembled then raised three fingers into the air and loudly repeated the following words, which they had memorized beforehand: 'I swear to almighty God that I will be faithful, brave, and obedient to my superiors, that in the common war with the German armed forces, under the command of the leaders of Great Germany, [the] SS units and the police, I will faithfully fulfil my duty to my Slovene homeland, which is a part of free Europe, against bandits and Communism as well as their allies. For this I am prepared to sacrifice even my life. So help me God!'[30] As president, Rupnik played a critical and visible role in organizing the oath. Following the ceremony, he and his wife Olga hosted a *Kammeradschaftsabend* in Ljubljana to celebrate the shared bonds between the Germans and anti-Communist Slovenes. Along with German occupational authorities and the Croatian General Consul, the invited guests included Provincial Administration ministers; the directors of the postal service, the railway, the theatre, the opera, the police, and the banks; the customs administrator; the district attorney; and the editors of various newspapers.[31] The image of Home Guard members swearing allegiance to the Third Reich, and Provincial Administration officials and the Bishop of Ljubljana smiling and rubbing shoulders with the German occupiers left a sharply treasonous impression.

Interpretations over the intent and meaning of the oaths have been predictably diverse. At his trial, Rösener insisted that the initiative came from 'the units themselves, the headquarters of the Home Guard, and was supported by Bishop Rožman.'[32] Vizjak, on the other hand, noted that the oath was not a 'real' oath but rather a 'promise' and that the previous Yugoslav military oath to King Peter remained in force.[33] This was also Bishop Rožman's understanding apparently.[34] Émigré writers claimed that the Germans had toyed with dissolving the Home Guard, as they were concerned with increasing anti-German sentiments among its members. The oath would, thus, 'prove' their loyalty.[35] Émigrés also noted that the term 'allies' referred to the Partisans as 'allies of Communism,' although Rösener insisted that it referred to the Anglo-Americans.[36] The Liberation Front and the Communist Party of Slovenia, predictably, viewed this as the worst treachery: an oath to Hitler to destroy Slovene freedom fighters.

To understand the oath, none of these rationalizations or interpretations is sufficient on its own. Although it is true that the oath was not a direct pledge of allegiance to Hitler – the wording did not mention his name – reference to him certainly could be inferred from the 'leaders of Great Germany.' There was growing evidence of anti-German sentiment on the part of some members of the Home Guard and the Police Corps, and the oath undeniably did force waverers to publicly compromise themselves. On the other hand, the oath also gave, as Mlakar pointed out, 'great symbolic, national, and political exposure to this central anti-Partisan formation.'[37] This was especially urged by those, such as Rupnik and Kociper, who saw the Home Guard as a unified response to Slovenia's political sectarianism: the harbinger of a new and stronger 'Slovene man.'

Regardless of how it is interpreted in retrospect, the oath had some immediate consequences. It further discredited the anti-Partisan units in the eyes of the Western Allies, And it widened a rift among SLS representatives in the government-in-exile. On one side, Kuhar, Snoj, and Izidor Cankar were supporting the position that all Slovene anti-Partisan units should join the OF in a united front. Opposing them stood SLS leader Miha Krek, now the representative of the Yugoslav government-in-exile to the Allied Advisory Council for Italy, and Monsignor Franc Gabrovšek, who believed such a move was suicidal for the units, and sought desperately to portray the Home Guard as an anti-occupier and pro-Allied formation.[38] The oath obviously undermined their position. In Slovenia, the oath deepened the ideological rift between the Liberation Front and its opponents, and it made a number of rank-and-file members of the Home Guard very uneasy. Metod Milač sensed this, writing, 'I felt pain and despair that day, knowing that many of my friends, acquaintances, and schoolmates who participated had no intention of pledging any alliance to the Third Reich, nor did the majority of those taking part. However, the Germans did not allow us any choice. It was agonizing to see a detachment of the SS marching the Home Guard to and from the oath-taking ceremony, even though we had to admire the parade perfection of the SS troops.'[39] Rudolf Hirschegger, a former VS and Home Guard member from Polje, stated that the Home Guard had been forced to swear the oath, taking part only because it had been ordered to do so. He criticized both its Slovene leadership and Rupnik, in particular, for their ignorance of the true 'national mindset.'[40] But were German suspicions of the 'national mindset' justified? Was there actual resistance within collaboration in the Home Guard that needed to be inoculated with the public shaming of the oath?

The Home Guard was surely aware of earlier German atrocities committed in Štajerska and Gorenjska. Nevertheless, there is only anecdotal evidence of tensions between the Home Guard and its masters before the spring of 1944. The young Home Guardsman Franc Golob, for example, recalled how the Germans had cruelly ridiculed his new unit as they learned to march.[41] Not surprisingly, the Home Guard and Germans had occasional scuffles. One such 'unhappy incident,' as Krener optimistically described it, occurred when his men attempted to keep order among rowdy German troops celebrating New Year's.[42] Dissension over check-point protocol led to some unfriendly incidents. In one case, German officers cursed and threatened to shoot the Home Guardsman who had the nerve to search their Slovene female companions.[43] On numerous occasions, Rösener threatened sanctions against Home Guard members who did not properly greet German officers and troops.[44] For their part, Home Guard internal correspondence occasionally recorded German indignities against Slovene cultural objects, as when drunken German soldiers vandalized a roadside shrine in Vrhnika.[45]

The Police Corps, too, sometimes had an ambivalent or even hostile attitude towards its German superiors. For example, some police found required German language classes offensive, despite the small honorarium they received for attending. In June 1944, Police Corps headquarters complained that no one in the Kočevje unit could write in German, reminding them that language instruction was 'not forcible Germanization, but permits the PVZ [Police Security Corps] rank to receive its allowance.'[46] Some police officers were evidently sympathetic to the Liberation Front, a trend that was noted not only by the Germans but also by Slovene anti-Communists. The Slovene Legion's intelligence service accused the Novo Mesto police of being pro-Partisan, and Home Guard and Police Corps units occasionally came to fist fights over this issue.[47] In response, Police Corps members were at times dismissed on account of their Communist sympathies.[48]

These acts of petty insubordination were overshadowed in the spring of 1944 by growing German concern over the increasing links among the Home Guard, the Četniks, non-Communist politicians, and the Allies. The Slovene Četniks had recovered somewhat from Grčarice, and similar to their machinations among the Anti-Communist Volunteer Militia the previous summer, they now attempted to wean Home

Guardsmen into their anemic ranks. As early as February 1944, Krener was aware of agitators urging Home Guard members to defect and join what he called 'some anti-Communist illegal' outfit that would fight the Partisans in Ljubljana. Krener warned these conspirators that they would be 'put before a court and a gun.'[49] A more significant windfall appeared later that same month when Janez Marn (alias Črtomir Mrak), a Christian Socialist unhappy with the Dolomite Declaration and its implications, defected to the Četniks with most of his Partisan battalion. Operating mostly in Dolenjska (Mirna region), the unit attacked the Partisans and their sympathizers; initially, it appeared to be a legitimate alternative to the Liberation Front. Marn's 20 April proclamation highlighted his independent policy: 'We former Partisans and *skrivači* [literally 'those who hide'] reject cooperation with the occupiers; therefore, we cannot step into the Home Guard ranks, and we remain therefore further in the forests, fighters for a shining ideal, which must fill each good Slovene and Yugoslav.'[50]

Additional Slovene Četnik detachments were cobbled together in the ensuing months – including small units in Notranjska, Gorenjska, and Primorska. Their total force numbered only a few hundred strong. Moreover, individual Četnik units often operated independently of Colonel Ivan Prezelj (alias Andrej), successor to Major Karel Novak, General Mihailović's representative in Slovenia. Lacking a territorial base, attacked by the Partisans, and shunned by a number of Home Guard officers and Provincial Administration officials, their most intransigent leaders were arrested by the Germans beginning in the spring of 1944. Indeed, Prezelj himself fled underground in the summer to avoid arrest and operated for a time with the Notranjska and Primorska detachments.[51]

Most of the Četniks who survived did so because of local arrangements with the Germans. Marn's unit struck a deal with the Germans already in April 1944, resulting in a supply of arms and permission to carry out hunt-and-kill missions against the Partisans. Indeed, Marn's doggedness earned him a particularly bloodthirsty reputation in the eyes of the Partisans, with his unit unmasked as the organizers of the Black Hand.[52] Other Četnik detachments held out longer, among them the Štajerska formation led by Jože Melaher (alias Zmagoslav), which by some estimates was 'the only anti-revolutionary military unit that attacked the occupiers with arms' on a consistent basis.[53] A follower of the Slovene People's Party, Melaher began recruiting already in 1942, acquiring a force of two hundred by 1944, composed mostly of Slovene deserters from the German army. Operating primarily in the Slovenske gorice, in Haloze, and on the plains of Ptuj, this unit received British airdrops well into the summer of 1944.[54] Melaher's position was made clear in his brief *Kri in zemlja* (Blood and Earth), in which he identified his enemies as 'Germans, Germanophiles, and Communists.'[55] Only in early 1945 did he, along with Prezelj, agree to local ceasefires with the Germans.

The passivity of the Četniks and, in some cases, their open collaboration with the occupiers contributed to their abandonment by the Western Allies. Nevertheless, the Germans remained very concerned about them and their intelligence networks. Rupnik claimed that, as late as 1943, the Germans were primarily concerned with Mihailović's cooperation with the English.[56] Rösener, too, rankled his postwar prosecutors by refusing to paint the Četniks as his lackeys, stressing that they had been part of the resistance: 'I understand the question, and I would like to respond to it. Mihailović's units fought against the Germans. Even Marn in the beginning fought against the Germans. They saw in us some kind of lesser evil, and they worked out a cease-fire with us.'[57] According to Vizjak, Rösener 'did not want to hear any talk' of Četniks operating among the Home Guard or the Slovene National Security Corps.[58] Despite these prohibitions, some ties did develop, as some Home Guard officers moonlighted for Mihailović and some others defected to the Četniks.[59] This simmering subversion did not escape the attention of foreign intelligence operatives. On 5 April 1944, John Fistere of OSS Morale Operations instructed Major Lindsay: 'Don't indulge in indiscriminate attacks upon the Slovenian Domobranchi [sic] or White Guard. While their leaders are Quislings and may be attacked, the rank-and-file have strong pro-Allied sympathies and should not be alienated by blanket indictments.'[60]

German suspicions only increased with the uncovering of the Zagreb branch of Vauhnik's BBZ intelligence web, in April 1944, a network that included a number of leading Četniks and Home Guardsmen. What is more, the BBZ was only one of several non-Communist intelligence webs operating in 1944. The Četniks ran their own network called the National Intelligence Service (Državna obveščevalna služba, DOS), which had descended from the Slovene Information Service, a pro-Allied military intelligence operation that had existed during the Italian occupation.[61] Members of the Slovene Legion and committed anti-Communists led by the chaplain Franc Glavač also operated a distinct spy network known as the Secret Intelligence Service (Tajna obveščevalna služba, TOS). TOS had emerged from M-7, a semi-legal intelligence network that had had the difficult task of maintaining contact between the Anti-Communist Volunteer Militia, the leadership of the Yugoslav Army in the Homeland, and the Italian command.[62] Under pressure from the Germans and bleeding personnel, by the end of 1944, TOS had essentially become a branch of President Rupnik's German-friendly anti-Partisan intelligence service, the Information Office of the Provincial Administration (Informativni urad, IU).[63]

Both the DOS and the TOS spied on their non-Communist political rivals and the occupiers, yet their main target was the Liberation Front. These anti-Communist credentials did not, however, assuage German concerns of a larger conspiracy among pro-Allied elements in the Province of Ljubljana. International events only heightened the Germans' suspicions. Rome was taken by Allied forces, on 5 June, triggering debate among Anglo-American military commanders on whether the southern invasion of the German Reich should come via the Po Valley and the Ljubljana Gap.[64] Although resources were eventually diverted to the liberation of southern France, that Slovenia was the lynchpin of a potential Allied invasion route made the Germans understandably nervous and concerned about any pro-Allied plotting in the Operation Zone Adriatic Littoral. The D-day landings, and the assassination attempt against Hitler on 20 July, only reaffirmed the need for vigilance against treason at this clearly pivotal point in German military fortunes.

The first purge of disloyal Home Guardsmen and Četniks – the 'democratic elements' in the anti-Communist camp, according to Vauhnik, who himself was forced to flee to Switzerland in June after the penetration of the BBZ – came in late spring.[65] Partisan intelligence corroborated this, noting that approximately '200 Mihailovićists' from the ranks of the TOS, the DOS, and the Home Guard were arrested on suspicions of plotting a future uprising against German rule, although it blamed these organizations for betraying their own.[66] On 28 June, a number of Četnik propagandists were arrested in Ljubljana, as they celebrated Vidovdan. Many were subsequently tortured and sent to concentration camps, among them Major Andrej Glušič, head of the DOS, and his colleague Ladislav Križ.[67] Arrested by the Gestapo in Trieste and sent to Buchenwald was another notable intelligence operative, Hrvoj Maister, son of General Rudolf Maister – the hero of the 1919 frontier war against Austria. In July, it was the Home Guard's turn. The OSS Alum Mission reported, on 12 July, 'that the Germans are taking away from the White

Guards all heavy machine guns and heavy and light mortars,' and four days later, that the 'Jerries imprisoned 500 White Guards whom they consider to be unreliable in Ljubljana.'[68] Perhaps most shocking was the Flotsam Mission report of 24 July: 'Partisans report Germans left Novo Mesto yesterday for north of Sava. Home Guard killed one German officer here yesterday. Have been clashes between Home Guard and Germans in three local villages in last two days.'[69]

These purges were accompanied by changes to how the Home Guard was organized and operated, bringing it under closer German supervision. For example, from Easter 1944 to the autumn of 1944, the SS ended Home Guard control over roadblocks into Ljubljana.[70] In the spring, the Germans also transformed the Home Guard organizational 'headquarters' (*organizacijski štab*) into an organizational 'branch' (*organizacijski oddelek*), directly subordinated to Rösener's 'anti-Bandit' headquarters. Krener lost the title of commander and became instead a *Leiter* (head/leader) of the organizational branch.[71] Accusing propagandists of nationalist 'excesses' and of 'ignoring the Germans,' the previously relatively unsupervised Home Guard propaganda was placed on a shorter leash.[72] In June, Rösener ordered Section VI of the Home Guard's Organizational Headquarters – responsible for the 'world-view and political cultivation of the Home Guard' – to be placed under SS Untersturmführer Franz Wolfs and the 'orders of the national leadership of the SS.'[73] Added to pre-existing limitations on the Home Guard's use of heavy weaponry and radio communication, these growing tensions between the Germans and the Home Guard made OSS agent Robert McDowell's conclusions appear less surprising: 'It is claimed, and the undersigned believes correctly, that with the exception of a small number of senior officers, including of course Rupnik, this force is thoroughly anti-German. It definitely is Nationalist and strongly anti-Communist.'[74]

Two political developments in the late summer and autumn of 1944 further challenged the modus vivendi between the Germans and their Slovene auxiliaries. On 1 September, Mihailović, despite just having had his post as supreme commander abolished by royal decree – an action that led to further desertions from Četnik to Partisan ranks – issued an order for a general mobilization: 'In the name of King Peter II, in accordance with our great coalition, and on the basis of the authority vested in me, I proclaim as of zero hour September 1, 1944, total mobilization of the whole nation against all enemies.'[75] His decision was spurred on by the imminent liberation of Belgrade and much of Serbia by the Red Army and the Partisans. His subsequent actions against the Germans and Bulgarians were far from spectacular and were made even more difficult by the launch of a Partisan offensive against the Četniks in western Serbia. By publicly turning against the Germans, however, Mihailović made his affiliated formations in Slovenia, and any Home Guard cooperation with them, all the more suspect in German eyes.

The second destabilizing political development was the establishment of a resurrected National Committee for Slovenia (Narodni odbor, NO), in December 1944, a coalition of Slovenia's non-Communist political parties, chiefly the Slovene People's Party, the Liberals, and the Socialists. Its inaugural declaration, backdated to the national holiday of 29 October – the date in 1918 when the South Slavs of the Austro-Hungarian Empire announced their union and desire to merge with the Kingdom of Serbia – described the National Committee as the 'provisional national representation of the national state of Slovenia.'[76] Highly secretive, the document was signed by three hundred prominent Slovenes, using pseudonyms. The National Committee had three critical aims: unite all anti-Communist forces in Slovenia, prevent a Partisan seizure of power, and at the 'opportune moment' rise up against the occupiers in coordination with an envisaged Anglo-American liberation. Like its Slovene Covenant predecessor, the National Committee called for a future Slovenia that incorporated all ethnic Slovenes within a federated and socially progressive Yugoslavia. Organizationally, the National Committee contained a Central Committee of thirteen with the Slovene People's Party having a controlling seven members.[77] Its president was the financier Jože Basaj, and both Šmajd, who only recently had been released from Gestapo incarceration, and the Liberal Marjan Zajec played important roles in the Central Committee's formation, the latter as its executive secretary. Prezelj would not declare his loyalty to the National Committee until 6 April 1945; however, a number of prominent Home Guard officers were involved in its preparations, particularly in acquiring and hiding undeclared weapons.[78]

German retaliation was not unexpected and was made clear in a captured Partisan letter from early 1945: 'Germans have begun to cleanse the Home Guard ranks; they do not trust them much anymore.'[79] Already in October, a hounded Prezelj warned Ernest Peterlin, the chief of staff of the organizational headquarters of the Home Guard, that his underground activities had made him a target of the Germans. In addition to his work in support of the National Committee, Peterlin claimed to have instructed Krener after the failed assassination attempt against Hitler to 'place the Home Guard on high alert, and especially in Ljubljana and its surroundings, the Vrhnika group and battalions. If the proper opportunity reveals itself attack the Germans.'[80] The alleged spark was the Germans' discovery of a Slovene Legion arms cache in Ljubljana, in December.[81] Ivo Krmavner, commander of the Slovene Legion, and Ladislav Bevc, head of the Sokol War Council that commanded the Sokol Legion, were arrested, as was Peterlin, who was sent to Dachau.[82] Dežman, too, the outspoken critic of the Turjak disaster and commander of the Novo Mesto Home Guard, whose strident royalist convictions and relations with the Četniks had alienated many of his Slovene subordinates, was arrested and imprisoned in Dachau; he was killed while in transit between camps in 1945, 'a victim,' in the estimatation of the anti-Communist émigré Janez Grum, 'of the German Nazi aggression.'[83]

In early 1945, the German purge expanded outside the borders of the Province of Ljubljana, with the arrest of a number of leading members of the Gorenjska Self-Defence who were suspected of pro-Allied allegiances and of plotting an uprising. An assassination order was issued for Slavko Krek, who managed to elude the Gestapo and remained in hiding until the end of the war.[84] According to many of those arrested and their sympathizers, they had been betrayed to the Gestapo by Liberation Front agents who had infiltrated the anti-Partisan ranks.[85]

Resistance to the Germans was not limited to some high-profile Home Guard officers. Rank-and-file members, such as Rudolf Hirschegger and his companion Tone Suhadolc, ignored Krener's warnings and attempted to hide a group of downed American pilots, or 'ours' as he described them, from the Germans.[86] In 1947, one of the pilots, Captain Maurice Brash, issued a sworn affidavit for Hirschegger, who at the time was still in a Displaced Persons camp in Italy, acknowledging his heroism and that of other Četniks, Home Guardsmen, and civilians:

> In November 1944 I was serving my country as a First Lieutenant with the 79th Fighter Group, 87th Squadron, 12th Air Force. I was Pilot of a P47 Thunderbolt, Attack dive-bomber, based in Ancona, Italy. While carrying out a reconnaissance mission on the Zalog-Ljubljana line, November 19, 1944, I was shot down by German anti-aircraft fire over Ljubljana. Although my plane caught fire and I was badly burned about the face and hands, I parachuted to safety with the Chetniks and Domobranska troops.

> This is to certify that Hirschegger, Rudolf, did all in his power, at great risks to his life, and the lives of his family and friends to aid me during my distress. He gave me directly or indirectly and of most importance, security from the Germans, excellent medical care, plentiful amounts of food, and shelter from the cold. His Christian kindness and courageous acts of bravery gave me and my (14) fourteen comrades great hope and inspiration to carry on in our struggle to return to our forces. It was through no fault of his or the other Chetniks and civilians who helped me that we were captured, for some of them were captured with me and were treated worse than my comrades or myself.[87]

Hirschegger was eventually forced into hiding over the affair.

Nevertheless, it is important to note that the majority of these acts of resistance were covert. The conspirators did not break off relations with the Germans and remained at their posts fighting the Partisans with the occupiers' arms. Their supporters claimed that this was merely feigned cooperation – that they could accomplish more as 'partners' of the Germans than they could as their open opponents. This was also Peterlin's position. At his postwar trial, he enumerated his record of resistance, including nineteen intercessions on behalf of imprisoned Partisans, who were consequently spared deportation to Dachau, and a number of sabotage attempts against the Germans. 'The list [of resistance activities] is not long,' he stated, 'but without self-congratulations, I could say, that of all those, who are not OF, no one's is longer.' The Germans 'took me to be totally equal as an enemy, to those who outside the Home Guard worked for the NOV [National Liberation Army].'[88]

The vast majority of the Home Guardsmen did not engage in behaviour that would warrant their arrest and deportation. They remained immune to considerable pressure exerted by the Western Allies (especially the British), the Yugoslav government-in-exile, and Tito to make common cause with the Partisans. In the spring of 1944, discussions between Ivan Šubašić, the prime minister of the fractured government-in-exile, and Tito led to the first of several agreements that would ultimately culminate in a United Yugoslav Government that was Communist in all but name, on 7 March 1945. Tito's key demand in these convoluted negotiations was that the new government should not contain elements hostile to Tito's National Liberation Army (the NOV) and must do all in its power to organize aid for the Partisans. Mihailović and all other forces operating outside of the NOV, including the various collaborating formations, were evidently becoming a greater burden to the government-in-exile. On 29 August 1944, King Peter abolished Mihailović's position as supreme commander of the Yugoslav Army in the Homeland. Tito was, thus, designated the sole leader of resistance forces in Yugoslavia, as made clear in King Peter's 12 September broadcast from London, in which he called upon 'all Serbs, Croats, and Slovenes to unite and join the National Liberation Army under the leadership of Marshal Tito.' He further stated,'None […] who remain deaf to this appeal shall escape the brand of traitor before his people and before history. By this message I strongly condemn the misuse of the name of King and the authority of the Crown by which an attempt has been made to justify collaboration with the enemy and to promote discord amongst our fighting people in the very gravest days of their history, thus, solely profiting the enemy.'[89]

With this succinct response to collaboration, Slovene representatives of the Šubašić government tried desperately to have the Home Guard and other similar formations recognize that the die had been cast and that their only salvation lay in joining the Partisans. Kuhar and Boris Furlan, later dean of the Ljubljana Law Faculty, made a number of such appeals over the BBC. Provincial Administration and Home Guard propaganda replied by giving Furlan the moniker of 'The Screamer from London'; Kuhar was dismissed as a paid mercenary of Tito who had no right 'to judge and to estimate us.'[90] Snoj went to even greater lengths, parachuting into occupied Slovenia, in August, in a bid to persuade the Home Guard to change course. His Partisan 'hosts' kept him incommunicado, and his mission a failure, as he 'could not convey anything to anybody.'[91] Krek, on the other hand, opposed the Tito-Šubašić agreement and conveyed his fears already in the fall of 1944 to Prezelj and the Home Guard that they risked repatriation to Tito's forces. Krek's perceptiveness did not emerge from thin air; he was merely repeating what the Partisans were promising in their propaganda. One day after King Peter's move against Mihailović, and cognizant of the approaching operation to liberate Belgrade, Tito offered an amnesty under the slogan 'Last Warning':

> Although numerous warnings have been sent to all Croatian Home Guard, Slovene Home Guard, and misled Četniks, that they immediately desert the occupiers and join the NOV, it nevertheless appears that those whom the warning was addressed to did not understand and that they are not aware of the repercussions that await them.

Therefore I declare the following:

1. All those who will be found on 15 September 1944 in the military units of the Home Guard, Četniks, and others, which are fighting against the NOV and POJ [Yugoslav Partisan Detachments], will be placed before a national court as traitors and will be harshly punished. Lighter conditions will be taken into consideration only for individuals and only in exceptional cases.
2. Enlistment in the NOV and POJ and the surrender of weapons can be carried out everywhere, as all of our units have received exact instructions on this issue.[92]

This amnesty, as well as the subsequent one of 15 January 1945, had generally mixed but overall disappointing results for the Partisans in Slovenia. Its greatest impact was on the Slovene National Security Corps (SNVZ), who were already beset with chronic recruitment problems facilitated by Primorska's widespread rejection of collaboration with the occupiers. Many units were halved by subsequent desertions to Tito's National Liberation Army.[93] The impact on the Home Guard was far less dramatic, as described by Lindsay: 'After the failure of large numbers of the opposition [Home Guard] to come over during the September amnesty, the Partisans may have realized that their postwar position was not as secure as they had thought. They are very anxious that the extent of the opposition and the anti-Partisan feeling not be known to us, hence the attempt to isolate us.'[94] SOE operative Peter Moore drew similar conclusions in his assessment of the January amnesty: 'The amnesty of 15 Jan. did not secure a single desertion.'[95]

Such disparate results raise the obvious question of morale within the collaborating military and police formations, as well as the related and controversial issue of motivation. That a majority of members of the Home Guard, Police Corps, and Gorenjska Self-Defence ignored the amnesties, and remained at their posts, even when they had no reasonable chance of success suggests, perhaps, that a number were, indeed, ideologically committed to the struggle or, at least, too suspicious of the Partisans to trust their promises. That Slovenes joined these anti-Communist units out of deeply held convictions should not come as a surprise. Fear and even hatred of the Liberation Front and its Communist ideology was real and, as chapter 2 demonstrates, it pre-dated the Second World War. Among a people who were still largely devout Catholics, the position of priests mattered. Bishop Rožman's presence at the Home Guard oaths and his and his officials' frequent denunciations of the Liberation Front were clear indications of where the Church in the Province of Ljubljana stood with regard to the NOV. The marriage of religious fundamentalism and political extremism was perhaps most apparent in Hacin's rather bizarre behaviour. Justifying his order to arrest those who swore in public and particularly those who cursed the Church and the Catholic faith, Hacin explained that the Church had 'been in the forefront of the war against Communism' and that a number of priests had already 'laid their lives down for the nation.'[96] In addition to the Church, anti-Communism was a central tenant of the pre-war Yugoslav political establishment and the royal army. Vizjak recalled that, as a Yugoslav soldier, he had been taught that Communism was the sworn enemy of the state.[97]

For others who joined the collaborating ranks, this lesson came from experience and the tit-for-tat killings and reprisals of guerilla *and* civil war. Not surprisingly, victimization was most commonly cited by anti-Communist émigrés as the motivation behind military collaboration. Kociper depicted the recruits as mostly honest, politically uneducated peasant boys and men who reacted to the Communists that had 'burned the roof over their heads.'[98] The commander of the 72nd Home Guard Company in Vrhnika reported that many of his fighters had had their homes burned and families killed by the Partisans.[99] Indeed, the refugees who had fled the fighting between the occupiers, the collaborators, and the Partisans produced a rich harvest of recruits for the Home Guard. Mostly from Dolenjska and Notranjska, thousands streamed into Ljubljana where the Church and the civil administration offered them help finding housing and food. Their official representative, Škulj's Committee for Dolenjski Refugees, worked closely with the Provincial Administration's Peasant Office (Kmečka pisarna) and the Action Committee (Akcijski odbor), which was responsible for recruitment notices that urged eligible male refugees to join the Home Guard. Over a thousand Home Guardsmen were recruited in this manner.[100] Some refugees, undoubtedly, joined out of antipathy towards the Liberation Front, but their dependence on the Church and the Provincial Administration also acted as a coercive factor; volunteering was, thus, seen as 'paying back' the care offered to them and their families.

Ubiquitous anti-Communist propaganda had an impact on recruitment, although an 'accurate measure,' as the historian of Nazi propaganda Ian Kershaw has noted, 'is naturally impossible.'[101] For the Home Guard, propaganda was neatly packaged in its official bilingual

German – Slovene publication *Slovensko domobranstvo* (Slovene Home Guard), first issued in August 1944. Propaganda was disseminated during Sunday mass and weekly 'morality hours,' which Home Guardsmen were obliged to attend. The Liberation Front was portrayed as 'godless' and a mortal threat to the Catholic identity, traditions, and culture of the nation. Propagandists seized upon the defence of traditional gender roles and the 'honour' of women. The OF's 'liberation' of women was viewed with suspicion by conservative Slovenes, and female Partisans were routinely described as prostitutes. As one Home Guard – affiliated propaganda piece declared, Partisan women 'understand all this swinishness [female emancipation] as something completely natural, they think [. . .] this is sanctioned by equal rights and some imaginary equality.'[102] In contrast, Home Guard propaganda abounded with recurring images of the pure Slovene mother in traditional garb, sitting near the hearth and surrounded by religious motifs. This presentation of the 'traditional' woman was, as the historian Kevin Passmore observed, common 'all over Europe [to] movements and regimes of the extreme right [and] idealized the chaste mother in peasant costume.'[103] Other recruits may have been convinced that service in the anti-Communist ranks was in Slovenia's national interests. The oft-repeated Home Guard slogan – 'God-Nation-Homeland' (*Mati-domovina-Bog*) – was a conservative and nationalist antidote to the OF's slogan of 'Death to fascism, Freedom to the people.' The Liberation Front, it was claimed, served only the Comintern and would destroy Slovenia's national individuality were it to seize power.

Slovene National Security Corps propaganda played its nationalism 'card' in a rather unique manner. The SNVZ claimed that the Germans rewarded their cooperation with national concessions that were unthinkable under the Italians, such as language rights, Slovene programming on Radio Trst, Slovene schools, and a degree of self-administration in Primorska (especially in the Province of Gorizia).[104] Pushing the envelope on Rainer's self-serving program of ethnic diversity in the Operation Zone Adriatic Littoral, some SNVZ displays of overt nationalism led to sporadic inter-ethnic disturbances with Italian forces, something the Germans were keen to avoid. The Postojna SNVZ reported, in June 1944, that 'there are always incidents' between SNVZ and the Fascist militia.[105] On 3 July 1944, a gun battle almost erupted between Italians and an SNVZ regiment in Pivka that was parading and waving Slovene flags and singing Slovene songs.[106] Thus, joining the SNVZ, its propaganda trumpeted, furthered the process of Slovene national emancipation in Primorska, suggesting that Italian forces would be removed once the Slovenes had firm control over the region's security. Indeed, in point ten of the inaugural agreement that created the Slovene National Security Corps, Globocnik dangled this very possibility: 'When the Security Committee [SNVZ] will be constructed in such a shape that it can guarantee [...] unconditional peace, the security units of other nationalities will be removed from the territory in question.'[107] In contrast, SNVZ propaganda accused the Liberation Front of planning to attach Primorska to an Italian Communist republic.[108]

Aside from these more earnest motivations, the collaborating units attracted those enterprising and unscrupulous individuals who, in the detritus of war, see opportunities for self-enrichment. Such behaviour was hardly unique to Slovenia, and as Paul Jankowski demonstrated in his study of the collaborationist French Legion des Voluntaires Française contre le Bolchevisme, many of its recruits, as in Slovenia, 'were unhappy or unemployed or at loose ends, people to whom collaboration offered tempting opportunities, and even the chance to change their lives.'[109] Incidents of ill-discipline were hardly rare among the SNVZ, the Police Corps, the Gorenjska Self-Defence, and the Home Guard. The Police Corps took advantage of certain 'fringe benefits' of policing, practising bribery and reportedly lying about having illegitimate children in order to collect additional child stipends.[110] On 6 March 1944, in Postojna, 13,700 lira, livestock, and alcohol were stolen by SNVZ troops, and not for the first time, SNVZ Deputy Inspector Major Ferenčak warned his units against 'looting and robbery, requisitions of livestock, firewood, food, [and] vehicles.'[111] As the Home Guard commander in Vrhnika pointed out, war also presented lucrative financial opportunities to those 'personal advantage seekers' among the Home Guard.[112] Some incidents were relatively minor – stealing chickens, for example. Others were far more serious and impinged on morale. A particularly gruesome report from the Metlika region accused the Home Guard of severing the fingers of dead Partisans in order to confiscate their rings.[113] Home Guardsmen manning roadblocks were accused of accepting bribes, and some rank and file as well as officers were employed in the black market.[114] There were reports of Home Guard members extorting money from suspected Liberation Front sympathizers.[115] In response, on 6 May 1944, Krener denounced Home Guardsmen who, rather than pursuing the Partisans into the forest after a battle, pilfered the booty left behind.[116] He repeated this criticism on 16 August, accusing some members of the Home Guard of being far more interested in personal enrichment than in the larger aim of destroying 'banditry.'[117] The Germans also responded, with Rösener reminding Krener that he was personally responsible for any looting and even manslaughter committed by his men.[118] Partly to curb theft, the Germans prohibited independent searches of homes by the Home Guard, already in November 1943, an order that would be repeated several times.[119] Evidence exists of Home Guardsmen using the authority vested in them by a gun and a uniform to settle scores with personal or political enemies. This was not limited only to OF sympathizers, as anti-Communists of a different political persuasion were reportedly also denounced as OF supporters or members.[120]

Indeed, this sampling of errant behaviour suggests that for some collaborators, their service was little more than a means of personal enrichment or a way to bide their time in relative security until the end of the war. The frequent complaints of administrative laxity across all collaborating units, therefore, were hardly surprising. Hacin's prohibition against public cursing, for example, had to be repeated often, and that few were actually arrested for it was indicative of a larger phenomenon of selective responsiveness and insubordination among the Police Corps.[121] According to a report by the Velika Lašče Home Guard, officers allowed their men to 'shirk' their duties, and this 'cancer' inevitably eroded morale and discipline.[122] Krener complained often of uniform violations, public drunkenness, gambling, or improper salutes to superiors. He criticized Home Guard members who exploited their authority by stopping trains in order to receive free rides into Ljubljana.[123] Indeed, Krener's authority was itself ridiculed, and his rather portly stature often became the butt of Home Guard jokes.[124] The Police Corps, too, was forced to admonish its ranks for their lack of respect for one another and for higher officials. In May 1944, Police Corps headquarters was forced to circulate photos of Hacin to ensure that the men recognized and properly greeted him.[125] Reports of unauthorized leaves were not uncommon among Slovene collaborating formations. The interrogation of Anton Kukman, who left his Žužemberk Home Guard unit without authorization to spend five days with his family, in November 1943, confirmed the impression of lax discipline. When asked, 'What made the decision for you [to go AWOL]?' Kukman replied, 'I never really thought about my actions, but I was also of the opinion that military rules will not be so strongly applied in the Home Guard army.' As if to vindicate Kukman's impression, he was never penalized.[126]

Service in the anti-Partisan forces appeared, indeed, to be a safer way of enduring the war, at least until its final days. This was anecdotally evident in an incident involving the Dravlje Home Guard, in which a member was shot by his own sentry as he made his way to the latrine one evening. The report emphasized that this simplemindedness was expensive, 'as more Home Guardsmen fall as a result of carelessness, than in battle.'[127] The Police Corps were, according to the Home Guard, even more risk averse. The Home Guard detachment in Horjul complained that the police 'eat and sleep in the security of the Home Guard' and that they were unwilling to place themselves in dangerous situations.[128] These cases appear almost comical in comparison with the fugitive existence of the Partisans or the thousands of Slovenes from Štajerska and Gorenjska who were forcibly conscripted into the Wehrmacht and who lost their lives, primarily on the Russian front. Not surprisingly, well over three hundred members of the Gorenjska Self-Defence were former Wehrmacht members.[129] Indeed, the leadership of the Gorenjska Self-Defence arranged that some Slovenes in the Wehrmacht, who were on leave and who wanted to join their ranks, would have news sent back to their commanders indicating that they had joined the Partisans.[130] It was not a bad decision for the vast majority of them: fewer than fifty Gorenjska Self-Defence members were killed in engagements with the Partisans during the Second World War.[131] Wehrmacht deserters were not alone in this regard. An analysis of 897 Gorenjska Self-Defence members revealed that over 40 per cent of them had served previously with the Partisans, and a quarter had served with both the German Army and the Partisans.[132] This 'shopping around,' as it were, was hardly indicative of ideological commitment and pointed, perhaps, to more immediate concerns of personal safety. Franc Tuljak, a Partisan deserter, testified during his interrogation that he had wanted to join the Slovene National Security Corps because the Liberation Front would kill him if he returned to his home. Franc Švirt, another formerly mobilized Partisan, joined the Home Guard and pleaded not to be stationed in 'a place where I am recognized.'[133]

The Germans and the Home Guard assuaged this fear of potential Partisan deserters and recruits by promising that they would not be harmed, and they offered financial incentives of 200 lira for every gun and 1,500 lira for every machine-gun that they surrendered.[134] Recruitment propaganda exploited the regular contact that Home Guardsmen had with family and friends to the loneliness and homesickness that was inherent in Partisan service: 'Your family lives in bitter lack and difficult longing! [. . .] And you are still wandering the forests and fighting. Why?'[135] In fact, Krener was forced to allow 5 per cent of each unit to return home for a maximum of fifteen days to do field work.[136] Partisan command fought against this 'marketing' by poisoning, for example, the greener grass of SNVZ service with rumours that the SNVZ was to be sent to Germany or to the Russian front.[137] Nor were they unsuccessful: the Postojna SNVZ reported, in August 1944, that such rumours had contributed to a poor recruitment drive.[138]

Of course, the ability to serve near one's home was not the monopoly of any one faction. The Liberation Front controlled large swaths of rural countryside and even a number of smaller towns – collaborators from these areas could not return home. Yet, for a number of recruits, the prospect of serving close to home was enticing. The Slovene National Security Corps had a particular love-hate relationship with this 'local patriotism.' The SNVZ used it as a carrot in recruitment, insisting that recruits could 'serve near your village or another piece of our beautiful fatherland.'[139] Its members responded in kind, requesting numerous leaves of absence or simply going temporarily AWOL, like Kukman, in order to visit their families or work in their own fields.[140] Some SNVZ members simply returned to the Province of Ljubljana from which almost half of their ranks originally hailed or disappeared. As a result, their commanders were forced to fight against this local patriotism, for example, using lectures to implant in their men 'a love for their entire home – Slovenian soil, and slowly to destroy that narrow-hearted love for their home – their village.'[141] Local patriotism remained strong also among the Home Guard. Vizjak testified that most AWOLs among the Home Guard could be attributed to local patriotism. He offered the example of the Polhov Gradec unit, which had been dispersed among various units as punishment for black marketeering. All of these men eventually deserted and returned to Polhov Gradec.[142]

Service in collaborating units offered modest financial rewards, which were appealing in the economic uncertainty of war. SNVZ recruitment posters promised 'food, footwear and clothes, and all other needs and those of your family will be taken care of.'[143] Home Guardsmen were offered pay according to rank, as well as free food and clothes, free health care, and assistance for family members.[144] The families of Home Guard members who were killed in battle received rudimentary 'life insurance' payments coordinated by the Provincial Administration's welfare branch, Social Aid (Socialna pomoč). As with the Anti-Communist Volunteer Militia, service in the anti-Partisan units allowed petitions on behalf of arrested family members or friends. Indeed, its sheer volume forced Krener, in December 1943, to prohibit Home Guardsmen from approaching police headquarters or the German staff on behalf of prisoners.[145]

In addition to their meagre wage and supplements of illicit income, simple bureaucratic inertia may have induced many in the Police Corps to remain at their posts following the occupation or to seek re-employment as policemen. It is instructive that older and retired policemen and political agents were considered particularly trustworthy by the occupiers, a view that Hacin shared in his recruitment of the Police Corps.[146] The case of Alojzij Šuštar, who had joined the Yugoslav police in January 1938, is indicative of this trend. Following the Italian occupation, he remained at his post until March 1942, when the Italians imprisoned him in Gonars for over a year. In September 1943, he served one month with the Partisans before deserting. Hiding at his home, Šuštar requested to join the Police Corps, in April 1944.[147] Despite his year-long imprisonment by the occupiers, Šuštar still sought re-employment in a police force that was under their control.

'Safety,' however, was a relative term in wartime, and numerous accounts still emphasized the perils of anti-Partisan service. Bitter cold, hunger, homesickness, and suicides gnawed at the ranks. Although encounters with the Partisans were far from continuous, violence was ever present. In March 1944, the local Police Corps unit disapproved of Gestapo orders to search homes in the outlying areas of Kočevje, where Partisan influence was strong, as it was dangerous work for which they were improperly armed.[148] Liberation Front executions of collaborators certainly made such work 'dangerous.' Desertions increased when conditions within collaborating units began to deteriorate, as they did in the final months of the war. The Germans did not look kindly on this trend. A young Partisan in Dolenjska told the OSS Arrow Mission, in April 1944, 'that White Guards who would like to join the Partisans, primarily because they think they are on the losing side now, are afraid to do so because the Germans would harm their families.'[149] Golob recalled how a German officer threatened to shoot anyone in his unit who abandoned his post.[150]

Yet, in some cases, examining the motivations of military collaborators is redundant, as a number of them were forcibly mobilized. This was perhaps most evident with the Wehrmannschaft in Štajerska and Gorenjska, despite the fact that postwar Slovene courts would, nonetheless, conclude that some Slovenes were too eager to join the force and, thus, could be counted as volunteers (see chapter 8). The wartime intelligence of the Liberation Front was more charitable, as seen in this assessment from late 1944: 'In the Wehrmannschaft were accepted all those, who according to their racial and political profile were seen as politically trustworthy or at least neutral. The Wehrmannschaft is otherwise a voluntary organization, but it was organized under the worst terror and whoever did not want to enter into their organization was threatened with penalties the mildest of which was expulsion and confiscation of property or concentration camps.'[151] Similarly, despite orders that the Gorenjska Self-Defence, the Slovene National Security Corps, and the Home Guard were to be voluntary associations, the intensification of the civil war led to forced mobilizations. However, unlike with the Wehrmannschaft, the impetus came more from Slovenes rather than their German leaders who, like Rösener, equated the practice with Communist tactics.[152] The escalation of violence obliged every 'conscious Slovene,' a rather flexible description, to join the anti-Partisan ranks. A typical summons for the anti-Partisan units, issued on 17 June 1944, revealed that this 'with us or against us' polarization left few real choices: 'We ask that you immediately appear at the Home Guard office in Gorenja vas and with this place yourself on the side of the Home Guard and the Slovene nation. We want clarity. There is no middle path. In the event that you do not respond to the summons, we will regard you as a member of the OF, and we will treat you as such.'[153] One method of forced recruitment was revealed in Franc Golob's diary: when his hometown of Šentjernej was surrounded by the Home Guard in January 1944 and all eligible males – Golob was only sixteen at the time – were pressed into service.[154] In the case of the Slovene National Security Corps, forced mobilization was virtually the only way to fill the ranks – indeed, only six volunteers had signed up a month and a half after the SNVZ's inauguration.[155] Exhibiting a veneer of voluntarism, recruitment for the SNVZ almost 'as a rule' became 'forced recruitment.'[156]

It appears that few individuals in the collaborating military and police units joined because they wanted to fight for Hitler and Nazism; nevertheless, that many ultimately did reveals the fatal irony of collaboration and the shortcomings of the 'Defence against Communism.' However, the anti-Partisan military and security formations that were created during the sunset of German military power, and which fought shoulder-to-shoulder with them against fellow Slovenes, were only the most visible face of Slovene collaboration. Behind them stood a much larger but less well-known collection of civilian administrators, religious representatives, and supportive ordinary Slovenes whose stories also reveal the controversies, difficulties, and even banalities of life under occupation.

8 The Banality of Civilian Collaboration, September 1943–December 1944

> My children, it is permitted you in time of grave danger to walk with the devil until you have crossed the bridge.[1]
>
> President F. D. Roosevelt

In a confidential remark to the press, President Franklin D. Roosevelt used this old Balkan proverb to justify the maintenance of U.S. relations with the collaborating Vichy regime. Roosevelt insisted that ties with Pétain were not to be interpreted as an endorsement of the Vichy government. Rather, the relations with Vichy served American interests, as the French government had secretly reorganized its intelligence service and made pertinent information available to the Americans.[2] Indeed, the very same proverb could have been used to justify the relations many ordinary Slovenes had with the occupiers during the Second World War.

For Slovenes, Italy's capitulation, on 8 September 1943, appeared to be of immediate importance only to the Province of Ljubljana and Primorska where civilians awaited the arrival of German jackboots with a mix of trepidation and curiosity. For the Slovene inhabitants of Gorenjska and Štajerska, it appeared to be merely one more day in a German occupation that was nearing its two and a half year anniversary, and another notch in the much longer oppression of the Slovene minority of Carinthia. Yet, here as well, 1943 would mark a change in the relationship between Slovenes and their German occupiers. As in Primorska, the end of 1943 would witness the spread of the civil war into Gorenjska, fanned by the creation of the Gorenjska Self-Defence (*samozaščita*). In Štajerska, 1943 would see a lightening of German oppression, if we understand 'lightening' to mean that 'only' fifty-seven hostages were shot that year and that the unsuccessful mass deportations of 'racially inferior' Slovenes, which had ended in 1942, would not be restarted.[3] Even Hungarian-occupied Premkurje was impacted by the events of 1943, insofar as Italy's collapse led the Hungarian government to accelerate efforts to extricate the country from the war.[4] These negotiations – a betrayal to Hitler – led to the German occupation of Hungary, Operation Margarethe, in March 1944, bringing all Slovene lands under de facto German control. This expansion of German authority *and* its growing pragmatism, a result of the Germans' dual attempt to simultaneously squash the spreading Partisan resistance and its ever more desperate attempt to mobilize the human and economic resources of Slovene regions in defence of the Reich, opened new opportunities not only for military collaboration but also for Slovene civilian collaboration. Thus, this chapter explores civilian collaboration in the period from September 1943 to early 1945 region by region. Beginning with an examination of the territories where opportunities for civilian collaboration expanded least (or even decreased), the chapter concludes with the area where it grew the most: the Province of Ljubljana, the heartland of Slovene collaboration in the Second World War.

Prekmurje

Prekmurje's Magyarization continued unabated through 1943. However, for those who were not deemed active proponents of Slovene nationalism or leftist resisters, everyday life in Prekmurje remained bearable. Most had, as Godina concluded, enough food and clothing and, significantly, did not have to carry the burdens of an uprising against the occupiers. The Italians' scorched earth policies in the summer of 1942 and widespread German reprisals against alleged OF sympathizers and hostages were not common in Prekmurje.[5]

The lack of anything more than a skeletal OF presence in Prekmurje also insured against a robust anti-Partisan reaction, and thus, Prekmurje escaped the worst of the the civil war that was tearing central parts of Slovenia asunder. Attempts to create a 'White Guard' were mostly limited to the distribution of some propaganda, led by the lawyer and SLS member Franc Bajlec and some Salesian monks.[6] Their isolation was credited to the 'restraint of the Catholic priesthood of Prekmurje [who] decisively influenced the fact that in Prekmurje the White Guard was not formed and that the mutual settling of accounts never came to be, as happened in other parts of Slovenia.'⁷ Indeed, according to Communist reports, some lower clergy supported the Liberation Front, facilitated no doubt by their demands for national liberation.⁸

Some settling of accounts did occur, and the Hungarian authorities relied on a web of civilian informants to assist them in pursuing OF supporters. Most informants tended to be ethnic Hungarians or Protestants, the new elite under Hungarian rule. Some Slovenes also took part. For example, Amalija Ambruž, whose husband was killed by the Liberation Front, was convicted after the war of denouncing a Partisan Gustav Gašparin to the Hungarian authorities. Gašparin was later executed.⁹ Nevertheless, denunciations appear to have been rare, as most Slovenes in Prekmurje accommodated quietly to the realities of life under Hungarian occupation – attending Hungarian schools, selling goods to Hungarian officials, and shouldering their military responsibilities. Some 415 Slovenes lost their lives as forcibly mobilized members of the Hungarian armed forces.¹⁰

The pivotal year for the Slovenes of Prekmurje was 1944, as Operation Margarethe brought the German army and a right-wing Hungarian government under General Döme Sztojay into power. The Jews of Prekmurje – the core of Slovenia's tiny pre-war Jewish community of slightly less than one thousand individuals were impacted almost immediately.¹¹ They had already suffered the loss of civil rights, confiscation of their property, the imposition of a numerus clausus in education, and deportations to labour camps in Hungary and Ukraine and to the brutal Bor copper mine in occupied Serbia.¹² The new regime now required Jews to wear the yellow Star of David. Survivor Elizabeta Fürst of Lendava recalled, 'After this date my friends, with one exception, did not want to walk with me in the street anymore.'¹³ In a series of arrests, in April 1944, Hungarian gendarmes ordered the remaining Jews of Lendava and Murska Sobota to gather in the local synagogue. An estimated 460 Jews from Prekmurje would eventually be deported to Auschwitz from which only sixty-five returned.¹⁴ In total, some 550 Jews from Slovenia perished in Nazi concentration camps.¹⁵ Unlike the Province of Ljubljana, where the Home Guard was involved in the arrest of its few remaining Jews, the existing literature points to the Nazis, Arrow Cross thugs, and the Hungarian gendarmes as the perpetrators of Prekmurje's Holocaust.¹⁶ Nevertheless, interwar Prekmurje saw Jews attacked in the Catholic press for their assumed wealth, Bolshevik sympathies, and identification with Hungarian culture; incidents of exploitation and the robbing of Jewish refugees in pre-1941 Prekmurje also occurred.[17] During the deportations of April, smuggler Franc Matjašec recalled, 'Some people were in favour of deportations because they were already thinking of taking their property. Without mercy. But there were also goodhearted people.'[18] The postwar dispossession of Jewish property in Prekmurje and elsewhere in Slovenia by neighbours and Communist officials would represent another black mark in the treatment of Slovenia's surviving Jewish community.

The new order, after March 1944, and in particular the rise to power of Ferenc Szalasi's Arrow Cross that autumn, also impacted the non-Jewish population of Prekmurje, eroding what had been a bearable Hungarian occupation. Curfews were reintroduced, corn fields were ordered cut down to deny safe havens to deserters and Partisans, and civilians were relocated away from rail lines.[19] Szalasi's call for 'total mobilization' made all citizens between the ages of twelve and seventy eligible for labour or military service.[20] Civilians were dragooned into constructing defensive works in a frantic attempt to slow the approach of the Red Army. However, desertions unravelled these efforts, and in the final months of the war, an increasing number of Slovene boys threw their lot in with the Partisans rather than fight for the lost cause of the Hungarian Army.[21]

Opportunities for civilian collaboration decreased in Prekmurje in the period from 1943 through 1944, particularly since a Slovene bureaucracy along the lines of the Provincial Administration (PU) in the Province of Ljubljana was never established. The return of sheer coercion after March 1944 and the changing fortunes of war undermined the accommodation that had characterized the response of most Slovenes to the Hungarian occupation. Civilian collaboration was left primarily to the Hungarian ethnic community, some Hungarian sympathizers among ethnic Slovenes (*madžaroni*), and a handful of wealthier Slovenes with an economic stake in the occupation.

Štajerska

Growing German losses on the European battlefields and the increased premium placed on mobilizing rather than expelling the human resources of the Third Reich can account, in part, for the easing of Štajerska's occupation in 1943. In addition to executing fewer hostages and suspending plans for the racial reorganization of Štajerska, the punitive deportations of families and relatives of Partisans and executed hostages would cease in the spring of 1943.[22] Nevertheless, the Germans continued to exploit Štajerska's industries, coal mines, viniculture, agriculture, and forests for their own needs.[23] As the Alum Mission reported in the summer of 1944, however, the Germans were allowing farmers to carry on unmolested in Gorenjska, Štajerska, and Koroška, requisitioning only from front-line areas 'in order to break Partisan control.'[24] This relative easing of repression would not last. With the Allies and Soviets approaching the underbelly of the Reich, in August 1944, Himmler declared Štajerska, Koroška, and Carinthia a special security zone.[25] No resistance would be tolerated.

The tentative retreat from the more ideologically driven policies of earlier years was hardly universal – the intensified hunt for Jews being the most glaring exception – yet, more pragmatic German military and civilian leaders, nonetheless, attempted to mobilize the human potential of their occupied territories using less draconian and self-defeating measures. The toll of a two-front war on German manpower was striking. By 1944, the average age in the German army was thirty-one and a half years, a full six years older than in the U.S. Army.[26] Considered part of the Reich, the Slovenes of Štajerska and Gorenjska continued to be inducted into the Wehrmacht, while the gendarmes and Wehrmannschaft were called on to undertake more anti-Partisan operations. Indeed, the Germans were so short of men for garrison duty that they brought five hundred metropolitan policemen from Vienna to strengthen their stations in Štajerska.[27] At the end of the year, the Germans would also use Ustaši and Croatian *domobran* (Home Guard) – the regular armed forces of the Independent State of Croatia – in anti-Partisan operations in the Kozjanska area of southern Štajerska.

Aggravating the military's manpower shortage were the Reich's labour requirements. Slovenes had been compulsorily recruited into the Reich Labour Service since 1942, with demand only growing in 1943 and 1944. For example, in 1943 eligibility expanded to men between the ages of sixty and sixty-five and women between the ages of seventeen and forty-five.[28] With the Reich's southern frontier recognized as a potential invasion route, on 26 July 1944, Hitler ordered Gauleiter Uberreither to build defensive installations in Štajerska along the Hungarian and Croatian borders, with a similar request issued to Rainer for the Operation Zone Adriatic Littoral (OZAK). At its height, a multinational contingent of some 150,000 to two hundred thousand people was mobilized under the auspices of Organisation Todt to complete these projects.[29] These labour demands upon Slovenes were hardly unique. By December 1944, a third of Germany's workforce was foreign, a large portion of it consisting of prisoners of war, deportees, and slaves.[30] The most notorious use of slave labour in Slovenia, albeit using mostly French and other foreign labour, was in the construction of the Ljubelj Tunnel in Gorenjska that marked the shortest route between Austria and the Adriatic. The project was completed in 1944 by inmates of the Ljubelj South Concentration Camp, a subsidiary of Mauthausen, and the only Nazi concentration camp located on Slovene territory.

Despite Štajerska's absorption into the Reich, civilian collaboration remained rare. As elsewhere in occupied Europe, intimate relations between Slovenes and Germans were not unheard of. Marija Pikalo, for example, was found to have defamed the honour of the nation for 'drinking and dancing with Nazis or [having] strolled with them.'[31] Unlike similar cases which were absolved because the women conveniently 'did not have healthy minds,' pleading that 'love is international' did not persuade postwar courts, and a number of women from Štajerska were sentenced to forced labour and loss of citizenship.[32] On balance, the Slovenes of Štajerska remained sympathetic towards the Liberation Front, even though few actually joined its ranks until the final phase of the war; a number of civilians, however, would be punished for betraying members of the resistance. Henrik Mohorič, for example, was accused of revealing a Partisan's location to German police in the town of Rače, in January 1945, and denouncing OF sympathizers; he was convicted by postwar courts to twenty years forced labour.[33] The lack of a sizable OF insurgency in Štajerska until the last months of 1944 also meant that its inhabitants, as in Prekmurje, largely avoided the reprisals and internecine violence that accompanied counter-insurgency operations in other parts of Slovenia. Despite the small OF presence and the inability or unwillingness of most Štajerci to join the fight, OSS Major Franklin Lindsay, who spent the latter half of 1944 with the Partisans in Štajerska, concluded that if 'the civilian population had been hostile,' and if it were not for 'an invisible screen of civilians – old men, women and children – to warn us of approaching German patrols, or of ambushes [. . .] we could not have survived for even a week.'[34]

The lack of civilian collaboration can also be explained by the fact that the Germans continued to offer few real opportunities to collaborate. They did not sponsor any avowedly Slovene collaborationist military units. Nonetheless, as a result of the labour and manpower shortage and the added administrative demands in occupying Italy, beginning in late 1943, Slovenes were given (and in some cases forced into) a larger role in Štajerska's bureaucracy – which was somewhat of a departure from the policies of 1941 and 1942, when Germans and Austrians mostly staffed its offices.[35] However, the bureaucracy remained identifiably German, and the Nazis refused to tolerate a Slovene civil service along the lines of the Provincial Administration. There is also no denying that the daily behaviour of Slovenes in Štajerska assisted the German occupiers. Slovenes, not entirely unlike the 'cowed and coddled' Czech workers in the Protectorate of Bohemia and Moravia, worked in German armaments industries, provided food and clothing for German troops, staffed their administration, and assisted in subduing insurgent activity.[36] The Germans monopolized the levers of coercion, and the Slovenes were forced to accommodate German demands. The temporary easing of German repression in 1943 notwithstanding, civilians clearly understood the danger that they and their families would be placed in should they refuse to cooperate with the occupiers. Collective punishment remained standard operating procedure for the duration of the war. Labour shirkers were pursued by the gendarmes, and Wehrmacht deserters were threatened with execution. The anxiety was palpable in Lindsay's memoir, as he described the welcome he and his Partisan escort received one evening after requesting rest and food from a local peasant: 'Finally a window opened a bit and a terribly frightened woman implored us hysterically to please go away. There were Germans nearby and she would be sent to a concentration camp or shot for having sheltered us. This time we heeded the anguished plea and slogged on in the dark night.'[37] In a few extreme cases, German coercion forced Slovenes to commit war crimes. Perhaps the most grotesque example was that of Joško Dajčar who, as a member of the 1st Alarmkompanie in Maribor, was ordered to execute twelve hostages in the village of Pameče near Slovenj Gradec, in July 1944. Postwar Yugoslav courts, however, found that he was forced at gunpoint to join the execution squad and that if he ever escaped the Wehrmannschaft and joined the Liberation Front, his wife and four young children would have been deported.[38]

Dajčar's case encapsulates the difficulties with branding what appears to be collaboration *as* collaboration. Recognizing that entrance into the Reich Labour Service, the Wehrmacht, the Wehrmannschaft, or the Heimatbund was rarely a voluntary exercise, a verdict of collaboration could only be reached after reviewing each case individually. Membership alone was not sufficient proof of collaboration just as the enrolment of fourteen-year-old Joseph Ratzinger (Pope Benedict XVI) in the Hitler Youth was not adequate evidence that he was a committed Nazi. This difficulty in assessing what constituted forced mobilization and what constituted collaboration bedevilled postwar trials in Štajerska. The regional court in Celje, for example, found that Leopold Krampršek had 'voluntarily' joined the Wehrmannschaft because he had earlier allegedly denounced a gendarme who had speculated that Germany would be defeated. The gendarme was deported and died in Mauthausen.[39] Slovenes serving in the Wehrmannschaft or the gendarmerie who denounced Partisans or who took part in thievery were also denied the defence of forcible mobilization.

Conversely, Štajerci who used their positions in Nazi organizations or beseeched German troops to assist or intervene on behalf of fellow Slovenes were often forgiven of what appeared to be evidence of collaboration. Greta Šarb, who owned a store and a tavern in Celje during the occupation, was originally sentenced to five years forced labour and the loss of citizenship rights for ten years for publicly escorting Germans and, thereby, having 'harmed the honour and reputation of the Slovene nation.'[40] This conviction was later overturned, when the court recognized that German troops gathering at a tavern was an unavoidable fact – an observation that could easily be extended to 'practically anybody else in German-occupied Europe who [. . .] ran a business.'[41] More importantly, the court also found that Šarb exploited her relations with the Germans to free her husband, who had been arrested on suspicions of being a Partisan. Her credibility was further enhanced when it was discovered that she had helped overturn the death sentences against two local Partisans and that she had provided the Liberation Front with food.[42] Similarly, Marija Žekelj, an official in the local Heimatbund in Gornji Grad, wove wreaths for fallen German soldiers and visited the injured in the hospital. She also allegedly threatened local members of the Liberation Front – a rather unhelpful record in postwar Communist Yugoslavia. However, the fact that Žekelj used her influence among the Germans to intervene on behalf of the politically suspect Kolenč family reduced her sentence to a two and half year loss of citizenship rights.[43] Forcible mobilization, thus, remained a slippery defence for Štajerci. In some cases, evidence that the accused cooperated passively and fulfilled compromising German orders only to avoid personal harm persuaded postwar courts. In others, prosecutors remained unmoved, replying that the 'large majority of the nation' took upon itself 'honourable suffering and the difficult liberation war.'[44] Far more effective in mitigating verdicts against Štajerci, who otherwise appeared to have taken to their responsibilities and duties in Nazi mass organizations with inordinate zeal, was proving that relations with the occupiers were cultivated to assist Slovenes and, above all, the National Liberation War.

Carinthia

Even more than the inhabitants of Štajerska, Carinthian Slovenes found themselves between a lethal rock and a hard place. Carinthia lay at the heart of Hitler's Austria; its 'solid Nazi historical credentials' were undisputed. Having suffered under Austrian chauvinism and with the Anschluss forced along with 'other, frightened, former Austrian citizens [...] to dissimulate and feign cooperation,' it is hardly surprising that Carinthia's Slovenes became adept at hiding their true sympathies.[45] Nationally conscious Slovenes who dreamed of unification with Yugoslavia made up only a portion of the Slovenophone population. Carinthia's more assimilated Slovenes along with the province's German majority continued, according to Barker, 'to support the Nazi system or at least not to lift a finger against it even after the initial period of prosperity had passed and the strains of war were all too evident, indeed until it collapsed under the concerted assault of its external foe.'[46] Most civilians in southern Carinthia, 'whatever their sympathies, [...] were terrified' of the rag-tag, tiny band of Partisans who had become more visible in 1944 'and even more terrified of the ruthless reprisals which they could expect from the German and Austrian security services if they were caught aiding' them.[47] These reprisals, which left in their wake burned homes and confiscated property, usually offered the peasants 'no recourse but to flee, many of them bitterly resentful toward the Partisans for the travail they were undergoing.'[48]

As Mlakar noted, it is also true, however, that in Carinthia there were not 'even the most elementary attempts at forming anti-revolutionary White Guard units.'[49] The Slovene priesthood, who in other parts of occupied Slovenia denounced the perceived atheistic credentials of the Liberation Front, did not come out strongly against the Partisans in Carinthia; indeed, a handful of them surreptitiously supported anti-Nazi activities. At worst, nationally conscious Slovenes who were, like many of their German neighbours, uncomfortable with the Communist character of the Liberation Front remained largely Centrists (*sredinci*), advocating patience in place of the Partisans' suicidal gamble.[50]

Indeed, SOE Major Charles Villiers, who in 1944 attempted to organize contacts on a potential 'back-door' Allied invasion of the Reich via the Ljubljana Gap, encountered among the isolated Partisans of Carinthia what he described as a 'religious enthusiasm for NOV and POS

(National Army of Liberation and Partisan Detachments), for the person of Tito and for the prospect of a Golden Age to follow the dismissal of the "Okupator."'[51] Yet, in actual manpower, Villiers' comrade Lieutenant Colonel Wilkinson described the Western Carinthian Partisan detachment as 'skeletal,' 'notional,' and 'scared out of their wits.' Their manner of warfare involved 'sending out fighting patrols and then hot footing it back to the southern Karawanken slopes,' that is, to the relative safety of Gorenjska, where much larger Partisan formations were located.[52] The few Carinthian Slovenes who were persuaded to join the Partisans did so, in many cases, to avoid more onerous alternatives, such as mobilization into the Wehrmacht and service on the Russian front. The Partisans were, thus, occasionally forced to recruit among slave-workers and prisoners of war.[53] In short, Carinthian Slovenes fell back on a strategy that had allowed them to survive on the southern marches of Germandom – reveal little and promise even less.

Gorenjska

Like Prekmurje, Štajerska, and Carinthia, the civilian population of Gorenjska appeared to sympathize with the Liberation Front, an estimate that even Home Guard intelligence was willing to concede.[54] Partisan activity was far more pronounced in Gorenjska compared with Slovene regions to the north and east. By 1944, it was inflicting real damage to industrial production in Gorenjska, not least by mobilizing valuable labourers.[55] The nature of guerilla resistance, with its requisitioning and inevitable reprisals, struck the civilian population hard and, in particular, the rural population living on the front lines – an amorphous zone where permanent German control appeared to end and liberated territory allegedly began. According to the SOE, Gorenjska remained 'more heavily garrisoned' by police and SS 'than any other Slovenian district.'[56] Normal German practice was to burn the houses where arms and ammunition were found. The deportation to concentration camps in Germany of the families and relatives of Partisans and executed hostages continued through 1943 and 1944.[57] Wilkinson reported that 'in the neighbourhood of Škofja Loka in early February 50 hostages were shot for the murder of one German Gestapo official,' describing such reprisals as 'a source of the greatest consternation to the Partisans.' The vulnerability of civilians was acute:

> The normal form is for the Germans to move down the valley, surround a village, shoot any Partizan who has been too idle to take to the hills, burn a

few houses of well-known Partizan sympathizers, requisition and pillage what they can, and then withdraw; perhaps taking a few boys and girls with them to send to forced labour in Germany. During this operation they may or may not be harassed by the local Partizan unit. Unless it is a definite encroachment into what the Partizans consider their safe areas, the chances are the village will be left to its fate.[58]

Yet, not all collective punishment was violent in nature. Some involved the loss of certain civilian privileges, which in the economic uncertainty of war were nonetheless burdensome. For example, in February 1944, the Germans decreed that cigarette coupons and bonuses for children would no longer be given to the inhabitants of several Gorenjska towns where OF activity had been reported, noting that they could 'thank the bandits for these measures.'[59] The lesson was clear in German propaganda, disassociating from the Partisans meant 'No more deportations! Each Gorenjec who fulfils his duties as a German citizen remains secure in his home.'[60]

As in Carinthia, this pervasive fear contributed to limited measurable support for the Liberation Front despite widespread sympathies for it. This was particularly evident in the Partisans' ongoing difficulties with recruitment. The postwar regime view of peasants and workers voluntarily and stoically taking to the forests made great propaganda but obscured the true nature of OF recruitment. As Wilkinson suggested, for many inductees, service with the Partisans was a way to 'evade German conscription or because their houses have been burnt or requisitioned, and they see in service with the Partizans an immediate means of livelihood and a possibility of saving something from the wreck after the war. Others have often been forcibly conscripted by methods reminiscent of the 18th Century Pressgang.' He continued, noting that 'apart from a sprinkling of young boys, they were most of them middle-aged farmers roused from their beds in the middle of the night and forced to fly for their lives – unshaven and frozen from their first night in the open, unarmed, resentful and thoroughly miserable, it seemed impossible they would ever make useful soldiers.'[61]

Unlike Prekmurje, Štajerska, and Carinthia, the Slovenes in Gorenjska did not have to 'choose' only between the foreign occupiers and their ethnic Partisan compatriots. Although the Germans were not ready to countenance the establishment of a White Guard Organization (Weissgardistische Organisation) when times were good, the deterioration of their military fortunes in 1943 and 1944 forced them to take a second look at harnessing a local solution to control the insurgency. The emergence of the Gorenjska Self-Defence made available a non-Communist and, unlike the Wehrmannschaft, a more identifiably Slovene option in the struggle for the hearts and minds of Gorenjska's population, notwithstanding its clearly compromised relationship with the Germans: 'Gorenjci! Decide for yourselves! Do you want to go with the murderers to a certain death and destruction or with a strong and orderly Greater Germany to a brighter future? Help the authorities and the *domobran* [Home Guard] in the destruction and extermination of the communist plague.'[62]

The Germans never followed up with the creation of a Slovene administration in Gorenjska that would, like the Provincial Administration (PU), buttress the Gorenjska Self-Defence and rally anti-Communist support. To do so, would give lie to the German claim that Gorenjska was a part of eternal Germandom. As a result, the opportunities for civilian collaboration in the region remained limited. Indeed, the impetus for the Gorenjska Self-Defence from the Slovene side was spearheaded mostly by a handful of anti-Communist politicians, Provincial Administration members, and Home Guard officers from the Province of Ljubljana. As noted earlier, Slavko Krek arrived in Gorenjska as Rupnik's representative, and despite German restrictions on joint operations between the Home Guard and the Gorenjska Self-Defence, the Home Guard continued to see the force as a subsidiary body. The Centre in Kranj remained largely a coordinating body for the Gorenjska Self-Defence. Their one 'outreach' function to the civilian population was the distribution of anti-Communist propaganda, which Krek rightfully described to be 'as important as weaponry, if not more.'[63] The Centre instructed each unit to have a 'good and responsible' propagandist who should have 'moral worthiness, who in his private life is also faultless,' and who would be responsible for spreading 'good Slovene literature.'[64] Indeed, a number of these 'good and responsible' propagandists such as Jože Bernik, who would later be arrested by the Germans for his Anglophilism, were sent to Gorenjska from Ljubljana, where they had been involved in propaganda work with the Home Guard. This appeared to have annoyed at least one Gorenjska Self-Defence unit, which contacted Kociper insisting that propagandists should come from Gorenjska, so that they could relate to the region.[65] Unlike the Province of Ljubljana, where there was considerable cooperation between Home Guard propaganda and the Slovene popular press, the Gestapo's restrictions on Slovene publishing in Gorenjska meant that the Gorenjska Self-Defence's propaganda was mostly an internal operation cut off from wider civilian participation. The Gorenjska Self-Defence was urged to disseminate pieces from the official German propaganda office of Carinthia (Reichspropagandaamt Kärnten); it also produced its own reviews in *Gorenjec*, *Zlatorog*, and *Gorenjsko domobranstvo*, in addition to distributing anti-Communist propaganda and newspapers from the Province of Ljubljana.[66]

Thus, the Gorenjska Self-Defence, whose units made up approximately 3 per cent of Gorenjska's population, remained far more isolated than the Home Guard.[67] In some cases, local inhabitants who sympathized with the Gorenjska Self-Defence would offer their farms, homes, or businesses (particularly taverns) as impromptu headquarters for local garrisons.[68] Such graciousness was risky, though, as the Partisans were known to pre-emptively burn these structures. Civilians in Gorenjska were not completely unresponsive to the Gorenjska Self-Defence's propaganda – the Mengeš and Litija units both reported that locals were enthusiastic about purchasing their newspapers.[69] Sunday mass was used as an opportunity to distribute propaganda, and Gorenjska Self-Defence patrols would gather locals together by singing traditional folk songs and Home Guard hymns, and, with their attention sufficiently secured, deliver short speeches critical of the Liberation Front.[70] However, having begun its campaign late in the final year of the war, the Gorenjska Self-Defence had an uphill battle against a population that had had its fill of German oppression. Partisan counter-propaganda and threats also took their toll, with the Gorenjska Self-Defence strike battalion reporting that forcibly mobilized Partisans preferred to surrender to the Germans because they had been told that the Gorenjska Self-Defence would pluck their eyes out.[71]

In short, even if some Slovenes of Gorenjska were willing to collaborate – and the vast majority were not – they were afforded but limited opportunities to collaborate. The Germans maintained a strong security presence and control over the administration of Gorenjska. This tight leash on Slovene activity was evident in the Gorenjska Self-Defence, where all of its activities including propaganda were under the close supervision of the Gestapo. Unlike the Province of Ljubljana, where the Home Guard and the Provincial Administration had considerable autonomy to engage the masses in the shared struggle against Bolshevism, in Gorenjska the Gorenjska Self-Defence was restricted primarily to its auxiliary military role of combatting the Partisans.

Primorska

The Germans had staked out Gorenjska for absorption into the Third Reich. Primorska, however, at least for the near future, was considered occupied territory to be exploited for the purpose of defending and provisioning the Germans. In the wake of the Italian capitulation, the Germans adopted a more accommodating occupation policy that took into account the ethnic diversity of the region and offered some hope to the Slovenes that the systematic discrimination they had endured for over two decades under Mussolini would end. This repression had forged a degree of political unity among the Slovene minority in Primorska. Yet, it was precisely the Germans' piecemeal national concessions – for example, permitting Slovene mayors in smaller towns and allowing schools to instruct in Slovene – that helped to somewhat fracture this cohesiveness. According to the historian Nevenka Troha, German concessions were politically divisive by appealing to Slovene Centrists who were 'anti-Communist, anti-Italian but waited for the arrival of the Western Allies.'[72] The Centrists did not advocate collaboration. They did, however, promise accommodation in return for a German occupation that refrained from abuse and ethnic discrimination. This attitude was clear in a letter from October 1943 that was written by a priest from Kal nad Kanalom, urging the new occupiers to open Slovene schools, release prisoners, and repair homes. In return, the 'people will become absolutely loyal to the German authorities, more than just loyal, they will be thankful for German order, which helped in its most difficult hour of national history and gave back freedom of language.'[73] Over and above the obvious willingness to accommodate, the patriotism of the request, tempered by twenty years of Italian oppression, is striking.

The German sponsorship of the Slovene National Security Corps (SNVZ), however, alienated a number of Centrists and forced many to side with the Liberation Front rather than risk fratricidal conflict. The experience of Engelbert Besednjak is instructive. A member of the so-called Centrists of Gorizia, Besednjak was a lawyer by training and had been involved in minority rights throughout the interwar era. A conciliatory Christian Socialist, he had served in the Italian parliament and had advised the Belgrade government on Yugoslav minority issues in Italy. Although uncomfortable with the Liberation Front, his position changed when the Germans demanded that Slovenes pacify the resistance in Primorska: 'They wanted that our people join with the Home Guard, for us to fight with them [. . .] The bloody battles between the National Liberation Army and the Home Guard became unbearable [. . .] For us their remained nothing else other than placing ourselves without hesitation squarely on the side of our *primorski* men and boys, who defended themselves against the Hitlerite – Home Guard attack from Kranjska, that is to say, without delay to join in the national liberation movement.'[74]

Besednjak's opinion that the Province of Ljubljana (Kranjska) had exported both collaboration and the civil war to Primorska was widely held and certainly not erroneous. Even more than the Gorenjska Self-Defence, the Slovene National Security Corps (SNVZ) was initially staffed primarily by Home Guardsmen and recruits from Ljubljana. Only in the summer of 1944 was the SNVZ made up of a majority of *primorci* (inhabitants of Primorska).[75] Anti-Communist rallies in Primorska were organized in part by officials from the Province of Ljubljana. For example, Kociper was the keynote speaker at a 'manifestation against Communism and its Stalinist, Titoist, Badoglioist, and plutocratic pact,' held on 8 June 1944 in Postojna, which celebrated the reopening of its famous nearby caves that had been damaged after the Partisans set fire to German fuel stored inside.[76]

Most Slovenes in Primorska, as in Gorenjska, refused to actively assist the anti-Partisan cause. An OSS assessment from 31 May 1944 highlighted this fact: 'In Slovenia more people are against him [Tito] then for him. In Slovene Italy, most are for Tito.'[77] Partisan policies certainly dissuaded collaboration, as entire families were often held collectively responsible for treason, although, as Mlakar noted, this punishment usually took the form of property confiscation.[78] Similarly, women who extended their amorous attentions to the occupiers had their heads shorn – a humiliating practice that has received much scholarly attention in France but that was evidently also practised by the Slovene Partisans.[79]

This reluctance to collaborate was not simply the product of the stick. The OF's promise of national liberation appealed to the long-oppressed Slovene minority of Italy. It even attracted some members of the Catholic clergy, potentially the most suspicious of the Liberation Front. Among the most responsive was Father Anton Bajt, who joined the OF's provincial committee in Primorska, in September 1943, and urged clergy to cooperate with the Partisans.[80] In contrast, the priesthood in Gorizia, a Catholic Slovene stronghold, adhered to Pius XI's verdict that Communism and Catholicism were incompatible and to the prohibition against cooperating with the Liberation Front announced by the archbishop of Gorizia Carlo Margotti.[81] Archbishop Margotti received Colonel Kokalj and offered him his blessings. A few priests assisted the SNVZ by delivering anti-Partisan sermons.[82]

The existence of a relatively autonomous Slovene administration in the Province of Ljubljana did not extend to Primorska, nor was there a significant 'trade- and industry-oriented middle class' among the mostly rural Slovenes there, which, according to the historian Gianmarco Bresadola, 'could have seen Nazi Germany as an advantageous trading partner justifying collaboration.'[83] Some Slovene officials were promoted into responsible positions; however, they remained under close German supervision or, in some cases, were scrutinized by a residual Italian Fascist administration. In Trieste, under the control of the Fascist Italian Prefect Bruno Coceanu, very few anti-Slavic measures were repealed, despite the efforts of Kokalj, who met with Coceanu in April 1944.[84] Indeed, the Germans' continued reliance on Italian officials in many areas of Primorska undermined Slovene trust in the Germans and, by extension, the SNVZ. In January 1944, the SNVZ in Postojna complained that its inability to attract recruits was due to the presence of an Italian mayor, Italian bureaucrats, and a Fascist militia in the town, which was often seen mingling in public with German troops. The SNVZ were, thus, seen as tools of the hated Italians.[85] The SNVZ's attempt to have the Italian mayor replaced with one of its officers ended in failure, further eroding its credibility.

The Slovene National Security Corps tried hard to cloak itself in the revered mantle of Slovene nationalism, particularly with its pervasive anti-Italian propaganda. Commemorating the one-year anniversary of the SNVZ, Staff Sergeant Franc Kervin lionized Kokalj for his brave decision to go into the countryside, 'where for a quarter century Slovenian brothers were enslaved under a foreign hell' and for having 'planted the Slovene flag on Primorska soil.'[86] Perhaps most surprising was how candidly Major Ferenčak described the organization's irredentist and nationalist objectives. In an address issued to all SNVZ units, on 4 July 1944, he wrote:

> Our present organization is, of course, primarily military. However, beyond this, our organization also has its cultural mission among the local Slovene population, above all it is the duty of each member of our organization to assist the national consciousness of our people, a consciousness, which in the last years under heavy pressure has fallen into slumber, which we have to rouse, that it will not fall asleep forever. The duty of

each of our soldiers is, therefore, that he firmly be conscious that he is in the first sense a Slovene [...] all over our beautiful Primorska soil the Slovenes are in the greatest majority, that is, without any admixture of foreigners, and only in Trst is there a non-indigenous minority, which is strong enough, that we can place great hope in it.[87]

The Slovene National Security Corps attacked Tito's forces for their cooperation with the Italian 'Garibaldi' Partisan brigades and their talk of Slovene-Italian brotherhood. In a pamphlet entitled 'New Evidence of How the OF Wants to "Liberate Us,"' the SNVZ ridiculed OF 'patriotism':

Who does not remember the many atrocities, which were committed against our nation by the Badoglian *makaronarji* [derogatory term for Italians]? Who does not know, how all of a sudden overnight the oppressors of our nation's blood became 'liberators' – and this only by having pinned on a red star? Our Slovene men and women have not forgotten the names: Rab, Gonars, Renicci, Padova, Ustica, and many others, where the Savoy devil repressed our strength. They know very well, that from the Savoys, nothing good can come – be this under this or that flag or sign. But someone did forget! Someone spit on their own national pride and our honour![88]

These themes and others were disseminated in a number of SNVZ publications. The most professional was *Straža ob Jadranu* (Watch along the Adriatic), issued in Postojna, along with *Glas izpod Krna* (The Voice below Krn Mountain), *Tolminski glas* (The Voice of Tolmin), and *Vipavec*, the publication of the Vipava valley, published in Ajdovščina. The Germans also provided SNVZ propagandists with a half-hour slot every other day on Radio Trieste.[89]

It is difficult to judge how effective SNVZ propaganda was in swaying *primorci* from their overall sympathetic attitude towards the Liberation Front. There were pockets of support for the Slovene National Security Corps: the Dolomite region and the area surrounding Idrija was considered pro-SNVZ, but allegiances in the Vipava valley and its centre of Ajdovščina fluctuated.[90] A patchwork pattern of local support extended into the Soča valley, where the SNVZ could claim the loyalty of the clergy in Kobarid, yet, less than twenty kilometres upriver in Bovec, it concluded that the 'priesthood is [...] against us and is very active for the Partisans.'[91] Boris Mlakar has cautioned that support for the SNVZ did not mean 'explicit enthusiasm' for them, but often passive resistance to the politics and practices of the Liberation Front, 'the reasons' for which 'were usually entirely local.'[92] Indeed, the nature of guerilla warfare, as in other regions of Slovenia and occupied Europe, could alienate the local inhabitants, particularly if they bore the brunt of reprisals, as they did in the village of Strmec where sixteen male inhabitants were executed and the village destroyed, in the fall of 1943, after local Partisans had killed a German officer. For much of 1944, an unofficial modus vivendi generally limited the Germans to the major towns, railways, and roads, while the Liberation Front held sway in the forested and mountainous hinterlands.[93] However, the Partisans did not look charitably upon civilians facilitating German incursions into their areas of control. For example, the SNVZ reported that the Liberation Front had taken the livestock and burned the house in the village of Mirna where the Germans had billeted some two days earlier.[94] Switching roles, in the village of Dolenja vas, the Germans executed six civilians and torched the local tavern after Partisans were spotted.[95] It is hardly surprising, then, that the inhabitants of Dornberk pleaded with the Partisans, in May 1944, not to attack the Germans.[96] In the village of Landol, outside of mostly pro-Partisan Postojna, an SNVZ report from February 1945 alleged that people are 'full up to their throats with the Partisans and tell the SNVZ their numbers and where they are hiding.'[97] Overall, however, even SNVZ sources admitted that numerous parts of Primorska were solidly behind the Liberation Front, as in the Pivka valley, which was described in one report as 'hermetically sealed by the Partisans.'[98]

The SNVZ was never more than a sideshow in the overall security apparatus of the Operation Zone Adriatic Littoral. There were, however, some spin-offs in the equipping and servicing of the SNVZ that involved some local cooperation, such as in the case of the Postojna ironware company, which provided kitchen supplies to the officers' mess, in November 1944.[99] A far greater demand for Slovene labour and skills was required in the building of fortifications in the OZAK to prevent the Allies from penetrating into Austria. At their height in the summer of 1944, some hundred and twenty thousand labourers of various nationalities were used to construct these installations, which were concentrated along the Soča and further south along the Čičarija range in northern Istria.[100] This mobilization, as elsewhere during the sunset of Nazi military might, cannot be seen as collaboration. Indeed, Rainer demanded compulsory mobilization of the OZAK's population into labour units, although those that joined the Slovene National Security Corps were spared this obligation.[101] Most *primorci* wisely refused Rainer's 'gracious' offer. Some, like the captured forcibly mobilized Partisan Marjan Zaro, in fact, requested to be allowed to 'work in Germany' rather than return home 'because the Partisans would again mobilize' him.[102] The exactions that five years of war had wrought upon Primorska's population were evident in an SNVZ report from January 1944, which described villages bereft of their male population, where only some 20 to 30 per cent of men aged eighteen to forty years remained.[103] The others had either been captured by the Allies in Italian uniform or had been mobilized by the Partisans and Germans. In comparison, the Slovene National Security Corps and open collaboration could only claim a tiny fraction of Primorska's human capital.

The Province of Ljubljana

The Province of Ljubljana was identified as a unique environment in the first phase of the occupation of Slovenia that ended in September 1943. The Italians' initial relatively lenient and haphazard occupation incubated the fledgling Liberation Front, just as the shift to a more draconian military response in 1942 assisted in the rise of the anti-Partisan units. The Province of Ljubljana's distinction as the epicentre of the Slovene civil war and collaboration held fast in the period after September 1943. Unlike the other regions surveyed so far, only in the Province of Ljubljana was there a structure for civilian collaboration that was both sanctioned by the Germans and, to a certain extent, supported by Slovenes. In other words, Slovenes were given the most opportunities to collaborate in the Province of Ljubljana, and more Slovenes than anywhere else seized these opportunities.

The Provincial Administration (PU) was the only allowable and identifiably Slovene bureaucracy during the occupation. Too small and weak to be a 'true' puppet state such as Slovakia or the Independent State of Croatia, the Provincial Administration perhaps most closely resembled the Czech administration in the Protectorate of Bohemia and Moravia, although with far more truncated areas of responsibility. Indeed, the Provincial Administration's authority only extended as far as those towns and surrounding rural environs that were garrisoned by either the Germans or the Home Guard. As Wilkinson made clear, in his April 1944 report, these were few indeed: 'In Notransko [sic] and Dolenjsko apart from the main railways and a few hedgehogs such as

Novo Mesto and Kocevje [sic] there are no permanent German garrisons.'[104]

The Provincial Administration encompassed a number of departments that serviced rather mundane daily needs of Slovenes in the province, many of which would appear to have had little to do with the Germans or collaboration. The Provincial Administration helped organize athletic events, social clubs, and cultural events. It played an important role in the restoration of the education system to something that neared its pre-war format by purging it of its Italian influence. However, the ideological agenda of education was evident in the increased prominence of German language instruction and anti-Communist lectures.[105] Similarly, despite the seemingly innocuous mandate of the Department for Social Politics and National Health – it was in charge of health care in the province – the Germans were known to interfere in its workings. Gauleiter Rainer, for example, demanded that doctors and pharmacists report the details of any injured Partisan to the nearest police command. The fact that Dr Hubad, the chief of the PU's Department of Internal Affairs, had to 'repeatedly warn' the province's medical association, in October 1944, to adhere to these stipulations suggests that the order was being ignored, and this despite Hubad's threat that 'every doctor and every pharmacist who will waive declaring these injuries will be strictly penalized by the authorities.'[106]

The Provincial Administration was partially responsible for assisting displaced Slovenes in the province. The first wave of refugees in 1941 and 1942 had fled German oppression in neighbouring Gorenjska and Štajerska. Already before the Italian capitulation, an increasing number were internally displaced within the province, seeking refuge from fighting associated with the Partisan insurgency or exiled from OF-held liberated territory. Responsibility for their welfare was divided between the PU's Peasant Office and charities associated with the Catholic Church. The demands of the refugees were often quite basic. In April 1944, the Committee for Suha Krajina Refugees petitioned Leon Rupnik for food, drinking water, and milk-bearing animals.[107] Housing was urgently required.[108] The PU's Novo Mesto office complained of being overwhelmed by the need to feed and house fifteen hundred anti-Communist refugees, in October 1944.[109]

Thus, in the midst of a difficult occupation, the Provincial Administration provided a Slovene body of appeal where solutions to a plethora of difficult and even commonplace grievances could be sought. That the Provincial Administration was seen as an intermediary between the occupied and the occupiers was evident in the numerous requests and intercessions that were addressed to President Rupnik or, as he was occasionally referred to, 'our protector.' For example, a number of Home Guardsmen asked Rupnik for assistance in having a university semester recognized despite their absence.[110] The villagers of Devica Marija v Polju requested Rupnik to restore access to their pastures and forests which had been cut off by the frontier between the Province of Ljubljana and Štajerska.[111] Others urged the Provincial Administration to mollify German demands, as in the letter from an inhabitant from Šentjernej who, in November 1943, pleaded that Rupnik save innocent lives and property by persuading the Germans to employ a trusted local translator.[112] The success of many of these requests remains unclear.

Yet, despite some genuine administrative initiative and its Slovene veneer, the Provincial Administration was clearly dependent on the occupier. The Germans controlled the issuance of travel passes that allowed PU officials to move about the province. The staging of PU – sponsored cultural events and commemorations, including a mass scheduled for October 1943 in remembrance of the victims of the First World War, required German clearance. Similarly, when a PU minister attempted to organize a military cinema for the Home Guard, he was told by the managers of the three largest cinemas in Ljubljana to contact Hans Breiner, head of the Reich Film Board in Trieste, as they carried out their duties 'only according to his orders.'[113]

Administering hospitals, schools, and social assistance was hardly objectionable and, in fact, was part of the occupier's obligation 'to restore, and ensure, as far as possible, public order and safety, while respecting, unless absolutely prevented, the laws in force in the country,' as stipulated by Article 43 of the 1907 Hague Convention.[114] Far less certain were the unnecessary steps taken by a number of PU officials and departments to ingratiate themselves with and assist the Nazis' wider war aims. This was most evident in the work of the PU's Information Office (Informativni urad, IU). The Information Office was established in October 1943, and despite a number of organizational changes, it would remain the PU's central office for intelligence and anti-Communist propaganda. Information Office intelligence, and the IU's ever-closer relationship with the Slovene Legion's Secret Intelligence Service (TOS) network, sought to establish the political convictions of Slovenes in the province, as well as the number and distribution of Partisans and their sympathizers. To assist them, the Information Office established, in 1944, the Nationality Report (Narodnostni referat, NR) to act as district branch offices in Novo Mesto, Kočevje, Logatec, Črnomelj, and the suburbs of Ljubljana. The Nationality Report compiled detailed card indexes of the political sensibilities of individual Slovenes; for example, the Logatec NR characterized suspicious individuals with the following three abbreviations: CPS – communist party member; OF – active member of the Liberation Front; or SOF – sympathizer of the Liberation Front.[115] Lists were also created of OF sympathizers working within Provincial Administration branches, including the post office, tax office, and the railway system.[116] The intimate details of these reports, although disconcerting, are not entirely unexpected. The population of the province was small and mostly distributed in villages and market towns where everyone knew each other's business. This familiarity was clear, for example, in the NR's description of Julka Taborski from Zalog: 'Sister of a political commissar, one of the worst *terencev* [literally translated as 'one in the field'] who already has several murders on his conscience. In the forest she has four brothers, all volunteers. People say that she does not deserve to live.'[117] Beyond identifying OF members and sympathizers, the Nationality Report provided summaries of local Partisan movements, the morale of the population, and their relations with the Home Guard. Intelligence was also exchanged with the Police Corps and the Home Guard, with whom the Provincial Administration worked in close cooperation.

The Provincial Administration's identification of OF members and their supporters assisted the Germans and the Home Guard in their dismantling of the insurgency. The Provincial Administration was intimately involved in the expulsion of 'untrustworthy' citizens. For example, on 14 June 1944, the PU district office in Novo Mesto recommended that fifty-nine OF sympathizers be exiled from Novo Mesto to Partisan regions. This was allegedly in retaliation for thirteen families that had been recently expelled to Novo Mesto by the Liberation Front.[118] Rupnik endorsed this suggestion, on 1 July 1944, but added that simple exile did not solve the problem; instead, he recommended that they be imprisoned.[119] In the end, ten allegedly pro-OF families were exiled from Novo Mesto, on 21 July, and their property seized to help provide for anti-Communist refugees.[120] This would not be the first time Rupnik recommended the arrest of Slovenes.[121]

The PU's Propaganda Department, which became a separate entity from the Information Office, in November 1943, and its German advisers worked energetically to convince inhabitants of the Province of Ljubljana that the Osvobodilna fronta were not national liberators but rather in the service of international Communism and the Jewish world conspiracy. The Partisans were portrayed as cowards, who lived in largesse by preying on the hard-working devout peasant population and as atheistic, sexual deviants who dishonoured chaste Slovene women and corrupted naïve youth. Headed initially by Ludovik Puš, the Propaganda Department had sections devoted to print, culture, radio, and film. Aside from the ubiquitous leaflets and pamphlets, a number of anti-Communist books were also published including the *Črna bukva*, which was a compendium of OF crimes, their victims, and the settlements and cultural institutions that it had destroyed, that was distributed among anti-Partisan forces and the general population. Beginning in November 1943, the Germans made radio time available to PU propagandists, albeit censored by the German News Service.[122] Radio Ljubljana's daily schedule heavily favoured German newscasts, but there was also a mixed Slovene program of music, literature readings, and dramatic series.[123] There were only two weekly half-hour propaganda broadcasts aired called the 'Slovenian People's Broadcast.'[124] Nevertheless, despite this limited exposure, the PU's Propaganda Department delivered a total of sixty-six broadcasts by 30 April 1944, including the Home Guard procession that followed the April oath-taking ceremony.[125]

One of the Provincial Administration's more sensationalist attempts at spreading anti-OF ideals was the anti-Communist manifesto campaign. Drawn up on 23 December 1943, inhabitants of the Province of Ljubljana – prominent civil servants, intellectuals, and 'nationally conscious sons of Slovene mothers of all classes of our nation' – were encouraged to sign the petition that described the anti-Communist movement in highly patriotic terms: 'Our fight is a Slovene fight, for our Slovene soil and for our Slovene ideals.'[126] The Information Office's special actions branch, which was in charge of the campaign, claimed success, as 40,131 individuals had signed the memorandum.[127] The staging of large anti-Communist gatherings was another attempt, like the petition, to mobilize the masses behind the Provincial Administration. At these assemblies, prominent anti-Communist speakers like Stanko Kociper would denounce the Liberation Front, and anti-Partisan literature would be distributed. The largest such assembly was held in the city of Ljubljana on 29 June 1944, although PU bureaucrats were obliged to attend. Others were held in the smaller centres of the province – in Vrhnika in April 1944, in Borovnica, Ježica, and Grosuplje in May, and in Rovte in August.

Professional PU propagandists also targeted the province's workers, civil servants, students, and peasants with more specific anti-Communist and pro-German campaigns. Lectures for workers were organized by Maks Jan, and from December 1943 to the middle of 1944, 911 lectures were delivered before an audience of 147,400 industrial workers, thirty-three lectures to 21,600 craftsmen and tradesmen, and seventy-seven lectures in 'continuing education' classes.[128] Many of these lectures were presented in the factories and would bear such titles as 'Working Conditions in the USSR,' 'Working Conditions in Germany,' and 'Jews – Carriers of the Capitalist Crime.'[129] Larger public 'anti-Communist workers' gatherings were also held. One, on 30 May 1944, was attended by Rupnik and twenty-five hundred workers.[130] Lectures targeting the peasantry and bearing titles such as 'War against All that Is Ungodly' and 'The Organization of the Peasantry in Germany' began in December 1943. Regular anti-Communist 'lessons' in schools were offered as early as November 1943. By April 1944, the PU's Propaganda Department estimated that it had delivered lectures to some 11,200 students in forty-eight institutions.[131] Particular focus was directed at high school students who, because of their rebellious age, were believed to be drawn towards the Liberation Front.

The Provincial Administration assisted the Germans by helping them mobilize the province's economic and human resources. Some aid appeared rather inconsequential – in February 1944, the Provincial Administration requested the municipality of Šmihel-Stopiče to provide three good wagons and the necessary number of horses for the German forces.[132] Other assistance was far more ambitious. To prevent Tito's forces from attacking Ljubljana from the south, the Provincial Administration was called on, in October 1944, to provide Organisation Todt 'Krain' with the labour required to build defensive works in Dolenjska and Notranjska. Rupnik dutifully responded, calling on all Slovenes regardless of class or sex to help defeat 'the Bolsheviks and their allies' by volunteering for the National Pioneers (Narodni Pionirji).[133] Rupnik and his officials were evidently aware that patriotism alone – particularly one that acted against the Partisans – would motivate few to enlist in this labour unit. As a result, they also promised volunteers financial incentives such as 'family assistance,' room and board, and weekly prizes of food or tobacco that they could 'send to their loved ones.' Armed units would provide security for work duties. In the end, most 'volunteers' were sent to projects near Ribnica and Postojna, as the insurgency hampered construction in most other areas of the province.[134]

In summary, the Provincial Administration certainly provided necessary and uncontroversial services to the beleaguered inhabitants of the Province of Ljubljana; nevertheless, it also went above and beyond this mandate by informing on its own citizens, promoting hatred of the Liberation Front and allegiance to Nazi Germany, and assisting in the exploitation of Slovene labour. Collectively, these actions lifted some of the burden of occupation off the shoulders of the Germans.

The Provincial Administration was staffed by a diverse group of former Yugoslav bureaucrats and officials, as well as inexperienced, youthful, and opportunistic Slovenes from the political right. Topping this administrative edifice was President Leon Rupnik. His supporters, as well as Rupnik himself, interpreted his role in a fashion similar to the 'old soldier' Pétain or the plodding Hácha – a selfless martyr who swallowed his pride and took on the thankless task of shielding his unlucky nation from the full impact of the occupation. Rupnik claimed that his family 'lived humbly, without luxury and well below the so-called average bourgeois standard.'[135] The use of sweet words and compliments to the occupiers were degrading to him, and yet for his nation 'that was stuck between communist horrors and the occupiers' repression, he would "eat excrement."'[136] The remaining pre-war political establishment largely avoided public fraternization with Rupnik; after all, Rupnik was seen, and not only by the Partisans, as a German puppet. Nevertheless, a number of his critics retained their employment within the Provincial Administration. Ladislav Bevc, for example, remained a senior engineering counsellor for the Provincial Administration with a monthly salary of 4,000 lire – considered a well-paid amount – at the same time that he was head of the Sokol War Council and in communication with the Yugoslav Army in the Homeland.[137] Rupnik, Kociper, and other prominent collaborators criticized this duplicity, denouncing such individuals as political 'speculators' who avoided standing firm with the Provincial Administration, Home Guard, and the occupiers for 'sectarian' calculations.[138] Rupnik maintained that, of all the pre-war politicians, he only knew the former governor (*ban*) of Drava Province and head of the National Council (NS) Marko Natlačen well and had a less than flattering view of the rest.[139] Rupnik's supporters lifted him above the political fray. Ignacij Hren observed that Rupnik 'did not understand political games.' Stanko Kociper praised his father-in-law's ability 'to fight and also how to take defeat,' adding that 'he did not know how to shove a knife in the back. He was not a politician! At least in this meaning he was not. He was a soldier, only a soldier!'[140]

Why Leon Rupnik remained loyal to the Germans until the end is open to speculation. The numerous requests Rupnik received from Slovenes urging him to intercede among the occupiers on their behalf appeared only to have reaffirmed his responsibility to collaborate. He wrote that 'countless people, emissaries, deputations from the city and the countryside, further large numbers of refugees and even politicians (Stare, Šmajd), all were beseeching, that I do something and as an old soldier I was not able to leave, rather I accepted all responsibility.'[141] Rupnik also had an exaggerated impression of German military strength. His suggestion of a Home Guard force, in September 1943, was predicated on the calculation 'that the war will continue for at least five more years, five to six years and in this time, using the excuse of an armed uprising, the occupier can exterminate [us] all.'[142] Rupnik, like collaborators throughout occupied Europe, also had an inflated view of the effectiveness of collaboration in winning concessions for the Slovenes of the Province of Ljubljana. He took comfort in Gauleiter Rainer's comments to him, after the Italian capitulation, that 'the wrongdoings done to your nation in 1941 will never again be repeated; instead, everything will be done that your nation will be able to further develop its individual originality.'[143] Rainer promised that Slovene refugees who had fled to the province to escape German oppression in Gorenjska and Štajerska in 1941 would not be hounded now that the Germans were in control and that Slovenes imprisoned in Italy could return home. His negotiations with the Germans in Klagenfurt, in September 1943, secured advantages for the province, which in Kociper's view appeared hopeful, especially in comparison with the Poles and even the Czechs – enhanced administrative autonomy, Slovene schools, exemption from German military service, and a hand in domestic security.[144] Rupnik believed that he had dissuaded the Germans from transforming the Home Guards into an SS division with his indignant response to Rösener: 'This you will not do because the entire nation would rise up against this and enter the forest. If in 1941 you had dealt with us properly and with kindness, you would today have had from us a complete elite corps.'[145]

Yet, if we pare away the apologetics of his supporters, there is the glaring reality that during his tenure as president of the Provincial Administration and inspector-general of the Home Guard the civil war intensified, the Germans were relieved of some of the burdens of providing 'security,' and the exploitation of the province's economic and human resources was accelerated. Rupnik was a politically ambitious creature, despite his professions to the contrary. The topsy-turvy world of a military occupation offered avenues to power for a discredited military general and his cohort of right-wing supporters, as well as the alluring prospect of refashioning what many of them saw as the decrepit and sterile world of interwar Yugoslav politics.

As Škerbec affirmed in his memoir, Rupnik surrounded himself with 'young people, with students, with young intellectuals, and with politically unripe people. We referred to them as the "Kindergarten."'[146] It attracted members of the Catholic right wing, including young *stražarji* (members of the Academic Club Straža) and *mladci* (Mladci Kristusa Kralja), as well as the Slovene members of Ljotić's pro-fascist movement. However, it was not a monolithic throng. The Catholic right, which included Kociper and Puš, attempted primarily to use the Germans to defend 'Christian Slovenia' against the Communist threat.[147] For example, Kociper claimed in his unapologetic memoir that it was not the Germans who exploited the Slovenes, rather it was the Slovenes who were too weak on their own against the Liberation Front who took advantage of German assistance.[148] He also claimed that it was his strident advocacy of Slovene nationalism that caused the Germans to reduce his influence in Home Guard propaganda in the middle of 1944. Nevertheless, beyond his anti-Communism and nationalism, Kociper and his companions sympathized with certain Nazi precepts including antisemitism, which was prominent in their wartime propaganda and in their less than charitable impression of the Jews after the Second World War, as well as the hoped-for creation of a vigorous, nationally conscious, new Slovene man that would rise above bickering sectarianism.[149] Indeed, Home Guardsman Milko Vizjak maintained that Kociper had an inordinate and negative influence on his pliable father-in-law, pushing him further to the right, not least by drafting many of his speeches.[150]

The Slovene Ljotićists Ljenko Urbančič, Izidor Cergol, Boris Smerdu, and others, like their Serb counterparts who became trusted German auxiliaries and policemen, unabashedly espoused the genius of National Socialism and maintained a very close relationship with the Gestapo.[151] They were 'probably the only Slovene political group that was also ideologically similar to national socialism, and also modelled on them.'[152] As the Germans grew increasingly suspicious of the loyalty of their Slovene auxiliaries, in 1944, and sporadically purged and arrested some, Slovene Ljotićists acquired more influence. For example, Cergol, who before the war was a Zbor activist in Celje, was elevated to head the PU's Propaganda Department, in late 1944, a platform from which he was able to spew his pro-Nazi and antisemitic vitriol, agitate for the national-socialist reorganization of Slovenia, and denounce the old political elite for their pathetic Anglophilism.[153] Like other European fascists, the Slovene Ljotićists attempted to forge a militant cult of personality around Rupnik and the Home Guard.[154] In a speech, on 30 January 1945, Cergol declared: 'The only true path is the path of General Rupnik and the Slovene *domobranstvo* [Home Guard] [. . .] Together with the German nation we have to fight against Bolshevism, which deceives Europe and the whole world.'[155]

Much less clear were the ideological and political views of mid- and lower-level PU bureaucrats. Some were career civil servants who may have been happy simply to hold employment, unlike their less fortunate colleagues in other regions of occupied Slovenia. Others, like Bevc, were far more political and still very much aligned with the pre-war elite on whose watch they had been hired. Indeed, as Mazower noted, 'the continuity of the state through the most violent ideological upheavals is one of the major unwritten themes of modern European history, and nowhere else was this more evident than during the Second World War.'[156] Far from being a well-oiled machine, and bureaucracies even in peacetime seldom are, the Provincial Administration was punctuated by laxness, disorganization, and at times a lack of enthusiasm for the anti-Communist struggle that was a job requirement. Indeed, OF members and sympathizers infiltrated the PU's ranks.[157] Rupnik needed to remind his bureaucrats to be tactful, sensitive, and gracious to anti-Communist refugees, rather than merely 'dull bureaucrats.'[158] Cergol circulated a letter to all branches of the Provincial Administration, in March 1945, chastising their selfish lack of ideological commitment and their administrative slovenliness. He demanded that officials look less at the clock and ensure that their duties were completed before going home.[159]

Avoiding the fawning idolization of Nazism exhibited by the more extreme members of Rupnik's circle, the Catholic Church in the Province of Ljubljana, nonetheless, remained unequivocal as to which side it supported in the civil war. After the German takeover of the province, Bishop Rožman did not sway from what he saw as the 'incompatibility of Christian doctrine with communist principles.'[160] On 30 November 1943, he issued his pastoral letter *O nevarnosti brezbožnega komunizma* (Of the Dangers of Godless Communism), in which he accused the Communists of attempting to seize power through a bloody revolution. For its part, the Liberation Front made little secret of its aim to reduce the Church's influence in a postwar Slovenia. In February 1944, the Liberation Front struck the first Commission for Religious Affairs in Yugoslavia, led by Father Metod Mikuž and a handful of pro-Partisan priests. Its goal was a separation of Church and state in Slovenia and the ending of the Church's practice of twinning religiosity with nationality – the view, shared by Bishop Rožman, that 'a non-Catholic could not be a good Slovene.'[161] However, in placing much of the blame for Slovenia's suffering on the shoulders of the Liberation Front, Rožman also refrained from publicly condemning the Germans for their role in the bloodshed. Moreover, as we have seen, Rožman's hard-line position was somewhat out of step with other occupied areas of Slovenia, where the priesthood remained far more neutral, if not supportive of the Partisan resistance.

Bishop Rožman's support for the Home Guard was patently evident in his 1944 'Christmas Letter to the Slovene Home Guard': 'You, Slovene Home Guard, are on guard to protect and defend not only the flock, that is the wealth of the Slovene nation, but also its life and the health of proper thinking, the holy and bright tradition, which we have received from our ancestors and which to each good Slovene is sacred and worthy of respect, [and also] faith in God, who sent his Son as the Saviour also to our nation.'[162] Rožman's appearance at both the April 1944 and January 1945 Home Guard oaths, which SS-Obergruppenführer Rösener claimed he participated in so 'that the Slovene nation would see him and that he would show his consent with German politics,' was taken as a sign of where the bishop stood in the conflict.[163] Equally compromising was Rožman's decision to allow military chaplains to serve within the ranks of the Home Guard, as he had also done with the Village Guards. In Rožman's view, this was not unusual, as attaching military chaplains to armed forces was standard practice in a number of countries and he, too, gave permission to Father Ilc to act as spiritual vicar in liberated areas. Rožman insisted that the principle duty of the military chaplains was 'spiritual shepherding [dušno pastirstvo], never [engaging] in military affairs.'[164] According to the 'Instructions on the Spiritual Care of the Home Guard,' issued in December 1943, by Rožman's office and signed by members of the Committee for the Social-Moral Renewal of Slovenia, which included among others Deacon Karel Škulj and Chief of the Police Corps Lovro Hacin, military chaplains were to keep the Home Guard occupied by offering daily religious instructions, holding regular masses, and administering the sacraments. The chaplains were to remain independent of the military leaders and ensure that people were not killed without reason, only those 'who really deserve death,' and that the condemned still had the opportunity to receive the sacraments, as did the wounded and dying on the battlefield.[165] The chaplains' pursuit of this fine and difficult balance of being ideologically opposed to the Liberation Front, while at the same time limiting the 'excesses' that were, in part, a product of this very opposition, was difficult. Bishop Rožman admitted as much, agreeing that there were 'bad' military chaplains that disregarded his orders to guard against excesses and crimes.[166] Vizjak told a different story at his trial, claiming that clerics did far more than simple spiritual shepherding and that they were involved in propaganda work and recruitment for the Home Guard.[167] In his response to his trial in absentia, Bishop Rožman denied playing any organizational or recruitment role for the Home Guard.[168] Nevertheless, Rožman's orders from January 1944 do suggest an organizational role for the chaplains, as they were to 'lift the morale and discipline of the men' and to maintain contact between Home Guard organizational headquarters and the bishop's ordinariat.[169]

Rožman justified his relationship with the Germans, as he did his relationship with the Italians, as an unavoidable necessity if the Church was to continue its independent existence and activity. Rožman's contacts allowed him to attempt intercessions on behalf of Slovenes and priests who had run afoul of the Germans. Indeed, SS-Obergruppenführer Rösener recalled the bishop requesting his intervention on behalf of two elderly imprisoned priests.[170] In all likelihood the two were Leopold Čampa and Franc Šiška, who Rösener felt were too sympathetic towards the Partisans.[171] Former member of both the Village Guards and the Home Guard Rudolf Hirschegger claimed that Rožman's resistance went even further, alleging that the bishop told him to protect the Allied airmen he was hiding 'like the greatest treasure.'[172] According to Ladislav Bevc, Rožman had shared situational circulars from the Yugoslav Army in the Homeland with him (he was a member of its organizational division), which the bishop had received from the Vatican.[173] As for his ideological opposition to the Liberation Front – a position that he emphasized was distinct from the actual armed defence against Communism and in which he played no role – Rožman made no apologies. He reiterated his stance that the vast majority of Slovenes were deeply religious and saw in Communism a great and justifiable danger. It was his priestly duty to wage ideological battle against it.[174]

Often as powerful as ideological motivations for collaboration were economic incentives. The Province of Ljubljana largely escaped the wholesale expropriation of Slovene-owned businesses that occurred in Gorenjska and Štajerska, in 1941 and 1942, where the disproportionately influential ethnic German merchants and industrialists were the main beneficiaries of the German occupation.[175] Not surprisingly, a number of Slovene companies and enterprises did business with the Germans and the Provincial Administration, including leather and construction firms, shoemakers, cabinet makers, glass workers, butchers, and Pivovarna Union (Union Brewery), among others.[176] Some, like Pavel Vrtačnik's company in Ljubljana, which made uniforms for the Slovene National Security Corps, assisted Slovene anti-Partisan units.[177] Property owners in Ljubljana also 'offered' room and board to German officers stationed there. Such activity did not escape the attention of OF agents, who dutifully recorded the landlords' names for future use.[178] Nevertheless, in drawing up lists of economic collaborators, the Partisans attempted to differentiate between active and coerced business dealings: 'It must be distinguished, who from their own inclination seeks and asks for orders directly from the Germans, or from the Technical Branch of the Provincial Administration, [or has] relations with the city chieftaincy [*mestno poglavarstvu*], which performs work for the army and the authorities – [and] who is forced [to do such work] [. . .] by the manner of his production.'[179] Slovenes took part in the province's active black market economy, particularly in the smuggling of cigarettes. The black market did not, as Davies has noted, *'have to* involve "collaboration"' – it could assist resisters as much as the occupiers – 'often they did go hand in hand.'[180]

On a much wider level, the economy of the Province of Ljubljana, as in the other regions of occupied Slovenia, continued to function and to assist the German war effort because of the decision – and, perhaps more accurately, the necessity – of tens of thousands of Slovenes to continue working. Trains were able to run because railway workers and engineers reported for duty, and food appeared at market because farmers continued to harvest and sell their produce. In most of these instances, however, collaboration becomes a rather unwieldy designation, as no individual could be denied the right to an income and sustenance just because his or her particular industry benefited the Third Reich, either directly or indirectly. Hundreds of thousands of Czechs, French, and indeed, a number of other occupied Europeans worked in German armament industries virtually until liberation.

The distinction appears to lie, as the Liberation Front noted above, in a somewhat subjective assessment of eagerness in seeking out the business of the occupier.

Just as doing business with the Germans did not necessarily correlate with collaboration, civilian sympathy for the Home Guard did not directly translate into treason. Sympathies for the Home Guard could mean approval of one or more of its defining characteristics, including its overt Catholicism and its supportive stance of traditional and conservative rural autarky. For civilian allegiance to translate into collaboration, evidence of active and measurable support for the Home Guard must be provided. However, even in these situations, support for the Home Guard could be given, as Mlakar noted in relation to the Slovene National Security Corps, for entirely local reasons that were divorced – at least in the civilian's mind – from the Home Guards' relationship with the Germans. In the thick of a civil war – and the rural regions of the Province of Ljubljana was its nucleus – questions about where the Home Guardsman received his weapons, pay, and orders were of far less importance to a peasant than was chasing away the Partisans who occasionally requisitioned food and livestock, billeted in their homes, or endangered their community with their very presence. 'Support,' therefore, could be passive or active, and it could be tactical, temporary and nominal, or committed and enthusiastic.

In addition to these interpretive difficulties, identifying regions of the Province of Ljubljana that supported or were not hostile to the Home Guard is an inexact science at best. No scientific surveys or polls of public sentiment were carried out on the occupied populace of Slovenia. Nevertheless, a number of anecdotal assessments suggest that the civilian population in the Province of Ljubljana, particularly its rural inhabitants, in comparison with other parts of occupied Slovenia, were most supportive of the anti-Partisan units and wary of the Liberation Front. A number of OSS and SOE reports identified Dolenjska and Notranjska, as well as parts of Bela Krajina, as being suspicious of the Liberation Front. In discussing the merits of a public denunciation of Leon Rupnik during Allied radio broadcasts, OSS Morale Operations wrestled with the question of public reactions: 'General Lav [sic] Rupnik, former officer in the Austro-Hungarian army, later colonel in the Yugoslav army, holds the same position in Slovenia as Nedich does in Serbia or Pavelich in Croatia. He is unquestionably a Quisling. A fairly large number of Slovenes, however, look upon him as a patriot who by his collaboration is concerned only with the safety of his people.'[181] OSS operative Major Franklin Lindsay was cautious of Partisan claims to unanimous civilian support: 'The Germans, playing upon the strongly conservative Catholicism of the Slovene population, had expanded the White Guard for the proclaimed purpose of defending the Church and conservative institutions against Communism. In this respect they were quite successful, they had probably recruited a greater number of Slovenes than had the Partisans.'[182] The OSS Fern Mission, which landed in Nadlesk west of Kočevje, reported on 30 August 1944, that 'many of the villages here are White Guard sympathizers and their sons and husbands are fighting with the White Guards on the German side.'[183] George Wuchinich, a second-generation American of Serbian descent who headed the OSS Alum Mission and who was criticized by Lindsay for having discarded all impartiality in his embrace of the Partisan cause, conceded, in August 1944, that the main strength of 'White Guard support' was Suha Krajina and Notranjska.[184] In addition to foreign intelligence operatives, the Partisans, too, admitted that these regions were not the friendliest of terrain. For example, an undated OF analysis concluded that seventeen villages in Suha Krajina were 50 per cent or more against the Partisans, nine villages were considered 50 per cent or more for the Partisans, and six villages were considered neutral.[185]

That the ever-shifting front lines between the core of the Slovene Partisan movement and the combined forces of the Germans and the Home Guard ran through these exact regions suggests that the actual fighting may have played a role in their greater than average support for the Home Guard. Although far from an iron-clad rule, the sources do suggest that inhabitants who had experienced Partisan control often wished them to be expelled, whereas areas under the rule of the Home Guard or the occupiers that had not tasted Liberation Front power viewed the OF as patriots and liberators. On a countrywide level, this generally held true, as it was the front line, mostly rural areas of the Province of Ljubljana where one found the greatest resistance to the Partisans, while those regions with a weaker OF presence such as Gorenjska, Štajerska, Koroška, and the well-defended urban areas of Ljubljana and Primorska harboured sympathies for the OF. SOE Brigadier Fitzroy Maclean described how the fluctuating front lines of guerilla warfare often left the rural civilians 'holding the bag' when the Partisans evacuated: 'For the Partisans to allow themselves to be forced into the role of a beleaguered garrison would have been a fatal mistake, as individual commanders were to learn on occasion by bitter experience.

And so towns and villages changed hands time after time with their inhabitants, and each time became more battered and lost more inhabitants in the process.'[186] For the peasants who provided food, manpower, and lodging to both sides in the conflict, and yet often suffered reprisals from each of them, their isolationism was an understandable reaction. The former Partisan Weiss-Belač was perhaps most poetic in describing the peasants' reaction to armed conflict:

> In a time of war, a peasant, already used to all kinds of difficulties, retreats into himself, he feigns, he removes himself from the war if possible. It is not certain who will be in power tomorrow [...] His slogan is, 'Land – not war.' No war, including the Partisan's, belongs to the peasant, only the peasant rebellion is his and even this is but a poor memory. Armies come from both sides, collect and depart, but the land suffers [and] the fields bear no fruit. All wars are the same, be they just, offensive or defensive, all are destructive [and] ruinous. The liberation war [is no different]. In war only the fallen fertilize the soil.[187]

Considering Weiss-Belač's perspective, it is perhaps less surprising that the Province of Ljubljana harboured a number of *skrivači* ('the hiders') – men who hid in order to avoid mobilization into the ranks of the Liberation Front, the occupiers, or the anti-Partisan units. They were, in part, the product of a localized political orientation that identified with neither the Communist nor the anti-Communist camp, but wanted above all to be left alone to survive the war. It is impossible to establish exactly how many skrivači there were in Slovenia, as most were not keen on being counted, and their numbers constantly fluctuated, as some were reluctantly persuaded to join the ranks of the competing factions. A safe estimate would place them in the low thousands, hiding in small bands or individually, most often at or near their homes. Their presence was most frequently reported later in the war, particularly in 1944, in the front-line areas of the Province of Ljubljana, one of the few areas of occupied Slovenia where men did not have to serve in the occupiers' armies and where there was still some 'choice' in not having to pick up a gun. Many skrivači were unarmed, but some did take more decisive actions to prevent mobilizations. In one Home Guard report from Suha Krajina, these men took on the role of 'village guards,' firing on and dispersing Partisans who had been interrogating villagers.[188] Yet, skrivači also feared and attacked, when necessary, the anti-Partisan forces. The Home Guard reported, on 6 March 1944, that a number of men who had deserted the Liberation Front were roaming the forests fearful of Partisans, but also of the Home Guard and the Germans, whom they killed on the spot.[189] Both the Liberation Front and the Home Guard treated the skrivači as a serious problem. Home Guard secret police attempted to assess their numbers and disciplined Slovene civilians who supported them. However, they also attempted to enlist skrivači, and the publication *Slovensko domobranstvo* contained photos of unkempt skrivači leaving the forests to join the Home Guard.[190] The Partisans took an increasingly draconian approach to them. At a meeting in Suha Krajina, on 7 February 1944, the Liberation Front identified 'the Home Guard, the *Ustaši*, the *Nedići*, the *Mihailovići* and *skrivači*' as their enemies, describing skrivači as 'local boys who hid before them, who do not want to go among them.'[191] In the same month, a Partisan brigade in Struge threatened to shoot any *skrivač* they found.[192]

This localized allegiance and suspicion towards outsiders was not new for the Liberation Front; it had been causing them grief in recruitment and provisioning since the birth of the movement. However, not all Partisans were as willing as the Slovene dissident Edvard Kocbek to understand this behaviour. Kocbek recorded in his diary an unnamed Partisan's explanation for this peasant 'attitude': 'Peasants are in the depth of their beings our enemies. To them we appear unwise, crazy, one-sided people, fanatics, at odds with life's experiences. It cannot be otherwise. Peasants are in essence conservative beings. On top of this they went through a clerical upbringing. If we win, they will be afraid of us, they will not have trust in us.'[193] For Father Mikuž, the source of the 'greater or lesser vacillations' of the peasants and their support for the White Guard was their ignorance.[194]

Denying the peasantry agency may have comforted Mikuž. Nevertheless, it appears that the peasants' decisions were based not on knowing too little but on knowing only too well what the arrival of the Partisans could mean. The intensification of the civil war after the Italian capitulation only multiplied examples of Partisan heavy-handedness and the frequency of reprisals inflicted as a result of their activities. For example, the 115th Home Guard Company reported somewhat self-servingly that although the population of Ribnica had been initially supportive of the Liberation Front, approximately 90 per cent of the population had come to support the 'disciplined' Home Guard, after having experienced excesses at the hands of the Partisans during their September 1943 'liberation.'[195] Partisan collective punishment was evident in one of their leaflets addressed to the Home

Guard: 'Have you not thought that you also have your own families, who are mostly in the service of Hitler like yourselves? Until now we have not persecuted them or committed reprisals against them, even though we could have! Thus, if you do not immediately release our families and end the denouncing and arrest of unarmed [nationally] conscious Slovenes, we will be forced to retaliate in kind!!'[196] Partisan threats escalated, in October 1944, when OF official Anton Mavec allegedly urged that 'all families in which there are Home Guardsmen must be killed, and their homes set aflame.'[197] The burning of Žvirče, in March 1945, as collective punishment for apparently concealing Home Guard artillery reveals that Mavec's advice was acted on.[198] By 1945, the peasants of Suha Krajina complained bitterly of having had all their livestock requisitioned by the Liberation Front.[199] Nor did the burden of Partisan liberation, as we have seen, end when the liberators left. For example, the Germans set aflame the village of Volavlje near Ljubljana, in August 1944, because of rumours that it was harbouring Partisans.[200]

Collectively, these Partisan practices and subsequent reprisals by the occupiers alienated some of the very people the Liberation Front was claiming to free. Thousands of civilian refugees fled the fighting to the relative security of German-occupied Ljubljana and other towns garrisoned by the occupiers or the Home Guard. As noted, many of the able-bodied men among them were urged to join the Home Guard. President Rupnik encouraged others to uncover Partisan hideouts and to 'cooperate with the German army and the Home Guard units [...] out of your own self-interest,' as you will 'in this manner protect your area from destruction.'[201] The 'carrot' that Rupnik dangled in his appeal is a reminder that similar to peasant 'support' for the Liberation Front, 'support' for the Home Guard and the Germans could also be tactical and fleeting – a necessary strategy to survive, to safeguard property, and to avoid 'destruction.' Indeed, how genuine was civilian compliance when a German leaflet issued during the autumn 1943 counter-insurgency in the Province of Ljubljana warned that 'for those who assist the bandits, we will deal with them as we would with the bandits'?[202] Likewise, incidents of indiscriminate and violent treatment of local inhabitants by the Germans and Home Guard – including requisitioning, looting, and murder – could quickly alienate them. Some Home Guard commanders were well aware that poor discipline destroyed public sympathy. The commander of the 15th Home Guard Company in Dravlje reminded his men, 'The people strongly and attentively watch all our steps, and parallel with this also approve or criticize our movement.'[203]

The Home Guard, unlike the Liberation Front, had more of an uphill battle in convincing a sceptical local population that they were not merely the Germans' puppets. This appeared an impossible task – distinguishing themselves from their sponsors who, as we have noted, kept their independence and, in particular, any manifestations of Slovene nationalism on a relatively short leash. Nevertheless, Home Guard and Provincial Administration propaganda developed strategies that exploited pre-existing divisions in Slovene society. They seized on peasants' fears about what Communism would mean for their family farms. In an article entitled 'The First Fighter,' the head of the PU's Propaganda Department, Ludovik Puš, declared that the peasant was the foundation of anti-Communism: 'At that moment, with a decisive step, the Slovene peasant stepped onto the field. He listened to the cries and groans of innocent people, watched the clouds of black smoke over the roofs of burning villages [. . .] To battle I go, and may the devil take the enemy! And he grabbed his gun and defended against the satanic crimes. Without the Slovene farmer there would never have been a village guard, without the village guard there would never have been a Slovene *domobranstvo* [Home Guard].'[204] Exploiting apprehensions about collectivization, a Home Guard pamphlet admonished peasants: 'Your fathers' fathers did not give you the fields so that you could waste them willy-nilly [. . .] Save your home and fields for your children.'[205] To drive their point home they also issued an illustration entitled, 'How the Communist Authorities Extort the Russian Farmer' that depicted a Communist wielding a whip and a gun over an exhausted peasant.[206]

Home Guard and Provincial Administration propaganda cast the 'warped intelligentsia' that spawned Communist ideology as the nemesis of this uncorrupted and nationally conscious peasant and rural class. This anti-intellectualism, seeded well before the Second World War, was visible in the Catholic Church's fear of being supplanted by liberal, socialist, and materialist ideologies. The writings of the theologian Aleš Ušeničnik, one of the ideological fathers of the Slovene People's Party and Slovene Christian Socialism, noted, 'Only a Catholic Slovene is a true Slovene, we cannot trust the others.'[207] Nor surprisingly, then, the pro-peasant and anti-intellectual bias of Home Guard and Provincial Administration propaganda was often expressed in an anti-urban discourse – a fear that cities like Ljubljana were the breeding ground of Communist values foreign to the Catholic and conservative traditions of most Slovenes. There was, as an earlier anti-Communist pamphlet had announced, a 'silent conspiracy of the Slovene cultural elite' in Ljubljana to refrain from denouncing OF murderers and their crimes.[208] This fear was not totally misplaced, as much of the Liberation Front's intellectual leadership had come from Ljubljana. Home Guard intelligence concluded that OF support was 'strongest in Ljubljana' – a view that was substantiated by the OSS Alum Mission, which estimated that in July 1944, 'over 90% of the people in Ljubljana are in favour of the Allies and the Partisans.'[209] Other evidence was more anecdotal – a drunken woman imprisoned for shouting abuses at Home Guardsmen, rumour mongering, and cruel jokes, particularly in certain taverns, at the expense of the Home Guard.[210] Similar, but less numerous observations of pro – Liberation Front sympathies were recorded in the province's other large towns including Grosuplje, Logatec, and Novo Mesto that were under the control of the occupiers.[211]

With such preconceptions, it is hardly surprising that Home Guard and Provincial Administration propaganda made little headway against the generally pro-Partisan bearing of Ljubljana's high school and university students. Indeed, the PU's Propaganda Department admitted as much, noting that they already 'knew at the beginning that the mass of high school students was OF-leaning or at least indifferent to the anti-Communist struggle.'[212] Their campaign did not appear to have significantly altered students' views, although boys' schools were found to be far more resistant to anti-Communist propaganda than girls' schools.[213] Some students were well behaved and attentive, but others accepted the lectures with disdain and ridiculed the ideas put forth. One lecturer admitted, 'It appears to me as if they think, speak whatever you want, you are lying anyway.' Another noted, 'They are holding themselves very coldly, almost with hatred.'[214]

Anti-Communist propaganda also encountered difficulties in appealing to the working classes, not least because they faced stiff competition from the Liberation Front which promised favourable pro-worker social reform in a postwar Communist Yugoslavia. Some attributed their cold and imperturbable attitude, as in the case of the Ljubljana Tobacco Factory, to Communist saboteurs who had infiltrated the workers' ranks: 'There are still some people, who secretly plot and in this way damage the effect of the lectures. It will be necessary to remove them.'[215] Railway workers were particularly suspect. One Home Guard report from 13 December 1944 stated that railway workers were spreading rumours that the Russians were coming and that they would settle accounts with the 'white dogs.'[216] Nevertheless, student and worker allegiances were not monopolized by any one side. Catholic student associations actively supported the Home Guard. Similarly, as chapter 4 noted, workers did not 'naturally' flock to the Liberation Front – their support needed to be earned – and they, too, were influenced by religious and local loyalties.

It can be concluded, on a general level, that active civilian support for the Home Guard in the Province of Ljubljana and, indeed, elsewhere in occupied Slovenia was influenced more by individual or local experiences with occupation and with the factions in the civil war than these individuals' specific professions or class identities. Socio-political categorizations have their limitations – an individual's occupation was only one of numerous identities that shaped his or her behaviour and responses to collaboration. Peasants supported the Home Guard in a number of front-line areas of the Province of Ljubljana. In other regions of occupied Slovenia and Yugoslavia, with little or no understanding of the complexities and nuances of Marxist-Leninist theory, peasants nonetheless, understood the need to liberate their homeland, and they sided with the Partisans. Moreover, as in wars everywhere, petty rivalries and jealousies played themselves out in collaboration and treason. A July 1944 police report from Novo Mesto concluded that spurious charges accounted for 80 per cent of those detained as suspected Communists and that it was 'easy to imprison someone, but harder to pin something on them, especially when the investigating individual sees that in many cases personal revenge plays the main role, or quarrels among former political parties, who attempt to blacken and remove one another with all possible and impossible means, because they seem to be dangerous for their further activities.'[217] The 42nd Home Guard Company in Polhov Gradec complained, in September 1944, that locals were willing to furtively denounce neighbours as Communists, yet 'nobody wants to stand as a witness.'[218] 'Poisoned pens' have always freed accusers from having their allegations publicly scrutinized. A more pressing fear, however, was the Partisan tendency to liquidate informants.

In closing, this chapter has revealed that it is crucial not to approach the issue of Slovene public opinion during the occupation as a zero-sum game. Refusal to decisively support the Liberation Front did not mean that those same civilians accepted the Germans, the anti-Partisan units, or the Provincial Administration. Conversely, aloofness towards the cause of the Home Guard, the Slovene National Security Corps, or the Gorenjska Self-Defence did not necessarily translate into a desire for a Communist Slovenia. As the civil war deepened, and as we enter the finals months and weeks of the Second World War, the tragic fact of the matter is that exactly this kind of polarized mentality came to dominate the thinking of radicals in both camps, leaving in its wake arrested, tortured, and murdered civilians. We now turn to this final showdown.

9 The Final Stand and Its Consequences, January 1945–May 1945

In our clean, white Ljubljana there is a strange atmosphere. The usually empty streets today are full of people. They gather in small groups and talk in subdued voices. Our people are very worried at news that the international Communist brigade, which goes under the name of the Yugoslav Army, has landed in Rijeka and is advancing towards Trieste and Ljubljana. The Partisans are coming down from the mountains and the first refugees have arrived in Ljubljana.[1]

Franc Pernišek, 4 May 1945

The arrival of 1945 brought into play the final act in the occupation of Slovenia. Only three and a half years had passed since Axis forces stormed across the frontiers of Yugoslavia; yet, the political landscape in Slovenia, as in the rest of the country, bore little resemblance to what it was in April 1941. Tito, a hounded fugitive before the war, was in firm control of the capital Belgrade and solidifying his grip over Serbia, Macedonia, Montenegro, and Dalmatia. Tito's National Liberation Army (NOV) was poised to continue the liberation of northern Yugoslavia, including Slav-inhabited areas of Italy and Austria. The former political elite were mostly in exile, in hiding, or had thrown their support behind Tito. The main towns and transportation routes of Slovenia were still firmly under German control, but the Partisans were, as Pernišek noted, preparing to come down from the mountains. The political polarization that had been developing since the early days of the occupation would come to a head in these last tumultuous five months of the Second World War.

The Liberation Front was a changed organization in 1945. Edvard Kocbek, an initially enthusiastic convert to armed resistance, would later agree: 'The Liberation Front of the first two years of its existence cannot be compared with any of its later phases, all are embarrassing expressions. The fact is that the Party with its exclusiveness buried the meaning and might of the Liberation Front, as she took over the entire cadre.'[2] Kocbek continued, claiming that in the 'last two years of the war and the first year after the war the Slovene Communists faithfully copied Soviet methods and Stalin's practices.'[3] Ideological and sectarian suspicions not only widened the chasm between the Communists and their opponents, but also between their allies and supporters. Pressure on Christian Socialists and other Catholic members of the Liberation Front to join the Communist Party of Slovenia intensified, with mostly younger members throwing their lot in with the Communists, whereas their elders – Kocbek among them – refused to join the CPS.[4] British and American missions also sensed a cooling of relations with the Liberation Front and, indeed, with Partisan formations throughout Yugoslavia. Already by late 1944, 'Lindsay and Moore had become thoroughly disillusioned with the SNLA [Slovene National Liberation Army] as a military force and were more certain than ever about Communist political objectives.'[5] In February 1945, the OSS alleged that the Partisans had mistreated Allied airmen and prevented them from contacting the American mission.[6] SOE agent Lieutenant Colonel Peter Moore remarked that 'Britain is regarded with intense dislike and suspicion by the Partisan authorities, who fear we may oppose their territorial claims or try and force them to moderate their internal policy.'[7] According to Moore, this attitude was in stark contrast to the rank-and-file and Slovene villagers, who were 'very grateful' towards the United States and Britain to the embarrassment of the Partisan authorities. Consistent with similar observations in 1944, Moore concluded that the Partisans continued to husband their resources for the final showdown with their domestic opponents at the expense of taking the fight to the Germans:

> The Slovene Pzns have lost interest in fighting the Germans as Germans as such and are conserving their forces for:
>
> I) The capture of Ljubljana and the liquidation of the White Guard after the defeat of Germany. Task 7 Corps.

II) The occupation of TRIESTE and all NE Italy up to the TAGLIAMENTO to permit a 'fait accompli' at the peace conference. Task 9 Corps.

III) The Occupation of KLAGENFURT and VILLACH. Task 4 Zone.[8]

In a January 1945 memorandum to Slovene Communist Boris Kidrič, the local Liberation Front in distant Prekmurje was also urging that in addition to sabotage and rebellion, it was 'important to "clean out" Quislings.'[9]

The Slovene Partisans were evidently buoyed by an expansion in their recruitment, which had increased their membership to some thirty to thirty-five thousand by late 1944.[10] This growth was in no small part a result of the widespread realization among Slovenes that the Germans were going to lose the war. By the beginning of February 1945, the Soviets had advanced to the River Oder and were some forty miles from Berlin. In Hungary, the Red Army had advanced to Lake Balaton. Only in Italy were the Allies making slower progress; the start of their final spring offensive in April still saw them overlooking Bologna some three hundred kilometres from Trieste. Moreover, the Yalta Conference held that same month reiterated the Big Three's shared conviction that there would be no separate peace with Germany and, ominously, that Soviet citizens would be returned to their respective homelands.

With Germany reeling on its last leg, one enters the world of the last-minute resister, a phenomenon common to all of the occupied states. Milač noted, 'When it became clear that the Liberation Front would be victorious militarily and politically, it seemed fashionable to join just to be on the winning side. One had to admit that the list of individual names, groups and organizations that joined the OF in the last year of the war was remarkable.'[11] Without denying genuine gratitude for their liberators, last-minute resisters also appear to have been motivated by an instinctual survival mechanism that would find them on the 'correct' side when all the proverbial chips had fallen. An overwhelming sense of apathetic weariness had gripped civilians who desired nothing more than a return to order and normalcy after four years of occupation and war. They were willing to support any side that could provide it. The OSS reported, in March 1945: 'Their favourite topic is when is the war going to end. They have had enough of it and want to be able to work their farms in peace. It seems that almost every family you run into has had losses of some sort.'[12] Moore concluded, in February 1945, that '75% of the population in liberated territory and the Army in Slovenia are war weary. The remaining 25% can think of little but the jobs they are going to get after the war.'[13] A Communist official in Ljubljana, according to Moore, 'admitted that the city which had previously been claimed as 75% for the Partisans, was now only 25% pro-Partisan, 20% for the White Guard and 55% apathetic.'[14]

This late influx into Partisan ranks impacted, albeit somewhat unevenly, Slovene anti-Partisan forces. The most dramatic desertions struck the Slovene National Security Corps (SNVZ), whose ranks deteriorated precipitously following the Partisan amnesty of September 1944. Those who remained were increasingly insubordinate and ill-disciplined. Colonel Anton Kokalj, the commander of the SNVZ, reported, in February 1945, that some SNVZ members refused to go into battle, as it was 'too dangerous' and 'they will not carry their heads in a bag.'[15]

The Slovene Police Corps, like the police in France and elsewhere in occupied Europe, also sensed that the tide was turning. Numerous reports in 1945 highlighted the Police Corps' lack of fervour in rooting out Communists and Partisans. In January 1945, Police Corps Chief Lovro Hacin criticized his men for concentrating only on criminal affairs – smuggling, alcoholism, and looting – while allowing Communists and their supporters to operate freely. Others were accused of fraternizing off-duty with known OF supporters, and prison guards brought extra food to OF prisoners or delivered their mail.[16] Indeed, some in the Police Corps criticized the Home Guardsmen for their subservience to the occupiers and dogmatic anti-Communism, claiming that they 'only imprison innocent people.'[17] On 5 March 1945, Hacin repeated his assertion that 'many among the ranks of the Police Corps are not aware of their main duty,' namely, the war against Communism.[18] There were genuine Partisan supporters among the Police Corps. Still, a change of attitude towards the Liberation Front was also a useful inoculation against future charges of treason.

Although far less dramatic than the bleeding of SNVZ ranks, desertions also increased among the Home Guard as the end of the war neared. Evidence of this quickening pace was revealed in the Rakek unit. It had five desertions in August 1944, nineteen in November, and fifteen in only the first half of December.[19] Increasing casualty rates and scarcer 'luxuries' such as proper clothing, food, and drink, sparked grumbling among the men.[20] The attempt to shore up discipline for the final showdown with the Partisans led some rank and file to protest against the 'strictness' of the officers.[21] Civilians became increasingly wary of associating with the Home Guard. A report from December 1944 noted a 'growing coldness and aloofness' among the population in burying fallen Home Guardsmen, stating that 'gratitude is lacking.' In Šentjurje, only those with family members in the Home Guard reportedly attended burial services, and even the priest was ambivalent and dragging his feet in burying them.[22] Highly emblematic of this shift was the town of Horjul, not far from where the first Village Guards units emerged in the summer of 1942. A February 1945 Home Guard report described it as, 'at the least neutral, but perhaps even majority pro-Communist.'[23]

Despite shifting public allegiance, however, the Home Guard could still rely on a fairly solid base of support in some of the rural regions of the Province of Ljubljana, where a number of their rank originated. Some of this support was in reaction to Partisan requisitioning during the lean winter months of 1944–45. Moore admitted as much, reporting that 'the peasants are holding out on the Partisans over food supplies. A natural reaction after four years of war.'[24] Others saw the Home Guard as desperately needed security at a time when various sundry collaborating units were moving northwards across the region ahead of the Partisans and the Red Army. This was made very apparent with the arrival in Dolenjska, in the spring of 1945, of the five hundred–strong Varjag/Wariag SS regiment, which claimed allegiance to General Vlasov's largely phantom Russian Liberation Army.[25] The Germans used them, the Home Guard, and an increasingly multinational force consisting of thousands of Cossack and Ukrainian Waffen-SS, Ustaši, Četniks, Ljotić's Serbian Volunteer Corps, and even collaborating Greeks in a last-ditch effort to hold off the National Liberation Army (NOV) and the Red Army advance across Slovenia towards Austria. Referred to as *vlasovci* in contemporary accounts, the Russians perpetrated an alcohol-fuelled terror campaign, looting, raping, and murdering civilians in Dolenjska. The Home Guard reported that in Žužemberk 'the people offer the Home Guard food and drink just so they will stay and protect them from the Vlasovists.'[26]

The final months of the occupation in Slovenia, however, witnessed not only desertions from collaborating ranks and growing professions of allegiance to the Partisans, but also a considerable hardening of ideological lines. This was already apparent in the inability to win over many in the Home Guard during earlier Partisan amnesties. Some in the Home Guard may have doubted the sincerity of the

Partisans' offer of clemency; nevertheless, the fact that so many refused to change sides suggests a considerable degree of ideological discipline and commitment among their rank and file. Their decision to stay also marked them as committed enemies of the NOV – from now until the end of the Second World War it truly was a life-and-death struggle.

This polarization eradicated any last vestiges of a non-Communist Slovene resistance. The Slovene Četniks, who had always ridden a convenient line between collaboration and resistance, were forced by increasing Partisan military pressure to rely ever more closely on the Germans. Ivan Prezelj (alias Andrej), who had been elevated to the rank of general by the Yugoslav Army in the Homeland, in December 1944, worked out ceasefire negotiations with the Germans, in January 1945. The depth of their cooperation was revealed when Prezelj's Četniks handed over fifteen Allied airmen to the German police in the same month, ostensibly to release a number of their own who were in German custody.[27] In Štajerska, Jože Melaher's Četniks were also forced by Partisan pressure to hold ceasefire negotiations with SS Colonel Franz Steindl, at the end of January 1945. Nevertheless, Melaher's unit continued to hide fugitive Allied airmen despite their 'legalized' existence under the umbrella of the German police.[28]

The upshot of having burned their proverbial bridges to the Liberation Front was a renewed determination and cohesiveness among anti-Partisan units. In the aftermath of the Partisans' failed January 1945 amnesty, Moore concluded:

> The morale of the White Guard has risen remarkably in spite of their apparent hopeless position as 100% collaborationist. The personnel of at any rate the POKRETNE [mobile] Battalions who are all volunteers are man for man of higher morale than the Pzns [Partisans]. Reasons are bad Pzn food, Pzns resigning the initiative, and the high standard of training in Pzn warfare, which the Germans have taught them, including the use of strong ski patrols. The POKRETNE Battalions have definitely established an ascendancy over the Pzns in large areas of wooded country previously considered Pzn preserves. The amnesty of 15 Jan did not secure a single desertion and the Slovene Pzns admit that the White Guard are as tough a proposition or even tougher than the Ustashi. White Guard troops fought stubbornly in defence of Ribnica and Kočevje and are capable of bold offensive action as shown by this raid on Črnomelj in November.[29]

In March 1945, the OSS mission echoed these sentiments in a report on the morale of the joint German–Home Guard forces in Slovenia: 'Judging by the enemy activity out of their garrisons, they don't act very much like one that are losing the war or expect to be surrendering soon. They are very aggressive and will put up with no monkey business near their garrisons or along the communication lines. They seem always on guard, on the alert and go after the Partisans about as often, if not more so, than the Partisans go after them.'[30] As late as April 1945, the Germans, along with the Home Guard, launched an offensive to push the NOV's VII Corps out of the Suha Krajina, Kočevje, and Bela Krajina regions and, thus, protect the southern approaches to Ljubljana. During these final weeks, the Home Guard solidified its military presence in the immediate environs of Ljubljana, dispatching more than 250 patrols in the Krim region.[31] The OSS reported German and Home Guard counterattacks as late as 4 May.[32] Besides revealing the Home Guard's cohesiveness – and desperation – these final offensives also highlight continued cooperation with the Germans. Their concerns about the loyalty of the Home Guard, evident in the sporadic arrests and reorganization of the Home Guard into smaller, more reliable units intermixed with German and other Axis troops, do not appear to have been realized.[33] In these final weeks, the Home Guard needed German military assistance against the Partisans as much as the Germans required Home Guard help in securing a safe passage north to the Reich.

The Home Guard continued to fight shoulder-to-shoulder with the Germans, although Leon Rupnik and his administration was facing a coup by the National Committee for Slovenia (NO), which had determined that the opportune moment to make common cause with the Western Allies had arrived. Rupnik's support for the German arrests that had struck the National Committee and the anti-Partisan forces, in late 1944 and early 1945, irreparably damaged his reputation in their eyes. Rupnik, who was never fond of the pre-war political elite, had urged his Home Guard, in January 1945 – and he truly did believe that they were *his* force – to oppose any kind of 'illegal' organizing: 'All officers, non-commissioned officers and soldiers of the Slovene Home Guard should concern themselves that these elements, which destroy the trust of the German authorities in the Slovene Home Guard, be removed from the Slovene Home Guard.'[34] He thanked SS-Obergruppenführer Rösener for the 'painful but necessary' imprisonment of some disobedient Home Guardsmen, who were attempting to 'shake up' the force under the influence of 'advantage-seeking politicians. These elements had to know that the German authorities, who enabled the Home Guard to form, would not peacefully tolerate the organization of a plot against them from within the Home Guard!'[35]

Chastened by these arrests, the National Committee nevertheless, continued its underground preparations. On 21 February 1945, it formally re-established the Slovene National Army (SNV).[36] Although merely a reorganized paper army of the anti-Partisan units that were at present fighting alongside the Germans, the National Committee both naively and optimistically hoped that it would be recognized by the Allies. The Slovene National Security Corps was, thus, secretly incorporated into the Slovene National Army, as an envisaged Primorska division; the Gorenjska Self-Defence was to become the *gorska* (mountain) division; and the Home Guard was to be reincarnated as the SNV's Ljubljana division.

These moves did not alleviate the National Committee's international isolation. The new twenty-eight-member United Yugoslav Government, appointed by the Regency Council under British auspices, on 7 March 1945, effectively ended the influence of King Peter and that of non-Communist politicians on developments in Yugoslavia. Only three politicians were considered unaffiliated with the Partisans, and all would leave the government before the end of the year.[37] Slovene politicians in exile remained divided with some such as the diplomat Izidor Cankar returning to Yugoslavia (Cankar would later be appointed ambassador to Greece). Others would remain in exile, such as Miha Krek, who would continue to advocate on the National Committee's behalf until the end of the war before heading the Yugoslav Welfare Society in Rome which championed the plight of Yugoslav political refugees.

On 17 April, two weeks before Hitler committed suicide in his bunker in besieged Berlin, the National Committee declared that the Slovene National Army, with General Prezelj at its head, would not fight the anticipated Anglo-American liberation of Slovenia alongside the Germans.[38] This envisaged fraternal Allied invasion of Slovenia was, however, the product of their deluded optimism and fervent anti-Communist world-view. The tanks of the British Eighth Army would not storm across the Ljubljana Gap. The Red Army, too, went no further than Prekmurje. The task of liberating Slovenia was solely in the hands of the NOV – its allies. Undaunted, the National Committee initiated negotiations with the Germans and Rupnik. With Bishop Rožman acting as an intermediary, or in his words as a 'witness,' Rupnik was invited to meet with the National Committee, on 28 April 1945, at the bishop's residence.[39] The demands were clear: Rupnik must resign, the administration must be transferred to the National Committee, and the Germans were to surrender all heavy and automatic weaponry to the Home Guard. In return, the Germans would receive safe passage across the Karavanke mountains into Austria. Rupnik baulked at the demand that he step down, noting that the Germans could still reverse the military situation by releasing their Werewolves, the largely imaginary Nazi guerila units that were to fight on behind enemy lines.[40] Instead, with SS-Obergruppenführer Rösener's assent, Rupnik proclaimed himself supreme leader of the Home Guard two days later, declaring in the 3 May special edition of *Slovensko domobranstvo* that, finally, 'we have conclusively become a Slovene military unit under our own leadership.'[41] However, Rupnik was not completely obstructionist. He allegedly secured a meeting between the National Committee and Rösener, on 30 April. The German commander agreed to tolerate the committee's 'illegal work' with the proviso that it not demonstrate its rule without his assent.[42]

Four days after the meeting at the bishop's residence, the National Committee trumped Rupnik. Meeting at the Sokol hall in the Tabor section of Ljubljana, and with Bishop Rožman present, the National Committee declared itself a provisional Slovene parliament under the presidency of Franc Kremžar, a former SLS deputy in the Yugoslav parliament. *Slovenec* finally bucked its subservience to the occupier's editorial agenda by splashing the Tabor Declaration across its front page the following morning:

UNITED SLOVENIA RISES!
Ljubljana, 3 May. During the historic and important meeting of last night, the following proclamation was adopted enthusiastically:

TO THE SLOVENE PEOPLE!
In the spirit of the Atlantic Charter and other solemn declarations of the Democratic Allies concerning the free determination and democratic organization of nations,

THE NATIONAL COMMITTEE OF SLOVENIA
In the decisive, critical and historic hour of the Slovene people,

DECLARES

That, encompassing the whole territory on which Slovenes live, the National State of Slovenia is established, as a part of the democratic and federated Kingdom of Yugoslavia.

The National Committee for Slovenia empowers the provisional Slovene government as the highest governmental body on the territory of the National State of Slovenia.

The Slovene National Army has taken upon itself to secure order and peace in the state and it will take possession of the frontiers. The Slovene National Guard and other national armed forces place themselves at the disposal of the National Committee for Slovenia; having pledged allegiance to the King and the Slovene people, they become the Slovene National Army and a part of the Royal Yugoslav Army in the Homeland.

In the National State of Slovenia, every party is entitled, according to the principles of freedom and democracy, to the free development and promulgation of its goals. Therefore, the National Committee for Slovenia invites all parties to cooperate with the Committee and, in this way, to facilitate the political and social consolidation of the Slovene people.

The National Committee for Slovenia urges the mutual reconciliation of all Slovenes, so that small and weakened national forces would not waste their energy in internecine strife; in this historic moment, unity and concord are indispensable for the realization of national interests. Therefore, the Committee appeals to all Partisan units to suspend immediately all actions against the Slovene National Army and the peace-loving Slovene people, and, by doing this, to bring to an end the terrible bloodshed among brothers.

The National Committee for Slovenia urges all Slovenes to maintain, in this decisive moment, national discipline, to assume a dignified attitude towards all, to stay away from the personal settling of accounts, and to carry out the orders of the National Government.

By reason of victorious arms and our efforts, Ljubljana, for the first time in history the capital of United Slovenia, must be in all respects the example of national consciousness, political wisdom, and civic discipline.

With trust in almighty God, who directs the destinies of nations, and with hope in the aid of the great Democratic Allies, the National Committee for Slovenia appeals to all Slovenes to cooperate for the good of the country, for its unity and accord, because only this cooperation assures the existence and the progress of the Slovene people.

Long live King Peter II
Long live the Federated Kingdom of Yugoslavia!
Long live the National State of Slovenia!
Ljubljana, May 3, 1945[43]

Many of the anti-Communists' and collaborators' naïve hopes and muddled, selective memories of four years of occupation were evident in this transformation of an unelected committee, some of whose members had either openly or furtively fought against the Liberation Front, into the 'highest governmental body' in the 'National State of Slovenia' – and one that saw itself as squarely on the side of the Western Allies. In their new liberationist role, the Slovene National Army – now headed by none other than Lieutenant-Colonel Franc Krener of the Home Guard, after Prezelj wisely relinquished authority over his impossible duties – were to be transformed from Nazi German auxiliaries into a national army that would seize control of the frontiers of an enlarged Slovenia. The Tabor Declaration called on Partisans to end their attacks on the SNV, as if they alone were the instigators of the fratricidal violence that had plagued the nation since 1942. No credit was given to the Partisans' armed resistance against the occupation. Instead, Slovenia had been freed thanks to ambiguous 'victorious arms and our efforts.' Despite the proclamation's commitment to Slovenia's long-held dream of a unified Slovenia (Zedinjena Slovenija) that would incorporate all areas 'on which Slovenes live,' Slovenia was to become part of a democratically reordered federated Kingdom of Yugoslavia. The notion bandied about in some postwar émigré circles that Tabor was a proclamation of Slovene independence ruthlessly snatched away by Tito's Communists is clearly unsubstantiated.

The Tabor assembly was held up by later émigrés as the pivotal moment in their struggle against a Communist revolution in Slovenia. Its immediate impact on events in May 1945, however, was minimal. SS-Obergruppenführer Rösener was not pre-informed of the declaration, and predictably, he reacted adversely, declaring martial law and halting the presses at *Slovenec*. Its editor, Matej Poštovan, was arrested and was later only released, according to Rupnik, through his intercession.[44] A number of the National Committee's members spent the next two nights in hiding.[45] However, with the Germans already evacuating Slovenia, Rösener was willing to compromise. He, along with Rupnik, called one final meeting with the National Committee at the handsome Kazina building on Congress Square in Ljubljana, on the morning of 5 May. Rösener listened to the committee's demands, and although he was willing to consider the release of any imprisoned anti-Communists, he refused to hand over the city's radio station and was unable to surrender Štajerska to the committee, as he had no authority over this region.[46] The tension between the National Committee and Rupnik was palpable. Rupnik noted that he 'greeted the individual gentlemen; however, they were like ice, so that it did not come to handshakes. The arrival of the Anglo-Americans seemed to me increasingly more possible, my evacuation increasingly more necessary.'[47] Rupnik agreed to resign and transferred to the National Committee authority over the Province of Ljubljana and Gorenjska, which Rösener and Rainer had only recently ceded to his control. Later that afternoon, Rupnik left Ljubljana by car for Austria, taking with him some three thousand cigarettes and 10,000 lire, although Ladislav Bevc, recalled that Rupnik refused to surrender control over the Home Guard until the end.[48]

Rupnik was ostracized. But other Slovenes who had collaborated or accommodated the occupiers were offered influential positions in the National Committee. The Home Guard and Police Corps rank and file came under the orders of the committee, and many of their officers including Krener, Vizjak, and Vuk Rupnik, Leon Rupnik's son, were elevated in rank.[49] In addition, a number of Provincial Administration bureaucrats were called on to contribute to the National Committee. Jože Osana, who was asked by the committee to compose the national hymn, had been a member of the Provincial Administration's cultural propaganda section.[50] Others, like former SLS deputy Albin Šmajd, and Marjan Zajec, who had been instrumental in helping to organize anti-Partisan units, were critically involved with the committee's establishment. Overnight, the former propaganda organs of the occupiers and the collaborators such as *Slovenec* (The Slovene), *Jutro* (Morning), and the Home Guard paper *Za blagor očetnjave* (For the Good of the Fatherland), along with their respective editors, had changed their tune and heralded the Allies as 'brothers-in-arms.'[51] For example, Kremžar, who was made president of the National Committee, was the editor of the paper *Domoljub* (Patriot) during the war; although its editorial policy was established by the occupiers, the Liberation Front had denounced Kremžar's employment as collaboration.[52]

In any event, the authority of the National Committee lasted mere hours – some members believed power had never officially been surrendered to them – as the decision was made later that day to go into exile.[53] Some of the NO elite were fortunate to make their way to the frontier in automobiles. Most of the anti-Communist officials and civilians, however, who for whatever reason feared the arrival of the Partisans enough to uproot their lives and gamble on an uncertain life as refugees, undertook the chaotic exodus on foot. Among the refugees was Bishop Rožman, who left Ljubljana and his bishopric by car, on 5 May, for Austria. Over two hundred priests and seminarians would follow his example.[54] Controversy has dogged Rožman's decision to leave, as it had not been approved by the Pope. From the Bishop of Klagenfurt's palace, where he sought refuge, Rožman attempted to explain his actions to the Holy See in a 1 August 1945 report that highlighted the actions of the Partisans and his responsibility to administer to the spiritual needs of Slovene refugees. Although he was never reassigned a formal position in the Church and was denied *ad limina* access to the Pope, to the frustration of the Yugoslav government, Rožman maintained his title as bishop until his death, in Cleveland in 1959.[55]

The urgency of the exodus was understandable. Although the National Committee made paper claims to ethnic Slovene lands, Tito's Fourth Army, which included the Slovene Partisan IX Corps, was in the process of winning them. The 'race for Trieste' ended when the NOV entered the city one day before the 2nd New Zealand Division, on 1 May, ushering in the city's dual occupation. Their offensive also effectively cut off the NO's 'Primorska division' – the Slovene National Security Corps – from Ljubljana. Some of the SNVZ's commanders had already taken authority into their own hands. An order issued on 29 April, by the commander of the 1st Slovene Strike Battalion in Ajdovščina, demanded all retreating German trucks be stopped and inspected for concealed weapons and material that could aid them in their struggle against Tito's National Liberation Army.[56] However, Partisan momentum was unstoppable – Ajdovščina fell on 5 May – and the remnants of the SNVZ, along with Četniks and Serbian Volunteer Corps units would surrender to the British in Italy. Although they would escape the Home Guard's fate, a number of those captured by the NOV were executed in the Trnovski forest east of Gorizia.[57]

While Primorska was being liberated, the NOV's 29th Hercegovina Division and the VII Corps were pushing towards Ljubljana from the south and west. Kočevje was liberated on 4 May, followed a day later by Rakek and Vrhnika, the latter town only some twenty kilometres west of the capital. Novo Mesto fell on 8 May. Cut off from Ljubljana, its Home Guard detachment along with some German units would be largely destroyed by the Partisans near Radeče. As the NOV had already reached the southern suburbs of Ljubljana, one of the first orders of the Slovene National Army was to prepare for a 'temporary retreat' to the relative security of Austrian Carinthia.[58] On the evening of VE day, they too, joined the thousands of Slovene civilians moving north towards the Karavanke mountain range and the Ljubelj Tunnel, sharing the road with retreating German troops and their allies. After some final engagements, in the early morning of 9 May, the NOV secured the Ljubljana train station, and a few hours later paraded into the city centre to the jubilant cheers of Ljubljana's populace. An eerie premonition of the bloody events that were still to unfold, the last edition of *Za blagor očetnjave* warned Tito's forces: 'We will return, this is a sure thing. We know what we are talking about, because we have assurances from the great Allied powers.'[59] Slightly more than two weeks later, they would return with the assurance of the British; however, not as the liberators *Za blagor očetnjave* envisaged, but rather as the walking dead.

Thousands fled the Partisan liberation, but many Slovenes antipathetic to Tito's regime remained behind. Marching north towards Ljubljana with the liberating Partisans in the last days of the Second World War, the Slovene economist and dissident Ljubo Sirc gave his impressions of the uneven welcome they received:

> At Kočevje, the castle in the middle of the town was in ruins and the population unwelcoming. They had had Partisans two years before, and regions liberated once before tended to be unenthusiastic about repeating the experience. This was Home Guard country [...] Public enthusiasm increased as we reached the suburbs. While communist Partisans frequently succeeded in occupying villages – for a while – Ljubljana had always remained firmly in the hands of their enemies, foreign or domestic. As a result the townspeople had no personal experience of Partisan rule and still harboured illusions about what was coming.[60]

Many of these 'unenthusiastic' civilians could not bear to leave their families, friends, and homes, as inertia generally prevailed over action.

Others felt that the rumours of impending revenge had been exaggerated. Indeed, Partisan radio broadcasts had stated that all those who did not have blood on their hands need not be afraid. This prediction bore itself out for some. Others, like the Ljubljana resident Jože Beranek, one of the Home Guard's most prolific propaganda illustrators, were less fortunate. Beranek's friends thought he was 'naïve and too honest, because he believed that after the war nothing bad would happen to him'; nevertheless, he was far more realistic with his wife, telling her that he would probably face five to fifteen years imprisonment.[61] Beranek was immediately arrested and imprisoned in Šentvid. Morbid rumours circulated that he had been tortured, his hands severed as punishment for his propaganda work. Government documents stated that he had been released in June 1945; however, only in 1969 was his wife given official notice that he had not lived past 1 June.[62]

Further north, a chaotic scene was enfolding, as thousands of civilian refugees, German troops, and their erstwhile Slovene and Axis collaborators surged into the narrow two-kilometre-long Ljubelj Tunnel, often squabbling over the right of way. Entering Austria, they discovered to their alarm that Tito's forces had already entered Klagenfurt, on 8 May, to stake their claim to southern 'Slavic' Carinthia. Of more immediate concern was their occupation of the town of Ferlach (Borovlje), which guarded the bridge across the Drava, blocking access to the British-held environs around Klagenfurt. Thus, on 11 May, three days after the war in Europe had officially ended, the Home Guard under Vuk Rupnik, with the assistance of German artillery and a battalion of collaborating Russians, joined forces for the last time in attacking the Partisan Bračičeva Brigade stationed in Ferlach. One hundred eighty Partisans were reportedly killed, with only a handful of casualties among the attackers.[63] Symbolically, the Bračičeva Brigade was the same unit that had assassinated Anton Dorfmeister, a leading Nazi official in Štajerska, which had led to the hanging of some hundred Slovene hostages in Frankolovo, a village near Celje, on 12 February 1945.[64] The 'Frankolovo crime' is considered to be one of the worst in a chilling dossier of Nazi war crimes perpetrated in occupied Slovenia.

With access over the Drava secured, we are returned to where this study started – on the eve of the forcible repatriation of members of the Home Guard from Vetrinje and their execution in Yugoslavia. We began with an attempt to understand why the British agreed to deport the Home Guardsmen and other Yugoslav collaborators and anti-Communists. Now, some words on why Tito's regime responded as it did. There is still no definitive 'smoking gun' to the question of who ordered the liquidations. Tito and his Slovene comrades Edvard Kardelj and Boris Kidrič were most certainly party to what appear to have been verbal orders.[65] Indeed, the only indictment of a Slovene official – issued in 2005 against former Yugoslav Prime Minister Mitja Ribičič, who headed a special branch of the feared OZNA (Oddelek za zaščito naroda, Department for the Protection of the People) – was dismissed for lack of evidence. The Communist Party seized the opportunity presented by the repatriations to permanently eliminate a considerable part of their most unrepentant opposition. That many of the executed Slovenes came from the Province of Ljubljana only highlights the regional uniqueness of the occupation. Since the Germans had already eliminated most of the pre-war political and religious elite in Štajerska and Gorenjska during the war, only in the Province of Ljubljana, where the occupation was less ambitious, could they survive in numbers threatening to the Communists in 1945. Moreover, having just recently seized control of Yugoslavia, and having orchestrated only the second successful Communist revolution in history, the Communists could at least be forgiven for feeling under siege. Yugoslavia had the makings of the first flashpoint between the capitalist West and the communist East in the stand-offs over Trieste and, to a lesser extent, Austria. Somewhere in the mountains of Bosnia, General Draža Mihailovič was still on the run, and from Croatia there emerged rumours of die-hard Ustaša Križarji (Crusaders) rebels who refused to surrender. Moreover, tens of thousands of anti-Communist Yugoslavs were residing in camps just across the frontier, in Austria and Italy. According to Yugoslav media, the bogy of Matthew's Army (Matjaževa vojska), an espionage and guerilla force established in Austria with the cooperation of Western intelligence, was attempting to overthrow the revolution. Nor can we discount, as the historian Mark Mazower noted in relation to Czechoslovakia's mass deportation of Germans, 'the fear that the Germans were only temporarily defeated and were preparing to launch their revenge.'[66] Complicating the matter further was Stalin's erratic and bullying attitude towards his Yugoslav protégé. These domestic and international tensions were amplified in a state where a million of its citizens had been killed and its infrastructure pilfered and destroyed.

Repatriations, widespread arrests, and mass executions after the Second World War were not unique to Yugoslavia, as Europe embarked, as put by the historian István Deák, on the largest attempt at judicial redress in its history.[67] Some two million Soviet citizens were repatriated with the full knowledge and assistance of the West. Collaborators – or at least those alleged to be collaborators – were executed, and many more were banished to early deaths in the Gulag. The Red Army raped an estimated two million German women, as it murdered and plundered its way to Berlin.[68] Some eleven to twelve million Germans were expelled from Eastern Europe in the first two years after the Second World War, and well over two million Poles and Ukrainians were exchanged across their new shared frontier. In Hungary, some three hundred thousand, or 3 per cent of the total population, suffered some sort of punishment for their wartime behaviour.[69] The more ethnically homogeneous and politically stable Western Europe escaped the worst of these atrocities; nevertheless, some ten thousand French citizens were executed for collaboration in impromptu settlings of accounts in the wake of liberation.[70] However, unlike France and other Western states, where 'the majority of the most severe "punishments" meted out for wartime activities were completed *before* formal or official tribunals had been set up to pass judgment,'[71] in Slovenia and Yugoslavia 'summary mass killings and convictions were unleashed by order of the new communist government.'[72] The proportional size of the victims in relation to Slovenia's small population was also unique: in postwar France, it would have been the equivalent of the government executing over 350,000 French citizens. In addition, unlike most of Europe, in Slovenia as in the rest of Yugoslavia (and in the Soviet Union), the most severe form of punishment – death – was applied, almost as a rule, to membership in collaborating units. Thus, in addition to the twelve thousand members of the Slovene Home Guard, thirty-six thousand Croats, five thousand Muslims, and thousands of Četniks were slaughtered at this time.[73] To this figure we can add the thousands of mostly Italian victims massacred in the immediate aftermath of the Partisan liberation of Trieste and Primorska, whose bodies, in a macabre dress rehearsal of the imminent massacres in central Slovenia, were disposed of in karst caves (*foibe* in Italian) that studded the surrounding mountains and hills.[74]

Nor was the bloody postwar settling of accounts entirely unexpected. From the outset, Tito was convinced that a Yugoslav Communist revolution would be born out of a successful war of liberation. Violence was, in the final assessment, the means to ensure success. As Tito told Milovan Djilas, before sending him to organize resistance in Montenegro, shoot anyone who 'wavers or shows a lack of discipline.'[75] Following the capitulation of Italy, in September 1943, the Liberation Front followed suit, executing many captured Village Guard and Četnik leaders and a number of the rank and file. OF propaganda, along with German and Home Guard propaganda, routinely spoke of eliminating, cleansing, and liquidating their opponents: 'Death to Fascism – Freedom to the People' and 'Death to Hitler and his Hirelings.' The Liberation Front and its supporters issued countless warnings to collaborators that 'heads would roll' at war's end, although most admittedly promised some form of judicial process.[76] Some were eerily accurate in their predictions. A Partisan leaflet from 1944 declared that the Teheran Conference, which was held in November 1943 and committed the Big Three to support Tito's forces, promised 'all who are responsible, or who freely took part in aggression, murder, and battles will be sent back to the place where they committed these crimes, to be judged by the liberated authority, which will be established there.'[77]

Foreign military missions also predicted a settling of accounts after liberation. SOE agent Moore prophesied as much in his February 1945 report: 'The KPS [read CPS] after 20 years of persecution are preparing to enjoy the sweets of office permanently, as is only natural [...] The present attitude of the Partisans should not however blind us to the fact that their regime is the only possible solution for SLOVENIA. However, a civil war of short duration and some discreditable excesses by the Partisans, are unfortunately only too likely after the departure of the Germans.' As a British officer, his following recommendation was particularly prescient: 'Missions from all organizations in SLOVENIA should be reduced to an absolute minimum, and in particular the number of senior officers should be reduced. Otherwise the goodwill we have earned with the civil population will be lost, by our being identified with possible excesses by the Partisans over whom we have no control whatever.'[78]

Promises of revenge continued to permeate the regime's pronouncements in the immediate postwar weeks. On 26 May – the day before repatriations of Home Guardsmen began from Austria – the OF's official organ *Slovenski poročevalec* (Slovene Reporter) declared: 'We have imprinted revenge in our hearts as a program and a core, in order to shatter and destroy this company of traitors and executioners [...] Victims must be avenged. Revenge must reach down to the deepest roots. We shall not only cut down the rotten tree, we shall dig up its roots and burn them, and the soil in which they grew we shall plough ten feet deep, so that not the least sprout remains of the tree.'[79] A speech given by Tito in Ljubljana, on the same day, is most often held up as proof of his guiding hand in the unfolding events: 'Regarding those traitors who were within the country itself [. . .] this is now a matter of the past. The hand of justice, the avenging hand of our nation has already reached a great majority; only a minority of traitors have managed to escape and be taken under the wing of patrons abroad. This minority will never again see our beautiful mountains and flowering fields, and even if this did happen, it would only last for a very short time.'[80]

Tito, his Partisans, and the Slovene masses had more than enough justification for urging harsh retribution against the Home Guard and its supporters. In his three-volume survey, published by the Writers Association of the History of the NOB, Silvo Grgič estimated that six thousand Slovene civilians were killed either directly by Slovene collaborators or as a result of surrendering them to the occupiers' penal systems.[81] Combined with Partisans killed, or who later died as a result of injuries sustained in combat against collaborators, his total estimate was approximately eleven thousand victims, including seven hundred women and 116 children and young people. More than a third of the civilian victims suffered some type of torture. As Grgič concluded, 'even the existing two volumes provide hundreds of examples that collaborators did not work in the spirit of an anti-Communist resistance, but rather in a crime-ridden, complete collaboration with the Nazi-Fascist occupiers. In fear of losing their power the collaborators inextricably bound themselves to the worst enemies the Slovene nation had had in its history.'[82] A number of historians have cast some doubt on Grgič's rather high figures. Tadeja Tominšek Rihtar, a professor and researcher at the Institute for Contemporary History in Ljubljana, who is taking part in a larger project to compile a detailed list of Slovenia's wartime and postwar victims, has estimated that the anti-Partisan units killed some twenty-seven hundred Partisans and fifteen hundred civilians, while the Partisans killed thirty-one hundred anti-Partisans and forty-five hundred civilians in wartime combat.[83] Overall, the Partisans paid a heavy price for their resistance. The twenty-eight thousand Partisans killed amounts to approximately 29 per cent of the ninety-six thousand victims that currently are estimated to have died in wartime and postwar violence in Slovenia. Together, about sixteen thousand Village Guards, Četniks, and Home Guardsmen were killed (the vast majority executed after the war), or 17 per cent of the total victims. The rest of Slovenia's victims were made up primarily of civilians (38,581 or 40%) and those forcibly mobilized into the occupier's armies (12,118 or 12.6%).[84]

This number crunching reveals, at least in part, why the Partisans believed that they, along with civilian victims whom they assumed cherished their anti-fascist ideals, carried the burden of Axis occupation. The desire for revenge spurred on by 'rightful indignation over the many acts of cruelty and treason committed by the collaborators' was understandable.[85] Less understandable was their abandonment of any pretense to a judicial process – which they had been promising in their propaganda – in the wholesale execution of the repatriated Home Guard.

Overall, the postwar massacres in Slovenia were greeted with silence in the international media. A cryptic exception was an address by Pope Pius XII to the College of Cardinals, on 3 June 1945: 'The present political and social situation suggests these words of warning to us. We have had, alas, to deplore in more than one region the murder of priests, deportations of civilians, the killing of citizens without trial or in personal vendetta. No less sad is the news that has reached us from Slovenia and Croatia.'[86] More formal judicial processes would replace the initial 'sheer frenzy' of violent retribution in Yugoslavia. Unlike the secrecy that enveloped the massacres, the trials that followed would attract far more attention. This was intentional, as the trials were designed to defend the righteousness of the National Liberation War (NOB) and the legitimacy of the new Communist government, as much if not more than its avowed goal of uncovering collaborators and traitors. For example, judges presiding over cases brought before the extraordinary Courts of National Honour (Sodišče narodne časti, SNČ) that were established to try more plebian cases of treason, were required to pledge the following oath: 'I swear upon the honour of my nation, that I will faithfully serve the nation and that I will judge lawfully and objectively, as a guardian and defender of the acquisitions of the national liberation war.'[87] This oath was emblematic of the revolutionary character of postwar justice. More regular civilian courts did exist, but most of the sentences meted out for collaboration in the initial year after the end of the Second World War were carried out either by irregular courts like the Courts of National Honour or military courts.[88] As part of their pledge to defend the NOB and assist in the Communization process, they aimed to vilify the pre-war political establishment that had remained largely on the sidelines in the heroic struggle against fascism. Thus, charges of collaboration smeared both genuine collaborators as well as political opponents of the regime. As confiscation of personal property was a deliberate and common punishment, the trials also gave a legal and populist veneer to the otherwise unpopular Communist programs of nationalization and collectivization.

Some of the first military trials against collaborators took place in Prekmurje, which had already been liberated in early April 1945. Shortly thereafter, military courts in Murska Sobota issued death sentences against the Hungarian sympathizers (*madžaroni*) Oskar Franko, Peter Toth, and Jožef Titan for crimes ranging from denouncing Liberation Front members to assisting in the Magyarization of Prekmurje.[89] In June, five members of the Arrow Cross, including the leader of the Murska Sobota branch, Jožef Kerčmar, were found guilty and executed for their role in the mass arrests and eventual deaths of thirty Slovenes.[90] The trials of the Arrow Cross were directed primarily against members of the Hungarian minority. There were trials against two influential Slovenes, the industrialist Jože Benko and the director of the Prekmurje Bank Jože Lipič. Benko, head of Prekmurje's largest meat processing and exporting company, was acutely involved in local politics and was closely associated with the Stojadinović government during the interwar era. He had greeted the invading Germans in 1941 and done business with the occupiers, and thus, his large commercial holdings and his political leanings were apparently the major factor in his trial.[91] Initially, the military court of Štajerska and Prekmurje gave Benko and Lipič twelve and six years of prison respectively; however, the Supreme Military Court in Ljubljana overruled this, sentencing both men to death, in June.[92] Benko was only posthumously acquitted, in 1993, and a street was named in his honour in Murska Sobota. On 23 June 1945, a disparate group of eleven whom the deputy head of the Department for the Protection of the People (OZNA), Mitja Ribičič, described as 'active members of the *Kulturbund* [...] unrepentant Germanizers, Hitlerites' were put before a military court in Ljubljana and sentenced to death.[93] Among them were Narte Velikonja, accused of being an ideological founder of 'White Guardism,' the Home Guard lieutenant Jože Bitenc, and the Black Hand organizer Franc Arhar. A few days later, another trial was held of twenty members of the Home Guard police, with sixteen sentenced to death and executed that same day.[94] As the historian Jera Vodušek-Starič has noted, many of the military trials were also held in secret, particularly if the accused were military men.[95] All of these trials followed questionable legal practices, were hastily constructed, and had significant direction from the Department for the Protection of the People.

Less bloody were the Courts of National Honour trials that were established in June and July 1945. They were as much exercises in political mobilization as they were a search for justice against those who, as

Slovenski poročevalec described them in June 1945, 'dirtied their national honour, at a time when each honest Slovene was required to place all of his energy at the disposal of the homeland and the fight for national freedom.'[96] The Courts of National Honour did not target ethnic or 'true Germans,' as they behaved in a manner that was consistent with their treacherous nationality and were, thus, not 'carriers of Slovene National Honour';[97] branded as aliens, they were imprisoned and expelled to Austria and Germany, beginning in the autumn of 1945, to join the millions of other Volksdeutsche erased from the map of Eastern Europe. The mass political designs of the Courts of National Honour often demanded mandatory public participation. This was evident in a poster for a SNČ trial in Kamnik on 18 July, which reminded locals that 'the duty of the population is to take part in the judgment of those who erred against the Slovene national honour.'[98] In the wake of liberation, a number of ordinary Slovenes responded, denouncing suspected collaborators as well as personal enemies in an officially sanctioned exercise in popular retribution.

Based in Ljubljana, the Courts of National Honour dispatched five-man senates to trial sessions in Kranj, Novo Mesto, Celje, Maribor, Ptuj, and Murska Sobota. Torture was officially disavowed during the interrogations of defendants, but other methods such as withholding food and cigarettes, imprisonment in 'disciplinary cells,' the use of fake witnesses, and threats of punishment were employed to extract confessions and ensure compliance.[99] In Štajerska, the SNČ pursued Slovene members of the Kulturbund, Steirischer Heimatbund, the Nazi Party, and those who 'blackened' the name of the Partisans and the National Liberation War or who cooperated with military or paramilitary Nazi formations, as well as women who had intimate relations with the Germans. The Courts of National Honour did not impose death sentences, instead handing down 'rehabilitative' punishments of forced labour (usually to a maximum of ten years), the confiscation of property, and the 'loss of national honour' for a prescribed period of time. The loss of national honour was not simply a semantic exercise but entailed 'exclusion from public activity, loss of rights to public office, employment and dignity, [and] loss of all national and political rights.'[100] Forced labour in postwar Yugoslavia was also a brutal experience, with high mortality rates because of overcrowding, unsanitary conditions, malnutrition, and beatings.

These events did not escape the attention of the Western media, which began to turn against their former darling Tito and cast rather unflattering verdicts on the prevailing atmosphere of paranoia and vindictiveness in the country. As early as 16 July 1945, the *New York Times* reported on the fate of some 250,000 former Yugoslav prisoners of war whom the Allies had repatriated: 'The majority naturally are not arrested, but those suspected of hostility towards the Government are sorted out upon arrival – and a very slight suspicion suffices. In Yugoslavia today the mere fact of having been a professional officer before the war is enough to cast doubts on a man, and everybody who was a prisoner of war during the occupation period, and therefore is unable to actively prove his allegiance to the Partisans, is likely to be a suspect.'[101] Another *New York Times* article lamented the 'branding of any form of opposition or criticism as "fascism." The term is no longer connected with any particular form of political organization or philosophy: it is anything that does not suit the new regime.' It highlighted the 'class warfare' in which 'landowners, industrialists, intellectuals, professional officers and pre-war officials are automatically suspect in the eyes of the present regime unless they proved themselves during the occupation and accept present policies without question.' Paranoia, the article concluded, was omnipresent: 'The result of all this feeling is that the atmosphere is heavy with suspicion and hostility. A large part of the population is keen to ferret out hidden enemies everywhere and another part lives in fear of denunciation for crimes they may or may not have committed. It is not conducive to peace of mind.'[102]

Conditions improved somewhat after the Yugoslav provisional parliament announced a general amnesty, on 3 August 1945, and the supplanting of the ad hoc military tribunals and the Courts of National Honour with more regular courts at the end of September.[103] The amnesty law applied to the following persons:

(1) All persons who had been members of Chetnik units, the forces of General Draja Mikhailovitch; Neditch units, those formed by the former Nazi puppet premier of Serbia, General Milan Neditch; units of Croat and Slovene Domobranstvo [Home Guard], the Moslem militia and other armed formations which had been employed in the service of the invader or had assisted him. It will also be granted to persons who had been members of political organizations or of the administrative or official system of that nature.
(2) Persons who had deserted from the Yugoslav Army or failed to respond to the call-up and who, up to the day of publication of the amnesty decree, had not gone over to the enemy side.

(3) Persons who had co-operated with the invader in cultural or artistic fields, provided their co-operation did not exceed the scope of normal professional activity.
(4) Persons who had slandered the Yugoslav Army or its representatives or people's administration or its organs.

The amnesty law did not apply to:

(1) Members of the Ustachi, the pro-Nazi force of Dr Ante Pavelitch, former puppet Premier of Croatia, or members of the Russian Volunteer Corps, except those who were mobilized by force after January 1942.
(2) Members of collaborationist organizations who committed crimes, such as arson, rape, murder, looting, etc.
(3) Informers, agents, officials and other persons employed by the Gestapo or secret political police in the service of the invader or courts of summary jurisdiction.
(4) Ideological initiators, organizers of collaborationist organizations or persons who financed them and persons who served in such organizations from the rank of battalion commander or leader upwards.
(5) Persons who fled abroad to escape responsibility before the people's administration.[104]

The devil obviously was in the details, and the magnanimity of the amnesty law was curtailed by a number of crucial exceptions. Civilians accused of 'petty collaboration' or who had accommodated the occupiers were, indeed, pardoned, partially annulling sentences meted out by the Courts of National Honour, reducing terms of forced labour, and converting the loss of civil rights to the loss of political rights – a less burdensome designation.[105] However, by not overturning verdicts of property confiscation and by not extending the amnesty to individuals found to have financed collaborationist organizations, the amnesty law did not dilute the regime's goal of 'patriotic nationalization.' Instead, it facilitated the nationalization of Slovenia's banking and industrial sectors that were disproportionately invested with German (and formerly some Jewish) capital and that were, arguably, least able to avoid collaboration of some form with the occupiers. Indeed, a number of Jewish properties in Slovenia were confiscated on the ground that its owners had previously considered themselves German, with the CPY's top brass helping themselves to some formerly Jewish-owned villas in Ljubljana.[106] By the end of 1946, the state had confiscated 70 per cent of the industrial sector, the majority of German property, and a large share of the Church's property, some of which was transferred to loyal Partisans and farmers, 'who had deserved well of the National Liberation Struggle.'[107] Moreover, the amnesty of the Home Guard was a macabre act of political theatre, as the vast majority of its members were already dead, and those who had managed to escape abroad had, wisely, no intention of returning. Indeed, trials against Home Guardsmen continued, with some 320 such trials held between 1948 and 1951.[108]

The most sensational trial in postwar Yugoslavia was against Draža Mihailović, who was captured in March 1946 near the Bosnian town of Višegrad and tried and executed in July. Its Slovene counterpart was undoubtedly the so-called Rupnik Trial against Leon Rupnik, Rösener, Vizjak, and Hacin, with Bishop Rožman and Krek tried in absentia. The British had surrendered the first three men to Yugoslav authorities after the war. The trial, which was held in Ljubljana before the military court of the Fourth Army, in late August 1946, was marked by procedural irregularities, not least of which was their joint trial despite their disparate positions and roles during the occupation. They were found to be collectively responsible:

> for the realization of the occupiers' imperialist plans to oppress and destroy the Yugoslav nations and the Slovene nation. Moreover, they organized, gave orders, executed and planned countless war crimes, such as: slaughter and extradition of the wounded to the occupier, murders and massacres, imprisonments, torture, deportations to concentration camps and forced labour, forced mobilization, burnings, robberies and destruction of public and private property, as well as other war crimes. Due to all this they are responsible for the death and suffering of tens of thousands of men, women and children.[109]

Hacin and Rösener remained defiant throughout the trial, with neither willing to admit his guilt. Not surprisingly, both were condemned to death by hanging. In contrast, Rupnik and Vizjak were remorseful, while also pleading ignorance to crimes that were committed by their subordinates. This did not save Rupnik, however; he was executed by firing squad on 4 September 1946. Vizjak received twenty years of forced labour, although he was released before he had served out this term. Rožman and Krek were sentenced to eighteen and fifteen years of hard labour respectively. Other significant trials included the so-called Christmas Trial of thirty-four members and organizers of the anti-Partisan units, held at the Ljubljana district court in December 1945. Several Home Guard officers were found guilty, and five were executed, including Peterlin.¹¹⁰ Friedrich Rainer, who had been captured by the British, was returned to Yugoslavia after having been compelled to testify at the Nuremberg war crimes trials. After a characteristically quick military trial in Ljubljana, in July 1947, Rainer was sentenced to death, although according to the historian Maurice Williams, 'he lived and worked for his captors until 1950, possibly later, writing hundreds of pages of history, political analysis and personality assessments.'¹¹¹

The severe sentence handed down to Bishop Rožman – and to Archbishop Stepinac – was part of a larger Communist offensive against the Catholic Church in Slovenia and Croatia in the immediate postwar years that did not abate until the early 1960s. In fact, diplomatic relations with the Vatican would be broken off from 1952 to 1970. Significant restrictions were placed on the Catholic press and on religious instruction in schools; Church properties were nationalized. Other forms of harassment included provisions preventing nuns from wearing habits in public and the firing of openly practising teachers.¹¹² The most sensational attack was inflicted on acting Ljubljana Bishop Anton Vovk, who was doused with petrol and set on fire at the Novo Mesto train station in January 1952, an act for which even the regime was forced to apologize.¹¹³ Although the Catholic Church in occupied Slovenia, as this study has revealed, was by no means united in opposition to the Partisan resistance, postwar persecution by the regime certainly eroded any remaining good will. Tito's government was particularly irked by Catholic officials who, even after liberation, assisted anti-Communist Slovenes and Croats to escape the country or who pastored their émigré communities. From 1946 until the early 1950s, numerous priests were tried for treason and collaboration, and others were accused of spying for the Vatican on behalf of Western imperialism. Fifty per cent of the wartime priesthood in the bishopric of Ljubljana – 266 out of 531 priests – were convicted of treason, along with eighty-eight priests from the bishopric of Maribor together with a handful of nuns.¹¹⁴ Seven were sentenced to death.¹¹⁵ The historian Tominšek Rihtar concluded that some fifty-seven priests were killed *without* trial from before liberation to February 1946.¹¹⁶

Again, although these measures against the Church were carried out partially in the belief that the 'higher clergy of certain religious communities took an active part in terroristic activities against the people and even committed grave crimes during the fascist occupation,' political expediency and ideology also played powerful roles.¹¹⁷ The Liberation Front had never taken a militantly atheistic line against the Catholic

Church – the Christian Socialists and priests who joined and remained within the OF until war's end are proof of this. The stance adopted was that religion was a stage in social progress; it would disappear when men no longer needed it.[118] However, for the revolution to be successful, the regime could not return to the pre-war days when the 'Roman Catholic Church made deep inroads into all aspects of social, public, cultural, educational and private life, seeking to establish its control over them and to subject them to its authority.'[119] Nor was this a view limited only to Communists. The interwar alienation of Christian Socialists, wary of the too powerful union between the Church and a rightward drifting Slovene People's Party, that continued into the war years with the reformist push by Mikuž, Kocbek, and other Catholic OF members to reach a healthier separation between Church and state and discard the supposed Catholic monopoly on Slovene national identity, was indicative of a broader questioning of the Church's place in politics. Thus, the revolutionary and pragmatic need to curtail the formidable power of the Church as an institution whose authority resided 'dangerously' in Rome, *combined with* the anti-Partisan stance of many of its clergy during the Second World War, best explains the battle of wills that developed between the Communist Party and the Church after 1945.

The number of trials against collaborators increased up until 1948. Many of these later judicial proceedings, however, were primarily show trials, mostly unrelated to actual collaboration during the Second World War. In Yugoslav show trials, as was the case with their Stalinist counterparts in Communist East Central Europe, collaboration with the fascist occupiers became shorthand for political opposition to the regime. Perhaps the most obvious example was the so-called Nagode Trial, named after Črtomir Nagode, the leader of a tiny group of leftist intellectuals who initially had joined with the Liberation Front before being expelled for refusing to sanction its growing sectarianism. Like Nagode, the fifteen co-accused were all progressive, liberal-minded members of the wartime 'Centre,' including Ljubo Sirc, SLS politician Snoj, and the dean of the Ljubljana Faculty of Law, Boris Furlan. Brought to trial at the end of July 1947, they were denounced as wartime collaborators and spies of Western imperialist warmongers. Nagode and two others were sentenced to death; Sirc, Snoj, Furlan, and others were given lengthy prison terms. A similar fate struck those tried in the 'Dachau trials,' so named because the defendants – all Communists and former members of the Liberation Front – had been arrested and sent to Dachau where, according to the charges, they began their careers as spies for the Gestapo and agents of the West. Reminiscent of the Stalinist paranoia that saw evidence of collaboration in the mere survival of Soviet prisoners of war, the Dachau trials would overlap with the Stalin–Tito split. Indeed, with the split in the summer of 1948, trials were reoriented to try suspected Soviet loyalists. These Informbiro 'criminals' were often leading Communists with rather heroic Partisan careers, but they, too, were 'ascribed suspicious past[s] from the period of the National Liberation War.'[120] Tito and the courts remained wary of arresting and convicting fellow Communists on the grounds of loyalty to the Soviet motherland, and evoking trumped-up charges of treason and collaboration during the National Liberation War was a convenient way of sullying the accused's reputation in anticipation of their inevitable conviction. Ever malleable, Cold War tensions with the West and, later, with the Soviet Union were inextricably linked with the occupation – the creation story of the revolution. If the state prosecutors *only looked deeply* enough, as countless postwar indictments revealed, they would find in wartime behaviour the seeds of later treason.

A more detailed expansion of these trials falls outside the scope of this study. Nevertheless, there is little doubt that they cast a long shadow over postwar Yugoslav society. Just as publicly professed religiosity limited one's upward mobility in Communist Yugoslavia, conviction for collaboration could also mean a sharp drop in economic and social status for those who survived its verdicts. To a certain extent, the stigma of collaboration resembled a biological entity, a virus, potentially infecting others with whom the collaborator came into contact. As a result, the families of alleged collaborators were also impacted – neighbours shunned them, they were denied employment and positions in the Communist Party, their children could be banned from entering institutions of higher education, and orphans of fathers killed in combat against the Partisans were allegedly denied places in state-run orphanages.[121] A few of the verdicts in the most egregiously political trials were reversed only in the late 1980s, as was the case for those convicted in the Dachau trials. Some found guilty on spurious and unfounded charges of collaboration would have to wait until the electoral defeat of Communism and Slovenia's independence for legal rehabilitation and the return of confiscated property.

The postwar trials, to say nothing of the summary executions of the Home Guardsmen and other anti-Partisan militiamen, can be criticized for a lack of impartiality and procedural irregularities. Nevertheless, it must not be forgotten that a number of of those sentenced were true collaborators who committed real acts of treason. Deák, in his overview of postwar retribution and trials in Europe, goes even further, submitting that those 'who were punished for good reason far outnumbered those who were punished unjustly.'[122] Understandably, for some Partisan veterans, the recent attempts to rehabilitate those they saw and continue to see as collaborators, such as Bishop Rožman, is viewed as a disgraceful insult to the heavy price that they and their fallen comrades paid for the liberation of their homeland. The passage of time has diminished what had been a sharp cleavage in Slovene society between the guardians of the National Liberation War and its betrayers; nevertheless, the question of collaboration can still draw battle lines among a new generation of Slovenes. Fortunately, unlike in their grandparents' day, these battles are no longer fought with guns but rather with pens.

Conclusion: The Verdict

> People living under German occupation would be damned if they resisted, and damned if they co-operated.[1]
>
> Rab Bennet, historian

On a dismal overcast day in Novo Mesto, in the winter of 1999, my cousin and I decided to climb Trdinov Vrh, the highest peak in the Gorjanci range (1,178 metres) that marks the frontier between Croatia and Slovenia. Ascending, we finally managed to break through the cloud cover into blazing sunshine and perfectly blue skies. Looking northwards, we could clearly make out the distinctive shape of Slovenia's highest peak Mount Triglav, which crowns the Julian Alps – *along the Austrian-Slovene border*. There are few countries in the world that allow one to gaze across its entire breadth. It reaffirmed that, unlike the unfathomable distances of Russia, Slovenia's tiny size and equally small population afforded little protection when it was invaded by its three Axis neighbours during the Second World War. Slovenia's tiny size and population also transformed the occupiers' ambitions to eradicate the Slovene nation into a frighteningly achievable aim. And, crucially, its small size also made the choice between collaboration and resistance for Slovenes strikingly personal. Made up of countless little towns and villages, with a capital city that counted fewer than a hundred thousand souls, most people knew one another's business. It was not unusual to find members of a single family serving in the Anti-Communist Volunteer Militia or the Home Guard facing their Partisan brothers and cousins in the Liberation Front. School friends became sworn enemies, children turned against their parents.

Today, among a generation fortunately untouched by war and living in countries that did not taste the bitterness of occupation, it remains difficult to comprehend how or why anyone would negotiate with representatives of Nazism and Fascism. These proponents of hate were responsible for a war that killed perhaps forty million Europeans, unleashed genocide against six million Jews, and inflicted incalculable material destruction. Yet, a number of Slovenes did collaborate with them and the stain of that association, like the blood on Lady Macbeth's hands, remains impossible to wash away.

Before verdicts can be passed on Slovene collaboration, it would, nevertheless, be wise to highlight a number of common myths of its spectral opposite – resistance. First, the notion that armed Partisan activity captured the enthusiasm of the nation, beginning in 1941, needs to be reappraised. Despite its deification in postwar Yugoslavia, armed resistance attracted, at least until the collapse of Italy and the changing tide of the war in late 1943, relatively few active supporters. The historians James Gow and Cathie Carmichael chose their words rather diplomatically in stating that the Liberation Front 'movement continued not to be as strong as it might have been' and that the 'numbers engaged with the OF remained relatively small till the latter stages of the war.'[2] Moreover, in Gorenjska, and particularly in Štajerska, where German repression against Slovenes was most acute, the Liberation Front was weakest. Here, as well as in other regions of Slovenia, fear of lethal collective punishment conditioned the population to be wary of actually supporting the Partisans, even though many sympathized with their aim of national liberation. Indeed, although sacrifice for the nation read heroically in leaflets and graffiti, it was a far messier and dangerous proposition in real life. In an atomizing occupation, behaving in accordance with what was in the best interest of one's local region, one's village, one's family, or indeed, one's self, could and did trump the distant abstraction of national allegiance. National identity was only one of several identities that made up a Slovene, and it rose and fell during the occupation in accordance with a whole host of factors, not least of which was how safely one could publicly express it.

This was also the case in many other occupied European countries. Bertelson, the Danish resister, remembered how 'the welfare of his family and friends at first meant more than the freedom of his native land.'[3] Mastny concluded that the Czechs were 'singularly defenceless against oppression' and hypothesized that perhaps 'in societies where too many people have too much to lose, comfort and affluence may become serious obstacles to resistance.'[4] Both Partisans and collaborators in Slovenia complained bitterly about the lack of national loyalty and the persistence of misguided 'local patriotism.' The Liberation Front could not understand why they, sacrificing all, had difficulty recruiting and why, in some areas, villagers would intentionally avoid them. Again, this was a common European response. In Greece, 'for villagers with seed to sow and fields to water, resistance was chiefly just another burden and drain on their time.'[5] In Italy, the German execution of twenty-five villagers from Ovaro in retaliation for a Partisan ambush in the dying days of the Second World War sent the furious villagers into the streets with 'shouts of "Death to Communist Partisans."'[6] In short, as Bennett has succinctly summarized, 'contrary to popular belief, resisters were initially regarded not as heroes or selfless patriots, but as reckless adventurers who at times needlessly endangered the lives of their fellow countrymen for acts of doubtful value.'[7]

What many Partisans truly and even fanatically believed was in the best interest of the nation, could – at times – be interpreted as lethal to the immediate concerns of Slovene civilians. This was particularly true of those who lived in the amorphous battle zones of guerilla warfare and paid the ultimate price for having harboured 'bandits.' Seen from the local level, it is understandable why a policy of accommodation may have appeared to be a less hazardous response to the occupation. The population did not instinctively rally behind the Partisan-led resistance; their acceptance came gradually and needed to be earned. That the resistance was denounced as communist by their opponents only made their task that much more difficult in a traditionally conservative society. Slovene civilians could and did think and decide for themselves how best to navigate and survive the occupation. And for some, despite the real threats of reprisal by the Liberation Front, it was collaboration. The thousands of Slovenes who served in the anti-Partisan units or in the occupiers' administration are proof that collaborators did not constitute only a handful of bourgeois traitors who had, according to the leading Slovene Communist Edvard Kardelj, 'never been able to receive any support among the Slovene nation.'[8]

For the remnants of the pre-war political and religious elite in the Province of Ljubljana, the only region in post-invasion Slovenia where they could exist, they initially practised what could only be described as passive resistance, a two-faced tactic of accommodating the occupiers while preparing for their future collapse. The existence of the various party legions and other underground political machinations was proof of this. They did cooperate with the occupiers when necessary, as in the case of the advisory committees (sosveti). Yet, they saw their compliance as a tit-for-tat exchange: they would urge order and calm among the general population in return for certain concessions and the lightening of the burden of occupation. Indeed, in comparison with the wholesale deportation of Slovenes in German-occupied Slovenia, the Magyarization of Slovenes in Prekmurje and the ongoing Fascist oppression of the Slovene minority in Primorska, the Province of Ljubljana was, at least in its first year of occupation, the only haven where Slovenes could still hope to be Slovene. For a small country that can be viewed clear across on a sunny day, it is understandable that the battered remnants of the Slovene national elite clung to the life raft of Italian concessions.

The emergence of a Communist-led armed Slovene resistance, spurred into action by Operation Barbarossa in June 1941, revealed that accommodation and cooperation was not the only national response to occupation. The OF's use of violence upset the non-Communist leadership's plans of lying low and biding time until liberation. Violence begot violence, and before long the policy of passivity was rendered useless in an environment of escalating disorder. The Liberation Front raised the bar of resistance to a height that the non-Communist elite were not willing to match. By declaring the Liberation Front the one and only true Slovene resistance movement, they also contributed to the definition of collaboration. Those who did not join or support the Liberation Front were not working for the liberation of Slovenes and were, thus, upholding the occupation and pigeon-holed as collaborators, or, at best, waverers. The crucial fact that the Liberation Front was spearheaded by the outlawed Communist Party ensured that a significant number of Slovene religious and political leaders, as well as civilians, would not respond to its rallying cry. For this reason the Axis invasion of the Soviet Union and the subsequent rise of Communist resistance movements throughout Europe, of which Yugoslavia and to a lesser extent Greece and Albania were the strongest examples, became such a pivotal moment in the development of European collaboration. As Niall Ferguson has concluded 'The occupation of Europe could now be reconfigured. Invasion of the Soviet Union was represented as a "crusade for Europe"; the entire continent could unite in a "European United Front against Bolshevism" [. . .] The Nazis' European rhetoric struck a chord with all those conservatives for whom German dominance seemed a lesser evil than Soviet Communism.'[9]

Indeed, for many conservative Catholic Slovenes conditioned by the pre-war rift between the political left and right, the Liberation Front was seen not as a liberationist movement – not as *their* resistance – but as an agent of international Bolshevism that had launched a revolutionary seizure of power in the midst of a national catastrophe. The Liberation Front's increasing sectarianism – the assassinations by the Security Intelligence Service (VOS), the Dolomite Declaration, and the jettisoning of coalition partners unwilling to toe the new Communist line – only confirmed these beliefs. Of course, the non-Communist camp hypocritically disregarded their own earlier sectarianism when they refused to allow 'illegal' Communists to join the National Council (Narodni svet) in April 1941. Unlike in Poland, the underground in Slovenia, as in the rest of Yugoslavia, was divided and fractured and could not speak with anything resembling a unified voice. In this environment, it was only a matter of time before the Italian occupiers and, somewhat later, a more pragmatic Germany were viewed as expedient partners in the suppression of the Communist bid for the postwar future of Slovenia. This was the slippery slope that led most Slovene collaborators to fight shoulder-to-shoulder with the Fascists and the Nazis – the Slovene contribution to Germany's common front against Bolshevism that would witness, among other unforeseen developments by war's end, nineteen of the thirty-eight Waffen SS divisions being made up of foreigners.[10] A number of those affiliated with Slovenia's non-Communist camp would, therefore, migrate to the anti-Communist camp and, by the summer of 1942, into the collaborationist camp, using the occupiers' weapons and their military superiority to kill and imprison fellow Slovenes. That the distance between these two outcomes was, as Gross has noted, remarkably short, and that within that limited time-frame the divide between what occupation should have and what it actually produced was so broad, only added to the disorientation as 'shielding' the nation almost overnight morphed into a betrayal of the nation.[11]

Collaborators such as Leon Rupnik and his Provincial Administration (PU) propagandists claimed to speak on behalf of all Slovenes; nevertheles, the reality was that collaboration, particularly in its most organized form of anti-Partisan military units and a collaborating administration, was very much a regional phenomenon centred, for the most part, in the Province of Ljubljana. Collaboration occurred in other regions of Slovenia, and the numerous Courts of National Honour (SNČ) verdicts bear witness to this, but these were most often individual acts of treason, unlike the more formal and widespread collaboration in the Province of Ljubljana. That this was the case had less to do with the socio-economic status and culture of the inhabitants of the Province of Ljubljana, and far more with the fact that the occupiers were most willing to countenance Slovene collaboration *as a policy* only in this area. The Province of Ljubljana was also the one region where Slovenes had the most *choice* in whether to collaborate. Service in the Wehrmacht in Štajerska and Gorenjska was not collaboration; there was no choice in the matter after conscription was introduced in 1942. Service in the anti-Partisan units, on the other hand, officially relied on volunteers. Finally, it was in the Province of Ljubljana where the Liberation Front was most active and where an ever-growing portion of the population came under its rule already during the war. This experience, particularly its more doctrinaire Communist measures, could be sobering. The infliction of reprisals on civilians for their alleged support for the insurgency could harden civilian support for the OF, but it could also lead to disavowal of the Liberation Front as agents of misfortune.

That collaboration took place within what many scholars have defined as a civil war brings us back to the question of definition posed at the beginning of this study: was the use of the occupiers to suppress the Partisans and their Communist program collaboration or self-defence? Indeed, all these years after the Second World War, this question remains contested and divisive. At first glance, it would appear that the actions of the OF's opponents smacked of both collaboration and self-defence. The behaviour of Tito's regime in the immediate post-war years – mass executions, disregard for any political opposition, assault against the Church, appalling show trials – reveal that there was, indeed, something to defend against. The argument employed by a number of scholars, not least Kocbek, that the Liberation Front and the Communist regime were two separate entities is specious and far too convenient, as the seeds for the Communist Party's actions after 1945 were already sown during the earliest stages of the Liberation Front and were inherent in the revolutionary ideology of the CPS and the CPY. As Geoffrey Swain reminded his readers in his recent biography of Tito, the marshal, and this could easily be expanded to his Slovene comrades, was first of all a Communist.[12] There is also some credence to the émigré view that although they were collaborating with the occupiers, a number of anti-Partisans were also working to undermine the occupation and preparing for its overthrow. Many in the Anti-Communist Volunteer Militia (MVAC) were less than enamoured with their Italian allies – indeed, a number had been imprisoned by them.

The Italians were also far from trusting of their Slovene partners. The Germans, too, periodically weeded out untrustworthy Home Guardsmen and kept a close watch over their activities. The Home Guard, as well as its MVAC predecessor, was infiltrated by pro-Allied espionage rings, and as Mlakar has noted, 'the vast majority of the Home Guard members remained politically and ideologically loyal to the positions of the Catholic Slovene People's Party.'[13] That these anti-Partisan units could be both collaborators and resisters speaks to the fatal division of the Slovene and Yugoslav underground. The 3 May 1945 'revolution' pales in comparison with the epic struggles of the outnumbered Partisans; it does appear, however, to have been bloodless, as envisioned in the original aim of the policy of passivity – one that eschewed unnecessary casualties until the 'opportune moment' revealed itself.

And yet, on 3 May 1945, the rechristened Slovene National Army and its supporters *did* have the blood of fellow Slovenes on their hands. The assistance that the anti-Partisan opposition offered the occupiers was far more significant than were its attempts at opposing them. Most important was its military contribution to suppressing the OF insurgency. In addition to hunting the Partisans and uncovering their networks of civilian support, the anti-Partisan opposition also guarded Slovenia's transportation lines and other crucial infrastructure targets, managed the prison system, and played a large role in creating and disseminating anti–Liberation Front and pro-occupier propaganda. Rupnik's administration was turned against fellow citizens who held unfavourable political views, mostly Communists and supporters of the Liberation Front but also some uncooperative non-Communists. In short, a significant portion of the anti-Communist camp took the occupiers' outstretched hand in common anti-Bolshevik solidarity in order to eliminate a vigorous upstart who was a threat to the postwar future of Slovenia and the wartime policy of passivity on which it was predicated. This was collaboration. What the Yugoslav gendarmerie and secret police could not achieve before the war, anti-Partisan Slovenes working in lockstep with the occupier would during the war.

Émigré writers have claimed that there was no alternative – that they were caught between two fires – and, more persuasively, that the Western Allies had, by late 1944, surrendered Yugoslavia along with the rest of Eastern Europe to Stalin. Yet, it must also be remembered that there were effective non-Communist resistance movements in other occupied European countries – the Home Army in Poland immediately comes to mind. Although the fate of the Home Army would hardly be reassuring for Slovene émigrés, the Poles largely avoided collaboration in 'a country without a Quisling,' while also minimizing, at least until the gory events of 1944, the unnecessary reprisals of a premature armed uprising.[14] Indeed, the Poles were offered fewer opportunities for collaboration, but the Poles also made it clear to the Germans, beginning with their resistance in September 1939 and evident in the sheer size, activity, and obedience owed to their underground state, that they would not tread the same path of conciliation that the Czechs had chosen some nine months earlier.[15] Closer to home, there was a non-Communist Slovene 'Centre' that, although very weak, opposed the Liberation Front and avoided collaboration with the occupiers. Unfortunately, there was hardly the most elementary attempt on the part of most Slovene non-Communist leaders to respond to the emerging but still weak Partisan forces in 1941 and 1942, either with their own armed anti-occupier units or serious attempts at seeking common cause with them. Old grievances, party allegiances, and ideological suspicions divided them not only from the Liberation Front, but also from Mihailović's forces. Instead, the non-Communist camp waited for outside assistance, fearful and paralyzed by the consequences their actions might entail, and in doing so, they allowed the Partisans to monopolize the forests. In response, they allied, albeit for the most part opportunistically, with the occupiers – thereby destroying their own image in the eyes of the Western Allies and ensuring their defeat.

Collaboration was not a harmless parlour game. Its consequences were real and deadly serious. Collaboration led to the imprisonment, torture, and murder of thousands of Slovenes. It facilitated the exploitation of Slovenia's human and economic resources which buttressed the occupiers' overall war effort and freed up more of their troops to fight the Soviets and the collaborators' alleged Anglo-American allies. Collaboration also placed Slovenes shoulder-to-shoulder with a Nazi regime that committed some of the worst atrocities in human history – crimes against humanity, war crimes, and genocide – crimes also inflicted on Slovenes. Conveniently and collectively 'denationalizing' the OF resistance as Communists and allies of Stalin's monstrous regime – in fact, rarely did émigré writers refer to the Partisans *as Slovenes* – was a desperate attempt at diminishing their morally fraught decision to side with the occupiers against their co-nationals.

There were, however, degrees of collaboration. As Davies has argued, 'In many ways [. . .] Nazi-occupied Europe resembled a laboratory. There was no uniform "system"; there were as many nuanced varieties of "collaboration" as there were European states. Indeed, if we use the term "collaboration" too often, it begins to lose its meaning. In some instances, the word just isn't appropriate.'[16] The Liberation Front and the postwar Communist regime had a penchant for reducing the complex responses to the occupation into a simple black-and-white formula of resistance or treason, tossing all opponents of the National Liberation War (NOB) onto the same traitorous heap. In reality, some Slovenes were guiltier than others; the degree of collaboration was relative to the nature of the particular collaborative relationship, who partook in it, when it took place, and what motivated the individual to engage in it. Motivation is always somewhat speculative, and far from an exact science, some general verdicts can be offered, nonetheless.

Most culpable were the handful of Dimitrije Ljotić's Slovene followers. These men eagerly sought positions in the Provincial Administration and actively promoted propaganda that was pro-German, opposed to the Western Allies and their Soviet partner, and viciously antisemitic. For them, suffocating the Liberation Front was not the only aim – they hoped for a German victory and the creation of a new fascist European order. They were modelled on and ideologically similar to National Socialism and remained committed to the Germans until the final days of the war, dutifully punctuating the airwaves with their shrill propaganda pronouncements. Their only saving grace was that their public support remained miniscule. Ljotić's Slovene followers operated on the political fringe before the Second World War and relied exclusively on the charitable tolerance of the occupiers for their inflated influence during the war. They were ostracized by both the Liberation Front and the Četniks, avoided by the political establishment, and condemned by the Allies.

Equally distressing were those otherwise unremarkable individuals who used the sudden vacuum of traditional political authority to gain a step up on their social, economic, or political rivals. They could be found throughout occupied Slovenia – indeed, they are common to almost all conflicts – their deeds recorded in memoirs and in the minutes of trial documents. Some were ethnic Germans and Hungarians, or at least they considered themselves to be, while others were Slovenes. Some were alleged to have joined the occupier's secret police, others guarded and mistreated imprisoned Slovenes. Their motivations may have been money, jealousy, or spite, but all operated from self-serving impulses.

Leon Rupnik was somewhat more politically and ideologically complex than the collaborationist Ljotićists, and as the highest-ranking pre-war military man, he was certainly a more influential individual. As mayor of Ljubljana under the Italians and as inspector-general of the Home Guard and 'president' of the Provincial Administration under the Germans, Rupnik acquired the ear of the occupiers and headed an administration that in addition to its everyday bureaucratic duties also uncovered OF members and their sympathizers. His pro-German, anti-Communist, antisemitic, and anti-Allied speeches were numerous and widely disseminated. However, Rupnik never shared the same fame as Pétain, and despite a rather pathetic attempt to foster a cult of personality around him, he became like the marshal, increasingly marginalized as the war drew to a close and dependent on the Germans. As the visual symbol of collaboration in Slovenia, however, Rupnik was denounced as a traitor by the Partisans, the Allies, and in the final weeks of the war, by non-Communist political leaders as well.

Leon Rupnik admired the Germans and had little regard for the pre-war Slovene political establishment, favouring instead, a new, unified, non-sectarian national movement that would coalesce around his Home Guard; still, he was not a Nazi. His exasperation with the political bickering of pre-war Slovenia was more in line with Pétain's nostalgic 'national revolution' and its conservative values of work, family, and patriotism. Like Pétain, who stated, 'I have had only one aim, to protect you from the worst [. . .] for if I could no longer be your sword, I wished to remain your shield,'[17] Rupnik claimed a similar goal of moderating the occupiers, who 'aimed to ruin as much of the Slovenes under the alibi of the war against Communism.'[18] Rupnik acted from a position of deep pessimism. He himself had been imprisoned by the Italians and believed that the war would be long and bloody. For a small nation like Slovenia, an armed uprising was tantamount to national suicide. Rupnik was also fiercely anti-Communist. His willingness to cooperate and negotiate was, in his mind and that of his supporters, a necessary ingredient in the creation and maintenance of the limited autonomy of the Province of Ljubljana. Yet, although his motives may have been originally for the 'good' of the Slovene nation – a rather malleable justification – Rupnik was led into an ever more compromising relationship that assisted the occupiers' exploitation of the province's resources and the suppression of its Partisan insurgency. In the end, Rupnik was not awarded a puppet state for his efforts. The Provincial Administration was not a Slovene version of the Slovak Republic: it remained under close German supervision, and its limited autonomy was not extended to other German-occupied Slovene territory.

Rupnik's administration was assisted by his so-called Kindergarten, comprised of mostly young, politically inexperienced men, many of whom came from the Catholic right. Although they were representative of the wider pre-war European trend of Fascist fellow-travellers, the later abuses of the occupiers – which included, in some cases, their imprisonment in Italian concentration camps – somewhat tempered this initial enthusiasm. However, their vicious opposition to Communism, which they blamed for the collapse of Yugoslavia and the occupiers' mounting reprisals, remained undiluted and ensured their vigorous participation in the Anti-Communist Volunteer Militia (MVAC), the Provincial Administration (PU), and the Home Guard. Along with Rupnik, members of this 'Kindergarten' despised the sectarianism of Slovene politics and weak-kneed liberalism that refused to decisively confront Communism. They also castigated the Western Allies for their self-serving alliance with the Partisans. Their radicalism, according to the anti-Communist Slovene poet and émigré Tine Debeljak, earned them the definition as, 'the revolutionary youth on the anti-revolutionary side.'[19] They did not see themselves as collaborators. Instead, they prided themselves on using the occupiers to expunge the Communist threat to the Slovene nation and creating, as Kociper noted, a 'new Slovene person [. . .] made in God's image.'[20]

Those who served within the ranks of the Village Guards (vaške straže), the Legion of Death, the Home Guard, the Slovene National Security Corps (SNVZ), and the Gorenjska Self-Defence (samozaščita) were undoubtedly collaborators, as were many of the remnant Četniks who eventually folded in with the occupiers. Their actions led to the death or imprisonment of thousands of their fellow countrymen, both active resisters and civilian supporters and sympathizers of the Liberation Front. Their visible collaboration was evident perhaps most shamefully at the Home Guard's oath-taking ceremonies. Both the Anti-Communist Volunteer Militia and the Home Guard were never able to extricate themselves from their dependence on the occupiers, which their supporters claimed was their true cloak-and-dagger intention. Most of the Village Guards refused to join the Četniks, even as the Italians were nearing collapse. Likewise, despite and perhaps because of their lost cause, most members of the Home Guard fought alongside the Germans to the very last days of the Second World War and, in the case of the attack on Ferlach, even after VE day.

This verdict does not disregard legitimate attempts at resistance from within the anti-Partisan ranks. A pervasive distrust certainly characterized their relationship with the occupiers; anti-Italian and anti-German espionage rings did operate in their midst, and plans for an uprising were planned, although never executed. Moreover, there is little doubt that the majority in their ranks were made up of men loyal to the Slovene People's Party (SLS) and other pre-war political creeds. Their motives for collaboration were certainly diverse. Some people were forcibly mobilized into the anti-Partisan ranks or were expected to join as 'repayment' for the care provided to them and their families by the Provincial Administration. At the other extreme were those who joined with criminal motives, to denounce, plunder, and profit and to wield the authority furnished by a gun. Between these two poles there existed a large number of men who were neither forced nor motivated to join by nefarious intent. Some had borne the brunt of Partisan attacks or the occupiers' reprisals. Others believed that service in the anti-Partisan units was the safest and least disruptive way to endure the war. Still others assumed Catholicism needed to be safeguarded. Thus, while not quite the selfless simple peasants defending their land and families against OF terror as émigré writers described them to be, neither were they the bloodthirsty, clerico-fascist traitors of Communist propaganda and historiography. Their motives do not erase their actions; however, and on balance, their assistance to the occupiers, whether in military undertakings against the Liberation Front, guard duty, or their propaganda value, handily outweighed their isolated, tardy, and frankly sporadic attempts at resistance.

The pre-war political elite, especially its representatives in Slovenia but also those in exile, were in a very precarious position after April 1941. As the strongest party in Slovenia before the war, the Slovene People's Party believed that it was responsible for the welfare of the nation during the occupation. The party influence of the SLS over Slovene society was effectively destroyed, however, by the ferocity of the occupation, especially in German-occupied territory. Horrified, the SLS attempted to engage the more accommodating Italians, as seen in the initial cooperation with the advisory committees (*sosveti*) – a move that was viewed by the Liberation Front as nothing short of treasonous. Nevertheless, the pre-war parties did not ignore the needs of an underground resistance. The Slovene and other party legions arose contemporaneously with the Liberation Front, but with the critical caveat that they would not engage in premature and reckless armed resistance. Confronted by an OF resistance that did not share their reservations and spurred on by the assassination campaign of the CPS's Security Intelligence Service (VOS), a number of the non-Communist representatives at home assisted in the organization of the anti-Partisan units. This only widened the gulf between them and some of their representatives in London, who they believed did not fully appreciate the difficult situation of being hemmed in by two enemies: the occupiers and the Liberation Front.

Although not opposed to the suffocation of the Liberation Front, the pre-war elite avoided Leon Rupnik and his circle, who they saw as far too eager to assist the occupiers. Their distrust, as we have seen, was mutual and only increased when it became obvious that the Germans were losing the war. As the historian Egon Pelikan has observed, however, émigré writers were also being hypocritical in foisting responsibility for collaboration only on the Catholic political right. As many of its young *stražarji* (members of the Academic Club Straža) and *mladci* (Mladci Kristusa Kralja) activists were killed after the war and could not respond to these charges – Stanko Kociper being the most vocal exception – the pre-war political establishment was able to conveniently deflect its own responsibility for wartime collaboration.[21] Nevertheless, the pre-war elite's belated and ultimately futile attempt to seize power near the end of the war was indicative of its attempt to walk the thin line between resistance and collaboration. Willing to support the anti-Partisan forces, it shared the Liberation Front's hope for a liberated and enlarged Slovenia within a federated, democratically reorganized Yugoslavia.

Unfortunately, its tight-rope antics failed on two counts. First, the Anti-Communist Volunteer Militia and then the Home Guard were unable to deal a death-blow to the Liberation Front and, second, the Western Allies never advanced beyond the Italian and Austrian frontiers. Riven by interparty squabbles, the non-Communist political remnants in the homeland were discredited in the eyes of the Partisans, the Allies, and some of their colleagues in exile. Moreover, most Slovene civilians, in recognizing the necessity to accommodate the occupiers, were also conscious that the Germans, the Italians, and the Hungarians were their national enemies. How could the Home Guard, who fought alongside the Germans for a year and a half, with a switch of a name at Tabor become their liberators?

The leadership of the Catholic Church in Slovenia, like the pre-war political parties, was also in a difficult position. Having a duty to protect and care for its parishioners and to ensure that religious life continued, it too was willing, indeed, almost compelled, to negotiate with the occupiers to fulfil these responsibilities. This was exceedingly difficult in German-occupied Slovenia, where the Church was attacked as a pillar of Slovene nationalism and where the deportation and imprisonment of priests left empty parishes. Conditions were far more stable for religious activity in the Province of Ljubljana, where the Church structure was left intact and priests expelled from the German zone could find refuge. Bishop Rožman, not surprisingly, advocated for a policy of accommodation and negotiation in order to preserve what was left of Slovene religious and cultural life. The majority of these exchanges were far from treasonous. Some, such as interceding on behalf of thousands of Slovenes imprisoned in Italian concentration camps, were heroic. Church officials were also among the first to document the occupiers' atrocities, and communication with the Vatican was used to disseminate information on what was occurring in Slovenia.

Yet, Bishop Rožman and a number of his priests publicly denounced armed resistance as misguided, not only for its allegedly pointless loss of life, but because it was led and organized by godless Communists. More than anywhere else in occupied Slovenia, the Church in the Province of Ljubljana visibly advocated on behalf of the anti-Communist cause in the civil war. In his September 1942 address to General Mario Robotti, Rožman offered advice on how Slovenes could assist in the suppression of the Partisan insurgency. Military chaplains were embedded among anti-Partisan units at the same time that Rožman condemned the handful of religious officials who sided with the Liberation Front – and in the case of Father Mikuž suspended him from offering the sacraments – chastising them on the grounds that 'no one can be both a Communist and a Catholic.'[22] From the pulpits, some priests engaged in what Rožman described as 'ideological war,' urging order and obedience to the occupiers' decrees at the same time that they demonized the Liberation Front as atheists and a mortal danger to the faith.[23] Bishop Rožman's presence at funerals for anti-Communist leaders and troops, as well as the mass he gave before the Home Guard oath in April 1944, spoke of his tolerance of the occupiers, his deep opposition to the Liberation Front, and his commitment to the anti-Communist cause.

Of course, the Church's ideological opposition to the Liberation Front must be seen in the context of its decades-long waning influence over society, not only in Slovenia but in Europe as a whole, which it blamed on encroaching liberalism, materialism, and of course, Communism. Well before the first shots in the civil war were fired, the priesthood was moulded to fear Bolshevism much more than Fascism and Nazism, which, as the Concordats revealed, the Church could apparently live with. As with the pre-war elite, the VOS assassinations in 1941 and 1942, which counted priests and Catholics among its victims, helped convince the Church that its long influence over Slovene society, indeed, its very survival as an institution, was at stake in the event of a Communist victory. The cumulative behaviour of Bishop Rožman and a number of his priests offers incontrovertible proof that over the span of the occupation they viewed the threat from the left as the greater evil.

Collaboration becomes even less useful when attempting to categorize the behaviour of those who served in the occupiers' civil administration or who maintained economic relations with them. Casting a net as wide as to include all those who 'accepted work in the organs of enemy rule' – one of the charges levied against Ivan Dolenec, principal of the Novo Mesto Gymnasium, in his postwar trial – would implicate tens of thousands of ordinary Slovenes from teachers to engineers, from street cleaners to the mobilized labourers in Organisation Todt, from railway workers to secretaries.[24] Indeed, Axis (or any) occupation by its very nature necessitates some degree of contact between occupiers and occupied. Employment within the occupier's administration or service in labour brigades was not proof of an individual's sympathy for his or her conquerors. Indeed, the civil administration of the Province of Ljubljana was thoroughly infiltrated with OF supporters. Police Corps files are filled with lists of suspected or suspicious employees in all branches of the civil service, from postal clerks to employees of the Justice Department, from pro-Communist professors to sympathetic medical doctors.[25] Documentary evidence reveals that police were suspicious of their own ranks.[26] Indeed, cases abound throughout occupied Europe of individuals and groups using their employment in the administrative organs of the enemy as cover for the underground. Of course, there were also Slovenes employed in the occupiers' administrative and economic superstructure who were neither members nor sympathizers of the Liberation Front, yet they were also not particularly fond of the occupiers, either.

Without a doubt, the cumulative efforts of Slovene administrators, workers, and farmers were of immense value to the occupation. If we consider an imaginary world in which stiff-lipped Slovenes contemptuously refused work in any position that even bore the slightest whiff of serving the occupiers, it is quite obvious that the latter would be burdened with providing hundreds of thousands of labourers from their nations' already scarce human resources. Such a fantastic scenario would also result in hundreds of thousands of unemployed Slovenes unable to provide for their families. In a choice between unemployment or employment in industries and services that directly or indirectly benefited the occupiers, most Slovenes chose the latter. By doing so, they were merely conforming to the millions of French, Dutch, Czechs, and other occupied Europeans who worked in the occupiers' administration and who continued to export food, raw resources, and industrial goods to them.

Here we are skirting the fuzzy divide between collaboration and accommodation, or what the historian Werner Rings has described as 'neutral collaborationism, a widespread attitude which eschewed politics as far as possible and construed itself simply as an unavoidable adjustment to adverse circumstances,' but one that also 'rendered invaluable service to the German war effort.' They did so 'not because they were National Socialists, but because they wanted to survive the war or acquire a better standard of living.'[27] The distance between accommodation and collaboration is significant. It allows, for example, two historians of wartime Poland to come to two very different verdicts on the behaviour of the majority of occupied Poles, with Klaus Peter Friedrich concluding that the 'bulk of the Poles cooperated and collaborated with the Germans as much as survival in the abnormal life of occupation required or allowed'[28] and John Connelly stating that 'Poland remains [. . .] in all of Nazi-controlled Europe, the place least likely to assist the German war effort.'[29] To expect civilians to adhere to strict non-cooperation with the occupiers was to set the bar of 'proper behaviour' so high as to imply that all who did not resist were collaborators. Even the Partisans were not so idealistic. They, for example, attempted to distinguish between Slovenes who actively sought out economic contracts with the occupiers and their collaborators, and those who completed them when asked – a nuanced but significant difference. Questions of culpability for civilian or everyday collaboration, therefore, must be assessed on an individual basis. Civilian propagandists for the anti-Partisan cause were certainly more culpable than Slovenes who worked for the Post Office. The artist Marjan Tršar, who was imprisoned after the Second World War, recounted his Communist interrogator's belief that 'artists who took part in propaganda were guiltier than those who fired guns.'[30] Yet, postal employees who took part in the censorship of correspondence were more culpable than those who delivered the mail. More difficulty arises with evaluations of teachers and principals, who while they implemented the Fascist and Nazi curricula, also educated Slovene children and offered them a refuge from the trying realities of occupation.

It is, thus, fitting to end this work that aimed, above all, to challenge the feuding black-and-white historiographies of Slovenia's occupation by pondering the perplexing grey world of accommodation that most Slovenes inhabited during these difficult times. True collaboration and resistance attracted only a minority of the population of Slovenia. Nor should one assume, as it certainly was assumed in postwar Communist Yugoslavia, that the resistance was the embodiment of pure ideals. Ideological fanaticism and aspirations for power were not only the preserve of Slovene collaborationists. Communist resistance leaders operated at times with what appeared to be an almost flagrant disregard for civilian casualties, and in the last two years of the war were transfixed by the prospect of power and concentrated their resources against their internal enemies. The postwar wholesale executions of approximately twelve thousand Home Guard members without even a façade of due process, speaks to this ruthless ambitiousness. Nevertheless, there was an epic quality to the dogged determination of the Partisans, who largely isolated and against great odds survived to liberate the homeland. This earned them the material and political support of the Western Allies and the gratitude of a significant and ever-increasing proportion of civilians. There was, of course, no shortage of ruthless ambition among collaborators either, particularly those who took advantage of Slovenia's prostrate status and enlisted on the side of the occupiers in pursuit of their own selfish interests or their own peculiar political agendas. In this sense alone were collaborationists and collaborators like Izidor Cergol, Stanko Kociper, and hardened Communist resisters similar, as they all emerged from the political fringes of pre-war Slovenia. Both Communists and collaborators saw an opportunity in the chaos of war to overturn the established order and to push their own 'revolutionary' programs. For most Slovenes, who were concerned perhaps above all with weathering yet another of the intermittent storms that have swept across East Central Europe's history, collaboration and, yes, even resistance, were by far the most extreme avenues in adapting to a world that had been turned upside down, once again.

Notes

Introduction

1. Graham Fraser, 'Threats Bound to Impact Policies: Spain, Britain Reacted to Attacks Very Differently,' *Toronto Star*, 8 June 2006, A6.
2. Stanley Hoffman, *Decline or Renewal? France since the 1930s* (New York: Viking, 1974), 26.
3. Edvard Kardelj, *Pot nove Jugoslavije: Čanki in govori iz narodnoosvobodilne borbe, 1941–1945* (Ljubljana: Državna založba Slovenija, 1946), 277.
4. Edvard Kardelj, *Tito and the Socialist Revolution of Yugoslavia* (Belgrade: Socialist Thought and Practice, 1980), 150.
5. Rodoljub Čolaković, *Winning Freedom* (London: Lincolns-Prager, 1962), 342.
6. Position paper, 'War Criminals, Traitors, and Quislings,' 12 Sept. 1947, Arrangement 25-0, Box 576, Entry 143, RG 153.13: Records of the War Crimes Branch, 1942–1957 (hereafter cited as RG 153), National Archives and Records Administration, Washington DC (herafter cited as NARA).
7. Miha Krek, 'Od Vetrinje do Koreje,' in *Zbornik koledar svobodne Slovenije* (Buenos Aires: Svobodne Slovenije, 1955), 14.
8. Stevan Pavlowitch, *Yugoslavia* (London: Ernest Benn, 1971), 20.
9. H. Seton-Watson, *The East European Revolution* (London: Methuen, 1956).
10. Tadeja Tominšek Rihtar, 'The Post-War Retribution in Slovenia: Its Death Toll,' *Slovene Studies* 28/1–2 (2006), 99.
11. Werner Rings, *Life with the Enemy: Collaboration and Resistance in Hitler's Europe, 1939–1945* (Garden City, NY: Doubleday, 1982) and Peter Davies, *Dangerous Liaisons: Collaboration and World War Two* (Harlow, UK: Pearson Longman, 2004).

12 Jan T. Gross, 'Themes for a Social History of War Experience and Collaboration,' in I. Deák, J. Gross, and T. Judt, eds., *The Politics of Retribution: World War II and Its Aftermath* (Princeton, NJ: Princeton University Press, 2000), 31.
13 Hoffman, *Decline or Renewal?*, 27.
14 Martin Conway, *Collaboration in Belgium: Leon Degrelle and the Rexist Movement, 1940–1944* (New Haven, CT: Yale University Press, 1993), 286.

1 The Battle Goes Postwar: The Historiographical Debate

1 *Slovenec* 73/101, 4 May 1945, in Borivoje M. Karapandžić, *Kočevje: Tito's Bloodiest Crime* (Munich: Iskra, 1970), 33–5.
2 John Corsellis and Marcus Ferrar, *Slovenia 1945: Memories of Death and Survival after World War II* (London and New York: I.B. Tauris, 2005), ix.
3 Ibid., 8.
4 Ibid., 7.
5 Tominšek Rihtar, 'Post-War Retribution,' 97. Note that Tominšek Rihtar's claim of 11,700 repatriates is significantly larger than the 8,263 Slovenes the British military claimed at the time to have returned. See Christopher Booker, *A Looking-Glass Tragedy: The Controversy over the Repatriations from Austria in 1945* (London: Duckworth, 1997), 256.
6 Nikolai Tolstoy, *The Minister and the Massacres* (London: Century Hutchinson, 1986), 204.
7 Julius Epstein, *Operation Keelhaul: The Story of Forced Repatriation from 1944 to the Present* (Old Greenwich: Devin-Adair, 1973), 13–14.
8 Convention between the United States of America and Other Powers, Relating to Prisoners of War, 27 July 1929, in *The Avalon Project: Documents in Law, History and Diplomacy*, Yale Law School.
9 Booker, Looking-Glass, 146.
10 Ibid..
11 Ibid., 147.
12 Ibid., 147.
13 Ibid., 197.
14 Corsellis and Ferrar, *Slovenia 1945*, 48–9.
15 Ferdo Godina, *Prekmurje, 1941–1945: Prispevek k zgodovini NOB* (Murska Sobota: Pomurska založba, 1980).
16 Metod Mikuž, *Zgodovina Slovencev* (Ljubljana: Cankarjeva založba, 1979), 777–8.
17 Branko Božič, *Zgodovina slovenskega naroda* (Ljubljana: Prešernove družbe, 1969), 201.
18 Ibid., 200.
19 Čolaković, *Winning Freedom*, 342–4.

20 Ivan Križnar, 'Slovensko domobranstvo v boju proti narodnoosvobodilnemu gibanju,' in *Osvoboditev Slovenije, 1945* (Ljubljana: Založba borec, 1977), 218.
21 Franček Saje, *Belogardizem* (Ljubljana: Slovenski knjižni zavod, 1952), and Štefanija Ravnikar-Podbevšek, *Sv. Urh: Kronika dogodkov iz narodnoosvobodilne vojne* (Ljubljana: Zavod borec, 1966).
22 Marjan Drnovšek, France Rozman, and Peter Vodopivec, eds., *Slovenska Kronika XX Stoletja, 1941–1995* (Ljubljana: Nova Revija, 1996), 350.
23 Ibid., 170.
24 See Louis Adamič, *My Native Land* (New York: Harper, 1943).
25 Ljubo Sirc, *Between Hitler and Tito: Nazi Occupation and Communist Oppression* (London: Andre Deutsche, 1989).
26 Ivan Korošec, *Prva nacionalna ilegala: Štajerski bataljon* (Ljubljana: Ilex-Impex, 1993).
27 See, e.g., Rudolf Čuješ and Vladimir Mauko, eds., *This Is Slovenia: A Glance at the Land and Its People* (Toronto: Slovenian National Federation of Canada, 1956); Matija Škerbec, *Krivda rdeče fronte* (Cleveland: Tiskarna Mohorjeve družbe, 1957); Tine Debeljak, *Začetki komunistične revolucije v Sloveniji: Ob 25-letnici prvih žrtev* (Buenos Aires: Svobodna Slovenija-Eslovenia Libre, 1968); Dr Jakob Kolarčič, *Škof Rožman: Duhovna podoba velike osebnosti na prelomnici časa*, 3 vols. (Klagenfurt: Tisk Mohorjeva družba, 1967, 1970, 1977); Karapandžić, *Kočevje*; Federation of Slovenian Anti-Communist Fighters, *The Slovenian Tragedy: For the 25th Anniversary of Betrayal of Vetrinje and Kočevski Rog Massacres* (Toronto: Author, 1970); Ivan Dolenec, *Moja rast* (Buenos Aires: Slovenska kulturna izdaja, 1973); Stane Kos, *Stalinistična revolucija na Slovenskem, 1941–1945*, vol. 1 (Rome: Samozaložba, 1984).
28 Škerbec, *Krivda rdeče fronte*, 11.
29 Milovan Djilas, *Wartime* (New York: Harcourt Brace Jovanovich, 1977), 447.
30 Edvard Kocbek, *Tovarišija: Dnevniški zapiski od 17 maja 1942 do 1 maja 1943* (Maribor: Založba obzorja, 1967), 347–8.
31 Boris Pahor and Alojz Rebula, *Edvard Kocbek: Pričevalec našega časa* (Trst: Zaliv, 1975), 150.
32 Božo Repe, *Slovene History: 20th Century: Selected Articles by Dr Božo Repe*. Danijela Trškan, ed. (Ljubljana: Ljubljana: Department of History, University of Ljubljana, 2005), 30. http://www.ff.uni-lj.si/oddelki/zgodovin/DANIJELA/HISTORY/_private/20th/bozorepe.pdf.
33 Dušan Željeznov, *Rupnikov proces* (Ljubljana: Cankarjeva založba, 1980).
34 Boris Mlakar, *Domobranstvo na Primorskem (1943–1945)* (Ljubljana: Založba borec, 1982), 222.
35 Tolstoy, *Minister*.

36 Spomenka Hribar, *Krivda in greh* (Maribor: ZAT, 1990), 53.
37 Gregorij Rožman, 'Škofa Rožmana odgovor,' *Nova revija* 11/93–94 (1990), 879–93.
38 Ivo Zajdela and Roman Leljak, eds., *Črne bukve: O delu komunistične Osvobodilne fronte proti slovenskemu narodu* (Maribor: Založba za alternativno teorijo, 1990), 1.
39 F. Gestrin, B. Grafenauer, and J. Pleterski, eds., *Slovenski upor 1941: Osvobodilna fronta slovenskega naroda pred pol stoletja* (Ljubljana: Slovenska akademija znanosti in umetnosti, 1991).
40 H. James Burgwyn, *Empire on the Adriatic: Mussolini's Conquest of Yugoslavia, 1941–1943* (New York: Enigma Books, 2005), 270.
41 Alojzij Žibert, *Pod Marijinim varstvom: Spomini Slovenca-Nemškega vojaka na drugo svetovno vojno v letih 1941–1945* (Kranj: Gorenski glas, 1995).
42 See Bojan Godeša, *Kdor ni z nami, je proti nam: Slovenski izobraženci med okupatorji, Osvobodilno fronto in protirevolucionarnem taborom* (Ljubljana: Cankarjeva založba, 1995); Boris Mlakar, *Slovensko domobranstvo 1943–1945: Ustanovitev, organizacija, idejno ozadje* (Ljubljana: Slovenska matica, 2003); Tone Ferenc, *Dies IRAE: Četniki, vaški stražarji in njihova usoda jeseni 1943* (Ljubljana: Modrijan, 2002); France Martin Dolinar, 'Sodni proces proti Ljubljanski škofu dr. Gregoriju Rožmanu od 21 do 30 avgusta 1946' (3 parts), *Zgodovinski časopis* 50/1–3 (1996); and Tamara Griesser, *Razdvojeni narod: Slovenija 1941–1945. Okupacija, Kolaboracija, državljanska vojna, revolucija* (Ljubljana: Maldinska knjiga, 2004).
43 See Mateja Čoh, 'V imenu slovenskega naroda: Krivi!' (Celje: Zgodovinsko društvo Celje) *Zgodovina za vse, vse za zgodovino* 9 (2000): 66–80 and Vera Kržišnik-Bukič, 'Legal Trials in Yugoslavia, Particularly in Slovenia, in the Aftermath of the Second World War' (Ljubljana: Inštitut za narodnostna vprašanja) *Razprave in gradivo* 32 (1997): 117–35.
44 Ferdo Gestrin, *Svet pod Krimom* (Ljubljana: Znanstveno raziskovalni center SAZU, 1993).
45 Also see Franc Perme, Anton Žitnik, and Davorin Žitnik, eds., *Slovenija: Zamolčani grobovi in njihovi žrtve, 1941–1948* (Ljubljana-Grosuplje: Društvo za ureditev zamolčanih grobov, 1998).
46 Stanko Kociper, *Kar sem živel* (Ljubljana: Založba mladinska knjiga, 1996), 44.
47 See, e.g., the newspaper *Družina*.
48 See Draga Ahačič, *Osvobodilna ali državljanska vojna?* (Ljubljana: Cankarjeva založba, 1992), and Gregor Tomc, 'Potret domobranca ali kako si pridobim prijatelje,' in Monika Kokalj-Kočevar, ed., *Mati, domovina, Bog* (Ljubljana: Muzej novejše zgodovine, 1999), 85–6.

49 Oto Luthar, 'Slovenia: History between Myths and Reality,' *Slovene Studies* 27/1–2 (2005): 117.
50 See Silvo Grgič, *Zločinov okupatorjevih sodelavcev: Monografija v treh knjigah* (Ljubljana: Piscev zgodovine NOB Slovenije, 1997); and Ivan Jan, *Škof Rožman in kontinuiteta: Zahteva po škofovi rehabilitaciji – ponoven izziv resnici* (Ljubljana: Samozaložba, 1998).
51 A few prominent examples include Robert Paxton, *Vichy France: Old Guard and New Order, 1940–1944* (New York: Columbia University Press, 1972); Hoffman, *Decline or Renewal?*; Rings, *Life with the Enemy*; Conway, *Collaboration in Belgium*; Madeleine Bunting, *The Model Occupation: The Channel Islands under German Rule, 1940–1944* (London: Harper Collins, 1995); Rab Bennett, *Under the Shadow of the Swastika: The Moral Dilemmas of Resistance and Collaboration in Hitler's Europe* (London: Macmillan, 1999); David Barrett and Larry Shyu, eds., *Chinese Collaboration with Japan, 1932–1945: The Limits of Accommodation* (Stanford, CA: Stanford University Press, 2001); Davies, *Dangerous Liaisons*.

2 Before the Deluge

1 Franc Rueh, *Moj dnevnik, 1915–1918* (Ljubljana: Slovenska matica, 1999), 8.
2 Dragotin Lončar, *Politično življenje Slovencev* (Ljubljana: Slovenska matica, 1921), 93.
3 Ivo Banac, *The National Question in Yugoslavia: Origins, History, Politics* (Ithaca, NY: Cornell University Press, 1984), 113.
4 Carole Rogel, 'In the Beginning: The Slovenes from the Seventh Century to 1945,' in Jill Benderly and Evan Kraft, eds., *Independent Slovenia: Origins, Movements, Prospects* (New York: St Martin's Press, 1994), 14.
5 Lončar, *Politično*, 92.
6 John Cox, *Slovenia: Evolving Loyalties* (London: Routledge, 2005), 25.
7 Lončar, *Politično*, 94.
8 Ferdo Gestrin and Vasilij Melik, *Slovenska zgodovina: Od konca osemnajstega stoletja do 1918* (Ljubljana: Državna založba Slovenije, 1966), 331.
9 Cox, *Slovenia*, 28.
10 Mitja Velikonja, 'Slovenia's Yugoslav Century,' in Dejan Djokić, ed., *Yugoslavism: Histories of a Failed Idea* (Madison, WI: University of Winsconsin Press, 2003), 89.
11 Ibid.
12 For simplicity, hereafter the term Primorska will also include this western strip of Notranjska.
13 Cox, *Slovenia*, 31.

14 Wanda Newby, *Peace and War: Growing Up in Fascist Italy* (London: Collins, 1991).
15 Cox, *Slovenia*, 33.
16 Ibid., 31.
17 Tone Zorn, 'A Contribution to the Problem Regarding the Nazi Denationalizing Policy in (Austrian) Carinthia and Occupied Upper Carniola from 1938 to 1943,' in Zivota Anič et al., eds., *The Third Reich and Yugoslavia, 1933–1945* (Belgrade: Institute for Contemporary History, 1977), 423–40.
18 Velikonja, 'Slovenia's Yugoslav Century,' 88.
19 Zdenko Čepič et al., eds., *Ključne značilnosti slovenske politike v letih 1929–1955: Znanstveno poročilo* (Ljubljana: Inštitut za novejšo zgodovino, 1995), 18.
20 Velikonja, 'Slovenia's Yugoslav Century,' 88.
21 Dimitrije Djordjević, 'The Yugoslav Phenomenon,' in Joseph Held, ed., *The Columbia History of Eastern Europe in the Twentieth Century* (New York: Columbia University Press, 1992), 319.
22 Velikonja, 'Slovenia's Yugoslav Century,' 88n8.
23 Cox, *Slovenia*, 34.
24 Velikonja, 'Slovenia's Yugoslav Century,' 88.
25 Ibid., 88–9.
26 Ibid., 89.
27 Djordjević, 'Yugoslav Phenomenon,' 321.
28 Ibid.
29 Ivo Banac, *With Stalin against Tito: Cominformist Splits in Yugoslav Communism* (Ithaca, NY: Cornell University Press, 1988), 70.
30 Cox, *Slovenia*, 38.
31 Boris Mlakar, 'Radical Nationalism and Fascist Elements in Political Movements in Slovenia between the Two World Wars,' *Slovene Studies* 30/1 (2009): 6.
32 Dimitrije Djordjević, 'Fascism in Yugoslavia, 1918–1941,' in Peter Sugar, ed., *Native Fascism in the Successor States, 1918–1945* (Santa Barbara, CA: ABC-Clio, 1971), 131.
33 Ibid.
34 Mlakar, 'Radical Nationalism,' 9.
35 Philip Cohen, *Serbia's Secret War: Propaganda and the Deceit of History* (College Station, TX: Texas A&M UP, 1996), 14.
36 Emil Kerenji, 'Ljotić, Dimitrije (1891–1945), in Richard Levy, ed., *Anti-Semitism: A Historical Encyclopedia of Prejudice and Persecution*, vol 2. (Santa Barbara, CA: ABC-CLIO, 2005), 431–2.
37 Cohen, *Serbia's Secret War*, 15.

38 Harriet Pass Freidenreich, *The Jews of Yugoslavia: A Quest for Community* (Philadelphia, PA: Jewish Publication Society of America, 1979), 173.
39 Cohen, *Serbia's Secret War*, 19.
40 Ivan Avakumović, 'Yugoslavia's Fascist Movements,' in Sugar, ed., *Native Fascism in the Successor States*, 136.
41 Cohen, *Serbia's Secret War*, 18; and Jovan Byford, 'Willing Bystanders: Dimitrije Ljotić, "Shield Collaboration" and the Destruction of Serbia's Jews,' in Rebecca Haynes and Martyn Rady, eds., *In the Shadow of Hitler: Personalities of the Right in Central and Eastern Europe* (London: Tauris, 2011), 297.
42 Burgwyn, *Empire on the Adriatic*, 100.
43 Čepič et al., *Ključne*, 18.
44 Ibid., 31.
45 Egon Pelikan, 'Vizije "Družbene prenove" v katoliškem taboru v tridesetih letih v Sloveniji,' in Peter Vodopivec and Joža Mahnič, eds., *Slovenska trideseta leta: Simpozij 1995* (Ljubljana: Slovenska matica, 1997), 63.
46 Ibid.
47 Djordjević, 'Yugoslav Phenomenon,' 321.
48 Pelikan, 'Vizije,' 62.
49 Čepič et al., *Ključne*, 20.
50 Burgwyn, *Empire on the Adriatic*, 101.
51 *Straža v viharju*, 20 May 1937, 114, in Pelikan, 'Vizije,' 64.
52 Mlakar, 'Radical Nationalism,' 13.
53 Pelikan, 'Vizije,' 64.
54 Peter C. Kent, *The Pope and the Duce: The International Impact of the Lateran Agreements* (London: Macmillan, 1981), 12.
55 Kolarčič, *Škof Rožman*, vol. 2, 166.
56 Dolinar, 'Sodni proces,' part I, 122.
57 Niall Ferguson, *The War of the World: Twentieth Century Conflict and the Descent of the West* (New York: Penguin, 2007) 231n.
58 John Cornwell, *Hitler's Pope: The Secret History of Pius XII* (London: Viking, 1999), 21.
59 Ibid., 39.
60 Kent, *The Pope*, 128.
61 Dolinar, 'Sodni proces,' part I, 125–126.
62 Cornwell, *Hitler's Pope*, 99.
63 Ibid., 114.
64 Kent, *The Pope and the Duce*, 154.
65 Cox, *Slovenia*, 37.
66 James Gow and Cathie Carmichael, *Slovenia and the Slovenes: A Small State and the New Europe* (Bloomington, IN: Indiana University Press, 2000), 20.

67 Branka Prpa-Jovanović, 'The Making of Yugoslavia, 1830–1945,' in Jasminka Udovićki and James Ridgeway, eds., *Burn This House: The Making and Unmaking of Yugoslavia* (Durham, NC: Duke University Press, 2000), 50, 54.
68 Rudolf Hribernik-Svarun, *Spomini: Klic svobode* (Ljubljana: Znanstveno in publicistično središče, 1995), 30.
69 Čepič et al., *Ključne*, 28–9.
70 Bojan Godeša, 'Odnos SLS do vprašanja rešitve državno pravnega položaja Slovenije po napadu sil osi na Jugoslavijo,' in *Slovenci in leto 1941: Znanstveni posvet, Šestdeset let od začetka druge svetovne vojne na Slovenskem: Ljubljana, 11.–12. april 2001* (Ljubljana: Inštitut za novejšo zgodovino, 2001), 97.
71 Ibid., 102.
72 Ibid., 95.
73 Jacob Hoptner, *Yugoslavia in Crisis, 1934–1941* (New York: Columbia University Press, 1963), 219.
74 Cohen, *Serbia's Secret War*, 23.
75 Hoptner, *Yugoslavia in Crisis*, 235–6.
76 Godeša, 'Odnos SLS,' 77.
77 Čepič et al., *Ključne*, 31.

3 Reality Subverted

1 Fred Singleton and Muriel Heppel, *Yugoslavia* (London: Ernest Benn, 1961), 175.
2 For the sake of simplicity and unless otherwise noted, hereafter references to German-occupied Gorenjska should be understood to include the Mežiška valley.
3 Fred Singleton, *A Short History of the Yugoslav Peoples* (Cambridge: Cambridge University Press, 1985), 185.
4 Drnovšek et al., *Slovenska*, 27.
5 Burgwyn, *Empire on the Adriatic*, 32, 97.
6 Drnovšek et al., *Slovenska*, 27.
7 Božo Repe, 'Odnos med Slovenci in nemško manjšin v Sloveniji v dinamiki okupacijskega leto 1941,' in *Slovenci in leto 1941: Znanstveni posvet, Šestdeset let od začetka druge svetovne vojne na Slovenskem: Ljubljana, 11.–12. april 2001* (Ljubljana: Inštitut za novejšo zgodovino, 2001), 238.
8 Tone Ferenc, 'The Austrians and Slovenia,' in F. Parkinson, ed., *Conquering the Past: Austrian Nazism Yesterday and Today* (Detroit, MI: Wayne State University Press, 1989), 208.

Notes to pages 54–8   263

9 Drnovšek et al.,*Slovenska*, 12.
10 Rudi Čačinovič, *Časi preizkušenj: Prispevki k zgodovini Prekmurja* (Murska Sobota: Pomurska založba, 1998), 11.
11 Burgwyn, *Empire on the Adriatic*, 45–8, 97.
12 Tone Kikelj et al., eds., *Slovenska narodna pomoč v okupirani Ljubljani med 1941–1945* (Ljubljana: Mestni odbor medvojnega aktiva OF, 1995), 23.
13 Hribernik-Svarun, *Spomini*, 31.
14 Galeazzo Ciano, *Ciano's Diary, 1939–1943* (London: Heinemann, 1947), 333.
15 Drnovšek et al., *Slovenska*, 11.
16 Marjan Žnidarič, *Do pekla in nazaj: Nacistična okupacija in narodnoosvobodilni boj v Mariboru, 1941–1945* (Maribor: Muzej narodne osvoboditve, 1997), 130.
17 Ibid.
18 SLS situation and political report from Prekmurje, 30 Aug. 1942, doc. 70508/09, fasc. 122, RG Arhiv Slovenija 1898 Slovenska ljudska stranka (hereafter cited as AS 1898), Arhiv Republike Slovenije, Inštitut za novejšo zgodovino, Ljubljana, Slovenia (hereafter cited as ARS.)
19 Čačinovič, *Časi*, 20.
20 Bennett, *Under the Shadow*, 9.
21 Vojtech Mastny, *The Czechs under Nazi Rule: The Failure of National Resistance, 1939–1942* (New York: Columbia University Press, 1971), 46.
22 Rings, *Life with the Enemy*, 60.
23 Čepič et al., *Ključne*, 22.
24 Godeša, 'Odnos SLS,' 79–80.
25 Ferenc, 'The Austrians,' 211.
26 See Slavko Ziherl, Zdenka Čebašek-Travnik, and Zvonka Zupanič-Slavec, 'The Extermination of Psychiatric Patients in Occupied Slovenia in 1941,' *International Journal of Mental Health* 36/1 (2007): 99–104.
27 Drnovšek et al., *Slovenska*, 13.
28 Ibid.
29 German propaganda leaflet, undated, fasc. 28, RG Arhiv Slovenija 1902 Zbirka tisk nasprotnikov NOB in politične sredine (hereafter cited as AS 1902), ARS.
30 Boris Mlakar, 'Repression over the Slovenian People by the German Nazism,' in Peter Jambrek, ed., *Crimes Committed by Totalitarian Regimes* (Ljubljana: Slovenian Presidency of the Council of the European Union, 2008), 120–1.
31 Ferenc, 'The Austrians,' 216.
32 The Croats were allowed to expel as many Serbs from Croatia to Serbia as the number of Slovenes they accepted. Jozo Tomasevich, *War in Yugoslavia,*

1941–1945: Occupation and Collaboration (Stanford, CA: Stanford University Press, 2001), 87.
33 Tomasevich, *War*, 87.
34 Zorn, 'A Contribution,' 423.
35 Tomasevich, *War*, 88.
36 Mlakar, 'Repression,' 117.
37 Helga H. Harriman estimated 55,000 Slovenes, *Slovenia under Nazi Occupation, 1941–1945* (New York: Studia Slovenica, 1977), 42. Ferenc estimated 83,000 were deported, but unlike Harriman, he also included those who fled on their own to the NDH and the relatives of Partisans and executed hostages who were deported to camps in Germany. Tomasevich, *War*, 90.
38 Dolinar, 'Sodni proces,' part I, 127.
39 Ferenc, 'The Austrians,' 214.
40 Drnovšek et al., *Slovenska*, 25.
41 Čačinovič, *Časi*, 11.
42 Ibid., 19.
43 Ibid.
44 'Kraljevi ukaz o ustanovitvi Ljubljanske pokrajine,' *Delavsko zavarovanje*, 19 July 1941, RG Arhiv Slovenija 1875 Rudolf Smersu (hereafter cited as AS 1875), ARS.
45 Davide Rodogno, *Fascism's European Empire: Italian Occupation during the Second World War* (Cambridge: Cambridge University Press, 2006), figures 17, 18.
46 Kikelj et al., *Slovenska*, 23.
47 Ciano, *Ciano's Diary*, 334.
48 Ibid., 334–6.
49 Rodogno, *Fascism's European Empire*, 267–8.
50 Ignacij Hren, 'Moja srečanja z generalom Rupnikom,' *Zbornik koledar svobodne Slovenije* (Buenos Aires: Svobodne Slovenije, 1967), 88.
51 Godeša, *Kdor*, 200.
52 Kos, *Stalinistična*, 113.
53 Ciril Žebot, *Slovenija včeraj, danes in jutri* (Klagenfurt: Družbe Sv. Mohorja, 1967), 11.
54 Željeznov, *Rupnikov*, 78.
55 Godeša, 'Odnos SLS,' 103.
56 Janez Arnež, *SLS: Slovenian People's Party, 1941–1945* (Ljubljana: Studia Slovenica, 2002), 408.
57 Marko Natlačen, 'Dr Marko Natlačen o svojem delovanju med 6. aprilom in 14. junijem 1941,' Historična dokumentacija. *Prispevki za novejšo zgodovino* 151/1 (2001): 143n62.

58 Marko Natlačen, 'Dr. Marko Natlačen, [Priloga] 18 Sept. 1941.' Historična dokumentacija. *Prispevki za novejšo zgodovino* 151/1 (2001): 146–8.
59 Memorandum, '*Sosvet za ljubljansko pokrajino*,' 10 June 1943, doc. 102547, fasc. 120A, Record Goup Arhiv Slovenija 1914 Četniki (herafter cited as AS 1914), ARS.
60 Dolinar, 'Sodni proces,' part I, 133.
61 Rožman, 'Škofa,' 881.
62 *Ljubljanski škofijski list*, 4–6, 31.7.1941, quoted in Tamara Griesser-Pečar and France Martin Dolinar, *Rožmanov Proces* (Ljubljana: Založba družina, 1996), 52.
63 Dolinar, 'Sodni proces,' part I, 131–2.
64 Rožman, 'Škofa,' 882.
65 Metod Mikuž, 'Donesek k zgodovini Osvobodilne fronte,' *Zgodovinski časopis* 15 (1971): 4.
66 Dolinar, 'Sodni proces,' part I, 130.
67 Rožman, 'Škofa,' 884–5.
68 Dolinar, 'Sodni proces,' part I, 128.
69 Ibid., 130.
70 Ferenc, 'The Austrians,' 210.
71 Minutes, Vrhovno sodišče Maribor, 24 Aug. 1945, fasc. 926 *Obsodbe narodnih izdajalcev vrhovno sodišče Ljubljana, Celje, Maribor, Prekmurje* (hereafter cited as fasc. 926) II, RG Arhiv Slovenija *Komisija za ugotavljanje zločinov okupatorjev in njihov pomagačev* (herafter cited as AS KUZOP), ARS.
72 Ferenc, 'The Austrians,' 211.
73 Minutes, Vrhovno sodišče Maribor, 8 Aug. 1945, fasc. 926 II, AS KUZOP, ARS.
74 Dušan Nećak, 'Nekaj osnovnih podatkov o usodi nemške narodnostne skupnosti v Sloveniji po letu 1945,' *Zgodovinski časopis* 3/47 (1993): 440–4.
75 Godina, *Prekmurje*, 25.
76 Minutes, Vrhovno sodišče Murska Sobota, 11 June 1945, fasc. 926 V, AS KUZOP, ARS.
77 Žebot, *Slovenija*, 11.
78 Janez Marolt et al. eds., *Slovenci skozi čas: Kronika slovenske zgodovine* (Ljubljana: Založba Mihelač, 1999), 342.
79 For more on the Sokol Legion, see Vladislav Bevc, ed., *Liberal Forces in Twentieth Century Yugoslavia: Memoirs of Ladislav Bevc* (New York: Peter Lang, 2007).
80 Marolt et al., *Slovenci*, 348.
81 Interrogation of Vizjak, fasc. 925a/IV, AS KUZOP, ARS, 53.
82 Arnež, *SLS*, 409.

83 Geoffrey Swain, *Tito: A Bibliography* (New York: I.B. Tauris, 2011), 30.
84 Tomasevich, *War*, 93.
85 Burgwyn, *Empire on the Adriatic*, 313.

4 The Emergence of Resistance

1 Walter R. Roberts, *Tito, Mihailović and the Allies, 1941–1945* (New Brunswick, NJ: Rutgers University Press, 1973), 26.
2 Sirc, *Between Hitler and Tito*, 33.
3 Korošec, *Prva nacionalna*, 9–10.
4 Sabrina Ramet, *The Three Yugoslavias: State-Building and Legitimation, 1918–2005* (Washington, DC: Woodrow Wilson Center Press, 2006), 142.
5 Ibid.
6 Swain, *Tito*, 37.
7 Drnovšek et al., *Slovenska*, 21.
8 Stevan Pavlowitch, *Hitler's New Disorder: The Second World War in Yugoslavia* (New York: Columbia University Press, 2008), 146.
9 Kocbek, *Tovarišija*, 74.
10 John Lampe, *Yugoslavia as History: Twice There Was a Country* (Cambridge: Cambridge University Press, 2000), 215.
11 Pahor and Rebula, *Edvard Kocbek*, 70.
12 Korošec, *Prva nacionalna*, 10.
13 Drnovšek et al., *Slovenska*, 52.
14 Kardelj, *Pot*, 447.
15 Pahor and Rebula, *Edvard Kocbek*, 69.
16 Drnovšek et al., *Slovenska*, 52.
17 Gregor Kranjc, '"Long Live Our Honest Girls": The Image of Women in Slovene Anti-Communist Propaganda, 1942–1945,' *Journal of Women's History* 18/1 (2006): 50–76.
18 Čepič et al., *Ključne*, 28–9.
19 Emil Weiss-Belač, *Ne hodi naprej* (Ljubljana: Slovenska matica, 1997), 90–1.
20 Tomasevich, *War*, 96.
21 Orchid Mission, 'Observations with a Slovene Partisan Unit in Slovenia, Koroška/Gorenjska Borderland,' 10 Feb. 1945, folder 248, box 18, Entry 154, RG 226, Records of the Office of Strategic Services (herafter cited as RG 226), NARA.
22 Lt. Col. PNM Moore, 'Report on Slovenia,' 14 Feb. 1945, PRO, FO 371/48811, R5717/6/92, quoted in Thomas Barker, *Social Revolutionaries and Secret Agents: The Carinthian Slovene Partisans and Britain's Special Operations Executive* (New York: Columbia University Press, 1990), 156–7.

23 Pahor and Rebula, *Edvard Kocbek*, 69–70.
24 Metod Milač, *Resistance, Imprisonment and Forced Labour: A Slovene Student in World War II* (New York, Peter Lang, 2002), 46.
25 Tomasevich, *War*, 97.
26 SLS situation, 29 Aug. 1942, doc. 70487, fasc. 122, AS 1898, ARS.
27 Žnidarič, *Do pekla*, 342.
28 Pahor and Rebula, *Edvard Kocbek*, 71.
29 Ramet, *Three Yugoslavias*, 143.
30 Tomasevich, *War*, 93.
31 Ferenc's figures, cited in Tomasevich, *War*, 90.
32 Ferenc, 'The Austrians,' 217.
33 Drnovšek et al., *Slovenska*, 20.
34 Tim Kirk, 'Limits of Germandom: Resistance to the Nazi Annexation of Slovenia,' *Slavonic and East European Review* 69/4 (1991): 652, 667.
35 Tomasevich, *War*, 91.
36 Gorazd Stergar, 'Kamniško-Zasavski narodnoosvobodilni partizanski odred in njegova vloga v narodnoosvobodilni vojni na slovenskem leto 1944,' *Vojaška zgodovina* 1 (2007): 90.
37 'Sovražne agenture na teritoriju Slovenije' (1944), *Prispevki za novejšo zgodovino* 38/1–2 (1998), 195–6.
38 Monika Kokalj Kočevar, 'Mother, Are the Apples at Home Ripe Yet?: Slovenian Forced and Slave Labour during the Second World War,' in Alexander von Plato, Almut Leh, and Christoph Thonfeld, eds., *Hitler's Slaves: Life Stories of Forced Labourers in Nazi-Occupied Europe* (New York: Bergahn, 2010), 140.
39 Minutes of Rösener trial, fasc. 925 a/V, AS KUZOP, ARS.
40 Drnovšek et al., *Slovenska*, 44.
41 Tomasevich, *War*, 91.
42 Žibert, *Pod Marijinim*, 310.
43 Tomasevich, *War*, 93.
44 Ibid., 94.
45 Čačinovič, *Časi*, 20.
46 MVAC intelligence report, 16 Aug. 1943, doc. 69197, fasc. 120, RG AS 1895 MVAC (hereafter cited as AS 1895), ARS.
47 Godina, *Prekmurje*, 51.
48 Čačinovič, *Časi*, 31.
49 In postwar 'elections,' Prekmurje voted against the regime candidate. Vienna, 'Political Situation in Slovenia: Government supporters and opponents,' p. 5, 9 May 1946, A-69024, roll 2, micro-1656, Entry 153A, RG 226, NARA.

50 Mlakar, *Domobranstvo*, 11.
51 Bogdan Novak, *Trieste 1941–1954: The Ethnic, Political and Ideological Struggle* (Chicago, IL: University of Chicago Press, 1955), 61.
52 Ibid.
53 Vladimir Vauhnik, *Nevidna fronta: Spomini* (Buenos Aires: Svobodna Slovenija, 1965), 210.
54 Ibid., 281–2.
55 Ibid., 210–11.
56 Burgwyn, *Empire on the Adriatic*, 295.
57 Ibid., 101.
58 Tomasevich, *War*, 98.
59 Ciano, *Ciano's Diary*, 419–20.
60 Burgwyn, *Empire on the Adriatic*, 103–4.
61 Drnovšek et al., *Slovenska*, 31.
62 Burgwyn, *Empire on the Adriatic*, 245.
63 Tomasevich, *War*, 98.
64 Ciano, *Ciano's Diary*, 471.
65 Vauhnik, *Nevidna fronta*, 305.
66 Tomasevich, *War*, 98.
67 Ibid., 103.
68 Burgwyn, *Empire on the Adriatic*, 112.
69 Ibid., 292.
70 Drnovšek et al., *Slovenska*, 40.
71 Burgwyn, *Empire on the Adriatic*, 137.
72 'Report from Ribniška valley,' 1942, doc. 69128, fasc. 120, AS 1895, ARS.
73 Drnovšek et al., *Slovenska*, 21.
74 Burgwyn, *Empire on the Adriatic*, 249.
75 Ibid.
76 Ibid., 290.
77 Drnovšek et al., *Slovenska*, 21.

5 The Emergence of Collaboration

1 Kardelj, *Pot*, 292.
2 Boris Mlakar, 'Vaške straže ter prostovoljna protikomunistična milica,' in Kokalj-Kočevar, ed., *Mati, domovina, Bog*, 8.
3 Saje, *Belogardizem*, 547–9; and *Zaveza* 1/1 (1991). http://www.zaveza.si/index.php/revija-zaveza/53-zaveza-t-01.
4 Mlakar, 'Vaške straže,' 9.
5 Željeznov, *Rupnikov*, 91.

6 This is how Ciril Žebot described the passive response of the Slovene prewar political establishment to the occupation in *Slovenija*, 11.
7 Rodogno, *Fascism's European Empire*, 269.
8 Gross, 'Themes for a Social History,' 24.
9 See the list of Slovene translators working for the Italians at the Ljubljana Court of Appeals: *Službeni list za Ljubljansko pokrajino* 105 (31 Dec. 1941), 496. http://www.sistory.si/publikacije/pdf/uradnilisti/Sluzbeni_list_1941/20-12-31-1941_105-Priloga.pdf.
10 Rodogno, *Fascism's European Empire*, 127, 268.
11 Theatre listings, *Slovenec*, 10 Jan. 1943, AS 1875, ARS.
12 Rodogno, *Fascism's European Empire*, 128.
13 Burgwyn, *Empire on the Adriatic*, 98.
14 Milač, *Resistance*, 39.
15 Dolenec, *Moja rast*, 85, 87.
16 Kocbek, *Tovarišija*, 15.
17 Verdict in trial of Franc Moškar, Vrhovno sodišče Celje, April 1946, fasc. 926 IV, AS KUZOP, ARS.
18 Rodogno, *Fascism's European Empire*, 441.
19 Ibid., 127.
20 Ivanka Tomšič, the mother of the Partisan National Hero Tone Tomšič, claimed that Bishop Rožman intervened, albeit unsuccessfully, to the Vatican to have Tone's death sentence overturned. He was executed in Ljubljana on 21 May 1942. Dolinar, 'Sodni proces,'part I, 133.
21 John Morley, *Vatican Diplomacy and the Jews during the Holocaust* (New York: KTAV, 1980), 151, 164.
22 Gregorij Rožman, 'Pismo v leto 1956,' *Zbornik koledar svobodne Slovenije* (Buenos Aires: Svobodna Slovenija, 1956), 11.
23 Rožman, 'Škofa,' 892.
24 Cornwell, *Hitler's Pope*, 255.
25 Jose M. Sanchez, *Pius XII and the Holocaust: Understanding the Controversy* (Washington, DC: Catholic University of America Press, 2002), 177.
26 Dolinar, 'Sodni proces,' part I, 139.
27 Roberts, *Tito*, 26-7.
28 Mark Mazower, *Hilter's Empire: How the Nazis Ruled Europe* (London: Penguin, 2008), 8.
29 Ramet, *Three Yugoslavias*, 157.
30 Božič, *Zgodovina*, 201.
31 Dolenec, *Moja rast*, 119.
32 Kocbek, *Tovarišija*, 32.
33 Burgwyn, *Empire on the Adriatic*, 247-8.

34 Djilas, *Wartime*, 339.
35 Kocbek, *Tovarišija*, 32, 42.
36 Mark Mazower, *Inside Hitler's Greece: The Experience of Occupation, 1941–44* (New Haven, CT: Yale University Press, 1993), 284.
37 Mastny, *Czechs under Nazi Rule*, 106.
38 Davies, *Dangerous Liaisons*, 62–3.
39 Rings, *Life with the Enemy*, 61, 198.
40 Chad Bryant, *Prague in Black: Nazi Rule and Czech Nationalism* (Cambridge, MA: Harvard University Press, 2007), 188.
41 Ibid.
42 Tomasevich, *War*, 97.
43 Ibid., 98.
44 Swain, *Tito*, 46.
45 Tomasevich, *War*, 100.
46 Drnovšek et al., 35.
47 Ferenc, *Dies IRAE*, 41.
48 'Osnove "Slovenske Zaveze,"' *Slovenska zaveza*, 7 May 1942, folder 17, box 529, Entry 92, RG 226, NARA.
49 *Slovenska zaveza*, 30 May 1942, doc. 71423, fasc. 71423, AS 1898, ARS.
50 Burgwyn, *Empire on the Adriatic*, 106.
51 Ibid., 267.
52 Kardelj, *Pot*, 279.
53 Oto Luthar, *The Land Between: A History of Slovenia* (Frankfurt am Main: Peter Lang, 2008), 431n.
54 Letter from Ciril Žebot to Pavla Verbica, Rome, undated, doc. 70147, fasc. 122, AS 1898, ARS.
55 Dolinar, 'Sodni proces,' part II, 259.
56 Tomasevich, *War*, 97.
57 Lambert Ehrlich, 'Razmere v "Ljubljanski pokrajini,"' quoted in Vrečar Marija, 'Spomenica za Vatikan 14. aprila 1942,' *Acta ecclesiastica Sloveniae* 24 (2002): 626.
58 Korošec, *Prva nacionalna*, 41.
59 Ibid., 9.
60 Ibid., 43.
61 Tomasevich, *War*, 98.
62 Antonio Munoz, *Slovenian Axis Forces in World War II, 1941–1945* (Bayside, NY: Axis Europa Books, 1998)
63 Novak, *Trieste*, 81.
64 Mlakar, 'Vaške straže,' 9.

65 List of 42 agents in Italian service, undated, doc. 69252, fasc. 120, AS 1895, ARS.
66 Žebot, *Slovenija*, 44.
67 Situation paper for Miha Krek, June 1942, fasc. 122, AS 1898, ARS.
68 Mlakar, 'Vaške straže,' 10.
69 Report: Miloš Stare to Rome, 3 Jan. 1943, doc. 102527, fasc. 120A, AS 1914, ARS.
70 SLS report, 'United national-political program of all Slovenes in the occupied homeland,' 30 Oct. 1942, doc. 70166, fasc. 122, AS 1898, ARS.
71 Burgwyn, *Empire on the Adriatic*, 108–9.
72 Instructions from SL leadership, 1942, 19 July 1942, doc. 69581, fasc. 120A, AS 1914, ARS,.
73 Ibid., 19 July 1942, doc. 69580.
74 Ibid., 1 Aug. 1942, doc. 69587.
75 Lists of imprisoned reserve officers and NCOs, undated, doc. 69249, fasc. 120, AS 1895, ARS; Mlakar, 'Vaške straže,' 9.
76 Munoz, *Slovenian Axis*, 2.
77 Report: Miloš Stare to Rome, 3 Jan. 1943, doc. 102527, fasc. 120A, AS 1914, ARS.
78 Interrogation of Ernest Peterlin, fasc. 925a/IV, KUZOP, ARS.
79 'Položaj v taboru Legiji smrti,' Aug. 1942, doc. 69122, fasc. 120, AS 1895, ARS.
80 Boris Mlakar, 'Vaške straže ter prostovoljna protikomunistična milica,' in Kokalj-Kočevar, ed., *Mati, domovina, Bog*, 10.
81 *Vesti*, 22 March 1943, doc. 60312, fasc. 110B, RG Arhiv Slovenija 1912 *Informativni urad – Tajna obveščevalna služba* (hereafter cited as AS 1912), ARS.
82 VS report, Topol, undated, doc. 69124, fasc. 120, AS 1895, ARS.
83 VS patrol log, 30 Aug. – 8 Sept. 1942, doc. 69341, fasc. 120, AS 1895, ARS.
84 Plans for the cooperation of MVAC units in the Christmas arrests 1942, doc. 69255-61, fasc. 120, AS 1895, ARS.
85 Report: Miloš Stare to Rome, 3 Jan. 1943, doc. 102527, fasc. 120A, AS 1914, ARS
86 Burgwyn, *Empire on the Adriatic*, 244.
87 List of the Legion of Death from the Novo Mesto region, 1943, doc. 22909-50, fasc. 120, AS 1895 MVAC, ARS.
88 'Vaške Straže,' *Živi izviri*, 12 June 1943, fasc. 4, AS 1902, ARS.
89 Rudolf Hirschegger, 'Resnica o naši borbi,' *Zbornik koledar svobodne Slovenije* (Buenos Aires: Svobodna Slovenija, 1966), 109–26.

90 Jan F. Triska, *The Great War's Forgotten Front: A Soldier's Diary and a Son's Reflections* (Boulder, CO: East European Monographs, 1998), 3.
91 Mlakar, 'Slovensko domobranstvo,' 12.
92 Gestrin, *Svet*, 91.
93 Letter from France Šeškar to G. Pregelj, undated, doc. A411981, fasc. 120, AS 1895, ARS.
94 Rožman, 'Škofa,' 893.
95 Editorial, *Goreči plamen*, 27 June 1943, fasc. 4, AS 1902, ARS.
96 Stella Alexander, *Church and State in Yugoslavia since 1945* (Cambridge: Cambridge University Press), 1979, 42.
97 Dolinar, 'Sodni proces,' part II, 282.
98 Chaplain 'Vesela's' request, Sept. 1942, doc. 69482, fasc. 120, AS 1895, ARS.
99 Rožman, 'Škofa,' 890.
100 Anton Šinkar's testimony, Kočevje, 28 Sept. 1943, AS 1851 GS NOV in POS *Kočevski process*, ARS.
101 Dolinar, 'Sodni proces,' part II, 284; and Dolenec, *Moja rast*, 106.
102 Karel Wolbang's sermon, 'Mladec – vzor borca Kristusa Kralja,' undated, doc. 95295, fasc. 165A, RG *K. Wolbang*, ARS.
103 Kolarčič, *Škof* II, 197.
104 Alexander, *Church and State*, 42.
105 Tomasevich, *War*, 519–20.
106 Burgwyn, *Empire on the Adriatic*, 263.
107 Ibid., 110.
108 Undated, doc. 70286-337, fasc. 122, AS 1898, ARS.
109 Sirc, *Between Hitler and Tito*, 34.
110 Ibid., 36.
111 Tomasevich, *War*, 521.
112 Čepič et al., *Ključne*, 28–9.
113 Pahor and Rebula, *Edvard Kocbek*, 71.
114 Gestrin, *Svet*, 60.
115 Hribernik-Svarun, *Spomini*, 64.
116 Ibid., 63.
117 Weiss-Belač, *Ne hodi*, 73.
118 Burgwyn, *Empire on the Adriatic*, 268.
119 Report by 2nd Lt. John Hamilton, Hacienda Mission, based on observations from 17 Aug. 1944–24 Sept. 1944, folder 615/A, box 69, Entry 144, RG 226, NARA.
120 Report for Ernest Peterlin, 'Položaj v taboru Legije smrti,' undated, doc. 69168, fasc. 120, AS 1895, ARS.

121 Burgwyn, *Empire on the Adriatic*, 110.
122 *Navodila*, 15 May 1943, doc. 69105, fasc. 120, AS 1898, ARS.
123 Novak, *Trieste*, 62.
124 Drnovšek et al., *Slovenska*, 51.
125 Željeznov, *Rupnikov*, 143.
126 Mlakar, *Domobranstvo*, 37.
127 SLS situation and political report, 1942, doc. 70450, fasc. 122, AS 1898, ARS.
128 Ibid., Sept. 1942, doc. 70457.
129 Novak, *Trieste*, 64–5.
130 Ferenc, 'The Austrians,' 217.
131 Minutes, Vrhovno sodišče Maribor, 12 April 1946, fasc. 926 II, AS KUZOP, ARS.
132 'Interrogation by James Van Tbor, to interrogate certain Yugoslav refugees at Amriya transit camp,' Feb. 1944, folder 93, box 5, Entry 154, RG 226, NARA.
133 Minutes, Vrhovno sodišče Maribor, 31 Dec. 1946, fasc. 926 II, AS KUZOP, ARS.
134 Ibid.
135 Ibid., 15 June 1946.
136 Ramet, *Three Yugoslavias*, 136; John Connelly, 'Why the Poles Collaborated so Little – And Why That Is No Reason for Nationalist Hubris,' *Slavic Review* 64/4 (2005): 774.
137 Minutes, Vrhovno sodišče Maribor, 18 Sept. 1946, fasc. 926 II, AS KUZOP, ARS.

6 The Collapse of Italy and a New Spirit of German Cooperation

1 Memorandum, 'Ustanovitev Slovenskega Varnostnega Zbora,' 26 Nov. 1943, doc. 1573, fasc. 5, RG AS 1878 *Slovenski narodni varnostni zbor v operacijski coni Jadransko primorje* (hereafter cited as AS 1878), ARS.
2 R.A.C Parker, *Struggle for Survval: The History of the Second World War* (Oxford: Oxford University Press, 1989), 177.
3 Drnovšek et al., *Slovenska*, 52.
4 Lampe, *Yugoslavia as History*, 221.
5 Seton-Watson, *East European Revolution*.
6 Tomasevich, *War*, 223.
7 Both Ferenc, *Dies IRAE*, and Arnež, *SLS*, interpret this episode in a similar manner.
8 Arnež, *SLS*, 410.

9 Drnovšek et al., *Slovenska*, 46.
10 Ferenc, *Dies IRAE*, 6–60.
11 Roberts, *Tito*, 98.
12 Lampe, *Yugoslavia as History*, 218.
13 Kosic, Krizman, 'Navodila za obveščevalno službo,' 14 April 1943, fasc. 120A, AS 1914, ARS.
14 Pavle Borštnik, *Pozabljena zgodba slovenske nacionalne ilegale* (Ljubljana: Mladinska knjiga, 1998), plates between pages 97 and 98.
15 MVAC report, 1943, doc. 69562, fasc. 120A, AS 1914, ARS.
16 Ferenc, *Dies IRAE*, 61.
17 Ibid., 84.
18 Ibid., 93.
19 Ibid., 95.
20 Ibid., 159.
21 Unauthored report, 1943, doc. 69566, fasc. 120A, AS 1914, ARS.
22 Ibid.
23 Ferenc, *Dies IRAE*, 157.
24 Novak, *Trieste*, 79.
25 Ferenc, *Dies IRAE*, 162.
26 Ferenc, *Dies IRAE*, 220–23; also summarized in memorandum, 9 August 1943, doc. 69192, fasc. 120, AS 1895, ARS.
27 Ferenc, *Dies IRAE*, 236–7.
28 *Vesti*, 10 Sept. 1943, doc. 61241, fasc. 111A, AS 1912, ARS.
29 Izjava podpolkovnik Josip Dežman, Ribnica, undated, fasc. 120, AS 1895, ARS.
30 Ferenc, *Dies IRAE*, 243–6.
31 Ibid., 247.
32 Izjava podpolkovnik Josip Dežman, Ribnica.
33 Ibid.
34 Ramet, *Three Yugoslavias*, 150.
35 Ibid., 157.
36 Novak, *Trieste*, 80–1.
37 Ferenc, *Dies IRAE*, 162.
38 Ibid., 192.
39 Ibid., 339.
40 Novak, *Trieste*, 80.
41 Tomasevich asserts that the number executed is probably somewhere between the 115 claimed by the Partisans and the over one thousand cited by émigrés. Tomasevich, *War*, 118.
42 Novak, *Trieste*, 80–1.

43 Luthar, *Land Between*, 435.
44 Lampe, *Yugoslavia as History*, 222.
45 Ramet, *Three Yugoslavias*, 157.
46 Dolenec, *Moja rast*, 112.
47 MVAC intelligence report, Novo Mesto, Feb. 1943, fasc. 120, AS 1895, ARS.
48 Home Guard report, Novo Mesto, undated, doc. 18561, fasc. 32, RG AS 1877 *Slovensko domobranstvo* (hereafter cited as AS 1877), ARS.
49 Novak, *Trieste*, 100–1.
50 Vauhnik, *Nevidna fronta*, 299.
51 Maurice Williams, 'The Nazis, German Nationalism, and Ethnic Diversity: The Adriatic Coastland under Friedrich Rainer,' *Slovene Studies* 17/1–2 (1995): 14.
52 Michael Thad Allen, *The Business of Genocide: The SS, Slave Labour, and the Concentration Camps* (Chapel Hill, NC: University of North Carolina Press, 2002), 133.
53 Mazower, *Hitler's Empire*, 391. For a discussion of Globocnik's disputed roots, see Joseph Poprzeczny, *Odilo Globocnik: Hitler's Man in the East* (Jefferson, NC: McFarland, 2004), 9–16.
54 Ferenc, 'The Austrians,' 220.
55 Paul Hehn, *The German Struggle against Yugoslav Guerillas in World War II: German Counter-Insurgency in Yugoslavia, 1941–1943* (New York: Columbia University Press, 1979), 2.
56 Williams, 'Nazis,' 14.
57 Ibid., 3.
58 Ibid., 19.
59 Novak, *Trieste*, 74–7, 86.
60 Ibid., 73.
61 Ibid., 72.
62 Ferenc, 'The Austrians,' 218.
63 Luthar, *Land Between*, 435.
64 Interrogation of Vizjak, 36.
65 Hren, 'Moja srečanja,' 92.
66 Željeznov, *Rupnikov*, 73.
67 Ibid., 119–20. Kociper, *Kar sem živel*, 178.
68 Drnovšek et al., *Slovenska*, 56.
69 Ibid., 60; Williams, 'Nazis,' 17.
70 Pamphlet, '*Slovenskemu delavstvu!*' 10 December 1943, fasc. 24 II, AS 1902, ARS.
71 Ramet, *Three Yugoslavias*, 157.
72 Connelly, 'Why the Poles,' 773.

73 Mlakar, 'Slovensko domobranstvo,' 11.
74 Željeznov, *Rupnikov*, 231.
75 Mlakar, 'Slovensko domobranstvo,' 11.
76 'Poziv za ustanovitev Slovenske domobranske legije,' Sept. 1943, fasc. 24/111, AS 1902, ARS.
77 Željeznov, *Rupnikov*, 231.
78 Rupnik, Order to Home Guard, 30 Sept. 1943, doc. 7498, fasc. 16, AS 1877, ARS.
79 Marolt et al., *Slovenci*, 402.
80 'Službena navodilo za generalnega inspektorja Slovenskega domobranstva,' 1 Jan. 1945, doc. 10158, fasc. 17, AS 1877, ARS.
81 Ibid.
82 Minutes of Rupnik's trial, fasc. 925 a/1, AS KUZOP, ARS.
83 Interrogation of Vizjak.
84 Rupnik's proclamation, 'Slovenci! Slovenke!' Sept. 1943, fasc. 24/II, AS KUZOP, ARS.
85 Tomasevich, *War*, 124.
86 Krener is also spelled Krenner in some sources.
87 Corsellis and Ferrar, *Slovenia 1945*, 51, 55.
88 Mlakar, 'Slovensko domobranstvo,' 15.
89 Home Guard membership list, 12 April 1944, doc. 10967–8, fasc. 18, AS 1877, ARS.
90 Nigel Thomas and K. Mikulan, *Axis Forces in Yugoslavia, 1941–45* (Oxford: Osprey, 1995), 35.
91 Instructions for Home Guard intelligence, undated, doc. 18769-70, fasc. 32, AS 1877, ARS.
92 Ordinary orders for 1944, 23 March 1944, doc. 7219, fasc. 16, ibid.
93 Vizjak's circular, 21 June 1944, doc. 9834, fasc. 17; 274, ibid.
94 Instructions for Home Guard propaganda, undated, doc. 11608-9, fasc. 19, ibid.
95 Riko Pollak, 'Riko Pollak's Story,' in Caterina Angi et al., compilers, *Task Force on Jewish Studies and Antisemitism – Jews and Antsemitism in Slovenia* (Ljubljana.Inštitut za narodnostna vprašanja). http://www.inv.si/psja/spomin/eriko_ziv.htm.
96 Vanja Martinčič, 'Ramo ob rami: Schulter am Schulter, Obleka naredi človeka, uniforma pa vojaka,' in Kokalj-Kočevar, ed., *Mati, domovina, Bog*, 54.
97 Daily reports to the intelligence branch, 25 March 1945, doc. 14353, fasc. 25, AS 1877, ARS.
98 Report of the Home Guard railway police, 16 April 1944, doc. 13469, fasc. 24, ibid.

99 Extracts, Nemškega državnega kazenskega zakonika, undated, doc. 7298, fasc. 16, ibid.
100 Rupnik's order to Home Guard, 2 Jan. 1945, doc. 7501 ibid.
101 Order from PZ Headquarters (HQ) to all units, 17 Aug. 1944, doc. 43356, fasc. 80, RG AS 1876 Policijska varnostni zbor (hereafter cited as AS 1876) ARS.
102 Order from PZ HQ, 6 June 1944, doc. 43302, ibid.; Davies, *Dangerous Liaisons*, 116.
103 Minutes of Hacin trial, fasc. 925/I, AS KUZOP, ARS, 2.
104 VOS intelligence from Gorenjsko, undated, doc. 56579, fasc. 105, RG AS 1888 Narodnosti referat Logatec (hereafter cited as AS 1888), ARS.
105 Minutes of Hacin trial, 1.
106 Ibid., 14.
107 Hacin's order to all PZ units, 11 June 1944, doc. 3050, fasc. 71, AS 1876, ARS.
108 Željeznov, *Rupnikov*, 165, 222.
109 Situation paper, PZ Kočevje, 29 March 1944, doc. 37242, fasc. 72, AS 1876, ARS.
110 Thomas and Mikulan, *Axis Forces*, 36.
111 Report, Home Guard Vrhnika, 29 Dec. 1944, doc. 24592, fasc. 44, AS 1877, ARS.
112 Special order from PZ HQ, 29 April 1945, doc. 35350, fasc. 69, ibid.;
113 Order from PZ HQ, 29 Oct. 1943, doc. 35436, fasc. 69, ibid.
114 PZ report, undated, doc. 43285, fasc. 80, ibid.
115 Order from PZ HQ, 13 July 1944, doc. 4117, fasc. 78, ibid.
116 Circular from PZ HQ to all PZ units, 16 Oct. 1944, doc. 36559, fasc. 70, ibid.
117 Instructions for air defence, 12 March 1945, doc. 40841, fasc. 77, ibid.
118 Report, Zadvor pri Dobrunjah, 25/26 March 1945, fasc. 75, ibid.
119 'Sovražne agenture,' 190.
120 Order from PZ HQ to all PZ units, 17 Nov. 1943, doc. 43321, fasc. 80, AS 1876, ARS.
121 Order from PZ HQ to all PZ units, 7 Dec. 1943, doc. 37169–70, fasc. 72, AS 1876, ARS.
122 Letter from Hacin to Rupnik, 9 Nov. 1943, doc. 40696, fasc. 77, ibid.
123 Ibid.
124 Verdict of Hacin trial, fasc. 925, AS KUZOP, ARS, 30.
125 Transport list of 193 prisoners bound for Ravensbrück, 17 March 1944, doc. 48270, fasc. 88; transport list of 51 prisoners bound for Dachau, 12 Sept. 1944, doc. 48314, fasc. 88, AS 1876, ARS.
126 Tomasevich, *War*, 125.

127 Mlakar, *Domobranstvo*, 95–6.
128 SNVZ membership list, Postojna, doc. 5861–5, fasc. 13, AS 1878, ARS.
129 Mlakar, *Domobranstvo*, 152.
130 Memorandum, 'Provisions for campaign against the enemy,' 28 Nov. 1944, doc. 1408, fasc. 4, AS 1878, ARS.
131 Intelligence report, Gorica, 5 July 1944, doc. 2648, fasc. 7, ibid.; Order, 13 Sept. 1944, doc. 1380, fasc. 4, ibid..
132 Lists of OF organizers, undated, fasc. 6, ibid.
133 Memorandum, 'Ustanovitev Slovenskega Varnostnega Zbora,' 26 Nov. 1943, doc. 1573, fasc. 5, ibid.
134 Order to all SNVZ units, 23 Aug. 1944, doc. 1375, fasc. 4, ibid.
135 Drnovšek et al., *Slovenska*, 54.
136 Monika Kokalj-Kočevar, 'Gorenjska samozaščita,' in *Mati, domovina, Bog,,* 32.
137 Report, *Udarna četa*, 12 Dec. 1944, doc. 94, fasc. 1, RG AS 1873 Gorenjsko domobranstvo (hereafter cited as AS 1873), ARS.
138 Kokalj Kočevar, 'Gorenjska samozaščita,' 28.
139 Ibid.
140 'Božično pismo,' doc. 32, fasc. 1853, AS 1873, ARS.
141 The term *domobranstvo* was at times used interchangeably with the *samozaščita*.
142 Memorandum, Dichtl, Kranj, 4 Dec. 1944, doc. 1–4, fasc. 1, AS 1873, ARS.
143 Ibid.
144 Ibid.
145 Interrogation of Vizjak, 34.
146 Ibid.
147 Minutes of Rösener trial, fasc. 925a/V, AS KUZOP, ARS, 40.
148 Order from Home Guard HQ, 24 April 1944, doc. 7235, fasc. 16, AS 1877, ARS; Order from SNVZ HQ, 6 Oct. 1944, doc. 1261, fasc. 4, AS 1878, ARS.
149 Mlakar, *Domobranstvo*, 97.
150 Kokalj-Kočevar, 'Gorenjska samozaščita,' 28.

7 Shoulder-to-Shoulder with the German Armed Forces

1 Kociper, *Kar sem živel*, 499.
2 Stergar, 'Kamniško-Zasavski,' 90.
3 Lindsay, *Beacons in the Night*, 73.
4 Linn M. Farish, 'Summary report on observations in Yugoslavia for the period 19 Sept. 1943 to 16 June 1944,' folder 198, box 14, Entry 154, RG 226, NARA.

5 R.H. Markham, 'Appraisal of Situation in Yugoslavia as of Aug. 1, 1944,' 31 July 1944, folder 319, box 23, Entry 154, RG 226, NARA.
6 Franklin Lindsay, 'Report of Operations Military Sub-Mission to Fourth Operational Zone Yugoslav Army of National Resistance' (14 May to 7 Dec. 1944, 15 Jan. 1945), PRO WO 202/309, quoted in Barker, *Social Revolutionaries*, 118–40.
7 Lt Col. P.A. Wilkinson, O.B.E. Royal Fusiliers, 'Memorandum on the Revolt in Slovenia,' 27 April 1944, PRO FO 371/44255, R98160, quoted in Barker, *Social Revolutionaries*, 107.
8 Drnovšek et al., *Slovenska*, 84.
9 Home Guard Intelligence centres, as of 26 March 1944, doc. 20463, fasc. 36, AS 1877, ARS.
10 'List of Home Guard informants,' undated, doc. 18333, fasc. 32, ibid.
11 List of *terencev*, activists, sympathizers of OF and members of the CPS with notes on their functions (Loški Potok/Novo Mesto), undated, doc. 17121–3, fasc. 30, ibid.
12 Home Guard interrogations of suspected OF sympathizers, 1944–45, fasc. 29; Judicial pronouncement, Commander of the 24th *četa*, 13 Jan. 1945, doc. 27996, fasc. 52, both ibid.
13 Report on Viktor Turnšek, undated, doc. 18423–7, fasc. 32, ibid.
14 Situation paper on the public's opinion of the Home Guard police, 1 July 1944, fasc. 37. ibid.
15 Daily reports to the intelligence branch, 22 July 1944, doc. 13743, fasc. 25, ibid.
16 Ibid., 10 March 1945, doc. 14321.
17 Interrogation of Vizjak, 57.
18 Alum Mission report to Bari, 26 May 1944, folder 402, box 36, Entry 136, RG 226, NARA.
19 Hirschegger, 'Resnica,' 120.
20 Daily intelligence reports, 13 Feb. 1944, doc. 13249, fasc. 24, AS 1877, ARS.
21 Christmas greeting by Maj. Fischer, 23 Dec. 1943, doc. 23497, fasc. 42, ibid.
22 Circular by Hacin, 24 May 1944, doc. 373782, fasc. 72, AS 1876, ARS.
23 Report from commander of 1st PZ Company Ljubljana, 24 May 1944, doc. 37383, ibid.
24 Order 1070/1 from the leadership of the PZ, 11 May 1944, doc. 3833, fasc. 69, ibid.
25 Instructions for prison guards, undated, doc. 35477, fasc. 69, ibid.
26 Željeznov, *Rupnikov*, 167.
27 Provisions in campaign against the enemy, udarnega polka, 28 Nov. 1944, doc. 1408, fasc. 4, AS 1878, ARS.
28 SNVZ report, 19 Aug. 1944, doc. 1517, fasc. 5, ibid.

29 Rožman, 'Škofa,' 888.
30 Krener's order to Home Guard commanders, 16 April 1944, doc. A437876, fasc. 17, AS 1877, ARS.
31 *Verzeichniss aller Gäste, die Eingeladen sind zum Kammeradschaftsabend am 20.4.1944 um 21 Uhr*, undated, doc. 9808–9, ibid.
32 Željeznov, *Rupnikov*, 236.
33 Interrogation of Vizjak.
34 Željeznov, *Rupnikov*, 236.
35 Ibid., 237–8.
36 Minutes of Rösener's trial, 55.
37 Mlakar, 'Slovensko domobranstvo,' 16.
38 Arnež, *SLS*, 426.
39 Milač, *Resistance*, 96.
40 Hirschegger, 'Resnica,' 122.
41 Franc Golob, 'Dnevnik domobranca,' in Kokalj-Kočevar, *Mati, domovina, Bog,*, 98–115.
42 Order from Krener, 5 Jan. 1944, doc. 7180, fasc. 16, AS 1877, ARS.
43 Daily reports to the intelligence branch, 25 July 1944, doc. 13751, fasc. 25, AS 1877, ARS.
44 Order from Krener, 28 Dec. 1943, doc. 7174; Order from Krener, 15 April 1945, doc. 7486, fasc. 16, ibid.
45 Home Guard intelligence report, 8 Feb. 1944, doc. 18430, fasc. 32, ibid.
46 Order from PZ HQ to Kočevje PZ, 24 June 1944, doc. 43307, fasc. 80, AS 1876, ARS.
47 *Novomeški Informator*, 4 Sept. 1944, doc. 54123, fasc. 100, RG AS 1889 Narodnosti referat Novo Mesto (hereafter cited as AS 1889), ARS; PZ report, 11 April 1944, doc. 36069, fasc. 70, AS 1876, ARS.
48 List of police members to be expelled, 5 March 1944, doc. 40752–5, fasc. 77, AS 1876, ARS.
49 Order from Krener, 29 Feb. 1944, doc. 09750, fasc. 17, AS 1877, ARS.
50 Leaflet, 20 April 1944, fasc. 24, ibid.
51 Vauhnik, *Nevidna fronta*, 402.
52 'Sovražne agenture,' 194.
53 Drnovšek et al., *Slovenska*, 67.
54 'Štajerski Četniški odred,' *Kronika*, June 1944, doc. 69638, fasc. 120A, AS 1914, ARS.
55 'Poročila Štajerske,' *Kronika*, 27 Oct. 1944, ibid.
56 Željeznov, *Rupnikov*, 275.
57 Minutes of Rösener trial, 102.
58 Interrogation of Vizjak, 35.

59 Mlakar, 'Slovensko domobranstvo,' 17.
60 Instructions from John Fistere (MO) to Major Frank Lindsay, 5 April 1944, folder 319, box 23, Entry 154, RG 226, NARA.
61 'Sovražne agenture,' 191.
62 Ibid., 192, Nada Krpič, 'Ogranizacija obveščevalne službe NOV in PO Slovenije, 1941–1945' (diplomsko delo, Univerza v Ljubljana: Fakulteta za družbene vede, 2006)), 27–8. http://dk.fdv.uni-lj.si/dela/Krpic-Nada. PDF.
63 Griesser-Pečar, *Razdvojeni narod*, 325.
64 Parker, *Sruggle*, 191.
65 Vauhnik, *Nevidna fronta*, 402.
66 'Sovražne agenture,' 192.
67 Bevc, *Liberal Forces*, 162.
68 Alum Mission reports, 12, 16 July 1944, folder 401, box 36, Entry 136, RG 226, NARA.
69 'Messages Flotsam,' 24 July 1944, box 39, ibid.
70 Interrogation of Vizjak, 35.
71 Ibid., 34.
72 Kociper, *Kar sem živel*, 152.
73 Order from Rösener, 22 June 1944, doc. 10336, fasc. 18, AS 1877, ARS.
74 Mlakar, 'Slovensko domobranstvo,' 16; Report by Robert H. McDowell, Ranger Unit Mission, Summer 1944, folder 291, box 21, Entry 154, RG 226, NARA, 55.
75 Roberts, *Tito*, 259.
76 Marolt et al., *Slovenci*, 403.
77 Arnež, *SLS*, 430.
78 Interrogation of Vizjak, 53.
79 Captured Partisan letter, 24 Feb. 1945, doc. 21121, fasc. 37, AS 1877, ARS.
80 Interrogation of Peterlin, fasc. 925a/IV, AS KUZOP, ARS, 41.
81 Bevc, *Liberal Forces*, 162.
82 Ibid.
83 Janez Grum, 'Ob 20 letnici Turjaka,' *Zbornik koledar* (1964), 319.
84 Kokalj Kočevar, 'Gorenjska samozaščita,' 32.
85 Bevc, *Liberal Forces*, 166.
86 Hirschegger, 'Resnica,' 118; Corsellis and Ferrar, *Slovenia 1945*, 38.
87 Hirschegger, 'Resnica,' 125.
88 Interrogation of Peterlin, 44, 49.
89 Roberts, *Tito*, 260.
90 Corsellis and Ferrar, *Slovenia 1945*, 39; Home Guard pamphlet, 'Plačanci, roke proč od nas!' 1944, doc. 71608, fasc. 124, AS 1898, ARS.

91 Arnež, *SLS*, 427.
92 Tito, 'Zadnji poziv,' 30 Aug. 1944, doc. 5517, fasc. 13, AS 1878, ARS.
93 Mlakar, *Domobranstvo*, 193.
94 Lindsay, 'Report,' 134.
95 Moore, 'Report,' 152.
96 Order from Hacin, 27 Jan. 1944, doc. 36511, fasc. 70, AS 1876, ARS.
97 Interrogation of Vizjak.
98 Kociper, *Kar sem živel*, 140.
99 Report, 72 Company Vrhnika, 7 Feb. 1945, doc. 18645, fasc. 32, AS 1877, ARS.
100 According to Mlakar, Škulj claimed a thousand refugees joined (Mlakar, 'Slovensko domobranstvo,' 14), while Mlakar noted in his earlier work *Domobranstvo* (75–6) that as many as 5,000 Home Guard were recruited in this manner.
101 Ian Kershaw, 'How Effective Was Nazi Propaganda?' in David Welch, ed., *Nazi Propaganda: The Power and the Limitations* (London: Croom Helm, 1983), 181.
102 Memorandum, *Nove predloge za antikomunistična propaganda*, undated, doc. 66333–4, fasc. 115, AS 1912, ARS.
103 Passmore, 'Europe,' in Kevin Passmore, ed., *Women, Gender and Fascism in Europe, 1919–45* (Manchester: Manchester University Press, 2003), 237.
104 Drnovšek et al., *Slovenska*, 43.
105 Report, 7th SNVZ Company Postojna, 2 July 1944, doc. 4667, fasc. 11, AS 1878, ARS.
106 Order from Kokalj, 3 July 1944, doc. 5034, fasc. 12, ibid.
107 Memorandum, *Ustanovitev Slovenskega Varnostnega Zbora*, 26 Nov. 1943, doc. 1573, fasc. 5, ibid.
108 Leaflet, '*Nov dokaz, Kako nas hoče OF "osvoboditi,"*' 5 March 1945, doc. 4844, fasc. 11, ibid.
109 Paul Jankowski, *Communism and Collaboration: Simon Sabiani and Politics in Marseille, 1919–1944* (New Haven, CT: Yale University Press, 1989), 91.
110 Penalties against police, undated, fasc. 75, AS 1876, ARS.
111 Report from SNVZ Postojna, 6 March 1944, doc. 5567, fasc. 13; Order from Major Ferenčak to all SNVZ units, 25 Aug. 1944, doc. 1191, fasc. 4, both AS 1878, ARS.
112 Report on 72nd Home Guard Company in Vrhnika, 7 Feb. 1945, doc. 18645, fasc. 32, AS 1877, ARS.
113 Order from Krener, 31 July 1944, doc. 9757, fasc. 17, ibid.
114 Orders from Home Guard HQ, 9 July 1944, doc. 7279; early 1945, doc. 7436; 6 May 1944, doc. 7742, fasc. 16, ibid.
115 Order from Home Guard HQ, 21 May 1944, doc. 7248, ibid.

116 Ibid., 6 May 1944, doc. 7240.
117 Order from Krener, 16 Aug. 1944, doc. 9893, fasc. 17, AS 1877, ARS.
118 Ibid., 8 July 1944, doc. 9756.
119 Order from Vuk Rupnik, 31 Dec. 1943, doc. 23498, fasc. 42, AS 1877, ARS.
120 Order from Krener, 26 April 1944, doc. 9815, fasc. 17, ibid.
121 Order from PZ HQ, 6 June 1944, doc. 43302, fasc. 80, AS 1876, ARS.
122 Report, 29th Company Velika Lašče, 17 May 1944, doc. 28281, fasc. 52, AS 1877, ARS.
123 Order from Krener, undated, doc. 7195, fasc. 16, ibid.
124 Order from Home Guard HQ, 23 March 1944, doc. 7219, ibid.
125 Order from PZ HQ, 11 May 1944, doc. 36275, fasc. 70, AS 1876, ARS.
126 Interrogation of Anton Kukman, 16 Dec. 1943, doc. 23696, fasc. 42, AS 1877, ARS.
127 Report from 15th Company Dravlje, undated, doc. 26235, fasc. 48, ibid.
128 Report from PZ Dobrova, undated, doc. 18798–9, fasc. 32, ibid.
129 Kokalj-Kočevar, 'Gorenjska samozaščita,' 32.
130 Ibid.
131 Ibid., 33–4.
132 Breakdown of recruits for units of the Gorenjsko *domobranstvo*, undated, doc. 171–6, 196–204, 217–24, 253–68, 350–5, fasc. 1; doc. 385–9, 398–401, 420–4, 430–5, 509–16, 532–41, fasc. 2, AS 1873, ARS.
133 Interrogation of Franc Tuljak, undated, doc. 16252; Interrogation of Franc Švirt, doc. 16236, both fasc. 29, AS 1877, ARS.
134 Home Guard pamphlet, 1944, fasc. 24, AS 1902, ARS.
135 Ibid.
136 Order from Krener, 12 June 1944, doc. 7286, fasc. 16, AS 1877, ARS.
137 Report on Dolenje Vas, undated, doc. 1786, fasc. 6, AS 1878, ARS.
138 Report from Postojna SNVZ, 1 Aug. 1944, doc. 5491, fasc. 13, ibid.
139 SNVZ propaganda leaflet, '*S silo odvedeni mobiliziranec! Od obljub zapeljani prostovoljec!*' undated, doc. 1897, fasc. 6, ibid.
140 Report from SNVZ Gorica, undated, doc. 1106, fasc. 4, ibid.
141 Report, Maj. J. Cesar, Postojna, 23 May 1944, doc. 1356, ibid.
142 Interrogation of Vizjak, 54.
143 Recuitment poster, 'Primorski Slovenci!' 1943, fasc. 15, AS 1878, ARS.
144 Order establishing the Slovensko domobranstvo, Sept. 1943, fasc. 274, AS 1877, ARS.
145 Order from Krener, 28 Dec. 1943, doc. 7175, fasc. 16, ibid.
146 Željeznov, *Rupnikov*, 222; Minutes of Hacin trial, 17.
147 Assessment of Alojzij Šuštar, 5 April 1944, doc. 39330, fasc. 76, AS 1876, ARS.
148 Report from PZ Kočevje, 29 March 1944, doc. 37244, fasc. 72, ibid.

149 Report from Arrow Mission, 'About the Enemy,' 28 March 1945, folder 332, box 25, Entry 154, RG 226, NARA, 2.
150 Golob, 'Dnevnik domobranca.'
151 'Sovražne agenture,' 195.
152 Order from Rösener, 11 May 1944, doc. 9824, fasc. 17, AS 1877, ARS.
153 Pozivnice, Gorenje Vas, 17 Jan. 1945, fasc. 1, AS 1873, ARS.
154 Golob, 'Dnevnik domobranca.'
155 Mlakar, *Domobranstvo*, 71.
156 Ibid., 72.

8 The Banality of Civilian Collaboration

1 Kirk Ford Jr, *OSS and the Yugoslav Resistance, 1943–1945* (College Station, TX: Texas A & M University Press, 1992), 176.
2 Ibid.
3 Tone Ferenc, 'Nekaj značilnosti narodnoosvobodilnega boja na Gorenjskem,' *Zgodovinski časopis* 31/1–2 (1977): 119–31.
4 Jörg K. Hoensch, *A History of Modern Hungary, 1867–1986* (London: Longman, 1988), 155.
5 Godina, *Prekmurje*, 76.
6 Čačinovič, *časi*, 63; Godina, *Prekmurje*, 114.
7 Godina, *Prekmurje*, 68.
8 Ibid., 168.
9 Minutes, Vrhovno sodišče Maribor, 10 May 1946, fasc. 926/II, AS KUZOP, ARS.
10 Marjan Anidžarič, Jože Dežman, and Ludvik Puklavec, eds., *Nemška mobilizacija Slovencev v drugi svetovni vojni*, (Celje: Zveza društev mobiliziranih Slovencev v nemško vojsko, 2001), 104–19.
11 Marko Perić, 'Demographic Study of the Jewish Community in Yugoslavia, 1971–1972,' *Papers in Jewish Demography* (Jerusalem: Institute of Contemporary Jewry, 1977), 268.
12 Zdenko Levental, ed., *The Crimes of the Fascist Occupants and Their Collaborators against Jews in Yugoslavia* (Belgrade: Federation of Jewish Communities of the Federative People's Republic of Yugoslavia, 1957), 116.
13 Elizabeta Fürst, 'Elizabeta Fürst's Story,' in Angi et al., *Task Force on Jewish Studies and Antisemitism*. http://www.inv.si/psja/spomin/efurst.htm.
14 Oto Luthar and Irena Šumi, 'Living in Metaphor: Jews and Anti-Semitism in Slovenia,' in Wolf Moskowitch, Oto Luthar, and Irena Šumi, eds., *Jews and Slavs*, vol. 12, *Jews and Anti-Semitism in the Balkans* (Jerusalem, Ljubljana: Založba ZRC, 2004), 39.

15 See Damjan Hančič and Renato Podbersič, 'Nacionalsocialistično in komunistično pregajanje Judov na Slovenksem,' in Jože Dežman and Hanzi Filipič, eds., *Hitlerjeva dolga senca: Nacionalsocialistično državnoteroristično in rasistično preganjanje prebivalcev Slovenije in njegove posledice v Titovi Jugoslaviji* (Klagenfurt: Mohorjeva, 2007), 175–88.
16 Borut Bremen, *Na robu zgodovine in spomina: Urbana kultura Murske Sobote med letoma 1919 in 1941* (Murska Sobota: Pomurska založba, 1995), 53.
17 Franc and Helena Matjašec, 'Story of Franc and Helena Matjašec,' (Interviewed by Hannah Starman and Bojan Zadravec), in Angi et al., *Task Force*. http://www.inv.si/psja/spomin/ematjas.htm.
18 Ibid.
19 Godina, *Prekmurje*, 139.
20 Hoensch, *History of Modern Hungary*, 157.
21 Godina, *Prekmurje*, 139.
22 Tomasevich, *War*, 89.
23 Ferenc, 'The Austrians,' 217; Drnovšek et al., *Slovenska*, 79.
24 Alum Mission report, 22 Aug. 1944, doc. 301, folder 2, Entry 136, RG 226, NARA, 10.
25 Peter Wilkinson, *Foreign Fields: The Story of an SOE Operative* (London: I.B. Tauris, 2002), 204.
26 Parker, *Struggle*, 137.
27 Lindsay, 'Report,' 129.
28 Parker, *Struggle*, 137.
29 Marolt et al., *Slovenci*, 403.
30 Parker, *Struggle*, 137.
31 Čoh, 'V imenu,' 74.
32 Ibid.
33 Minutes, Vrhovno sodišče Maribor, 19 Jan. 1945, fasc. 926/II, AS KUZOP, ARS.
34 Lindsay, *Beacons*, 131.
35 Žnidarič, *Do pekla*, 131.
36 Bryant, *Prague*, 175.
37 Lindsay, *Beacons*, 212.
38 Minutes, Vrhovno sodišče Maribor, 30 Aug. 1946, fasc. 926/I, AS KUZOP, ARS.
39 Minutes, Vrhovno sodišče Celje, 29 Aug. 1946, ibid.
40 Ibid., 29 April 1946,.
41 Corsellis and Ferrar, *Slovenia 1945*, 8.
42 Minutes, Vrhovno sodišče Celje, 29 April 1946.
43 Ibid., 13 April 1946.

44 Čoh, 'V imenu,' 74.
45 Barker, *Social Revolutionaries*, 8.
46 Ibid., 11.
47 Kirk, 'Limits of Germandom,' 662; Wilkinson, *Foreign Fields*, 204.
48 Barker, *Social Revolutionaries*, 24.
49 Boris Mlakar, 'Review of Thomas M. 'Barker, *Social Revolutionaries and Secret Agents: The Carinthian Slovene Partisans and Britain's Special Operations Executive.* New York: Columbia University Press, 1990,' *Papers on Slovene Studies* 11/1–2 (1989): 234.
50 Drnovšek et al., *Slovenska*, 51.
51 Barker, *Social Revolutionaries*, 33.
52 Ibid., 19.
53 Ibid., 24.
54 See Ferenc, 'Nekaj značilnosti,' 127, and Mikuž, *Zgodovina*, 826.
55 Kirk, 'Limits of Germandom,' 665–6.
56 Wilkinson, 'Memorandum on the Revolt,' 106.
57 Tomasevich, *War*, 89.
58 Wilkinson, 'Memorandum,' 107–8.
59 German declaration, Feb. 1944, fasc. 24, AS 1902, ARS.
60 German propaganda leaflet, undated, fasc. 28, ibid.
61 Wilkinson, 'Memorandum,' 92, 102.
62 *Samozaščita* pamphlet, 'Grozotni doživljanji Gorenjskega fanta pri branitih,' undated, doc. 116–18, fasc. 1, AS 1873, ARS.
63 Krek, 7 Nov. 1944, doc. 130, fasc. 1, ibid.
64 Centra, 'Smernice za propag. službo v edinicah Gor. Domobranstva,' 9 Dec. 1944, doc. 22–3, ibid.
65 Črni vrh, 12 Aug. 1944, doc. 844, fasc. 3, AS 1873, ARS.
66 Centra, 'Smernice za propag. službo v edinicah Gor. Domobranstva,' 9 Dec. 1944, doc. 22–3, fasc. 1, ibid.
67 Kokalj-Kočevar, 'Gorenjska samozaščita,' 34.
68 Ibid., 32.
69 Mengeš, 29 Nov. 1944, doc. 62; Litija, 2–6 Dec. 1944, doc. 71, both fasc. 1, AS 1873, ARS.
70 Report from *udarna četa*, 29 June 1944, doc. 59, ibid.
71 *Udarna četa*, 12 Dec. 1944, doc. 94, ibid.
72 Nevenka Troha, 'Politične usmeritve med primorskimi Slovenci v coni A Julijske krajine (1945–1947),' *Zgodovinski časopis* 3/49 (1995): 455.
73 Letter, Stanko Žerjal to Rupnik, Gorica, 19 Oct. 1943, fasc. 274, AS 1877, ARS.
74 Troha, 'Politične usmeritve,' 455.

75 Ibid.
76 Agenda, Postojna, 8 June 1944, 1 June 1944, doc. 6595, fasc. 14, AS 1878, ARS.
77 R.H. Markham, 'A Report on the Situation as of May 31, 1944,' folder 319, box 23, Entry 154, RG 226, NARA.
78 Mlakar, *Domobranstvo*, 192.
79 Security agency Brda, 24 July 1944, doc. 1708, fasc. 5, AS 1878, ARS.
80 Novak, *Trieste*, 108.
81 Troha, 'Politične usmeritve,' 465.
82 Mlakar, *Domobranstvo*, 145.
83 Gianmarco Bresadola, 'The Legitimising Strategies of the Nazi Administration in Northern Italy: Propaganda in the Adriatishes Küstenland,' *Contemporary European History* 13/4 (2004), 445.
84 Novak, *Trieste*, 86.
85 Report, SNVZ *bojna skupina* Postojna, 11, 18–20 Jan. 1944, doc. 4989–90, fasc. 12, AS 1878, ARS.
86 Address, Staff Sargeant Franc Kervin, 19 Feb. 1945, doc. 6930, fasc. 15, ibid.
87 Order, Major Ferenčak, 4 July 1944, doc. 1554, fasc. 5, ibid.
88 Leaflet, 'Nov dokaz, Kako nas hoče OF "osvoboditi,"' 5 March 1945, doc. 4844, fasc. 11, ibid.
89 SNVZ propaganda leaflet, 'Primorski Slovenci!' undated, fasc. 15, ibid.
90 Mlakar, *Domobranstvo*, 140.
91 SNVZ report, 31 May 1944, doc. 6268, fasc. 14; Report, 9th SNVZ company Kobarid, 7 May 1944, doc. 4731, fasc. 11, both AS 1878, ARS.
92 Mlakar, *Domobranstvo*, 143.
93 Wilkinson, 'Memorandum,' 106.
94 SNVZ report, undated, doc. 1728, fasc. 6, AS 1878, ARS.
95 Ibid., undated, doc. 1786.
96 Report, SNVZ Gorica, 30 May 1944, doc. 6265, fasc. 14, AS 1878, ARS.
97 Report, II Strike Battalion, Landol, 10 Feb. 1945, doc. 6750, fasc. 15, ibid.
98 Report, SNVZ Postojna, 19 Sept. 1944, doc. 5315, fasc. 13, ibid.
99 Receipt, doc. 3506, fasc. 8, ibid.
100 Marolt et al., *Slovenci*, 403–4; Ferenc, 'The Austrians,' 220.
101 Williams, 'Nazis,' 19.
102 Interrogation report, doc. 16415, fasc. 29, AS 1877, ARS.
103 Report, SNVZ *bojna skupina* Postojna, 11 Jan. 1944, doc. 4989, fasc. 12, ibid.
104 Wilkinson, 'Memorandum,' 106.
105 Drnovšek et al., *Slovenska*, 43.

106 Dr Hubad, Oddelek za socialno politiko in narodno zdravje, 'Prijavljanje poškod—Zdravniški zbornici Ljubljana,' 18 Oct. 1944, doc. 50715, fasc. 93, RG Arhiv Slovenija 1891 Pokrajinska uprava (herafter cited as AS 1891), ARS.
107 Letter to Rupnik, 17 April 1944, doc. 50174, fasc. 92, ibid.
108 Correspondence between Committee for Dolenjski, Notranjski, and Belokranjski Refugees and Rupnik, undated, doc. 50172, ibid.
109 Report, PU district office Novo Mesto, 5 Oct. 1944, doc. 52982, fasc. 98, ibid.
110 Letter to Rupnik, undated, fasc. 92, ibid.
111 Letter to Rupnik, 14 Jan. 1944, doc. 50175, ibid.
112 Odbor za moralno-socialno obnovo Slovenije to Rupnik, 19 Nov. 1943, doc. 50171, ibid.
113 Correspondence, Kino Union, Kino Matica, Kino 'Sloga' and I. Suša, 13 Dec. 1943, doc. 50052, ibid.
114 *Convention (IV) Respecting the Laws and Customs of War on Land and Its Annex: Regulations Concerning the Laws and Customs of War on Land. The Hague, 18 October 1907*. International Humanitarian Law—Treaties and Documents, International Committee for the Red Cross. http://www.icrc.org/ihl.nsf/385ec082b509e76c41256739003e636d/1d1726425f6955aec125641e0038bfd6.
115 'Navodila za informativno in propagandno službo,' 1944, doc. 56085, fasc. 104, AS 1888, ARS.
116 Lists of OF sympathizers, 1943–1945, fasc. 106, AS 1912, ARS.
117 Intelligence report: Julka Tabor, 23 May 1944, doc. 54006, fasc. 100, AS 1889, ARS.
118 Novo Mesto district office, 14 June 1944, doc. 52587, fasc. 97, AS 1891, ARS.
119 Rupnik's reply to Novo Mesto district office's request of 14 June 1944, 1 July 1944, doc. 52589, ibid.
120 Novo Mesto district office, 21 July 1944, doc. 52590, ibid.
121 Rupnik's order for the arrest of Ivana Omahen, 23 Nov. 1943, doc. 49932, fasc. 92, AS 1891, ARS.
122 Report, 'O delu propagandnega odseka pokrajinske uprave od začetka do 30. aprila 1944,' doc. 65960, fasc. 115, AS 1912, ARS.
123 Radio Ljubljana program, *Slovenec*, 25 Nov. 1943, doc. 96404, fasc. 165B, RG AS Ivan Dolenec; 'Legenda po stanju 30. IV. 1944,' doc. 65959, ibid.
124 Summary of propaganda activities, 30 April 1944, doc. 66004–5, ibid.
125 Ibid.

126 *Manifesto to the Slovenes*, 23 Dec. 1943, folder 17, box 529, Entry 92, RG 226, NARA; Letter, Puš to all PU branch offices, doc. 64597, fasc. 112, AS 1896, ARS.
127 Summary of propaganda activities, 30 April 1944.
128 'Legenda po stanju 30. IV. 1944,' doc. 65959, fasc. 115, AS 1912, ARS.
129 Anti-Communist lectures for workers, 1943–1944, doc. 65979, ibid.
130 Listing of 'Public Performances,' undated, doc. 66011, ibid.
131 'Legenda po stanju 30. IV. 1944,' doc. 65959, ibid.
132 Order, Novo Mesto district office to Šmihel-Stopiče, 14 Feb. 1944, doc. 51691, fasc. 95, AS 1891, ARS.
133 Rupnik's proclamation, 'Slovenci! Slovenke!,' undated, fasc. 24/II, AS 1902, ARS.
134 Marolt et al., *Slovenci*, 404.
135 Željeznov, *Rupnikov*, 90.
136 Drnovšek et al., *Slovenska*, 57.
137 Bevc, *Liberal Forces*, 151–2, 162.
138 Rupnik, Order no. 2, 9 Oct. 1944, doc. 10123–4, fasc. 17, AS 1877, ARS.
139 Željeznov, *Rupnikov*, 91.
140 Hren 'Moja srečanja,' 92; Kociper, *Kar sem živel*, 100.
141 Željeznov, *Rupnikov*, 154.
142 Ibid., 134.
143 Ibid., 151.
144 Kociper, *Kar sem živel*, 51.
145 Željeznov, *Rupnikov*, 162.
146 Matija Škerbec, *Spomini in reminiscence*, quoted in Kociper, *Kar sem živel*, 85.
147 Mojca Šorn, 'Idejni in politični nazori Rupnikovega kroga,' *Prispevki za novejšo zgodovino* 153/1 (2003): 66.
148 Kociper, *Kar sem živel*, 98.
149 Ibid., 150, 178, 226–8.
150 Interrogation of Vizjak, 24.
151 Ibid., 36.
152 Drnovšek et al., *Slovenska*, 58.
153 Leaflet, 'Par 1000 mravljincev, ki v . . . marširajo . . . ,' undated, doc. 66291, fasc. 115, AS 1912, ARS.
154 Cergol's radio broadcast, 'Rupnik in Slovenski domobraci,' undated, doc. 71576, fasc. 124, AS 1898, ARS.
155 Cergol's speech, 30 Jan. 1945, doc. 18806, fasc. 32, AS 1877, ARS.
156 Mazower, *Hitler's Empire*, 432.
157 TOS lists, undated, fasc. 106, AS 1912, ARS.

158 Order from Rupnik, 26 Nov. 1943, doc. 50925, fasc. 94, AS 1891, ARS.
159 Cergol, circular to PU branch offices, 17 March 1945, doc. 66677, fasc. 115, AS 1912, ARS.
160 Dolinar, 'Sodni proces,' part III, 434.
161 Alexander, *Church*, 46.
162 Gregorij Rožman, 'Božično pismo slovenskim domobrancem,' *Slovensko domobranstvo*, 28 Dec. 1944, fasc. 6, AS 1902, ARS.
163 Minutes of Rösener trial, 41.
164 Dolinar, 'Sodni proces,' part II, 284.
165 Ibid., 284.
166 Rožman, 'Škofa,' 886.
167 Interrogation of Vizjak.
168 Rožman, 'Škofa,' 888.
169 Dolinar, 'Sodni proces,' part II, 285–6.
170 Minutes of Rösener trial, 40.
171 Dolinar, 'Sodni proces,' part II, 287–8.
172 Hirschegger, 'Resnica,' 120.
173 Bevc, *Liberal Forces*, 154.
174 Rožman, 'Škofa,' 890–1.
175 Before the war, almost half of the industrial enterprises in Slovenia consisted of German capital. Drnovšek et al., *Slovenska*, 119.
176 List, 'Podjeta, ki delajo za Nemce,' undated, doc. 007366–69, fasc. 304, RG Arhiv Slovenija 1895 BEGA—domobranstvo (hereafter cited as AS 1895 BEGA), ARS.
177 Receipts from A. Kassig and Pavel Vrtačnik, 7 March 1944, doc. 5743–4, fasc. 13, AS 1878, ARS.
178 Fasc. 304, AS 1895 BEGA, ARS.
179 List, 'Podjeta, ki delajo za Nemce,' undated, doc. 007366–9, ibid.
180 Davies, *Dangerous Liaisons*, 135.
181 V. Lazovich to Ben Ames, 'Leaflets concerning Rupnik and Rožman,' undated, folder 790, box 79, Entry 144, RG 226, NARA.
182 Lindsay, *Beacons*, 45.
183 Report from FERN mission, 'Tunic' operation, 30 Aug. 1944, folder 365, box 25, Entry 154, RG 226, NARA.
184 George S. Wuchinich, 'Political Appraisal of Slovenia,' 14 Aug. 1944, folder 301, box 22, Entry 154, RG 226, NARA.
185 Captured Partisan archive, undated, doc. 54014, fasc. 100, AS 1889, ARS.
186 Fitzroy Maclean, *Eastern Approaches*, (New York: Time-Life Books, 1949), 339.
187 Weiss-Belač, *Ne hodi*, 29.

188 Daily reports to the intelligence branch, 2 Sept. 1944, doc. 13852, fasc. 25, AS 1877, ARS.
189 Ibid., 6 March 1944, doc. 13331.
190 *Slovensko domobranstvo*, 3 Aug. 1944, fasc. 6, AS 1902, ARS.
191 Daily reports to the intelligence branch, 7 Feb. 1944, doc. 13225, fasc. 25, AS 1877, ARS.
192 Ibid., 9 Feb. 1944, doc. 13235.
193 Kocbek, *Tovarišija*, 346–7.
194 Mikuž, *Zgodovina*, 778.
195 Report, 115th Home Guard company Ribnica, 12 Feb. 1945, doc. 18647–8, fasc. 32, AS 1877, ARS.
196 Partisan pamphlet, 'Opozorilo domobrancem!,' 28 Nov. 1943, doc. 13264, fasc. 24, ibid.
197 Interrogation of Anton Mavec, 19 Oct. 1944, doc. 16499, fasc. 29, ibid.
198 Daily reports to the intelligence branch, 20 March 1945, doc. 14343, fasc. 25, ibid.
199 Ibid., 14, March 1945, doc. 14329.
200 Ibid., 4 Aug. 1944, doc. 13785.
201 Rupnik's proclamation, 'Slovenci! Slovenke!' Sept. 1943, fasc. 24/II, AS KUZOP, ARS.
202 German proclamation, 'Poziv!' 21 Sept. 1943, doc. 61318, fasc. 111a, AS 1912, ARS.
203 Order, Commander 15th Company Dravlje, undated, doc. 26197, fasc. 48, AS 1877, ARS.
204 Puš, 'Prvi borec,' 3 Aug. 1944, doc. 67130, fasc. 116, AS 1912, ARS.
205 SNVZ pamphlet, 'Slovenski kmet! Ti nosiš odgovornost,' fasc. 28, AS 1902, ARS.
206 Leaflet, 'How the Communist Authorities Extort the Russian Farmer,' fasc. 24/II, ibid.
207 Egon Pelikan, *Akomodacija ideologije političnega katolicizma na Slovenskem* (Maribor: Založba obzorja, 1997), 137.
208 Untitled doc., 1942, doc. 71495, fasc. 124, AS 1898, ARS.
209 Report by Alum Mission, no. 85, 21 July 1944, folder 401, box 36, Entry 136, RG 226, NARA; *Kartoteka partizanov in terencev*, undated, doc. 20004, fasc. 34, AS 1877, ARS.
210 PZ report, undated, doc. 43285, fasc. 80, AS 1876, ARS; Daily reports to the intelligence branch, 7 July 1944, doc. 13762, fasc. 25, AS 1877, ARS.
211 Report from Home Guard informants, 14 Feb. 1945, doc. 18615, fasc. 32; Daily intelligence reports, 3 March 1944, doc. 13319, fasc. 24, both AS 1877, ARS.

212 Report, 'O delu propagandnega odseka pokrajinske uprave od začetka do 30. aprila 1944,' doc. 65969, fasc. 115, AS 1912, ARS.
213 Report on progress of anti-Communist propaganda among students, undated, doc. 67063, fasc. 116, ibid.
214 Report on progress of anti-Communist propaganda among students, undated, doc. 67023, 67040, fasc. 116, ibid.
215 Report, 'O delu propagandnega odseka pokrajinske uprave od začetka do 30. aprila 1944,' doc. 65986, fasc. 115, ibid.
216 Order from Krener, 13 Dec. 1944, doc. 9949, fasc. 17, AS 1877, ARS.
217 Report from PZ Novo Mesto, 25 July 1944, fasc. 72, AS 1876, ARS.
218 Report from 42nd Company Polhov Gradec, 5 Sept. 1944, doc. 29267, fasc. 55, AS 1877, ARS.

9 The Final Stand and Its Consequences

1 Corsellis and Ferrar, *Slovenia 1945*, 6.
2 Pahor and Rebula, *Edvard Kocbek*, 133.
3 Ibid., 146.
4 Alexander, *Church and State*, 45.
5 Barker, *Social Revolutionaries*, 51.
6 Report, 17 Feb. 1945, folder 72, box 5, Entry 154, RG 226, NARA.
7 Moore, 'Report,' 158.
8 Ibid., 150.
9 Godina, *Prekmurje*, 139.
10 Drnovšek et al., *Slovenska*, 52.
11 Milač, *Resistance*, 185.
12 Report from Captain John Blatnik, Arrow Mission, 28 March 1944, folder 332, box 25, Entry 154, RG 226, NARA.
13 Moore, 'Report,' 156–7.
14 Ibid., 155.
15 Kokalj, secret memorandum, 9 Feb. 1945, fasc. 4, AS 1878, ARS.
16 Order from Hacin to all units, 11 Jan. 1945, doc. 3050, fasc. 71, AS 1876, ARS.
17 Fasc. 75, ibid.
18 Order from Hacin to all units, 5 March 1945, doc. 36835, fasc. 71, ibid.
19 Reports from 2nd Teške čete, Rakek, 5 Aug. 1944, doc. 32262; Nov. 1944, doc. 32167; doc. 32219, 15 Dec. 1944, all fasc. 62, AS 1877, ARS.
20 Daily reports to the intelligence branch, 16 April 1945, doc. 14401, fasc. 25; Report on 1st strike battalion, 12 Feb. 1945, doc. 18600, fasc. 32, ibid.
21 Daily reports to the intelligence branch, 4 Feb. 1945, doc. 14241, fasc. 25, ibid.

22 Ibid., 19 Dec. 1944, doc. 14131.
23 Report 115th Company Ribnica, 12 Feb. 1945, doc. 18647–8, fasc. 32, ibid.
24 Moore, 'Report,' 154.
25 Mile Pavlin, *Petnajsta brigada* (Ljubljana: Knižnica NOV in POS, 1969), 392.
26 Daily reports to the intelligence branch, 28 March 1945, doc. 14359, fasc. 25, AS 1877, ARS.
27 Marolt et al., *Slovenci*, 397.
28 Drnovšek et al., *Slovenska*, 67.
29 Moore, 'Report,' 152.
30 Report from Captain John Blatnik, Arrow Mission, 28 March 1944, folder 332, box 25, Entry 154, RG 226, NARA.
31 Gestrin, *Svet*, 113.
32 Reports from J-3, 29 April, 4 May 1945, folder 416, box 37, Entry 136, RG 226, NARA.
33 Munoz, *Slovenian Axis*, 24.
34 Rupnik, Order no. 5, 9 Jan. 1945, doc. 7502, fasc. 16, AS 1877, ARS.
35 Ibid.
36 Marolt et al., *Slovenci*, 403.
37 Roberts, *Tito*, 317.
38 Marolt et al., *Slovenci*, 410–11.
39 Rožman, 'Škofa,' 890.
40 Bevc, *Liberal Forces*, 172.
41 Rupnik's declaration, *Slovensko domobranstvo*, 3 May 1945, fasc. 6, AS 1902, ARS.
42 See Kociper, *Kar sem živel*, 294; and Željeznov, *Rupnikov*, 249–50.
43 *Slovenec* LXXIII / 101, 4 May 1945, quoted in Karapandžić, *Kočevje*, 33–5.
44 Kociper, *Kar sem živel*, 355; and Željeznov, *Rupnikov*, 257.
45 Bevc, *Liberal Forces*, 175.
46 Ibid.
47 Željeznov, *Rupnikov*, 259.
48 Kociper, *Kar sem živel*, 368; Bevc, *Liberal Forces*, 176.
49 Order from Hacin to all PZ units, 'Napuščanje postaj PZ brez povelja prepoveduje,' 4 May 1945, doc. 42827, fasc. 80, AS 1876, ARS; Memorandum, 'Establishment of the Slovenska narodna vojska,' 7 May 1945, doc. 69698, fasc. 120, AS 1895, ARS.
50 Drnovšek, Rozman and Vodopivec, *Slovenska*, 79; 'Legenda po stanju 30. IV. 1944,' doc. 65959, fasc. 115, AS 1912, ARS.
51 *Za blagor očetnjave*, 5 May 1945, fasc. 7, AS 1902, ARS.
52 Corsellis and Ferrar, *Slovenia 1945*, 136.
53 Bevc, *Liberal Forces*, 176.

54 Tomasevich, *War*, 518.
55 Ibid.
56 Order from commander of I Slovenski udarni polk na Primorskem, doc. 6375, fasc. 14, AS 1878, ARS.
57 Mlakar, *Domobranstvo*, 222.
58 Marolt et al., *Slovenci*, 410.
59 'Nazaj še pridemo!,' *Za blagor očetnjave*, May 6, 1945, fasc. 7, AS 1902, ARS.
60 Sirc, *Between Hitler and Tito*, 69.
61 Anja Čebulj and Ana Veršnik, *Jože Beranek: Vojno ustvarjanje* (Ljubljana: Univerza v Ljubljani, 2008), 13.
62 Čebulj and Veršnik, *Jože Beranek*, 13.
63 Drnovšek et al., *Slovenska*, 83.
64 See Stane Terčak, *Frankolovski zločin* (Ljubljana: Partizanska knjiga, 1971).
65 Corsellis and Ferrar, *Slovenia 1945*, 70.
66 Mazower, *Hitler's Empire*, 546.
67 István Deák, 'Introduction,' in I. Deák, J. Gross, and T. Judt, eds., *The Politics of Retribution: World War II and Its Aftermath* (Princeton, NJ: Princeton University Press, 2000), 12.
68 Mazower, *Hitler's Empire*, 541.
69 Deák, 'Introduction,' 11.
70 Tony Judt, 'The Past Is Another Country: Myth and Memory in Postwar Europe,' in Deák et al., *The Politics of Retribution*, 301.
71 Ibid.
72 Luthar, *Land Between*, 439.
73 Ramet, *Three Yugoslavias*, 160.
74 For an Italian perspective, see Arrigo Petacco, *A Tragedy Revealed: The Story of the Italian Population of Istria, Dalmatia, and Venezia Giulia, 1943–1956* (Toronto: University of Toronto Press, 2005).
75 Swain, *Tito*, 35.
76 Daily reports intelligence branch, 30 April 1945, doc. 14424, fasc. 25, AS 1877, ARS.
77 'Katoliški cerkveni dostojanstvenik pri Stalinu!' doc. 02910, fasc. 24, ibid.
78 Moore, 'Report,' 158.
79 Corsellis and Ferrar, *Slovenia 1945*, 71.
80 Drnovšek et al., *Slovenska*, 101.
81 Grgič, *Zločinov*, 551–2.
82 Ibid., 553.
83 Tominšek Rihtar, 'Post-War Retribution,' 96.
84 Ibid.
85 Deák, 'Introduction,' 3.

86 'Text of Pope Pius XII's Address to the Sacred College of Cardinals,' *New York Times*, 3 June 1945, 22.
87 Čoh, 'V imenu,' 66.
88 Jera Vodušek-Starič, 'Ozadje sodnih procesov v Sloveniji v prvem povojni letu,' *Prispevki za novejšo zgodovino* 32/1–2 (1992): 154.
89 Vojaško sodišče Prekmurje, Murska Sobota, fasc. 926 V, AS KUZOP, ARS.
90 Vojaško sodišče Maribor, 29 June 1945, fasc. 926 II, ibid.
91 For more on Josip Benko's life, see Branko Žunec, *Josip Benko – mit in resničnost, 1889–1945* (Murska Sobota: Franc-Franc, 1993).
92 Vodušek-Starič, 'Ozadje,' 143.
93 Ibid., 144.
94 Kržišnik-Bukič, 'Legal Trials,' 127.
95 Vodušek-Starič, 'Ozadje,' 144.
96 Čoh, 'V imenu,' 67.
97 Ibid., 73.
98 Drnovšek et al., *Slovenska*, 110.
99 Čoh, 'V imenu,' 70.
100 Ibid., 67, 74.
101 Sam Pope Brewer, 'Freed Yugoslavs Seized on Return,' *New York Times*, 16 July 1945, 3.
102 Sam Pope Brewer, 'All Tito Dissidents Branded Fascists,' *New York Times*, 18 July 1945, 11.
103 Vodušek-Starič, 'Ozadje,' 147–8.
104 'Amnesty Given Nazis' Puppets by Yugoslavia,' *Herald Tribune*, 6 Aug. 1945, file 25–10, box 577, Entry 143, RG 153, NARA.
105 Kržišnik-Bukič, 'Legal Trials,' 132.
106 Hančič and Podbersič, 'Nacionalsocialistično,' 181–5.
107 Drnovšek et al., *Slovenska*, 119.
108 Tominšek Rihtar, 'Post-War Retribution,' 100.
109 Kržišnik-Bukič, 'Legal Trials,' 127–8.
110 Tominšek Rihtar, 'Post-War Retribution,' 100.
111 Williams, 'Nazis,' 16.
112 Theresa Marie Ursic, *Religious Freedom in Post-World War II Yugoslavia: The Case of Roman Catholic Nuns in Croatia and Bosnia-Hercegovina, 1945–1960* (Lanham, Md: International Scholars Publications, 2001), 153n.
113 Alexander, *Church and State*, 89–90.
114 Drnovšek et al., *Slovenska*, 111.
115 Tominšek Rihtar, 'Post-War Retribution,' 101.
116 Ibid.,

117 Rastko Vidič, *The Position of the Church in Yugoslavia* (Belgrade: Zavod Jugoslavija, 1962), 9.
118 Alexander, *Church and State*, 47.
119 Vidič, *Position of the Church*, 19.
120 Kržišnik-Bukič, 'Legal Trials,' 126.
121 'Educational System in Yugoslavia,' 14 June 1946, Arrangement 70080, Roll 4, Microfilm 1656, RG 226, NARA.
122 Deák, 'Introduction,' 12.

Conclusion: The Verdict

1 Bennett, *Under the Shadow*, 118.
2 Gow and Carmichael, *Slovenia*, 46.
3 Rings, *Life with the Enemy*, 61.
4 Mastny, *Czechs under Nazi Rule*, 225.
5 Mazower, *Inside Hitler's Greece*, 284.
6 Bennett, *Under the Shadow*, 41.
7 Ibid., 5.
8 Kardelj, *Pot*, 277.
9 Ferguson, *War of the World*, 440.
10 Mazower, *Hitler's Empire*, 456.
11 Gross, 'Themes for a Social History,' 29.
12 Swain, *Tito*.
13 Mlakar, 'Radical Nationalism,' 12.
14 Connelly, 'Why the Poles,' 772.
15 Ibid., 774–5.
16 Davies, *Dangerous Liaisons*, 98.
17 Stephen Gilliat, *An Exploration of the Dynamics of Collaboration and Non-Resistance* (Lewiston: Mellen Press, 1990), 79–80.
18 Željeznov, *Rupnikov*, 122.
19 Drnovšek et al., *Slovenska*, 58.
20 Kociper, *Kar sem živel*, 150.
21 Pelikan, *Akomodacija ideologije*, 134.
22 Dolinar, 'Sodni proces,' part I, 140.
23 Rožman, 'Škofa,' 890.
24 Dolenec, *Moja rast*, 161–2.
25 PZ lists of suspected Communist sympathizers, 1943–1945, fasc. 90, AS 1876, ARS.
26 Evaluations of the political reliability of PZ members, 26 April 1945, doc. 40756–60, fasc. 77, ibid.

27 Rings, *Life with the Enemy*, 278.
28 Klaus Peter Friedrich, 'Collaboration in a "Land without a Quisling": Patterns of Cooperation with the Nazi German Occupation Regime in Poland during World War II,' *Slavic Review* 64/4 (2005): 744.
29 Connelly, 'Why the Poles,' 772.
30 Čebulj and Veršnik, *Jože Beranek*, 13–14.

References

Archival Sources

Arhiv Republike Slovenije (ARS, Archive of the Republic of Slovenia), Ljubljana

AS (Record Group) 1851: GS NOV in POS, Kočevski proces (The Kočevje Trial)
AS 1873: Gorenjsko domobranstvo
AS 1875: Rudolf Smersu
AS 1876: PVZ, Policijski varnostni zbor (Police Security Corps)
AS 1877: Slovensko domobranstvo
AS 1878: Slovenski narodni varnostni zbor v operacijski coni Jadransko primorje (Slovene National Security Corps in Operation Zone Adriatic Littoral)
AS 1888: Narodnostni referat, Logatec (Nationality Report, Logatec)
AS 1889: Narodnostni referat, Novo Mesto (Nationality Report, Novo Mesto)
AS 1891: PU, Pokrajinska uprava (Provincial Administration)
AS 1895: MVAC
AS 1895: BEGA-Domobranstvo
AS 1898: Slovenska ljudska stranka (Slovene People's Party)
AS 1900: Sodni spisi Črne Roke (Judicial Documents on the Black Hand)
AS 1902: Zbirka tisk nasprotnikov NOB in politične sredine (The Collection of the Publications of the Opponents of NOB and the Political Center)

AS 1912: IU – TOS, Informativni urad – Tajna obveščavalna služba (Information Office – Secret Intelligence Service)
AS 1914: Četniki
AS KUZOP: Komisija za ugotavljanje zločinov okupatorjev in njihov pomagačev (The Commission to Ascertain the Crimes of the Occupiers and their Collaborators)
- KUZOP, fascicle 925: Rupnikov proces (The Rupnik Trial)
- KUZOP, fascicle 926: Obsodbe narodnih izdajalcev, Vrhovno sodišče Ljubljana, Celje, Maribor, Prekmurje (Verdicts against National Traitors, Supreme Courts in Ljubljana, Celje, Maribor, and Prekmurje)

K. Wolbang, Fascicle 165A

National Archives and Records Administration (NARA), Washington

Record Group 153.13: Records of the War Crimes Branch, 1942–1957
Record Group 226: Records of the Office of Strategic Services (OSS)
- Entry 92: COI/OSS Central Files
- Entry 136: Washington and Field Station Files: Algiers, Austria, Bari, Burma, Cairo, Calcutta, Caserta, Denmark, Kunming, London, Paris and New York
- Entry 144: Field Station Files: Algiers, Austria, Bari, Belgium, Burma, Cairo and Calcutta
- Entry M153A: SSU Intelligence Reports: 1946
- Entry 154: Field Station Files: Bari, Bucharest, Burma, Cairo, Caserta, Kandy and Kunming

Published Primary Sources

The Avalon Project: Documents in Law, History and Diplomacy. Yale Law School: Lillian Goldman Law Library, 2008. http://avalon.law.yale.edu/:
- *Convention between the United States of America and Other Powers, Relating to Prisoners of War, 27 July 1929*

Convention (IV) Respecting the Laws and Customs of War on Land and Its Annex: Regulations Concerning the Laws and Customs of War on Land. The Hague, 18 October 1907. International Humanitarian Law – Treaties and Documents, International Committee for the Red Cross. http://www.icrc.org/ihl.nsf/385ec082b509e76c41256739003e636d/1d1726425f6955aec125641e0038bfd6.

Ehrlich, Lambert. 'Ehrlihova spomenica za Vatikan 14. Aprila 1942: Razmere v "Ljubljanski pokrajini."' In Marija Vrečar, ed. *Acta Ecclesiastica Sloveniae*

24 (2002): 619–39. (Ljubljana: Inštitut za zgodovino Cerkve pri Teološki fakulteti Univerze v Ljubljani.)
Lindsay, Franklin. *Report of Operations, Military Sub-Mission to Fourth Operational Zone, Yugoslav Army of National Resistance.* 14 May to 7 Dec. 1944, 15 Jan. 1945. Public Records Office [PRO], War Office [WO] 202/309. Quoted in Barker, *Social Revolutionaries and Secret Agents*, 118–40.
Moore, Lt. Col. Peter N.M. *Report on Slovenia.* 14 Feb. 1945. PRO, Foreign Office [FO] 371/4811, R5717/6/92. Quoted in Barker, *Social Revolutionaries and Secret Agents*, 146–8.
Natlačen, Marko. 'Dr Marko Natlačen o svojem delovanju med 6. aprilom in 14. junijem 1941.'; '[Priloga] 18 September 1941.' Historična dokumentacija. *Prispevki za novejšo zgodovino* 151/1 (2001): 121–48.
Rožman, Gregorij. 'Škofa Rožmana odgovor.' *Nova Revija* 11/93–94 (1990): 879–93.
Službeni list za Ljubljansko pokrajino 105 (31 Dec. 1941). http://www.sistory.si/publikacije/pdf/uradnilisti/Sluzbeni_list_1941/20–12–31–1941_105-Priloga.pdf.
Sovražne agenture na teritoriju Slovenije (1944). Prispevki za novejšo zgodovino 38/1–2 (1998): 179–94.
Sub-Source's Impression of Partisan Activities in Slovenia. No. 1 (U) Section C.M.F./ 28 March 1945. PRO, WO 202/309. Quoted in Barker, *Social Revolutionaries and Secret Agents*, 159–63.
Wilkinson, Lieut. Colonel P.A., O.B.E. Royal Fusiliers. Memorandum on the Revolt in Slovenia. 27 April 1944. PRO, FO 371/44255, R98160. Quoted in Barker, *Social Revolutionaries and Secret Agents*, 83–116.
Zajdela, Ivo, and Roman Leljak, eds. *Črne bukve: O delu komunistične Osvobodilne fronte proti slovenskemu narodu*. Maribor: Založba za alternativno teorijo, 1990. (Originally published Ljubljana, 1944.)

Period Newspapers and Periodicals Consulted

Čas kliče, Glas izpod Krna, Goreči plameni, Junaki, Jutro, Kri in zemlja, Kronika, Mi gremo naprej, Mi mladi Goričani, Mlada Slovenija, Na braniku, New York Times, *Novomeški informator, Poročila, Slovenec, Slovenija in Evropa, Slovenska straža, Slovenska zaveza, Slovenski poročevalec, Slovensko domobranstvo, Straža ob Jadranu, Svoboda ali smrt, Svobodna Slovenija, Tebi dekle, Tolminski glas,* Toronto Star, *Vesti, Vipavec, Za blagor očetnjave, Za Slovensko domačijo, Živi izviri*

Memoirs, Diaries, and Autobiographies

Angi, Caterina, Martina Bofulin, Damjan Franz, Matevž Košir, Attila Kovacz, Hannah Starman, Irena Šumi, Marjan Toš, Marta Verginella, and Bojan

Zadravec, compilers. *Task Force on Jewish Studies and Antisemitism: Jews and Antisemitism in Slovenia*. Ljubljana: Inštitut za narodnostna vprašanja. http://www.inv.si/psja/spomin/efurst.htm.

Bevc, Vladislav, ed. *Liberal Forces in Twentieth Century Yugoslavia: Memoirs of Ladislav Bevc*. New York: Peter Lang, 2007.

Ciano, Galeazzo. *Ciano's Diary, 1939–1943*. London: Heinemann, 1947.

Čačinovič, Rudi. *Časi preizkušenj: Prispevki k zgodovini Prekmurja*. Murska Sobota: Pomurska založba, 1998.

Djilas, Milovan. *Wartime*. New York: Harcourt Brace Jovanovich, 1977.

Dolenec, Ivan. *Moja rast*. Buenos Aires: Slovenska kulturna izdaja, 1973.

Fürst, Elizabeta. 'Elizabeta Fürst's Story.' In Angi et al., *Task Force on Jewish Studies and Antisemitism*. http://www.inv.si/psja/spomin/efurst.htm.

Golob, Franc. 'Dnevnik domobranca.' In Kokalj-Kočevar, *Mati-domovina-bog*, 98–115.

Hirschegger, Rudolf. 'Resnica o naši borbi.' *Zbornik koledar svobodne Slovenije*. Buenos Aires: Svobodna Slovenija, 1966, 109–26.

Hren, Ignacij. 'Moja srečanja z generalom Rupnikom.' In *Zbornik koledar Svobodne Slovenije*. Buenos Aires: Svobodna Slovenija, 1967, 88–95.

Hribernik-Svarun, Rudolf. *Spomini: Klic svobode*. Ljubljana: Znanstveno in publicistično središče, 1995.

Kardelj, Edvard. *Pot nove Yugoslavije: Članki in govori iz narodnoosvobodilne borbe, 1941–1945*. Ljubljana: Državna založba Slovenija, 1946.

– *Tito and the Socialist Revolution of Yugoslavia*. Belgrade: Socialist Thought and Practice, 1980.

– *Reminiscences: The Struggle for Recognition and Independence: The New Yugoslavia, 1944–1957*. London: Blond and Briggs, 1982.

Kocbek, Edvard. *Tovarišija: Dnevniški zapiski od 17 maja 1942 do 1 maja 1943*. Maribor: Založba obzorju, 1967.

Kociper, Stanko. *Kar sem živel*. Ljubljana: Založba mladinska knjiga, 1996.

Korošec, Ivan. *Prva nacionalna ilegala: Štajerski bataljon*. Ljubljana: Ilex-Impex, 1993.

Lindsay, Franklin. *Beacons in the Night: With the OSS and Tito's Partisans in Wartime Yugoslavia*. Stanford, CA: Stanford University Press, 1993.

Maclean, Fitzroy. *Eastern Approaches*. New York: Time-Life Books, 1949.

Matjašec, Franc, and Helena. 'Story of Franc and Helena Matjašec.' (Interviewed by Hannah Starman and Bojan Zadravec). In Angi, et al., *Task Force on Jewish Studies and Antisemitism*. http://www.inv.si/psja/spomin/efurst.htm.

Milač, Metod. *Resistance, Imprisonment and Forced Labour: A Slovene Student in World War II*. New York: Peter Lang, 2002.

Newby, Wanda (nee Wanda Škof). *Peace and War: Growing up in Fascist Italy.* London: Collins, 1991.
Pollak, Riko. 'Riko Pollak's Story.' In Angi et al., *Task Force on Jewish Studies and Antisemitism.* http://www.inv.si/psja/spomin/eriko_ziv.htm.
Rožman, Gregorij. 'Pismo v leto 1956.' In *Zbornik koledar svobodne Slovenije.* Buenos Aires, Svobodna Slovenija, 1956, 11–12.
Sirc, Ljubo. *Between Hitler and Tito: Nazi Occupation and Communist Oppression.* London: Andre Deutsch, 1989.
Vauhnik, Vladimir. *Nevidna fronta: Spomini.* Buenos Aires: Svobodna Slovenija, 1965.
Weiss-Belač, Emil. *Ne hodi naprej.* Ljubljana: Slovenska matica, 1997.
Wilkinson, Peter. *Foreign Fields: The Story of an SOE Operative.* London: I.B. Tauris, 2002.
Žibert, Alojzij. *Pod Marijinim varstvom: Spomini Slovenca-Nemškega vojaka na drugo vetovno vojno v letih 1941–1945.* Kranj: Gorenjski glas, 1995.

Secondary Sources

Adamič, Louis. *My Native Land.* New York: Harper, 1943.
Ahačič, Draga. *Osvobodilna ali državljanska vojna?* Ljubljana: Cankarjeva založba, 1992.
Alexander, Stella. *Church and State in Yugoslavia since 1945.* Cambridge: Cambridge University Press, 1979.
Allen, Michael Thad. *The Business of Genocide: The SS, Slave Labour, and the Concentration Camps.* Chapel Hill, NC: University of North Carolina Press, 2002.
Anderson, Robin. *Between Two Wars: The Story of Pope Pius XI (Achille Ratti) 1922–1939.* Chicago, IL: Franciscan Herald Press, 1977.
Anič, Z., R. Brčic, V. Glišič, V. Gozze-Gučetić, V. Kljaković, B. Križman, J. Marjanović, J. Mirnić, and P. Morača, eds. *The Third Reich and Yugoslavia, 1933–1945.* Belgrade: Institute for Contemporary History, 1977.
Anidžarič, Marjan, Jože Dežman, and Ludvik Puklavec, eds. *Nemška mobilizacija Slovencev v drugi svetovni vojni.* Celje: Zveza društev mobiliziranih Slovencev v nemško vojsko, 2001.
Arnež, John A. *SLS: Slovenian People's Party, 1941–1945.* Ljubljana: Studia Slovenica, 2002.
Avakumović, Ivan. 'Yugoslavia's Fascist Movements.' In Sugar, ed., *Native Fascism in the Successor States*,135–43.
Banac, Ivo. *The National Question in Yugoslavia: Origins, History, Politics.* Ithaca, NY: Cornell University Press, 1984.

– *With Stalin against Tito: Cominformist Splits in Yugoslav Communism*. Ithaca, NY: Cornell University Press, 1988.
Barker, Thomas M. *Social Revolutionaries and Secret Agents: The Carinthian Slovene Partisans and Britain's Special Operations Executive*. New York: Columbia University Press, 1990.
Barrett, David P., and Larry N. Shyu. *Chinese Collaboration with Japan, 1932–1945: The Limits of Accommodation*. Stanford, CA: Stanford University Press, 2001.
Benderly, Jill, and Evan Kraft, eds. *Independent Slovenia: Origins, Movements, Prospects*. New York: St Martin's Press, 1994.
Bennett, Rab. *Under the Shadow of the Swastika: The Moral Dilemma of Resistance and Collaboration in Hitler's Europe*. London: Macmillan, 1999.
Borštnik, Pavle. *Pozabljena zgodba slovenske nacionalne ilegale*. Ljubljana: Mladinska knjiga, 1998.
Božič, Branko. *Zgodovina slovenskega naroda*. Ljubljana: Prešernove družbe, 1969.
Bremen, Borut. *Na robu zgodovine in spomina: Urbana kultura Murske Sobote med letoma 1919 in 1941*. Murska Sobota: Pomurska založba, 1995.
Bresadola, Gianmarco. 'The Legitimising Strategies of the Nazi Administration in Northern Italy: Propaganda in the Adriatisches Küstenland.' *Contemporary European History* 13/4 (2004): 425–51.
Brewer, Sam Pope. 'Freed Yugoslavs Seized on Return.' *New York Times*, 16 July 1945, 3.
– 'All Tito Dissidents Branded Fascists.' *New York Times*, 18 July 1945, 11.
Bryant, Chad. *Prague in Black: Nazi Rule and Czech Nationalism*. Cambridge, MA: Harvard University Press, 2007.
Bunting, Madeleine. *The Model Occupation: The Channel Islands under German Rule, 1940–1944*. London: Harper Collins, 1995.
Burgwyn, James H. *Empire on the Adriatic: Mussolini's Conquest of Yugoslavia, 1941–1943*. New York: Enigma Books, 2005.
Cohen, Philip. *Serbia's Secret War: Propaganda and the Deceit of History*. College Station, TX: Texas A&M University Press, 1996.
Connelly, John. 'Why the Poles Collaborated so Little – And Why That Is No Reason for Nationalist Hubris.' *Slavic Review* 64/4 (2005): 771–81.
Conway, Martin. *Collaboration in Belgium: Leon Degrelle and the Rexist Movement, 1940–1944*. New Haven, CT: Yale University Press, 1993.
Cornwell, John. *Hitler's Pope: The Secret History of Pius XII*. London: Viking, 1999.
Corsellis, John, and Marcus Ferrar. *Slovenia 1945: Memories of Death and Survival after World War II*. London: I.B. Tauris, 2005.

Cox, John K. *Slovenia: Evolving Loyalties*. London: Routledge, 2005.
Čebulj, Anja, and Ana Veršnik. *Jože Beranek: Vojno ustvarjanje*. Ljubljana: Univerza v Ljubljani, 2008.
Čepič, Z., T. Ferenc, A. Gabrič, B. Godeša, D. Nećak, J. Prinčič, J. Prunk, B. Repe, A. Vidovič-Miklavčič, P. Vodopivec, and M. Ževart, eds. *Ključne značilnosti Slovenske politike v letih 1929–1955: Znanstveno poročilo*. Ljubljana: Inšititut za novejšo zgodovino, 1995.
Čoh, Mateja. 'V imenu slovenskega naroda: Krivi!' Celje: Zgodovinsko društvo Celje. *Zgodovina za vse, vse za zgodovino* 7/1 (2000): 66–80.
Čolaković, Rodoljub. *Winning Freedom*. London: Lincolns-Prager, 1962.
Čuješ, Rudolf, and Vladimir Mauko, eds. *This Is Slovenia: A Glance at the Land and Its People*. Toronto: Slovenian National Federation of Canada, 1956.
Davies, Peter. *Dangerous Liaisons: Collaboration and World War Two*. Harlow, U.K.: Pearson Longman, 2004.
Deák, István. 'Introduction.' In Deák et al., *The Politics of Retribution in Europe*, 3–14.
– 'A Fatal Compromise? The Debate over Collaborations and Resistance in Hungary.' In Deák et al., *The Politics of Retribution in Europe*, 39–73.
Deák, István, Jan T. Gross, and Tony Judt, eds. *The Politics of Retribution in Europe: World War II and Its Aftermath*. Princeton, NJ: Princeton University Press, 2000.
Debeljak, Tine. *Začetki komunistične revolucije v Sloveniji: Ob 25-letnici prvih žrtev*. Buenos Aires: Svobodna Slovenija-Eslovenia Libre, 1968.
Djordjević, Dimitrije. 'Fascism in Yugoslavia, 1918–1941.' In Sugar, ed., *Native Fascism in the Successor States*, 122–35.
– 'The Yugoslav Phenomenon.' In Joseph Held, ed., *The Columbia History of Eastern Europe in the Twentieth Century*. New York: Columbia University Press, 1992.
Dolinar, France Martin. 'Sodni proces proti Lubljanskemu škofu dr. Gregoriju Rožmanu od 21 do 30 avgusta 1946.' *Zgodovinski časopis* 50/1–3 (1996): part I, 117–44; part II, 255–90; part III, 411–34.
Drnovšek, M., F. Rozman, and P. Vodopivec, eds. *Slovenska kronika XX stoletja, 1941–1945*. Ljubljana: Nova Revija, 1996.
Epstein, Julius. *Operation Keelhaul: The Story of Forced Repatriation from 1944 to the Present*. Old Greenwich: Devin-Adair, 1973.
Federation of Slovenian Anti-Communist Fighters. *The Slovenian Tragedy: For the 25th Anniversary of Betrayal of Vetrinje and Kočevski Rog Massacre*. Toronto: Author, 1970.
Ferenc, Tone. 'Nekaj značilnosti narodno-osvobodilnega boja na Gorenjskem.' *Zgodovinski časopis* 31/1–2 (1977): 119–31.

- 'The Austrians and Slovenia.' In F. Parkinson, ed., *Conquering the Past: Austrian Nazism Yesterday and Today*. Detroit, MI: Wayne State University Press, 1989, 207–23.
- *Dies IRAE: Četniki, vaški stražarji in njihova usoda jeseni 1943*. Ljubljana: Modrijan, 2002.

Ferguson, Niall. *The War of the World: Twentieth Century Conflict and the Descent of the West*. New York: Penguin, 2007.

Ford Jr, Kirk. *OSS and the Yugoslav Resistance, 1943–1945*. College Station, TX: Texas A&M University Press, 1992.

Fraser, Graham. 'Threats Bound to Impact Policies: Spain, Britain Reacted to Attacks Very Differently.' *Toronto Star*, 8 June 2006, A6.

Freidenreich, Harriet Pass. *The Jews of Yugoslavia: A Quest for Community*. Philadelphia, PA: Jewish Publication Society of America, 1979.

Friedrich, Klaus Peter. 'Collaboration in a "Land without a Quisling": Patterns of Cooperation with the Nazi German Occupation Regime in Poland during World War II.' *Slavic Review* 64/4 (2005): 711–46.

Gestrin, Ferdo. *Svet pod Krimom*. Ljubljana: Znanstvenoraziskovalni center SAZU, 1993.

Gestrin, Ferdo, and Vasilij Melik. *Slovenska zgodovina: Od konca osemnajstega stoletja do 1918*. Ljubljana: Državna založba Slovenije, 1966.

Gestrin, F., B. Grafenauer, and J. Pleterski, eds. *Slovenski upor 1941: Osvobodilna fronta Slovenskega naroda pred pol stoletja*. Ljubljana: Slovenska akademija znanosti in umetnosti, 1991.

Gilliat, Stephen. *An Exploration of the Dynamics of Collaboration and Non-Resistance*. Lewiston: Mellen Press, 2000.

Godeša, Bojan. *Kdor ni z nami, je proti nam: Slovenski izobraženci med okupatorji, Osvobodilno fronto in protirevolucionarnem taborom*. Ljubljana: Cankarjeva založba, 1995.

- 'Odnos SLS do vprašanja rešitve državno pravnega položaja Slovenije po napadu sil osi na Jugoslavijo,' in *Slovenci in leto 1941: Znanstveni posvet, Šestdeset let od začetka druge svetovne vojne na Slovenskem* (Ljubljana: Inštitut za novejšo zgodovino, 2001), 97.

Godina, Ferdo. *Prekmurje, 1941–1945: Prispevek v zgodovini NOB*. Murska Sobota: Pomurska založba, 1980.

Gow, James, and Cathie Carmichael. *Slovenia and the Slovenes: A Small State and the New Europe*. Bloomington, IN: Indiana University Press, 2000.

Grgič, Silvo. *Zločinov okupatorjevih sodelavcev: Monografija v treh knjigah*. Ljubljana: Piscev zgodovine NOB Slovenije, 1997.

Griesser-Pečar, Tamara. *Razdvojeni narod: Slovenija 1941–1945: Okupacija, Kolaboracija, državljanska vojna, revolucija*. Ljubljana: Maldinska knjiga, 2004.

Griesser-Pečar, Tamara, and France Martin Dolinar. *Rožmanov Proces*. Ljubljana: Založba družina, 1996.
Gross, Jan T. 'Themes for a Social History of War Experience and Collaboration.' In Deák et al., eds., *The Politics of Retribution in Europe*, 15–35.
Grum, Janez. 'Ob 20 letnici Turjaka.' *Zbornik koledar svobodne Slovenije*. Buenos Aires: Svobodna Slovenija, 1964, 310–20.
Hančič, Damjan, and Renato Podbersič. 'Nacionalsocialistično in komunistično pregajanje Judov na Slovenksem.' In Jože Dežman and Hanzi Filipič, eds., *Hitlerjeva dolga senca: Nacionalsocialistično državnoterorističcno in rasistično preganjanje prebivalcev Slovenije in njegove posledice v Titovi Jugoslaviji*. Klagenfurt: Mohorjeva, 2007, 175–88.
Harriman, Helga H. *Slovenia under Nazi Occupation, 1941–1945*. New York: Studia Slovenica, 1977.
Hehn, Paul N. *The German Struggle against Yugoslav Guerillas in World War II: German Counter-Insurgency in Yugoslavia, 1941–1943*. New York: Columbia University Press, 1979.
Heppel, Muriel, and F.B. Singleton. *Yugoslavia*. London: Ernest Benn, 1961.
Hoensch, Jörg K. *A History of Modern Hungary, 1867–1986*. London: Longman, 1988.
Hoffman, Stanley. *Decline or Renewal? France since the 1930s*. New York: Viking, 1974.
Hoptner, J.B. *Yugoslavia in Crisis: 1934–1941*. New York: Columbia University Press, 1963.
Hribar, Spomenka. *Krivda in greh*. Maribor: ZAT, 1990.
Jan, Ivan. *Škof Rožman in kontinuiteta: Zahteva po škofovi rehabilitaciji – ponoven izziv resnici*. Ljubljana: Samozaložba, 1998.
Jankowski, Paul. *Communism and Collaboration: Simon Sabiani and Politics in Marseille, 1919–1944*. New Haven, CT: Yale University Press, 1989.
Judt, Tony. 'The Past Is Another Country: Myth and Memory in Post-war Europe.' In Deák et al., eds., *The Politics of Retribution in Europe*, 293–323.
Karapandžić, Borivoje M. *Kočevje: Tito's Bloodiest Crime*. Munich: Iskra, 1970.
Kent, Peter C. *The Pope and the Duce: The International Impact of the Lateran Agreements*. London: Macmillan, 1981.
Kerenji, Emil. 'Ljotić, Dimitrije (1891–1945).' In Richard Levy, ed., *Anti-Semitism: A Historical Encyclopedia of Prejudice and Persecution*, vol. 2. Santa Barbara, CA: ABC-CLIO, 2005.
Kershaw, Ian. 'How Effective Was Nazi Propaganda?' In David Welch, ed., *Nazi Propaganda: The Power and the Limitations*. London: Croom Helm, 1983, 180–204.
Kikelj, T., J. Kos, N. Lukež, and M. Žganjar, eds. *Slovenska narodna pomoč v okupirani Ljubljani med 1941–1945*. Ljubljana: Mestni odbor medvojnega aktiva OF, 1995.

Kirk, Tim. 'Limits of Germandom: Resistance to the Nazi Annexation of Slovenia.' *Slavonic and East European Review* 69/4 (1991): 646–67.
Kokalj-Kočevar, Monika, ed. *Mati-domovina-bog*. Ljubljana: Muzej novejše zgodovine, 1999.
– 'Gorenjska samozaščita.' In Kokalj-Kočevar, ed., *Mati-domovina-bog*, 28–37.
Kolarčič, Dr Jakob. *Škof Rožman: Duhovna podoba velike osebnosti na prelomnici časa*, 3 vols. Klagenfurt: Tisk Mohorjeva družba, 1967, 1970, 1977.
Korošec, Ivan. *Prva nacionalna ilegala: Štajerski bataljon*. Ljubljana: Ilex-Impex, 1993.
Kos, Stane. *Stalinistična revolucija na Slovenskem, 1941–1945*, vol. 1. Rome: Samozaložba, 1984.
Kranjc, Gregor. ' "Long Live Our Honest Girls": The Image of Women in Slovene Anti-Communist Propaganda, 1942–1945.' *Journal of Women's History* 18/1 (2006): 50–76.
Krek, Miha. 'Od Vetrinje do Koreje.' In *Zbornik Koledar Svobodne Slovenije*. Buenos Aires: Svobodna Slovenija, 1955, 12–14.
Križnar, Ivan. 'Slovensko domobranstvo v boju proti narodno-osvobodilnemu Gibanju.' In *Osvoboditev Slovenije, 1945*. Ljubljana: Založba borec, 1977, 186–219.
Krpič, Nada. 'Ogranizacija obveščevalne službe NOV in PO Slovenije, 1941–1945.' Diplomsko delo. Univerza v Ljubljani: Fakulteta za družbene vede, 2006. http://dk.fdv.uni-lj.si/dela/Krpic-Nada.PDF.
Kržišnik-Bukič, Vera. 'Legal Trials in Yugoslavia, Particularly in Slovenia, in the Aftermath of the Second World War.' *Razprave in gradivo* 32 (1997): 117–35. (Ljubljana: Inštitut za narodnostna vprašanja.)
Lampe, John. *Yugoslavia as History: Twice There Was a Country*. Cambridge: Cambridge University Press, 2000.
Levental, Zdenko, ed. *The Crimes of the Fascist Occupants and Their Collaborators against Jews in Yugoslavia*. Belgrade: Federation of Jewish Communities of the Federative People's Republic of Yugoslavia, 1957.
Lončar, Dragotin. *Politično življenje Slovencev*. Ljubljana: Slovenska matica, 1921.
Luthar, Oto. 'Slovenia: History between Myths and Reality.' *Slovene Studies* 27/1–2 (2005): 109–19.
Luthar, Oto, and Irena Šumi. 'Living in Metaphor: Jews and Anti-Semitism in Slovenia.' In Wolf Moskowitch, Oto Luthar, and Irena Šumi, eds., *Jews and Slavs*, vol. 12, *Jews and Anti-Semitism in the Balkans*. Jerusalem: Založba ZRC, 2004, 29–48.
Luthar, Oto, ed. *The Land Between: A History of Slovenia*. Frankfurt am Main: Peter Lang, 2008.
Marolt, J., D. Mihelič, M. Žvanut, F. Rozman, J. Prunk, F. Kresal, M. Kacin-Wohin, T. Ferenc and B. Repe. *Slovenci skozi čas: Kronika slovenske zgodovine*. Ljubljana: Založba Mihelač, 1999.

Martinčič, Vanja. 'Rama ob rami: Schulter am Schulter, Obleka naredi človeka, uniforma pa vojaka.' In Kokalj-Kočevar, ed., *Mati-domovina-bog*, 42–83.
Mastny, Vojtech. *The Czechs under Nazi Rule: The Failure of National Resistance, 1939–1942*. New York: Columbia University Press, 1971.
Mazower, Mark. *Inside Hitler's Greece: The Experience of Occupation, 1941–44*. New Haven, CT: Yale University Press, 1993.
– *Hilter's Empire: How the Nazis Ruled Europe*. London: Penguin, 2008.
Mikuž, Metod. 'Donesek k zgodovini Osvobodilne fronte.' *Zgodovinski časopis* 15 (1971): 3–30.
– *Zgodovina Slovencev*. Ljubljana: Cankarjeva založba, 1979.
Mlakar, Boris. *Domobranstvo na Primorskem (1943–1945)*. Ljubljana: Založba borec, 1982.
– 'Review of Thomas M. Barker. *Social Revolutionaries and Secret Agents: The Carinthian Slovene Partisans and Britain's Special Operations Executive*. New York: Columbia University Press, 1990.' *Papers on Slovene Studies* 11/1–2 (1989): 232–6.
– 'Vaške straže ter prostovoljna protikommunistična milica.' In Kokalj-Kočevar, ed., *Mati-domovina-bog*, 8–10.
– 'Slovensko domobranstvo v Ljubljanski pokrajini.' In Kokalj-Kočevar, ed., *Mati-domovina-bog*, 11–18.
– *Slovensko domobranstvo 1943–1945: Ustanovitev, organizacija, idejno ozadje*. Ljubljana: Slovenska matica, 2003.
– 'Repression over the Slovenian People by the German Nazism.' In Peter Jambrek, ed., *Crimes Committed by Totalitarian Regimes*. Ljubljana: Slovenian Presidency of the Council of the European Union, 2008, 117–24.
– 'Radical Nationalism and Fascist Elements in Political Movements in Slovenia between the Two World Wars.' *Slovene Studies* 30/1 (2009): 1–19.
Morley, John. *Vatican Diplomacy and the Jews during the Holocaust*. New York: KTAV, 1980.
Munoz, Antonio J. *Slovenian Axis Forces in World War II, 1941–1945*. Bayside, NY: Axis Europa Books, 1998.
Nećak, Dušan. 'Nekaj osnovnih podatkov o usodi nemške narodnostne skupnosti v Sloveniji po letu 1945.' *Zgodovinski časopis* 47/3 (1993): 439–51.
Novak, Bogdan. *Trieste 1941–1954: The Ethnic, Political and Ideological Struggle*. Chicago, IL: University of Chicago Press, 1955.
Pahor, Boris, and Alojz Rebula, eds. *Edvard Kocbek: Pričevalec našega časa*. Trst: Zaliv, 1975.
Parker, R.A.C. *The Struggle for Survival: The History of the Second World War*. Oxford: Oxford University Press, 1989.
Passmore, Kevin, ed. *Women, Gender and Fascism in Europe, 1919–45*. Manchester: Manchester University Press, 2003.

Pavlin, Mile. *Petnajsta brigada*. Ljubljana: Knjižnica NOV in POS, 1969.
Pavlowitch, Stevan K. *Yugoslavia*. London: Ernest Benn, 1971.
– *Hitler's New Disorder: The Second World War in Yugoslavia*. New York: Columbia University Press, 2008.
Paxton, Robert. *Vichy France: Old Guard and New Order, 1940–1944*. New York: Columbia University Press, 1972.
Pelikan, Egon. 'Vizije "Družbene prenove" v katoliškem taboru v tridesetih letih V Sloveniji.' In P. Vodopivec and J. Mahnič, eds., *Slovenska trideseta leta: Simpozij, 1995*. Ljubljana: Slovenska matica, 1997, 58–68.
– *Akomodacija ideologije političnega katolicizma na Slovenskem*. Maribor: Založba obzorja, 1997.
Perne, Franc, and Anton Žitnik, eds. *Slovenija: Zamolčani grobovi in njihove žrtve, 1941–1948*. Ljubljana-Grosuplje: Društvo za ureditev zamolčanih grobov, 1998.
Petacco, Arrigo. *A Tragedy Revealed: The Story of the Italian Population of Istria, Dalmatia, and Venezia Giulia, 1943–1956*. Toronto: University of Toronto Press, 2005.
Poprzeczny, Joseph. *Odilo Globocnik: Hitler's Man in the East*. Jefferson, NC: McFarland, 2004.
Prpa-Jovanovič, Branka. 'The Making of Yugoslavia, 1830–1945.' In Jasminka Udovićki and James Ridgeway, eds., *Burn This House: The Making and Unmaking of Yugoslavia*. Durham, NC: Duke University Press, 2000, 43–63.
Ramet, Sabrina. *The Three Yugoslavias: State-Building and Legitimation, 1918–2005*. Washington, DC: Woodrow Wilson Press, 2006.
Ravnikar-Podbevšek, Štefanija. *Sv. Urh: Kronika dogodkov iz narodno-osvobodilne vojne*. Ljubljana: Zavod borec, 1966.
Repe, Božo. 'Odnos med Slovenci in nemško manjšin v Sloveniji v dinamiki okupacijskega leto 1941.' *Slovenci in leto 1941: Znanstveni posvet, Šestdeset let od začetka druge svetovne vojne na Slovenskem*. Ljubljana: Inštitut za novejšo zgodovino, 2001, 237–42.
– *Slovene History – 20th Century: Selected Articles by Dr Božo Repe*. Danijela Trškan, ed. Ljubljana: Department of History, University of Ljubljana, 2005. http://www.ff.uni-lj.si/oddelki/zgodovin/DANIJELA/HISTORY/_private/20th/bozorepe.pdf.
Rings, Werner. *Life with the Enemy: Collaboration and Resistance in Hitler's Europe, 1939–1945*. Garden City, NY: Doubleday, 1982.
Roberts, Walter R. *Tito, Mihailović and the Allies, 1941–1945*. New Brunswick, NJ: Rutgers University Press, 1973.
Rodogno, Davide. *Fascism's European Empire: Italian Occupation during the Second World War*. Cambridge: Cambridge University Press, 2006.
Rogel, Carole. 'In the Beginning: The Slovenes from the Seventh Century to 1945.' In Benderly and Kraft, eds., *Independent Slovenia*, 3–23.

Rueh, Franc. *Moj dnevnik, 1915–1918*. Ljubljana: Slovenska matica, 1999.
Saje, Franček. *Belogardizem*. Ljubljana: Slovenski knjižni zavod, 1952.
Sanchez, Jose M. *Pius XII and the Holocaust: Understanding the Controversy*. Washington, DC: Catholic University of America Press, 2002.
Seton-Watson, Hugh. *The East European Revolution*. London: Methuen, 1956.
Singleton, Fred. *A Short History of the Yugoslav Peoples*. Cambridge: Cambridge University Press, 1985.
Stare, M., J. Krošelj, T. Debeljak, P. Rant, and P. Fajdiga, eds. *Zbornik Koledar Svobodne Slovenije*. Buenos Aires: Svobodna Slovenija, 1955–1967.
Stergar, Gorazd. 'Kamniško-Zasavski narodno-osvobodilni partizanski odred in njegova vloga v narodno-osvobodilni vojni na slovenskem leto 1944.' *Vojaška zgodovina* 1 (2007): 81–128.
Sugar, Peter, ed. *Native Fascism in the Successor States, 1918–1945*. Santa Barbara, CA: ABC–Clio, 1971.
Swain, Geoffrey. *Tito: A Biography*. New York: I.B. Tauris, 2011.
Škerbec, Matija. *Krivda rdeče fronte*, vol. 2. Cleveland, OH: Tiskarna Mohorjeve družbe, 1957.
Šorn, Mojca. 'Idejni in politični nazori Rupnikovega kroga.' *Prispevki za novejšo zgodovino*. 153/1 (2003): 65–74.
Terčak, Stane. *Frankovski zločin*. Ljubljana: Partizanska knjiga, 1971.
Thomas, Nigel, and K. Mikulan. *Axis Forces in Yugoslavia, 1941–45*. Oxford: Osprey, 1995.
Tolstoy, Nikolai. *The Minister and the Massacres*. London: Century Hutchinson, 1986.
Tomasevich, Jozo. *War and Revolution in Yugoslavia, 1941–1945: Occupation and Collaboration*. Stanford, CA: Stanford University Press, 2001.
Tomc, Gregor. 'Potret domobranca ali kako si pridobim prijatelje.' In Kokalj-Kočevar, ed., *Mati-domovina-bog*, 84–97.
Tominšek Rihtar, Tadeja. 'The Post-War Retribution in Slovenia: Its Death Toll.' *Slovene Studies* 28/1–2 (2006): 95–106.
Triska, Jan F. *The Great War's Forgotten Front: A Soldier's Diary and a Son's Reflections*. Boulder, CO: East European Monographs, 1998.
Troha, Nevenka. 'Politične usmeritve med primorskimi Slovenci v coni A Julijske krajne (1945–1947).' *Zgodovinski časopis* 49/3 (1995): 455–69.
Ursic, Marie T. *Religious Freedom in Post-World War II Yugoslavia: The Case of Roman Catholic Nuns in Croatia and Bosnia-Hercegovina, 1945–1960*. Lanham, MD: International Scholars Publications, 2001.
Velikonja, Mitja. 'Slovenia's Yugoslav Century.' In Dejan Djokić, ed., *Yugoslavism: Histories of a Failed Idea*. Madison, WI: University of Winsconsin Press, 2003, 84–99.
Vidič, Rastko. *The Position of the Church in Yugoslavia*. Belgrade: Zavod Jugoslavija, 1962.

Vodopivec, P., and J. Mahnič. *Slovenska trideseta leta*. Ljubljana: Slovenska matica, 1997.
Vodušek-Starič, Jera. 'Ozadje sodnih procesov v Sloveniji v prvem povojni letu.' *Prispevki za novejšo zgodovino* 32/1–2 (1992): 139–54.
Williams, Maurice. 'The Nazis, German Nationalism, and Ethnic Diversity: The Adriatic Coastland under Friedrich Rainer.' *Slovene Studies* 17/1–2 (1995): 3–23.
Zaveza. Revija za duhovna, kulturna in politična vprašanja sedanjosti in prihodnosti – s posebnim ozirom na krizo slovenstva po boljševiški revoluciji in državljanski vojni. Ljubljana: Nova slovenska zaveza. 1, 2009. http://www.zaveza.si/index.php/revija-zaveza/53-zaveza-t-01.
Ziherl, Slavko, Zdenka Čebašek-Travnik, and Zvonka Zupanič-Slavec. 'The Extermination of Psychiatric Patients in Occupied Slovenia in 1941.' *International Journal of Mental Health* 36/1 (2007): 99–104.
Zorn, Tone. 'A Contribution to the Problem Regarding the Nazi Denationalizing Policy in (Austrian) Carinthia and Occupied Upper Carniola from 1938 to 1943.' In Anič et al., eds., *The Third Reich and Yugoslavia*, 423–40.
Žebot, Ciril A. *Slovenija včeraj, danes in jutri*. Celovec: Družbe sv. Mohorja, 1967.
Željeznov, Dušan. *Rupnikov proces*. Ljubljana: Cankarjeva založba, 1980.
Žnidarič, Marjan. *Do pekla in nazaj: Nacistična okupacija in narodnoosvobodilni boj v Mariboru, 1941–1945*. Maribor: Muzej narodne osvoboditve Maribor, 1997.
Žunec, Branko. *Josip Benko – mit in resničnost, 1889–1945*. Murska Sobota: Franc-Franc, 1993.

Films

Ophuls, Marcel. *The Sorrow and the Pity : Chronicle of a French City under the Occupation*. Chatsworth, CA: Image Entertainment, 2001, ©1969.
Štiglič, France. *Na svoji zemlji*. Ljubljana: Viba film, 1948.

Index

Academy of Commerce (Ljubljana), 67
accommodation, 3–5, 12, 31, 45, 51, 55, 64, 91–4, 1 72, 182, 240–1, 251, 253–4
Action Committee, 160
Action Française, 39
Adamič, Louis, 21
Adlcešič, Juro, 56, 61, 108
Adriatic Sea, x–xi, 30, 121, 142, 174
advisory committee (sosvet), 62–3, 93, 100, 241, 249
Africa, 78, 80
Ahčin, Ivan, 48
Ajdovščina, 185, 221
Alarmkompanie, 75, 175
Albania, x, 241
Alexander, Harold, 17
Alexander, King, 36, 38–40, 47
Allied Advisory Council for Italy, 149
Allies, 13, 16, 18, 22–3, 33, 67, 79, 86, 90–1, 95, 107, 112, 115, 117–18, 120, 123, 140, 142–4, 147–50, 152, 155–7, 173, 182, 186–7, 200, 206, 211, 215, 217, 219–20, 222, 231, 244–8, 250, 254; airmen, 144–6, 198, 210, 214; anticipated liberation of Yugoslavia, 121, 124, 153, 177, 216
Ambruž, Amalija, 171
Ancona, 79, 156
Anti-Communist Volunteer Militia (MVAC), 85, 98–104, 107–9, 110, 114, 117–23, 131, 135, 137, 139, 150, 153, 165, 238, 243–4, 248, 250
Anti-Fascist Council of the National Liberation of Yugoslavia (AVNOJ), 83, 122
Anti-Imperialist Front, 67, 69
antisemitism, 39–40, 42, 48, 132, 195. *See also* Jews
Argentina, 16
Arhar, Franc, 229
Arrow Cross, 77, 171–2, 229
Asia, 28
Atlantic Charter, 217
Auschwitz, 132, 171
Australia, 16
Austria, 3, 15–18, 25, 31–2, 34, 46, 51, 53, 57, 59, 65, 69, 75, 126–7, 138, 141, 153, 174–5, 186, 209, 213, 217, 220–1, 223–4, 226, 230, 238, 250; Anschluss, 35, 40, 177

Austrian Littoral Crown Land, 34
Austro-Hungarian Empire, 4, 31–2, 37, 48, 53, 126, 155; Army, 126, 130, 200
Avsenek, Ivan, 120
Axis, x, 4, 6, 20, 22, 30, 36, 40, 46, 48, 52, 63, 67, 79, 215, 223, 228, 252; invasion of Yugoslavia, 3–4, 30, 37, 41, 49, 51, 65, 67–8, 238

Badoglio, Pietro, 115, 119, 183
Bajlec, Franc, 170
Bajt, Anton, 183
Bajuk, Marko, 88
Balkan Pact, 40
Balkans, 4, 14, 31, 38, 48–9, 79, 86, 102, 117, 121, 124, 131, 143–4, 169
Basaj, Jože, 155
Battle of Britain, 3
Bavarians, 4
Baza, 20, 83
BBC (British Broadcasting Corporation), 70, 158
BBZ (*Berliner Börsen-Zeitung*; code name for Vladimir Vauhnik's espionage ring), 79, 100, 120, 152–3
Bela Krajina, xi, 26, 52, 108, 142, 145, 200, 215
Belgian barracks (prison), 135–6
Belgians, 11
Belgrade, x, 4, 16, 36, 46, 48–9, 51, 79, 90, 182, 209; liberation of, 143, 154, 158
Belzec, 124
Beneš, Edvard, 92
Benko, Jože, 229
Beranek, Jože, 223
Berlin, 59, 79, 211, 216, 225
Bernik, Jože, 180
Bernot, Zvonimir, 37

Bertleson, Aage, 93, 239
Besednjak, Engelbert, 182–3
Bevc, Ladislav, 156, 193, 196, 198, 220
Bevc, Vid, 146
Bežigrad, 52
Biber, Dušan, 24
Bihać, 83
Bilten, 39
Biro, Josip, 65
Bitenc, Jože, 229
Black Hand, 20, 151, 229
Bled, xi, 59, 125, 138
Bleiburg, 15
Blitz, 3
Blue Guard, 67, 117
Boh, Ivan, 118
Böhme, Franz, 75
Boj, 39
Bologna, 79, 211
Bolshevism, 42–3, 45, 106, 128–9, 130, 171, 192, 196, 242, 252; anti-, 41, 127, 130, 181, 241, 244
Bor, 171
Borci, 39
Borovnica, 146, 191
Bosnia-Hercegovina, 6, 83, 117, 122, 146, 224, 233; Muslims of, 128, 225
Bousquet, René, 28
Bovec, 185
Božič, Branko, 19, 91
Brash, Maurice, 156
Bratislava, 48
Breiner, Hans, 189
Brulc, Alojz, 120
Buchenwald, 153
Buenos Aires, 21
Buffarini, Guido, 61
Bulgaria, x, 38, 40, 51–2, 155

Canada, 3, 16
Cankar, Izidor, 149, 216
Carabinieri, 102
Carinthia, xi, 14–15, 17, 35, 42, 52–3, 56–9, 62, 64, 73, 78, 111, 144, 169, 173, 177–9, 222–3; German propaganda office of, 181; Homeland Service, 35; Political and Economic Association of, 35; Provincial Assembly, 35; Security Police and Security Service for, 125, 133, 138
Carniola, 31, 34, 127
Carstanjen, Helmut, 53
Catholic Action (KA), 43, 94, 104, 118
Catholic Church, 21–3, 25, 31, 36, 41–3, 45–6, 48, 60, 71, 77, 89, 95, 100, 102–4, 118, 123, 125, 132, 159–61, 170, 188, 195–7, 200–1, 205–6, 210, 234–5, 242, 244, 248–52; press, 28, 171; priesthood, 19, 43, 45–6, 48–9, 58–9, 63–4, 71, 89, 90, 103–4, 107, 111, 118, 159–60, 170, 177, 182–5, 197–8, 213, 221, 228, 234–5, 251–2; student groups, 66, 104, 207
Celje, xi, 53, 56, 62, 126, 176, 195, 223, 230
Central Leadership of Home Resistance (UVOD), 93, 95
Centre (Gorenjska Self-Defence), 138, 180
Centrists (*sredinci*), 21, 235, 245
Cergol, Izidor, 195–6, 254
Channel Islands, 93
China, 5
Christian Socialists, 23, 41, 71, 95, 123, 151, 182, 205, 210, 235
Christmas Trial, 233
Churchill, Winston, 16–17

Ciano, Galeazzo, 54, 61, 63, 80–1, 87, 111
Cleveland, 21, 221
Coceanu, Bruno, 184
Cold War, 5, 22, 236
College of Cardinals, 228
Comintern, 37–8, 41, 67, 69, 161
Command Staff for the Suppression of Guerillas Ljubljana, 130, 146, 154
Commission for Religious Affairs in Yugoslavia, 197
Committee for Dolenjski Refugees, 127, 160
Committee for Suha Krajina Refugees, 188
Committee for the Social-Moral Renewal of Slovenia, 197
Communism, 7, 22, 27, 40–7, 69, 73, 77, 99, 107, 120, 141, 144, 148, 191, 196, 236, 241, 247–8, 252; anti-, 9, 22, 29, 36, 39, 41, 45, 104, 108, 120, 132–3, 139, 146, 148, 160, 167, 183, 195, 198, 201, 205, 212
Communist Party of Slovenia (CPS), 24, 26, 38, 41, 67, 70–3, 94, 108, 116, 126, 148, 190, 210, 226, 243, 250; Central Committee, 83, 94
Communist Party of Yugoslavia (CPY), 6, 18, 37–8, 41, 47, 67, 69–70, 95, 232, 243; Central Committee, 67; Politburo, 70
Concordat (1933), 45, 252
Convention of Delegates of the Slovene People, 122
Corfu Declaration, 32
Cossacks, 25, 127, 213
Courts of National Honour (SNČ), 228–32, 242
Cres, 34

Croatia, 4, 32–4, 36–8, 49, 56, 58, 79, 89, 121, 124, 128, 142–3, 146, 158, 173, 200, 224–5, 228, 234, 238, 263f
Croatian domobran, 158, 173, 231
Croatian Peasant Party, 49
Cvetković-Maček government, 48
Czechoslovakia, 22, 224; government-in-exile, 92
Czechs, 4, 55, 92–3, 103, 175, 187, 194, 199, 239, 245, 253
Čampa, Leopold, 198
Četniks, 26, 68, 90–1, 98, 112, 117–18, 121, 128, 130, 139–40, 144, 150, 152, 154–5, 158–9, 213, 221, 225, 231, 246; Slovene, 21, 70, 95, 97–8, 104, 116–23, 139, 150–3, 156–7, 214, 226–7, 248. *See also* National Intelligence Service
Čičarija mountains, 186
Čolaković, Rodoljub, 6
Črna bukva, 25, 191
Črnomelj, 190, 214

D-day, 153
Dachau, 145, 156–7, 236
Dachau trials, 235–6
Dajčar, Joško, 175
Dalmatia, x, 34, 110, 122, 209
Danube River, 48
Darlan, Françoise, 92
Debeljak, Janko, 119
Debeljak, Tine, 138, 248
Democratic Opposition of Slovenia (DEMOS), 25
Denmark, 92, 115
Department for the Protection of the People (OZNA), 224, 229
Devica Marija v Polju, 189
Dežman, Josip, 121–2, 156

Dichtl, Erich, 138–9
Displaced Persons camps, 15, 156
Djilas, Milovan, 23, 91, 225
Dolenec, Ivan, 88, 91, 123, 252
Dolenja vas, 186
Dolenjska, xi, 26, 30, 52, 72, 82, 97, 109, 118, 142, 151, 160, 166, 187, 192, 200, 213
Dolinar, France, 27, 64
Dolomite Declaration, 116, 151, 242
Dolomite region, 185
Domenis, Giovanni, 102
Domoljub, 221
domobranstvo. *See* Home Guard
Dorfmeister, Anton, 223
Dornberk, 186
Doujak, Hermann, 126
Drašković, Milorad, 37
Drava Province, 53–4, 193
Drava River, 52, 223
Dravlje, 164, 204
Družin, Ivan, 114
Duscha, Paul, 133

East Central Europe, 3, 28, 48, 65, 93, 235, 254
Eastern Europe, 5, 14, 116, 225, 230, 244
Ehrlich, Lambert, 42, 47, 96–7, 99, 104
Egypt, 52
émigrés, 7, 17–18, 21, 23, 28–9, 32–3, 121, 156, 160, 234, 248; school (historiography), 7–9, 21–3, 25, 28–9, 43, 85, 101–2, 131, 148, 219, 243–5, 249–50, 274f
Erpić, Franc, 138
Evans, Julian, 3

Fajfar, Tone, 71, 123
Fanouš-Emer, France, 94

Farish, Linn, 144
fascism, 5–6, 38, 41–3, 47, 78, 161, 226, 228, 231, 239, 252; Italian, 15, 87, 124–5, 184
Fascist Youth Organization of Ljubljana (GILL), 88, 96
Ferdinand, Franz, 33
Ferenčak, Major, 162, 184
Ferfolja, Jože, 112
Ferlach (Borovlje), 223, 249
First World War, 3–4, 30–3, 39, 42, 56, 59–60, 103, 189
Fistere, John, 152
Foss, Erling, 93
France, 5, 9, 16–17, 28, 39, 45, 70, 115, 118, 126, 153, 174, 183, 199, 225, 253; Vichy, 11, 39, 92, 162, 169, 212
Franko, Oskar, 229
Frankolovo, 223
Franks, 4
Freemasons, 38, 42
Furlan, Boris, 158, 235
Fürst, Elizabeta, 171

Gabrovšek, Franc, 149
Galicia, 124
Gambarra, Gastone, 119
Garibaldi division, 121, 185
Gašparin, Gustav, 171
Gaullism, 5
Generalplan Ost, 57–8
Geneva Convention (1929), 16
German army (Wehrmacht), 27, 51, 55, 72, 76, 112, 124, 129–30, 133, 143, 147–8, 152, 164, 171, 173, 175, 178, 204, 243; High Command, 74
German Center Party, 45
German National Penal Code, 132

German News Service, 191
Germany, x–xi, 3, 5, 38–40, 45, 48, 52–5, 57–9, 67, 75, 79, 92, 102, 114, 125, 127, 129, 132, 137, 140, 143, 145, 148–9, 165, 172, 174, 176, 178–80, 182, 184, 187, 192–3, 199, 210–11, 230, 242, 264f
Gestapo, 59, 65, 114, 133, 138–9, 146, 153, 155–6, 166, 178, 180–1, 195, 232, 236
Glas izpod Krna, 185
Glavač, Franc, 152
Glazer, Karel, 113
Globocnik, Odilo, 35, 115, 124–5, 130, 135, 137, 162, 275f
Glušič, Andrej, 153
Golob, Franc, 150, 166–7
Gonars, 83, 166, 185
Gorenja vas, 167
Gorenjec, 181
Gorenjska, xi, 14, 20, 52–3, 56–9, 61–2, 64–6, 73–6, 88, 111–12, 116–17, 124–5, 135, 137–40, 143–4, 147, 150–1, 164, 166, 169, 173–4, 178–83, 188, 194, 199, 201, 220, 224, 239, 243, 262f
Gorenjska Self-Defence, 135, 137–40, 147, 156, 159, 162, 164, 167, 169, 180–1, 183, 208, 216, 248
Gorenjsko Domobranstvo, 181
Gorizia, xi, 34, 62, 82, 124–6, 161, 182–4, 221
Gorjanci mountains, 238
Gornji Grad, 176
Gošar, Andrej, 95, 99
Grafenauer, Niko, 25
Graz, 53, 59
Grazioli, Emilio, 56, 60–3, 80–1, 96, 106
Grčarice, 104, 121–2, 139, 150

Great Britain, 3, 6, 15–17, 23, 25, 34, 48–9, 72–3, 117, 141, 152, 157, 210, 216, 221–3, 226, 233–4, 256f; Eighth Army, 17, 216; Foreign Office, 16; Joint Staff Mission, 16; V Corps, 17
Great Depression, 40, 44
Greece, x, 5, 23, 52, 92, 213, 216, 240–1; Greek National Liberation Front (EAM), 92
Grosuplje, xi, 145, 191, 206
Guardia Civica, 98, 101
Gulag, 225

Hácha, Emil, 92, 193
Hacin, Lovro, 133, 135, 146–7, 160, 163, 166, 197, 212, 233
Hague Conventions, 16, 189
Haider, Jörg, 35
Haloze, 152
Hamilton, John, 110
Hartner, Ferdinand, 65
Heeren, Viktor von, 39
Heimatbund, 57, 75–6, 175–6, 230
Heydrich, Reinhard, 57–8, 93
Hirschegger, Rudolf, 102, 149, 156–7, 198
Hitler, Adolf, 35, 39–40, 45, 48–9, 53, 55–7, 63, 68, 72, 89, 115, 118, 124, 147–9, 153, 155, 167, 170, 173, 177, 204, 216, 226, 229; *Mein Kampf*, 42
Hitler Youth, 76, 175
Hitlerites, 55, 183, 229
Hlinka Guard, 132
Holocaust, 57, 89, 171
Home Guard (*domobranstvo*), 9, 14, 123, 126, 131–4, 136–42, 144–6, 158–60, 164–7, 171, 173, 178, 180–3, 187, 189–90, 196, 212, 215–17, 219–20, 222–3, 238, 244, 247–8, 250, 282f; anti-German activity of, 150, 152–7; Catholic Church and, 197–8; civilian reaction to, 200–7, 213; creation of, 128–30; historiography of, 23–5, 27–8, 102; ill-discipline of, 162–3; oath, 147–9, 251; propaganda, 130, 160–1, 195, 205–6; Provincial Administration and, 191, 193–4; repatriation and execution of, 9, 15–18, 23, 221, 223, 225–8, 236, 254; postwar trials, 229, 231, 233
Home Guard Organizational Headquarters, 130, 154–5, 198
Horjul, 46, 54, 164, 213
Hradetzky, Franz, 125
Hrastnik, 15
Hren, Ignacij, 126, 193
Hribar, Spomenka, 25
Hribernik-Svarun, Rudolf, 46, 54, 109
Hubad, Dr, 188
Hungarian Army, 60, 171–2
Hungarian Educational Organization for Prekmurje, 60
Hungarian Soviet Republic, 37
Hungary, x, 3, 5, 18–19, 22, 40, 51–5, 59–61, 65, 72, 77, 87, 111–12, 114, 170–3, 211, 225, 229, 246, 250

Idrija, 34, 136, 147, 185
Ig, 109
Ilc, Anton, 103, 197
Illyrian movement, 31
Independent Democratic Party, 95
Independent State of Croatia (NDH), x–xi, 52, 56, 58, 77, 148, 173, 187, 232, 264f
Information Office (IU), 153, 189–91
Informbiro, 236

Internal Macedonian Revolutionary Organization, 38
Isonzo front, 4, 30
Istanbul, 67
Istria, 34, 186
Iška vas, 109, 119
Italian Army, 63, 78, 82, 105, 108, 121, 161–2; Second Army, 60, 118; XI Corps, 60; summer offensive (1942), 81–5, 91, 96, 100–1, 106, 108, 111
Italian front, 131, 142
Italian Cultural Institute in Zagreb, 62
Italian High Commissariat, 56, 61–4, 81, 94, 97, 106
Italian National Olympic Committee, 87
Italy, x–xi, 3, 4–5, 14–15, 18, 30, 32–3, 40, 45, 48, 52, 54, 60, 62–3, 69, 83, 86, 89, 96, 102, 111, 127, 132, 139, 143–4, 156, 182–3, 194, 209, 211, 221, 224, 240; Slovene resistance to, 78–81; Yugoslav minority in, 34, 46, 78, 123; capitulation of, 114–22, 124–5, 127–8, 135, 169–70, 174, 225, 239

Jacklin, Friedrich, 126
Jajce, 122
Jan, Maks, 192
Jarman, Jože, 114
Javornik, 114
Javornik, Mirko, 25
Jews, 38–9, 42, 45, 52, 79, 127, 173, 191–2, 195, 232, 239; Croatian, 48, 89; of Trieste, 124; Polish, 124; Slovene, 55, 132, 171–2, 232; Yugoslav, 48. *See also* antisemitism
Ježica, 191

Judenburg, 15
Julian Alps, 76, 82, 143, 238
Jutro, 220

Kal nad Kanalom, 182
Kamnik, 112, 139, 230
Kamniške mountains, 143
Karadjordjević dynasty, 13, 32
Karavanke mountains, 178, 217, 222
Kardelj, Edvard, 6, 38, 70–2, 83, 85, 94, 109, 145, 224, 240
Katyn, 17
Kazina building, 220
Keitel, Wilhelm, 74
Kek, Canon, 123
Kerčmar, Jožef, 229
Kervin, Franc, 184
Kidrič, Boris, 19, 38, 71, 145, 211, 224
Kikelj, Jaroslav, 104
Kingdom of Serbia, 155
Kingdom of Serbs, Croats, and Slovenes, 4, 31–3, 35–7, 78
Klagenfurt, 15, 21, 59, 103, 194, 211, 221, 223
Klekl, Josef, 59, 77
Klinar, Anton, 101
Kobarid, 34, 185
Kocbek, Edvard, 23–4, 26–7, 41, 62, 71–4, 88, 91–2, 123, 145, 203, 210, 235, 243
Kociper, Stanko, 27–8, 127, 141–2, 149, 160, 180, 183, 191, 193–5, 248, 250, 254
Kočevari (Gottscheer), 58
Kočevje, xi, 58, 121–2, 134, 142, 145, 150, 166, 188, 190, 201, 214–15, 222
Kočevje trials, 104, 122–3
Kočevski Rog, 15, 20, 25–6, 69, 81, 83, 109, 143

320   Index

Kokalj, Anton, 120, 129, 135, 137, 184, 212
Korea, 22
Korošec, Anton, 32–3, 36, 41–3, 47–9
Korošec, Ivan, 70, 72, 97–8
Koroška, 111, 143, 173, 201
Kostanjevica, 103, 144
Kovač, Štefan, 77
Kozjansko, 173
Kragujevac, x, 90, 95
Kramperšek, Leopold
Kranj, xi, 43, 113, 138–9, 180, 230
Kranjc, Milan, 119
Kranjska, 183
Krek, Miha, 7, 55–6, 94, 99, 138, 149, 158, 216, 233
Krek, Slavko, 138, 140, 156, 180
Kremžar, Franc, 217, 220–1
Krener, Franc, 129–30, 146, 148, 150–1, 154–6, 162–3, 165–6, 219–20, 276f
Krim, 109, 215
Križ, Ladislav, 153
Križarji, 224
Krmavner, Ivan, 156
Krošl, Anton, 67
Kučan, Milan, 26
Kuhar, Alojzij, 50, 56, 61, 149, 158
Kukman, Anton, 163, 165
Kulovec, Franc, 43, 49, 51
Kulturbund, 53, 65, 113, 229–30; Swabian-German, 65
Kursk, 115
Kutschera, Franz, 20, 57

Lake Balaton, 211
Landol, 186
Lane, Arthur Bliss, 49
Lateran Agreement, 45
Lebensraum, 54

Legion des Voluntaires Française contre le Bolchevisme, 162
Legion of Death, 98–9, 101–2, 110, 112, 117, 119, 122, 131, 248
Lenček, Ignacij, 103
Lendava, 65, 171
Leskovšek, Franc, 38, 70
Ležaky, 93
Liberals, 21, 27, 31, 36–7, 41–4, 62, 66–7, 94, 100, 107, 119, 155, 205, 235, 248, 252
Liberation Front (OF), 5–6, 8–9, 13–14, 34, 47, 52, 66–7, 70, 85, 87, 89–93, 111, 122, 127, 142–3, 150, 165, 175, 187, 190, 195, 210, 212, 219, 221, 243, 252; Bračičeva Brigade, 123; Cankar Brigade, 144; Catholic Church and, 103–4, 106, 160–1, 197–8, 251; civil war and, 94–5, 97–9, 102, 107, 116–18, 120, 131, 135, 138–40, 151, 153, 156, 159, 161–2, 164–6, 181, 191, 193, 211, 214, 238–42, 244, 245–6, 248–9; civilian reactions to, 74, 77–8, 108–10, 112–13, 123, 137, 174, 176–9, 182–3, 185–6, 192, 200–7; historiography of, 18–29; Home Guard oath and, 148–9; Italian summer offensive (1942) and, 81, 83, 96; postwar retribution, 225–6, 229, 234–5; Pohorski Battalion, 76; rise of, 69, 71–3
Lidice, 93
Lienz, 15
Lika, 121
Lindsay, Franklin, 143–4, 152, 159, 174–5, 201, 210
Linz, 57
Lipič, Jože, 229
Litija, 181

Little Entente, 40
Ljotić, Dimitrije, 39–40, 128, 195, 213, 246; Slovene Ljotićists, 195–6, 247
Ljubelj Tunnel, 15, 174, 222–3; South Concentration Camp, 174
Ljubljana, x–xi, 13, 20, 25, 49, 52–3, 54, 61–3, 74, 77–83, 85, 88, 96–8, 101, 105, 108–9, 120–2, 124, 126, 128–9, 131–6, 138, 140, 142, 145–8, 151, 153–4, 156, 160, 163, 180, 183, 189–92, 199, 201, 204–6, 209–10, 212, 215, 217–23, 226–7, 229–30, 232–4, 269f; bishopric of, 25, 43–4, 64, 147–8, 234; mayor of, 24, 56, 61, 108, 127, 134, 247; Supreme Military Court in, 229; Tobacco Factory, 206. *See also* Province of Ljubljana
Ljubljana Gap, 153, 177, 216
Ljubljana Points / Slovene Declaration (1932), 36, 47
Ljutomer, 74
Logatec, 74, 206
Loh, Maks, 134
Lokve, 126
London, 3, 16, 52, 70, 93, 99, 158; Yugoslav government in, 22, 67, 90, 95, 99, 112, 117, 122, 250; Treaty of, 33
Lovrič, Jože, 138
Lošinj, 34
Loška valley, 145
Loški Potok, 85
Lubej, Franjo, 71
Lubran, General, 119

M-7, 153
Macedonia, 38, 46, 209
Maclean, Fitzroy, 201
Maček, Vladko, 48–9
Maginot Line, 126
Main State Security Office (Reichssicherheitshauptamt), 57, 59, 93
Maister, Hrvoj, 153
Maister, Rudolf, 153
Majdanek, 124
Malnar, Franciška, 134
Margotti, Carlo, 184
Maria Elend, 15
Maribor, x–xi, 52–5, 59, 74, 113–14, 175, 230; bishopric of, 63, 234
Markham, Reuben, 144
Marn, Janez (Črtomir Mrak), 151–2
Marseille, 40
massacres (postwar), 5, 9, 15, 17–18, 20–1, 23–6, 221, 223–9, 233, 236, 243, 254
Matjašec, Franc, 172
Matthew's Army (Matjaževa vojska), 224
Maurras, Charles, 39
Mauthausen, 132, 174, 176
Mavec, Anton, 204
May Declaration, 32
McDowell, Robert, 154
Megušar, Anton, 138
Melaher, Jože (Zmagoslav), 151–2, 214
Mengeš, 181
Messner, Rudolf, 138
Metlika, 162
Mežiška valley, 52, 57, 124, 262f
Mihailović, Draža, 21, 66–7, 90–1, 95, 100, 117–18, 123, 142, 144, 151–5, 157–8, 203, 224, 233, 245
Mikuž, Metod, 19, 64, 71, 107, 123, 197, 203, 235, 251
Milač, Metod, 88, 149, 211
Milan, 79
Mirna, 186; valley, 118, 151

Mladci Kristusa Kralja, 42–3, 195, 250; *Mi mladi borci*, 42
Mladina, 25
Mohorič, Henrik, 174
Mohorjeva družba, 21
Molotov-Ribbentrop Pact, 22, 41, 47, 67
Montenegro, 38, 46, 71, 90–1, 117, 209, 225
Moore, Peter, 73, 159, 210–14, 226
Moscow, 18, 37
Mount Triglav, 238
Munich, 79; Agreement, 92
Mura River, 59
Muravidék, 49
Murska Sobota, 53–5, 65, 171, 229–30
Mussolini, Benito, 34, 40, 45, 54, 61–3, 80, 82, 89, 115, 119, 182

Nadlesk, 201
Nagode, Črtomir, 95, 99, 107
Nagode Trial, 235
Naša Žena, 72
National Committee for the Liberation of Yugoslavia, 122
National Committee for Slovenia (NO), 13, 155, 215, 218–19, 221
National Council (NS), 65, 193, 242
National Defence, 74, 80
National Intelligence Service (Četniks, DOS), 152–3
National Legion, 67
National Liberation Army (NOV), 13, 157–60, 177, 183, 209–10, 213–16, 221–2; Fourth Army, 221, 233; VII Corps, 142, 215, 222; IX Corps, 221; 29th Hercegovina Division, 222
National Liberation War (NOB), 5, 18–21, 28–9, 177, 227–8, 230, 236–7, 246

National Pioneers, 192
National State of Slovenia, 13, 155, 218–19
Nationality Report (NR), 189–90
National Socialism (Nazism), 5, 35, 57, 75, 89, 96, 111, 128, 146–7, 177, 223, 239; Catholic Church and, 45, 252; propaganda, 55, 126, 241; Slovene (Yugoslav) admiration of, 39–40, 42, 126, 167, 176, 195–6, 230–2, 246–7. *See also* Germany
Nationalsozialistische Volkswohlfahrt (NSV), 57
Natlačen, Marko, 54, 56, 61–3, 87, 93–4, 100, 193
Nedić, Milan, 39, 47, 128, 200, 203, 231
Netherlands, 77, 253
New Slovene Covenant, 27
New Zealand, 2nd Division, 221
North Africa, 83, 117
Notranjska, xi, 26, 34, 52, 108–9, 118, 142, 151, 160, 192, 200–1, 259f
Novak, Karel, 95, 97–8, 101, 116–19, 121, 139, 151
Novo Mesto, xi, 88, 104, 120, 122–3, 134, 142, 144–5, 150, 154, 156, 188, 190, 206–7, 222, 230, 234, 238, 252
Nova Revija, 25
Nuremberg Trials, 234

Oder River, 211
Office of Strategic Services (OSS), 73, 117, 143–4, 154, 174, 183, 200, 210–1, 215; Alum Mission, 146, 153, 173, 201, 206; Arrow Mission, 166; Fern Mission, 201; Flotsam Mission, 154; Hacienda Mission, 110; Morale Operations, 152, 200
Officers Group (Častniška skupina), 67

Operation Reinhard, 124
Operation Zone Adriatic Littoral (OZAK), 124–8, 130, 132, 137–8, 142, 147, 153, 161, 173, 186
operations: Barbarossa, 20, 22, 65, 67, 69–70, 85, 240–1; Beehive, 17; Frühlingsanfang, 147; Margarethe, 170–1; Plan Primavera, 81, 108; Winterende, 147
Ophuls, Marcel, 5
Organisation Todt, 132, 134, 173, 192, 252
Organization of the University of Ljubljana, 88
Organization of Yugoslav Nationalists (ORJUNA), 34, 38
Osana, Jože, 220
Ottoman Empire, 4, 33
Ovaro, 240

Palestine, 52
Pameče, 175
Pannonian plain, 52
Pan-Slavism, 73
papal encyclicals, 43, 103; *Caritate Christi* (1932), 44; *Divini Redemptoris* (1937), 44; *Mit Brennender Sorge* (1937), 45; *Quadragesimo anno* (1931), 44; *Rerum Novarum* (1891), 44
Papon, Maurice, 28
+Partisans, 5, 46, 54, 63, 65, 67, 70–8, 85–6, 88, 90–1, 93–4, 96–106, 109–13, 127–31, 134–8, 141–2, 147–8, 151, 153–5, 159–62, 164–6, 170–9, 181, 183, 185–93, 197–204, 206–7, 210–16, 218–19, 238–40, 243–5, 247–51, 253–4, 264f, 274f; casualties, 227; historiography 6, 8, 11, 18–20, 22–3, 26–8; Italian capitulation, 115, 117–18, 120–4;

Italian summer offensive, 82–4; liberation, 13–15, 143, 209, 221–6; origins of, 70–3; postwar retribution and, 226–7, 230–7; relations with government-in-exile, 157–8; Supreme Headquarters, 70–1, 81, 123, 142
Paul, Prince (regent), 49, 52
Paulus, Friedrich, 115
Pavelić, Ante, 52, 89, 200, 232
Peasant Office, 160, 188
People's Liberation Committees, 83, 142
People's Radical Party, 95
Perne, Alojz, 138
Pernišek, France, 15, 209
Persterer, Alois, 138
Pétain, Marshal, 114, 169, 193, 247
Peter II, King, 13, 49, 52, 95, 122, 148, 154, 158, 216, 219
Peterlin, Ernest, 101, 120–1, 129–30, 155–7, 234
Pikalo, Marija, 174
Pivka, 136, 161, 186
Po Valley, 153
Pobratim, 67
Pohorje massif, 76
Poland, 17, 41, 66, 110, 114–15, 194, 225, 242, 244–5, 253; government-in-exile, 70; Home Army, 70, 244
Polhov Gradec, 83, 165, 207
Police Corps (PZ), 133–6, 139, 145–7, 149–50, 159, 162–4, 166, 190, 197, 212, 252
Police Security Corps (PVZ), 150
Polje, 102, 149
Pollak family, 132
Pope, 25, 63, 221; Leo XIII, 44; Pius X, 44; Pius XI, 44–5, 183; Pius XII, 45, 89, 103, 228
Popular Front, 38, 40–1, 43, 45, 47, 70

Postojna, xi, 34, 135, 161–2, 165, 183–6, 192
Poštovan, Matej, 220
Praprotnik, Avgust, 94
Prekmurje, x–xi, 18, 52–5, 59–60, 65–6, 77, 111–12, 143, 170–2, 174, 178–9, 211, 216, 229, 241
Prezelj, Ivan, 101, 151–2, 155, 158, 214, 216, 219
Primorska, xi, 14, 20, 25, 34, 66, 77–8, 82, 87, 108, 110–13, 116, 122–4, 135–7, 139–40, 142, 151, 159, 161–2, 169, 182–7, 201, 222, 225, 241, 259f
prisoners of war, 16–17, 141, 174, 178, 231; Soviet, 236
Protectorate of Bohemia and Moravia, 92–3, 175, 187
Protestants, 60, 171
Province of Ljubljana, xi, 10, 14, 24, 76–9, 116, 122, 160, 165, 170–2, 180–1, 183–4, 194, 196, 199–202, 220, 224, 240–3, 247, 251–2; under German occupation, 124–8, 130, 133, 135, 138–46, 153, 156, 169, 187, 189–91, 204, 207, 213; under Italian occupation, 52, 54, 56, 58–66, 80, 83, 85–8, 91–4, 100–1, 106, 108–13
Provincial Administration (PU), 126–7, 134, 145, 148, 151, 153, 158, 160, 165, 172, 175, 180–1, 187–90, 192–4, 196, 199, 207, 220, 242, 246–9; Department for National Health, 188; Department of Internal Affairs, 188; Propaganda Branch (Department, PO), 125, 190–2, 196, 205–6; Technical Branch, 199
Provincial Workers Union, 87
Ptuj, 52, 114, 152, 230

Pucelj, Ivan, 62, 100
Pukl, Srečko, 114
Pula, 124
Puš, Ludovik, 191, 195, 205

Quebec Conference, 117
Quislings, 6, 16, 128, 152, 200, 211, 245

Rab, 83, 185
Rače, 174
Radeče, 222
Radgona, 114
Radio Ljubljana, 56, 191
Radio Trst/Trieste, 161, 185
Radovljica, 112, 139
Railway Police, 132, 134
Rainer, Friedrich, 35, 57, 124–8, 161, 173, 186–8, 194, 220, 234
Rakek, 145, 212, 222
Rašica, 74
Ratež, 98
Ratzinger, Joseph, 175
Ravna Gora, 90
Red Army, 16, 18, 72, 77, 86, 115, 143, 154, 172–3, 211, 213, 216, 225. *See also* Soviet Union
Red Justice, 37
regime school (historiography), 5–9, 18–20, 23–4, 26–9, 64, 73, 91, 179. *See also* émigrés
Regional Committee for Gorenjska, 138
Reich Film Board, 189
Reich Labour Service (Reichsarbeitsdienst), 76, 124, 135, 137, 145, 173, 175, 186–7, 192–3, 252
Reichspropagandaamt Kärnten, 181
Renicci, 83, 185

repatriation, 6, 158, 231; from Austria, 9, 15–17, 25, 223–4, 226, 256f; of Soviets, 16–17, 25, 224
Ribičič, Mitja, 224, 229
Ribnica, 145, 192, 203, 214
Ribniška valley, 83
Rijeka, xi, 34, 124, 209
Risiera di San Sabba, 124
Roatta, Mario, 82, 106, 110
Robotti, Mario, 60, 80–2, 85, 100, 105, 119, 251
Rode, Franc, 69
Romania, x, 51, 124
Rome, 45, 62–3, 79, 153, 216, 235
Roosevelt, Franklin, 169
Rosenbach, 15
Rösener, Erwin, 75–6, 125, 128–30, 132, 140, 148, 150, 152, 154, 163, 167, 194, 197–8, 215, 217, 219–20, 233
Rovte, 191
Rožman, Gregorij, 6, 28, 43, 58, 62, 71, 221, 237, 251–2; and Home Guard, 147–8, 159, 197–8; and MVAC, 103–4, 106; opposition to Partisans, 44, 103–4, 196–8; relations with Germans, 147–8, 159, 197–8, 217; relations with Italians, 63–4, 89, 97, 100, 106; trial, 25, 233–4
Rožman-Stane, Franc, 20
Rueh, Franc, 30
Rupnik, Leon, 27, 86, 108, 122, 126–7, 133, 138, 141, 147, 152, 180, 188–9, 192, 195, 200, 242, 244, 247–8, 250; and Home Guard; 128–30, 148–9, 196; Line, 126; negotiations with NO, 215, 217, 220; opposition to Partisans, 190, 204; relations with Germans, 126, 148, 153–4, 193–4;

relations with Italians, 62–3, 111, 127; Trial, 24, 233
Rupnik, Olga, 148
Rupnik, Vuk, 220, 223
Rus, Jože, 71
Russian Civil War, 19
Russian Front, 72, 83, 86, 115, 164–5, 178
Russian Liberation Army, 128, 213
Russian Volunteer Corps, 232
Russians, 17, 25, 82, 207, 213, 223, 238. *See also* Soviet Union

Salvini, Luigi, 62
Salzburg, 59
Sava River, 48, 52, 143, 154
Schutzstaffel (SS), 20, 75, 124–5, 129, 137–8, 147–9, 154, 178, 194, 197–8, 213–15, 217, 219; Waffen-, 213, 242; XVIII Military District, 75, 129
Secret Intelligence Service (TOS), 152–3, 189
Security Intelligence Service (VOS), 94, 97, 104, 112, 126, 133, 242, 250, 252
Security Service (Sicherheitsdienst), 59, 145, 177; for Carinthia, 125, 133, 138
Seeler, Oberst von, 14
Semi, Francesco, 54
Semič, 145
Serbia, 4, 18, 31–3, 36–9, 46–7, 49, 52, 58, 71, 75, 79, 89–90, 98, 128, 146, 154–5, 158, 171, 195, 200–1, 231, 263f
Serbian State Guard, 128
Serbian Volunteer Corps, 128, 213, 221
Seton-Watson, Hugh, 9, 116
Sicily, 115

Silesia, 124
Simović, Dušan, 49
Sirc, Ljubo, 21, 70, 107, 222, 235; trial of, 235
skrivači, 151, 202–3
Slavič, Matija, 62
Slovak Republic, 42, 48–9, 126, 132, 187, 248
Slovene Covenant (SZ), 94–5, 97, 99, 116–17, 119, 155
Slovene Information Service, 152
Slovene Legion (SL), 66–7, 78, 100, 103, 107, 118, 120, 131, 138, 140, 150, 152, 156, 189
Slovene National Army (SNV), 14, 101, 120–1, 216, 218–19, 222, 244
Slovene National Council in Trieste, 112
Slovene National Liberation Committee (SNOO), 71, 83, 107
Slovene National Security Corps (SNVZ), 135–40, 147, 152, 159, 161–2, 164–5, 167, 182–7, 199–200, 207, 212, 216, 221, 248
Slovene People's Party (SLS), 31–3, 36–8, 40–3, 45–51, 55–6, 59, 62, 66–7, 74, 94–5, 98–100, 107–8, 117–20, 127–8, 130, 135, 138, 140, 149, 151, 155, 170, 205, 217, 220, 235, 244, 249
Slovenec, 41, 48, 138, 217, 220
Slovenj Gradec, 175
Slovenski dom, 25
Slovenski poročevalec, 226, 230
Slovensko Domobranstvo, 161, 203, 217
Smerdu, Boris, 195
Snoj, Franc, 56, 149, 158, 235
Sobibor, 124
Social Aid, 165

Social Democrats, 37
Socialists, 31, 155
Society for Slovene Studies, 88
Soča River, 34, 142, 185–6
Sokol, 66, 71; hall, 13, 217; Legion, 66, 71, 95, 99, 156; Military Committee, 66; War Council, 156, 193
Sorrow and the Pity, The (film), 5, 28
South Slavs, 4, 32, 155
Soviet Union, 8, 16, 20, 22, 25, 38, 40–1, 48, 67–8, 73, 127, 173, 192, 210–11, 225, 236, 241, 245–6; citizens, 16, 224; mission to Partisans, 123. *See also* operations: Barbarossa; Red Army; repatriations; Russians
Spanish Civil War, 43, 45
Spanish Falange, 42
spazio vitale, 54
Special Operations Executive (SOE), 73, 117, 143, 159, 177–8, 200–1, 210, 226
Spittal, 15
Split, 34, 79
St Veit, 15
Stalin, Joseph, 8–9, 25–6, 183, 210, 224, 235–6, 244–5
Stalin-Tito split, 236
Stalingrad, 115
Stara Pravda, 95
Stare, Miloš, 94, 99–101, 107, 194
Steindl, Franz, 214
Stepinac, Alojzije, 89, 133, 234
Stevenson, Ralph, 16–17
Stojadinović, Milan, 36, 40, 47, 229
Straža, 42, 66, 99, 104, 195, 250
Straža ob Jadranu, 185
Straža v viharju, 42
Strmec, 186
Struge, 203

Sturmabteilung (SA), 59, 75
Stuttgart, 53
Suha Krajina, xi, 108–9, 201–4, 215
Suhadolc, Tone, 156
Supreme Allied Command, Mediterranean, 17
Sveta Barbara v Halozah, 114
Sveti Urh, 20, 23
Sveti Vid, 85
Switzerland, 79, 153
Szalasi, Ferenc, 172
Szombathely, 59
Sztojay, Döme, 171
Šarb, Greta, 176
Šentjernej, 167, 189
Šentjošt nad Horjulom, 85
Šentjurje, 213
Šentvid, 145–6, 223
Šeškar, Franc, 103
Šinkar, Anton, 104
Šiška, 52
Šiška, Franc, 198
Škerbec, Matija, 43, 195
Škofja Loka, 138–9, 178
Škulj, Karel, 127, 160, 197, 282f
Šmajd, Albin, 138, 155, 194, 220
Šmihel, 103–4; -Stopiče municipality, 192
Šolar, Jakob, 95
Štajerska (Styria), xi, 52–4, 56–9, 61, 63–6, 72, 74–7, 82, 98, 111–12, 121, 124–5, 128, 137, 140, 143, 150–1, 164, 166, 169, 172–8, 179, 188–9, 194, 199, 201, 214, 220, 223–4, 229–30, 239, 243
Štajerski Battalion, 97–8, 117
Šubašič, Ivan, 157–8
Šuštar, Alojzij, 166
Šuštar, Alojzij (Archbishop), 26

Šušteršič, Ivan, 32–3
Švirt, Franc, 164

Tabor Declaration, 13–14, 22, 217, 219, 250
Taborski, Julka, 190
Tagespost, 53
Teharje, 15
Teheran Conference, 226
TIGR, 34, 78
Tiso, Joseph, 42, 48
Titan, Jožef, 229
Tito, Josip Broz, 6, 15, 17–18, 20–1, 26, 38, 41, 67, 70–1, 90, 94, 118, 122–3, 142, 144, 157–8, 178, 183, 209, 224–7, 230, 236, 243
Todt, Fritz, 132. *See also* Organisation Todt
Tolminski glas, 185
Tolstoy, Nikolai, 25
Tomažič, Ivan, 63
Tomec, Ernest, 42, 47, 104
Tomišelj, 109
Tommasini, Amedeo, 102
Toronto, 3, 21
Toško Čelo, 101
Toth, Peter, 229
Touvier, Paul, 28
Trbovlje, 38, 74
Trdinov Vrh, 238
treaties: London, 33; Rapallo, 33; Saint-Germain, 35; Versailles, 42
Treblinka, 124
Trebnje, 101
Trieste, xi, 13, 24, 34, 62, 79, 112, 120, 123–5, 135, 142, 153, 184–5, 189, 209, 211, 221, 224–5
Tripartite Pact, 49
Triska, Jan, 103
Trnovski forest, 221

Tršar, Marjan, 253
Tuljak, Franc, 164
Turjak, 121–2, 156
Turnšek, Viktor, 145

Uberreither, Siegfried, 57, 63, 173
Udine, 124
Ukraine, 104, 108, 171, 213, 225
Union Brewery, 199
Union of Industrialists, 94
United Nations, 6
United States, 6, 16, 18, 21, 49, 72–3, 88, 91, 117, 120–1, 128, 144, 148, 153, 155, 169, 201, 210, 216, 220, 245; airmen, 146, 156; Office of War Information, 144
United Yugoslav Government, 157, 216
University of Ljubljana, 26, 42, 46, 62, 88, 206; Faculty of Law, 158, 235
Urbančič, Ljenko, 195
Ustaša, 38, 52, 89, 133, 173, 203, 213–14, 224
Ušeničnik, Aleš, 205
Užice, 71

Varjag/Wariag SS Regiment, 213
Vas, 59
Vatican, 45, 62, 64, 67, 89, 97, 198, 221, 234, 251, 269f
Vauhnik, Vladimir, 79, 100–1, 120, 152–3
Velike Lašče, 145, 163
Velikonja, Narte, 229
Venezia Giulia, 34
Vetrinje, xi, 15, 223
Vidmar, Josip, 71
Vidovdan, 153; Constitution 33
Vidussoni, Aldo, 80

Vienna, 79, 114, 124, 142, 173
Vietnam, 22
Village Guards (VS), 85, 97–103, 112, 117–20, 131, 146, 149, 197–8, 202, 205, 213, 226–7, 248
Villiers, Charles, 177–8
Vipava valley, 136, 185
Vipavec, 185
Višegrad, 233
Vizjak, Milko, 126, 129–30, 140, 146, 148, 152, 160, 165, 195, 198, 220, 233
Vlasov, Andrey, 213
Vlasovists, 213
Volavlje, 204
Volksbund, 57, 75–6
Volksdeutsche, 53, 55, 58, 65, 75, 121, 128, 199, 230, 246
Volkssturm, 143
Vovk, Anton, 234
Vrhnika, xi, 119–20, 126, 145, 150, 156, 160, 162, 191, 222
Vrtačnik, Pavel, 199

War Council (SNV), 101
Washington, DC, 16
Wehrmannschaft, 75–6, 112, 143, 166–7, 173, 175–6, 180
Weiss-Belač, Emil, 73, 109, 202
Windisch (vindišari) theory, 53–4, 57, 86
Werewolves, 217
Western Europe, 5, 225
White Guard, 19–20, 67, 146, 152, 154, 166, 170, 177, 179, 201, 203, 210, 212, 214, 229
Wilkinson, Peter, 144, 178–9, 187
Wolbang, Karel, 104
Wolfs, Franz, 154
Wolfsberg, 141

Wolsegger, Dr, 124
Workers Anti-Communist Action, 127
Wuchinich, George, 201

Yalta Agreement, 16, 211
Young Pioneers, 20
Yugoslav Action, 39
Yugoslav Army (under Tito's command), 17, 209, 231–2
Yugoslav Army in the Homeland, 21, 90, 117, 153, 158, 193, 198, 214, 218
Yugoslav Club, 32
Yugoslav Committee, 32
Yugoslav Constituent Assembly, 37
Yugoslav Crown Council, 49
Yugoslav government-in-exile, 7, 22, 55, 67, 70, 79, 90, 95, 99, 112, 117, 122, 127, 140, 149, 157–8, 250
Yugoslav National Party, 95
Yugoslav Partisan detachments (POJ), 159
Yugoslav People's Army, 46
Yugoslav Radical Union, 36
Yugoslav Royal Army, 39, 47, 51–2, 54, 67, 71, 81, 96, 118, 120, 126, 130–1, 135, 200
Yugoslav Welfare Society (in Rome), 216
Yugoslavia, Kingdom of, 3, 10, 33–4, 36–42, 46–9, 60, 68, 72, 133, 218–19. *See also* Kingdom of Serbs, Croats, and Slovenes
Yugoslavism, 31, 33, 38

Za blagor očetnjave, 220, 222
Zadar, 34
Zagreb, x, 24, 52, 62, 79, 89, 152
Zajc na Gorjancih, 98
Zajec, Marjan, 155, 220
Zala, 59
Zalaegerszeg, 59
Zalog, 156, 190
Zapotok, 122
Zaro, Marjan, 187
Zasavje, 74
Zbor, 39–40, 47, 128, 195
Zbornik koledar svobodne Slovenije, 21
Združeni slovenci (United Slovenes), 95
Zedinjena Slovenija (unified Slovenia), 69, 219
Zidani Most, 143
Zlatorog, 181
Žabnice, 42
Žebot, Ciril, 99, 269f
Žekelj, Marija, 176
Žibert, Alojzij, 27, 76
Župančič, Oton, 37, 46
Žužek, Franc, 127
Žužemberk, 145, 163, 213
Žvirče, 204

www.ingramcontent.com/pod-product-compliance
Lightning Source LLC
Chambersburg PA
CBHW020352080526
44584CB00014B/998